THE NEW GERMANY
SOCIAL, POLITICAL AND CULTURAL
CHALLENGES OF UNIFICATION

THE NEW GERMANY

SOCIAL, POLITICAL AND CULTURAL CHALLENGES OF UNIFICATION

edited by

Derek Lewis and John R.P. McKenzie

UNIVERSITY
of
EXETER
PRESS

First published in 1995 by
University of Exeter Press
Reed Hall, Streatham Drive
Exeter EX4 4QR
UK

British Library Cataloguing Publication Data
A catalogue record for this book is
available from the British Library

Hardback ISBN 0 85989 494 0
Paperback ISBN 0 85989 442 8

Printed and bound in Great Britain, by Short Run Press Ltd, Exeter

Typeset in Times New Roman
by M. Lewis
Ottery St Mary

Contents

Part III: The Cultural and Artistic Challenges

Maps

Tables

Acknowledgements

The editors gratefully acknowledge the co-operation and patience of the contributors to this book. They are also grateful for the encouragement and advice of Mr Simon Baker and Dr Richard Willis of the University of Exeter Press, and for the assistance of Mrs Mary Lewis in producing numerous drafts and in typesetting the final copy. Thanks are due to members of the Department of German, University of Exeter, to Professor Dieter Herberg of the Institute of German Language in Mannheim, and to the staff of the libraries of the Universities of Exeter and Würzburg. The map on the front cover is supplied by courtesy of Professor Mark Blacksell of the University of Plymouth.

Derek Lewis and John R.P. McKenzie

Contributors

Mark Blacksell
Professor of Geographical Sciences
University of Plymouth

Martin Brady
Lecturer in German
King's College
University of London

Dagmar Flinspach
Lector in German
University of Leeds

Helen Hughes
Lecturer in Linguistics and
International Studies
University of Surrey

Charles Jeffery
Senior Research Fellow in
German Studies
University of Birmingham

Karl Koch
Professor of Modern Languages
University of South Bank
London

Derek Lewis
Lecturer in German
University of Exeter

John R.P. McKenzie
Senior Lecturer in German
University of Exeter

James Mellis
Lecturer in German
University of Aberdeen

Edward Neather
Senior Lecturer in German
School of Education
University of Exeter

Gerald Opie
Lecturer in German
University of Exeter

Michael Patterson
Professor of Visual and
Performing Arts
De Montfort University

Jochen Rohlfs
Lecturer in German
University of Exeter

John Sandford
Professor of German
University of Reading

Ingrid Sharp
Lecturer in German
University of Leeds

Jürgen A.K. Thomaneck
Professor of German
University of Aberdeen

Germany: the Federal States and their Capital Cities

Introduction

The Background

'We never thought that unification would be like this,' wrote former Federal Chancellor Helmut Schmidt some three years after the unification of East and West Germany (Schmidt 1993a:15). The Federal Republic of Germany (FRG) formally merged with the German Democratic Republic (GDR) at midnight on 2–3 October 1990. This date marked the conclusion of the *Wende*, the 'turning-point' or period during which the East Germans displaced the Communist regime that had ruled them for forty years, and elected a provisional government to negotiate the dissolution of their own state. For Germans in the old FRG unification represented the fulfilment of a long-standing constitutional commitment that was embodied in the Basic Law of 1949 (indeed, the term 'Basic Law' had been deliberately chosen to denote the provisional nature of the West German state pending re-unification). For citizens of the former GDR unification brought, not the prosperity they had anticipated (and had been promised), but unemployment and insecurity. Disillusionment was not confined to the east. Concerned that the Berlin Wall continued to exist in the hearts and minds of Germans in both east and west, Schmidt demanded that the nation as a whole confront the issues raised by unification. For it is now clear that between 1989 and 1990 most observers and politicians seriously underestimated the long-term challenges of merging two different societies. This book investigates the nature of these continuing challenges and the responses to them.

The book devotes particular attention to the experiences of Germans in the 'new federal states', as the territory of the former GDR is now known in Germany. The terminology is telling: it reflects how unification has left the structures and institutions of the old FRG largely intact and how the citizens of the former East Germany have had to adapt, abruptly and often painfully, to Western conditions. At first Germans in the east welcomed with enthusiasm the prospect of radical system change: they looked forward in particular to more democracy and to increased wealth within a free market economy. The question here is whether the existing structures and institutions of western Germany can actually meet the long-term challenges of absorbing the eastern states and satisfy the aspirations of their inhabitants. In areas such as literature, education, and women's rights, eastern Germans have proved in varying degrees less eager to surrender their cultural heritage to Western values. Indeed for many Germans in both east and west unification is perceived as a lost or at best a mismanaged opportunity, and the painful transition has reinforced feelings of alienation and division. Such feelings have found particular expression in literature and in the arts. In addition to the internal problems of economic, cultural, and social integration, Germany has also discovered that unification has created problems that extend beyond its national frontiers. As the largest and economically most powerful country in Europe Germany is having to assess the international implications of its new status and, in particular, to re-examine its role in the European Union and NATO.

The Structure of the Book

In presenting these issues the book aims to give the reader a variety of perspectives into unification and its aftermath. Students following an arts-based German or European Studies degree course and requiring background information about contemporary Germany will find it especially useful. It will also interest general readers who wish to deepen their knowledge of German institutions and culture. The contributions provide both description and analysis, and concepts that may be unfamiliar to the reader are explained in full.

The book has three Parts, arranged according to topic area. Individual chapters review particular aspects of Germany's transition to a unified state. The chapters may be read individually and in any order, although the reader is advised to consider each contribution within the context of its topic area in order to gain a comprehensive picture.

Part I sets the scene by focusing on the revolution of 1989–90 and on how unification affected the citizens of the former GDR. Chapter 1 is based on case study material compiled from interviews with members of a family living in the east German town of Rostock. It demonstrates what unification has meant for ordinary men and women in the new federal states. Although they belong to the same family the interviewees present a variety of responses to unification in terms of gender, education, and professional background. As a snapshot of the immediate social consequences of unification, this case study is recommended as a useful starting-point for the reader. Again from a personal, and predominantly east German perspective, Chapter 2 recounts the events of the 1989 revolution as perceived by those who observed it or participated in it. The sources range from journalists and politicians to ordinary people, including East Germans who were sympathetic to the Communist regime. The picture here is of a set of individuals who display wide-ranging and often confused responses to the abrupt political changes, a view that to some extent counteracts the later image of a people single-mindedly pursuing the goal of unification. Chapter 3 concludes Part I with a brief account of the political system of the old GDR and of the way in which this affected and controlled the everyday lives of East German citizens; the chapter also recounts the events that led up to unification and considers some of the ways in which the new Germany is coming to terms with the legacy of the former Communist state. In particular, the notion that East Germany was a positively criminal regime rapidly gained currency during the *Wende*. This issue raised a number of fundamental questions for the new, united Germany: above all there was a need to provide justice for the victims of Communist repression by placing the leaders of the former GDR before a court of law while at the same time avoiding political show trials.

Part II considers the wider political, economic, and social issues of unification. The starting-point is a review of the human and political geography of united Germany, with particular reference to Germany's role as a European power (Chapter 4). Chapter 5 examines the implications of integrating the eastern federal states into the existing political structures of western Germany and considers developments in German foreign policy. A key factor in the fall of East Germany was its failure to match the economic performance of the FRG: Chapter 6 explains the principles of the West German social market economy and assesses how it is responding to the demands of integrating the new federal states. Chapter 7 analyses changes in the education system, and Chapter 8 investigates the implications of unification for women in the new Germany.

Part III is devoted to the media, the arts, and culture. Chapter 9 shows how unification has scarcely affected the press and broadcasting industries in western Germany while producing dramatic changes in the east. Although few would advocate a return to the state-controlled media of the GDR days, the emergence of large commercial media corporations and of satellite and cable television is posing a serious challenge to traditional Western values of political pluralism and freedom of expression. Unification has also generated a lively debate in Germany about the role of literature. Chapter 10 raises the question of whether the literature of the former GDR was too closely defined by the conditions in which it was produced to survive the demise of Communism, while Chapter 11 assesses the reactions of German writers as a whole to the Western takeover; assertions by critics in the old FRG that some East German writers had been too supportive of the Communist regime have actually deepened the sense of cultural division between east and west after unification. Chapter 12 considers the beneficial and adverse effects of unification on German theatre, in particular the response to the lifting of censorship in the east and the challenge of having to adapt to a commercial environment. Chapter 13 provides a survey of German documentary and feature films after the *Wende*. Part III ends with a description of the unique role which language has played in the unification process and how it has reflected the problems of transition (Chapter 14).

Editorial Policy

The book observes the following editorial conventions. First, the terms 'east Germany' and 'west Germany' are used as synonyms for the new and the old federal states respectively, as they are now constituted after unification. The capitalized forms 'East Germany' and 'West Germany' refer to the former GDR and FRG before October 1990. Where the distinction is immaterial (for instance, when referring to east Germans before and after 2 October 1990), the lower-case forms are used. Second, English terms for German institutions are normally employed in the chapters (thus 'federal state' for *Land* and 'People's Chamber' for *Volkskammer*). A German term is used if attention is being drawn to the cultural context (as in referring to 'the *Länder*-system of the FRG') or if there is no recognized translation equivalent (for example, many German school types fall into this category). In the case of titles of books and films an English translation accompanies the first occurrence of a title within a chapter; thereafter the German title is used. The intention throughout has been to make the book as accessible as possible to readers who are not familiar with the German language. The only exception to this principle is Chapter 14, where the subject matter necessarily presupposes some knowledge of German on the part of the reader. At the end of the book there is a Chronology of Events in Germany from the *Wende* to December 1994 (pages 321–28) and a Glossary of principal institutional terms and abbreviations (pages 329–35). Where appropriate, suggestions for further reading and pointers to the relevant specialist literature are included for each chapter. A comprehensive Bibliography is also provided (pages 336–54).

Derek Lewis and John R.P. McKenzie,
Exeter,
Summer 1995

Part I

Setting the Scene:
The Demise of East Germany

1

From Euphoria to Reality
Social Problems of Post-Unification

JÜRGEN A. K. THOMANECK

1.1 The K. family and the aftermath of 9 November 1989

The K. family lives in the city of Rostock in the state of Mecklenburg-West Pomerania, one of the five new federal states in the north of the former GDR. The following study is based on interviews conducted with various members of the family between the summer of 1989 and the autumn of 1993 (the current time of writing is mid-1994). The interviews provide a profile of experiences and attitudes that throw a human light on the profound changes that took place in eastern Germany after the fall of the GDR. The chapter also attempts to place the individual responses of the members of the K. family within the wider context of political, economic, and social developments in eastern Germany.

The family comprises five brothers, all married and with children (one brother left for Schleswig-Holstein in January 1990, two months after the opening of the Berlin Wall). On 9 November 1989 the family was gathered for a family celebration in one of the homes when, almost by accident, they saw on television Politburo member Günter Schabowski making the historic announcement that travel restrictions for East Germans had been abolished. In an atmosphere of incomprehension and near disbelief one of the brothers and his wife decided there and then to travel by car to Berlin. They returned to Rostock the following morning and, together with the rest of the family, continued to witness the indescribable scenes on West German television. *Wahnsinn* was the word commonly used to express the mood of those days. The dictionary defines the word as meaning madness, or lunacy, but this fails to convey the euphoria that gripped both East and West Germans in the autumn of 1989. The word was used largely in response to the fact that something totally unexpected had happened. Nobody had foreseen the opening of the East–West border, let alone planned for unification. Neither the rulers of the GDR nor their secret police, the *Stasi*, foresaw the train of events that had been set in motion; the same is true for politicians and academics in the West (Krockow 1993:7–8). The well-known East German author Günter de Bruyn wrote in retrospect in 1991 that the debate conducted in the previous decade about unification now appeared ludicrous. Even as the day of unification approached, many intellectuals were convinced, like de Bruyn, that the venture was unrealizable, dangerous, and futile. They regarded those who welcomed unification as nationalists or dreamers; realists considered merger with the FRG to be either impossible or undesirable. Such scepticism was not confined to the East: in late 1989 a leading West German journalist advised his readers to leave the skeleton of German unification firmly in the cupboard (Bruyn 1991:7).

The K. family was caught up in this frenzy of *Wahnsinn*, and they, like many other Germans, had no notion of where events would lead. They were unaware that 9 November signalled the start of a historical epoch and that unification was on the doorstep. Just four months after the fall of the Wall, when the first free national elections in the history of the GDR were held on 18 March 1990, the CDU and its allies gained a momentous victory which paved the way for unification later that year. Thereafter events moved quickly and optimism was the order of the day. The Federal Chancellor, Helmut Kohl, repeatedly assured the people that the eastern part of the new Germany would become 'a flourishing land' within two years (Schmidt 1993a:17). Later, as the economic situation deteriorated, economists, journalists, politicians, and ordinary people were not slow to remind the self-proclaimed *Einheitskanzler* ('Unity Chancellor') of his promise. Former Chancellor Helmut Schmidt, writing in the respected national weekly *Die Zeit*, pointed out that Kohl, in his desire to win the first elections in a united Germany, had promised both prosperity for Germans in the east and no tax increases for citizens of the old FRG (Schmidt 1993b). When he made his promise Chancellor Kohl might well have believed that the nation would experience a second economic miracle. But the 'flourishing land' failed to materialize and tax rises proved unavoidable. The economic miracle of the 1950s and 1960s could not simply be re-enacted. Even worse, the former GDR was threatened with large-scale de-industrialization. The contrast between Kohl's promise and the economic reality was stark: the Federal Minister of Education, Rainer Ortleb, speaking at an FDP Party Congress in eastern Germany in 1992, foresaw the north of the former GDR turning into a 'national park with hot-dog stalls' (*Naturschutzgebiet mit Würstchenbude*).

At the time it was widely acknowledged that Ortleb's projection could well have become reality: in common with the European Union, Germany as a whole was undergoing an economic crisis. The situation was particularly acute in the former GDR, where factories and plants were closing, productivity was falling, and investment had failed to materialize; at the same time crime and racism were on the increase. In 1993 the British journalist Allan Saunderson questioned the reliability of economic forecasts by German economists, predictions which the average German, including the K. family, treated with the same credulity as the long-range weather forecast (Saunderson 1993). Saunderson reported that many German banks and economic researchers were 'wary of overstating their forecasts for 1994'. This new-found caution was a reaction to the grossly optimistic predictions of the previous two years: in 1993 'virtually all components of the west German economy performed far worse than economists expected'. With only 0·5% real growth, no recovery at all was projected for 1994. Although output in the five eastern federal states increased by 7·5% during 1993, the total production accounted for only 8% of the eleven western states.

What continued to affect most ordinary people, especially in the former GDR, was unemployment. In September 1993 unemployment in the west stood at 7·4% (2,288,100) and 15·2% (1,159,200) in the east. Additional factors meant that the figures were even worse than they appeared. First, the number of short-time workers was 590,400 in the west and 143,400 in the east. Second, 1·05 million east Germans were undergoing training or taking part in job creation schemes. Finally, almost one million workers in the east found themselves more or less forced into early retirement. It is unlikely that there will be any increase in the number of people in work before the year 2000. The cost to the taxpayer of financing the jobless and early retirements in the first half of 1993 alone was 65 billion DM (Kühl 1993:11). An examination of the distribution of unemployment in July 1993 revealed that each of the five new states outstripped the western states in terms of the percentage of unemployed (*General-Anzeiger* 1993:1).

To the costs of unemployment in the former GDR must be added those of rebuilding the infrastructure, of privatizing companies, and of cleaning up the environment. The public purse provided a total of 182 billion DM in 1993 for the eastern states. Part of this sum was raised by an increase in direct taxation—a 7% surcharge for those who earned enough to afford it. The surcharge directly affected the spending power of the individual and produced resentment, particularly in the west.

The official unemployment figure of 15·2% in the east during 1993 is part of a much larger picture of continuing social upheaval. Before unification there were 9·6 million jobs in the former GDR. More than half of these have disappeared. Some areas have been particularly badly affected; of the 800,000 people who worked in agriculture, for example, only 200,000 remain. The situation in farming has been exacerbated by over two million claims for restitution lodged by former landowners who were expropriated by the GDR authorities or who fled westwards when their land was collectivized. The claims mean that hundreds of thousands of east Germans are experiencing insecurity as they are threatened by the loss of flats, houses, and land to which they had enjoyed rights of ownership and use for decades. For ideological as much as economic reasons, large job losses have also occurred in science, education, and culture: of the 2·2 million who used to work in these sectors, more than half have left or have lost their jobs. Over half a million people formerly employed in governmental institutions have seen their posts disappear because they are identified with the old regime.

Since unification employment patterns in the east have been greatly affected by type of work and geographical location. Unemployment has been highest in Saxony-Anhalt (17·6% in 1993) and Mecklenburg-West Pomerania (17·4%). In the predominantly agricultural region of Mecklenburg-West Pomerania, ship-building used to be the biggest industry before unification. In the town of Wolgast, for example, 3,800 jobs existed in the dockyards before unification; today only 850 are left, many of these short-term. In Wismar 5,000 people used to be employed in ship-building; in 1993 the 1,400 remaining workers were anxiously awaiting new orders for ships. In Rostock, the once proud Warnow and Neptun shipyards have to all intents and purposes been closed down. Indeed, without the financial support of the Federal Government, unemployment would not have stood at 17·4% but at 38% (McLaughlin 1993).

1.1.1 *Brigitte K: the working woman*

Before unification all five brothers of the K. family and four of their wives were in full employment in Rostock. Today the brothers still have jobs but none of their wives is employed. Before unification Brigitte K., now in her late forties, worked as a quality surveyor in the Neptun shipyards, where she headed a team of seven men. For eighteen months until September 1993 she either worked a short-time week or was engaged on one of the government work-creation schemes; since 1993 she has been out of work. Before 1990 Brigitte K. was one of the 12,600 employees in the Rostock shipyards. After unification the workforce was drastically reduced and by November 1991 40% of the workers had left the shipyards to find jobs elsewhere in Rostock or in western Germany. Apart from those who left the shipyards voluntarily, a further 30% took early retirement. This affected not only ship-building but also training, social facilities, cleaning contracts, and carpentry, which were either dissolved or taken over by western firms (for a detailed study of the situation of employees at the Neptun shipyards see Häußermann and Heseler 1993).

In 1991 a Bremen shipyard offered Brigitte K. work as a quality surveyor. For a number of reasons she refused the post: she was concerned about the uncertain employment situation of her husband; her teenage daughter had obtained a place as an apprentice in Rostock; and she and her husband were closely attached to their home city. Since her dismissal in September 1993 Brigitte K. has been unable to find a new job and she has abandoned all hope of starting a new career. Together with her husband she lives in a state of social isolation on the twenty-first floor of a multi-storey building. Her comment—'What am I to do all day long in our flat for the rest of my life?'—illustrates one of the most significant social consequences of unification: unemployment in the east has hit women far more forcefully than men. One year after unification 59% of the unemployed in the new federal states were women, a figure which has since increased. Whereas many of Brigitte K.'s male colleagues at the Neptun shipyards have obtained new jobs, women have generally found this far more difficult, if not impossible.

Brigitte K.'s case illustrates how women in particular have become victims of unification. Not only are women with lesser vocational skills and in lowly positions the first to be made redundant and the last to be re-employed: the highly qualified are also affected (Kolinsky 1992:275). Brigitte K. had worked from the day she left school; the GDR's comprehensive child-care facilities ensured that she did not have to interrupt her career to bring up her two children. Apart from providing child-care, workplaces in the GDR—even more so than in other countries—were places of social interaction and community life. As Eva Kolinsky points out:

> One of the legacies of the GDR has been to link social environments, leisure pursuits and activities to employment. In the new *Länder* the unemployed find themselves isolated from their familiar social networks while replacements have been slow to emerge. [...] Isolation and despondency seemed to be the dominant impact of unemployment as women struggled to cope with the post-socialist uncertainties. (Kolinsky 1992:276)

Although never an SED member, Brigitte K. has always been politically active. As in previous years, she participated in the (poorly attended) May Day Demonstration in Rostock in 1993. However, the personal, economic, and social dislocation which she has experienced since unification has killed any interest she might have had in participatory politics. Since 1990 she has not joined a party or any other political organization, although she now votes for the SPD. Brigitte belongs to what is a new social type characteristic of post-*Wende* east Germany. As a woman she has become economically dependent on her husband; her public persona is projected through him. Feeling an outcast, she has been unable to integrate herself into the new post-unification society and political system. Women like Brigitte K. have been marginalized and as a result have withdrawn from political activity:

> Women refrained from joining political parties or political participation. They opted for a contemporary replica of the traditional women's deficit in politics, retreating from activity and waiting for change. (Kolinsky 1992:277)

By contrast, at the time of unification, east German women were expected to thrive in the new Germany. They were, it was felt, equipped with special qualities that would enable them to do well in a capitalist society:

> The GDR woman will prove herself to be the most enduring species, the one and only product about which GDR culture can be proud. For western man, scarred by the battle of the sexes, she is a riddle: working, self-confident, decisive and still feminine—it is a mixture he fails to understand. (Schneider 1990:152)

Schneider's optimistic predictions have not materialized, but he based his views partly on the fact that, at 83%, female participation in the labour market was higher in the former GDR than in most other advanced industrial societies (the figure rises to 91% if those in full-time education are included). In 1989 88% of GDR women held a vocational and/or professional qualification, more than in any other country. Today, apart from feeling isolated and dependent, east German women strongly resent the fact that their hard-earned qualifications are under-valued. Brigitte K. sums up this feeling with the idiomatic expression, '*Alles für die Katz*' ('It's all been a total waste of time'). To make matters worse, Brigitte's generation was brought up in a system which stressed the importance and value of work: a basic tenet of Marxist ideology holds that human beings realized their full potential through creative work.

Given the experiences of women like Brigitte K. it is clear that the democratic model of the new Germany is in grave danger of losing the loyalty of a vast section of the population of the former GDR—unemployed women aged over twenty-five. The term democracy implies that there must be at least a modicum of 'ownership' in the sense of popular control over the existing power structures. It is this ownership, the sense of control over her economic and social situation, that Brigitte K. has lost with unification.

1.1.2 Gert K: the skilled worker

Until 1990 Brigitte K.'s husband, Gert, was a lift engineer. He held a responsible position in the city of Rostock's direct labour organization, which carried out installation and maintenance work in public buildings and housing estates. Soon after unification the organization was privatized and Gert found himself employed by a leading international lift company. No longer confined to Rostock, his job takes him all over the northern part of the former GDR and occasionally to western Germany. Most recently he spent several weeks in Hanover installing lift systems in a new luxury hotel. His absences from home have placed a further strain on Brigitte K.'s emotional state and have aggravated her sense of social isolation, all the more so since Gert is very much a family man who throughout his marriage has assumed an equal share of household work and established a good domestic partnership with his wife. As a direct result of his work pattern and her homebound existence their relationship is now changing. Gradually the couple are adopting a social pattern based on the traditional division of roles, in which the husband works to earn money and the wife performs domestic chores.

Financially Gert K. has done well out of unification: his income and spending power have increased substantially. But as a professional engineer and a committed trade unionist he finds two aspects of the new order disturbing. During his recent stay in Hanover a west German colleague took it upon himself to explain some technical aspects of the job. His manner left no doubt that he regarded Gert as professionally backward. Gert was particularly upset by the fact that his colleague had made no attempt to ascertain the level of his professional competence: he had automatically assumed that Gert's training was inadequate. Gert's comment is: 'It is a major problem in my job to have to deal with know-all west Germans.' Like many east Germans, Gert K. has grown accustomed to the paternalistic attitudes of westerners. Despite the disappearance of the Wall the fact remains that the barrier still exists in the minds of the German people. As Hans Modrow, briefly GDR Prime Minister after the fall of the SED, declared in 1990: 'Germany is united as a state, but the division persists' (Modrow 1993:5).

Despite earning more money after unification Gert K. also experiences wage discrimination: his western colleagues receive higher remuneration for the same work. The Unification Treaty between East and West Germany envisaged the progressive harmonization of wages and salaries (see Chapter 6, 6.5.1). This process was due to be completed by 1994. Currently wages in the eastern part of Germany lie between 50% and 70% of western levels. But even if wages reach 100% of western levels in most sectors by 1994, this will not mean that easterners will enjoy the same income, since holiday pay and Christmas bonuses are exempted from the agreement. Furthermore, wages in the east are depressed by the glut in the labour market, so that pay above the agreed basic rate, which is the rule in western Germany, is likely to remain the exception in the east. In the metal industry the gap in real incomes between east and west was estimated to remain at 30% by the end of 1994, although the cost of living would be much the same (Christ and Neubauer 1991:243). Recent projections talk of a convergence rate of thirty to forty years, depending on which economic and fiscal steps are taken. Two different models for convergence have been proposed. The first is that wage harmonization is slowed down and delayed well beyond 1994. The second involves government wage subsidies for jobs in the east. Whichever model is adopted, all projections envisage a German Mezzogiorno for some time to come (Zank 1993:31). This is likely to produce profound social and political problems.

There is more at stake than a long-term east–west social divide. Under threat is the almost unique German system of 'social partnership' between employers and workforce which politicians and social historians have seen as a mainstay of the West German economic miracle. German 'social partnership' has provided employees with good basic pay and conditions of service together with seats on the boards of larger companies. In return employers have enjoyed industrial peace. Since the 1950s this balance of interests has resulted in one of the highest productivity rates in the world alongside one of the lowest rates of industrial action.

A cornerstone of the social partnership is the 'tariff system' (*Tarifsystem*), in which employers' associations and trade unions jointly determine basic rates of pay and conditions of service for their particular industries for one or two years. Once reached, these agreements are legally binding on both parties. At present there are some 40,000 such agreements in existence. In the current industrial recession vociferous calls are being made for an overhaul of the *Tarifsystem*, which is seen as cumbersome, inflexible, and as hostile to free-market forces. There are even demands that it be scrapped altogether. Because of high wage levels and ancillary benefits many believe that Germany's competitiveness abroad is threatened. If German goods price themselves out of the market, even greater unemployment will result. The German employers' federation is currently arguing for increased flexibility and for the right in certain cases to pay wages at less than the agreed tariff level. Clearly the unions would not welcome this. Others argue that radical changes to the system will amount to the disappearance of the type of social market economy which has served the FRG so well. It has to be recognized that the process of dismantling the *Tarifsystem* has already started in the eastern states, where employers are negotiating directly with workers on site in order to reach localized agreements (Schulenberg 1993).

Gert K. was involved in one of the first major strikes over pay in the engineering sector that took place in the new federal states in 1993. Employers and trade unions eventually agreed that, because of high production costs and low productivity, companies could pay below the tariff in so-called 'hardship cases' in order to avoid insolvency. Consequently some twenty engineering companies now pay less than the national tariff. In other sectors it is reckoned that half of all east German companies now undercut the tariff. In many cases the practice is illegal and is not justified on grounds of hardship, as defined in the original agreement. However, local trade union officials feel that in the face of financial collapse and continuing unemployment in eastern Germany they have little option but to accept the inevitable reduction in rates of pay.

In order to by-pass the *Tarifsystem* altogether a number of companies negotiate directly with their workers at local level. In Dresden the large media conglomerate, Gruner & Jahr, have made negotiations outside the *Tarifsystem* a precondition for a 500 million DM investment. Although workers are paid less than tariff rates they can benefit from performance-related bonuses. So far, the arrangement has saved 700 to 800 jobs (Schulenberg 1993). Gruner & Jahr is not the only company in Dresden to tie its investment policy to circumvention of the *Tarifsystem*. The city's CDU mayor, Herbert Wagner, proudly points to the statistics of success: some two to three years after unification Dresden had the lowest unemployment rate in the five new states (11·8% in August 1993) and the highest tax income from business (63 million DM in 1992). Outside the east German context the figures are less impressive, a fact which Wagner himself readily admits: although Dresden's population is almost half a million, 'when compared to the west, this volume of tax income corresponds to a city with about 100,000 inhabitants' (Schayan 1993:24).

Individuals like Gert K. resent the long-term discrimination which such wage deals imply. They are particularly dissatisfied with those organizations which claim to represent their interests, the SPD and the trade unions. On a broader level they are also becoming more and more sceptical about the alleged benefits of the social market economy. In socio-political terms Gert K. falls into a category which was established in a recently published longitudinal study of the lives of individual Germans: 'It could very well be that, as happened after the Second World War to those born around 1920, these generation groups develop a "without me" syndrome with respect to political participation' (Huinink and Mayer 1993:167). Indeed, the spread of this 'without me' attitude towards participatory politics could alienate whole sections of the east German population:

> A not unrealistic scenario is that the upheaval of GDR society will result in a series of 'lost generations'. The loss is four-fold: pensioners will experience a relative material loss compared with other age groups; older people who are no longer working and who supported the former regime will undergo a loss of status and a loss of identity; finally, virtually everyone will find that their qualifications are devalued. (Joas and Kohli 1993:167–68)

Brigitte and Gert K. could be considered as members of a 'lost generation' in the sense that they are lost to participatory democracy in the Western European sense. While not necessarily hostile to democracy, such citizens are not active participants in the democratic process. The apathy and resignation that will probably emerge is already evident in the final comment by Brigitte and Gert K.: *'Wir haben unser Auskommen'* ('We get by. We don't complain').

1.1.3 Dirk K: the middle manager

On 25 September 1989 the first Monday Demonstrations took place in Leipzig with only a few thousand participants. The following week an estimated 20,000 demonstrators appeared on the streets. On 9 October the number had grown to 70,000, and on 16 October to 120,000. One week later, the number exceeded 200,000. On 30 October 300,000 took to the streets and on 6 November the numbers reached their peak with half a million. The Thursday Demonstrations in Rostock began later than those in Leipzig and were never as large. But the mood and the slogans were the same. For six weeks the cry was *'Wir sind das Volk'* ('We are the people'); after 13 November the predominant slogans were *'Wir sind ein Volk'* ('We are one people') and *'Deutschland, einig Vaterland'* ('Germany, one Fatherland', a quotation from the GDR national anthem). The slogans indicated a shift away from demands for internal reform towards a desire for unification. Some four years later an article in *Die Zeit* carried the headline 'Wir waren das Volk' ('We were the people'; Kurbjuweit 1993). Clearly, between 1989 and 1993 the east Germans' enthusiasm for unification had changed profoundly. What happened during this period to affect east Germans' perceptions of the unification process will be analysed with reference to the K. family.

Dirk K., now in his late thirties, and his wife Jutta took part in the Rostock demonstrations from the very beginning. Neither had been SED members and they joined the reformist New Forum in the early stages in Rostock. Dirk K. had left school with the *Abitur* and planned to study German literature, a subject in which the competition for university entrance was intense. To improve his chances of university entry and give himself a solid financial basis for study, he volunteered for a nine-year term in the GDR navy as an NCO. During his service he met his future wife. She soon became pregnant and the couple married. Both felt that it would be preferable for Dirk to take a job on leaving the navy. Aged twenty-eight, he began working with the GDR state-owned oil and petrol company, Minol, and by 1989 he had risen to a middle management position within the local Rostock structure. He now holds a managerial position with a petrol company. The job takes him to Berlin for the working week and he sees his family only at weekends. His wife, who trained as a florist, stopped working after the birth of the second of their three children, two of whom were attending primary school in 1994.

Dirk K. had always taken a strong interest in the study of Marxism-Leninism, and long before the collapse of the GDR he had hoped for a 'socialism with a human face'. Despite his engineering background and career as a technocrat he still sees himself as a political thinker and intellectual (his own term). He is an avid reader of *Die Zeit* and sympathizes with most of the findings of the article 'Wir waren das Volk'. The article contains statements by a number of leading demonstrators on the occasion of the fourth anniversary of the Leipzig demonstrations. One statement recalls a line by the Leipzig poet Heinz Czechowski, who parodies the speeches of the French Revolution: 'We have done too little, the revolution is eating its young; they are guzzling bananas, who could blame them?' The reference to the revolution consuming its own young is echoed more prosaically by other demonstrators, who also declare that they did too little and made grave tactical and strategic mistakes. For instance, instead of negotiating with politicians theoretically still in power, the intellectuals leading the civil rights movement should have shown the old guard the door and simply taken over the reins of power themselves. But as one of them says: 'We were not used to power.'

Although Dirk K. does not share the bitterness expressed in the article, he is concerned about how the revolution passed out of the hands of its originators and supporters. First, he regrets how, four years after the *Wende*, the aims of the revolution and the process of unification have become confused. In his view they have both been usurped by the self-proclaimed Unity Chancellor and his propagandists. Dirk firmly believes that the revolution was the property of the intellectual dissidents, for the most part members of New Forum. He also points out that, even after the fall of the Berlin Wall, when the dissidents' influence declined rapidly, it was the East German population that insisted on unification. In no sense did West Germany either instigate the revolution or provide the popular impetus for unification. According to Peter Schneider the Western attitude was at best reactive: there was not a single demonstration for unification in West Germany. It is true that public opinion polls there in the late autumn of 1989 indicated 80% support for Kohl's unification plans, but in March 1990, when West Germans were asked whether they would be prepared to make personal financial sacrifices for unification, only 61% said yes, and by May 1993 the figure had fallen to 28% (Schneider 1990:137). Second, Dirk K. highlights the fact that the GDR elections of March 1990 were largely West German affairs. The election processes, ranging from paper supplies to the choice of speakers, were in effect controlled by the West German parties. The poor showing of the New Forum and the other opposition groups underlined the sense of loss, if not to say theft, experienced by the East German intellectuals who had been the motor of the revolution.

1.1.4 *Uwe K: the intellectual*

In the wake of unification the intellectuals of the former GDR felt disappointed and depressed. Those who had refused to align themselves to 'real existing socialism' (the official GDR term for the achievements of the socialist state) experienced an acute sense of having lost control of the revolution. Dirk K. points out that intellectuals played a key role in the early stages of the *Wende*; Jens Reich, co-founder of New Forum and a leading dissident, describes the autumn of 1989 primarily as an intellectual protest movement. The public climax of this movement was the mass meeting on the Berlin Alexanderplatz on 4 November, at which leading authors such as Christa Wolf and Stefan Heym welcomed the political changes and presented their vision of a reformed but independent East German state. Soon afterwards the intellectual reformers were pushed aside, even ridiculed. Clearly they had not anticipated such a reverse. They had become the victims of a two-fold illusion: first, that the people would endorse their aims and elect them as leaders; and second, that the West would recognize their role (Reich 1992:23).

But it was not only the actively dissident intellectuals who found themselves in a political vacuum during the unification process. There were many intellectuals in the GDR who, politically inactive, were not included in the nomenclature (the national register of approved key personnel in the former GDR). These suffered disproportionately from unemployment, enforced early retirement, and the often painful process of *Abwicklung*, the procedure by which positions and organizations in the former GDR have been evaluated to establish whether they will be retained after unification. *Abwicklung* has led to wholesale restructuring and job losses, not only in industry, trade, and commerce, but also in universities, further education institutions, research institutes, schools, and public administration (Reich 1992:13). As a consequence a class of disillusioned intellectuals is emerging in the east, either unwilling or unable to support the new democracy. An uncomfortable historical parallel with the Weimar Republic comes to mind: a major reason advanced to explain the downfall of the Republic is that it was a democracy without democrats, specifically a democracy that did not enjoy the support of the intellectuals.

Uwe K., the oldest brother in the family, and his wife Doris belonged to the intelligentsia of the former GDR. Both had been members of the SED since their student days. As a Communist Doris's father has been persecuted during the twelve years of Nazi rule. Until his death in the late 1960s Uwe's father had been a member of the SED and a leading trade unionist. Uwe studied chemistry at undergraduate and postgraduate level at the University of Rostock. During his student days he had also served for a year as secretary of the university branch of the national youth movement, the FDJ. In 1968, with the invasion of Czechoslovakia and the suppression of the Prague Spring, Uwe suffered severe political doubts for the first time in his life. It was not merely that he sympathized with Alexander Dubcek's reformist aspirations; he found the participation of East German troops in the invasion particularly odious since it evoked memories of Hitler's annexation of Czechoslovakia and their entry into Prague in March 1939. Seeking a more acceptable alternative to the Stalinist system in the GDR, Uwe actively studied other forms of socialism such as those practised in China, Cuba, and more recently in Zimbabwe. After Gorbachev came to power in 1985 Uwe K. experienced new hope. He continued to believe, albeit mistakenly, that 'real existing socialism' could be reformed and remained an active SED member in his work's branch until the autumn of 1989. After gaining his Ph.D. he worked for some years in the Chemistry Department of Rostock University. Eventually he moved from teaching to research and became part of an internationally recognized team in the Clinical Section of the University which was involved in the construction of artificial organs. On account of its international reputation the members of the team belonged to the privileged travel cadre, a group of key personnel who were permitted to travel abroad. Uwe undertook business and research trips to North Korea, Bulgaria, Finland, West Germany, Belgium, the USA, and Britain.

The SED group in the Clinical Section at Rostock University was predominantly pro-Gorbachev and in an act of no mean defiance sent a letter to the regional SED Party Secretary demanding to know why the authorities had banned the import of the Soviet satirical magazine *Sputnik*. Uwe and his wife Doris finally broke with the SED in January 1990, when the media exposed the widespread personal and organizational corruption in leading cadres of the Party. They also realized that the notion of the reformability of 'real existing socialism' had been a pipe-dream and that the SED, despite changing its name, could not reform itself. Uwe and Doris withdrew from active politics and are now SPD voters.

After unification and during the evaluations of staff at Rostock University (conducted as part of the *Abwicklung* programme) it emerged that two members of Uwe K.'s research team had been *Stasi* informers. One had already left the country for a research post in Austria; the other resigned. The team's leader, Professor T., an internationally acknowledged expert in his field, was also implicated in *Stasi* activities. While his collaboration was never proved, the University dismissed him because of his high-level contacts with the SED even though such contacts were routine for someone in his public position. Soon afterwards he took up a research position at the University of Bologna. For personal reasons Uwe declined to follow his professor's invitation to join him at Bologna: his two children were in their last years of secondary education. Uwe received official clearance after a university hearing had found that his political involvement was insufficient to recommend dismissal. But after the research team was dispersed, he did not want to continue as a research fellow in another, less prestigious field, and he left university employment. He joined a Hamburg-based pharmaceutical company as their representative for Mecklenburg-West Pomerania. His wife, who had worked as a chemist with the GDR Academy of Sciences in the field of artificial fertilizers, lost her job when the Academy was dissolved. After some time working on a job creation scheme she is now unemployed and unlikely to find another post.

Uwe and Doris K. are prime examples of how human expertise and resources were wasted after unification. They are also members of what they themselves call the second 'deceived generation' in twentieth-century German history, a generation that grew up in the GDR and believed in the ideals of socialism. But unlike the situation after the Second World War, they feel there is no space in the east for a communal pioneering spirit: the panacea of the free market commends only individualistic attitudes. Both Uwe and Doris have found that their social status has declined since unification, but they harbour no bitterness and their outlook is of realistic acceptance: 'The main thing is, the money's O.K.' They quote from the final strophe of the *Florian Geyer Lied*, a song from the Peasants' Revolt of 1525: 'Our grandchildren will make a better fight of it.'

When talking to Uwe and Doris K., it is difficult to get them to acknowledge what can only be described as the guilt complex of GDR intellectuals. Peter Schneider describes the nature of this complex:

> Not until they were subjected to the test of the October Revolution of 1989 did it become clear that the criticisms voiced by the literary 'dissidents' were almost always made within the bounds of a consensus: the legitimization of the socialist one-party state was never questioned, neither was the Party's claim to leadership. Criticism was levelled against the SED's misuse of power, never against its monopoly of it. The demand for more democracy did not imply free elections and a ('reactionary bourgeois') party pluralism but the abolition of censorship and a plurality of opinions within the socialist power structures. (Schneider 1990:68–69)

By acknowledging the leading role of the SED and its monopoly of power, the dissidents and critical intellectuals of the GDR placed themselves in a paradoxical position: they wanted *glasnost* but not a party democracy (Thomaneck 1984:80). Unsurprisingly, the feeling of guilt that accompanied this position gave way to relief once the pretence was over. Formerly active SED members, Uwe and Doris K. no longer have to defend a system which they knew to be imperfect and to some extent indefensible. Within their family and circle of friends they are now more open and relaxed than they had ever been before 1989.

1.1.5 *Detlef K: the senior manager*

Until 1989 Detlef K., the second oldest of the brothers, belonged to the GDR's class of senior managers: as such he was classed as a member of the intelligentsia. While he was in his first semester at the Leipzig Institute of Journalism, his girlfriend Ingrid gave birth to a son. The new responsibility prompted Detlef to drop his studies and start work as an electrician. Coming from a generation of school pupils in the GDR who had completed an apprenticeship while studying for their *Abitur*, he was already a qualified tradesman. While working he obtained an engineering degree through an evening and correspondence course and was rapidly promoted to the most senior managerial position of the direct labour organization in Rostock (*VEB Gebäudewirtschaft*).

During the course of his promotions Detlef K. was approached by the SED and invited to join the Party. His response was that he would rather join the Liberal LDPD (one of the Block Parties under the control of the SED); as town councillor for the LDPD he soon became active in local politics. In the autumn of 1989 he was one of the prime organizers of the Rostock Thursday Demonstrations, along with Pastor Joachim Gauck and Rainer Ortleb. Detlef was responsible for the absorption of the NDPD and the DBD (both former Block Parties) into the LDPD. He also played a leading role in the transformation of the LDPD into the liberal-orientated FDP in Mecklenburg-West Pomerania and for almost three years he was the FDP General Secretary for the region. In June 1993 he left this post and now works as a junior partner and managing director in a property company.

Detlef K. is the most positive of the whole family about unification. He has embraced the free market economy and its ideology wholeheartedly and earns by far the highest salary in the family. Politically he sees himself on the right of the FDP and maintains that nobody is worse off after unification.

1.1.6 *Olaf and Karin K: perceptions of unemployment and crime*

Olaf K. and his wife Karin live in Lüttenklein, one of the many soulless concrete housing schemes between Rostock and Warnemünde. Olaf is a lift mechanic and works for the same firm as his brother Gert. Olaf has always been apolitical and remains so after unification. He considers that little has changed in his life. His wife, who worked as a shop assistant with the HO (the *Handelsorganisation*, the state-owned food distribution and retail organisation for the GDR) now finds herself unemployed after participating in a number of job creation schemes. Since their three children are at secondary school, she would like to return to work. Together with her sister-in-law Jutta, she has applied for numerous jobs as a shop assistant. On occasion both women have reached the interview stage with large western supermarket chains which have established themselves in Rostock. However, they have found it disconcerting not to be asked primarily about their qualifications and expertise. The interviews have concentrated instead on their marital status and domestic life, their family income, and the age of their children. The women are convinced that the fact that they have children is the reason why they have not been appointed. Both freely acknowledge that they would have considerable difficulties in looking after their children outside school hours. In particular, Jutta would have to arrange day-care for the youngest child.

Before unification nearly 90% of children under ten in the GDR were accommodated in full-time day-care facilities. These have now virtually disappeared and as a result both Jutta and Karin K. feel not only under-valued as women and workers, but also penalized for being mothers. For these women the loss of access to child-care has produced the most drastic differences in their lives since unification. Previously they were highly re-garded members of GDR society, and their status was actually enhanced by the fact that they each had three children. The GDR positively pro-moted women and motherhood:

> East German women were humoured with exceptions, privileges, special measures and financial bonuses to embrace their family roles and especially motherhood more willingly. [...] Women in the GDR did not have as keen a sense of disadvantage as that which had emerged in the West. East Germans were inclined to accept the state administered place of women as securing equal opportunities, at least in the public sphere. Even after unification, a majority con-tinues to believe that equality had been achieved. (Kolinsky 1992:271–72)

For Jutta and Karin, both in their mid-thirties, the change in social attitude has occurred too suddenly and has been a deep shock to their psyches. Both women live on the sixth floor of a so-called *Wohnsilo* (literally: 'an accommodation silo', a pejorative term for large, anonymous apartment blocks). Socially isolated, they enjoy little contact with the outside world.

Jutta and Karin K. are acutely aware of the increasing crime rate in their neighbourhoods. This mostly takes the form of burglaries, car thefts, and vandalism to vehicles, but there are also attacks on women. The new crime wave is very much a topic of conversation in the family. Karin and her husband Olaf often refer back to the Honecker days, when criminality was less widespread and offenders were dealt with harshly. They favour the death penalty and would like to see draconian penalties for criminals. They would also welcome neighbourhood vigilantes. The couple blame the in-creased criminality on foreigners and young people. In their view, foreign-ers should be deported. As for the treatment of young people, they regret the disappearance of the authoritarian approach to education as formerly practised under 'real existing socialism'. At the same time they regret the closure of leisure facilities for young people who now have nowhere to go in their free time. Indeed, the lack of facilities for young people is a prob-lem throughout Germany. Faced by financial difficulties, many German towns and cities are closing down youth centres (Arntz 1993:22). The situation is much worse in the new federal states, which have virtually no money to spend on youth and community projects.

Karin and Olaf K. are undoubtedly correct in their perception that more crimes are being committed by young people in eastern Germany than in the GDR years. In 1992 7,461 juvenile crimes per 100,000 inhabitants were registered in the east. These figures indicate that the level of youth criminality there is now virtually the same as in western Germany. East German youths are also increasingly members of cliques, gangs, and sub-cultures. In Leipzig, for instance, there are about fifty gangs of twelve to fifteen-year-olds who squat in derelict buildings, often not returning home for several days. They specialize in muggings, burglaries, and car thefts. So far the east has been spared dramatic increases in drug-usage and drug-related crimes, although alcoholism is as widespread among young people as in the west (Malarski 1993a:5–8).

Statistics indicate that children of foreigners are responsible for a dis-proportionately high number of crimes. This is particularly true of street muggings (74%) and pickpocketing (35%). Overall, 30% of all crimes in Germany are committed by foreigners. Karin and Olaf K. are not alone in their view that foreigners should be discouraged from entering Germany. In the new federal states 75% of young people believe that Germany should restrict the number of foreigners, compared to 58% in the west; 55% of east German sixteen-year-olds feel that foreigners who already live in Germany should return to their country of origin; this compares with 33% in the west. These statistics are mirrored in the figures for violent crimes committed by right-wing extremists. In 1992 there were 2,584 such crimes, of which 33·5% occurred in the east. In the first six months of 1993 a total of 971 violent crimes was reported, of which 223 (23%) took place in eastern Germany. Both figures suggest that the rate in the new states is proportionally higher, where only one-fifth of the German population lives. Worst hit are Brandenburg and Mecklenburg-West Pomerania (Malarski 1993a:7, 10–11). The possibility of an increase in crime in the former GDR was predicted by Peter Schneider in 1990 in an essay entitled 'Are there two German cultures?':

> Regardless of how GDR-citizens now assess their forty-year experi-ence, compared to the Federal Republic they lived in a society of equals. It does not need much imagination to predict that their ex-periences may result in a social explosion. In an economic crisis east Germans will easily perceive themselves as second-class citizens. Given such a crisis, the culture of equality which they have inherited is undoubtedly more likely to provide a breeding ground for extreme

right-wing populists than for left-wing agitators. In any case, there
is bound to be a conflict. (Schneider 1990:149)

Clearly the disappearance of the culture of equality to which Schneider refers is not the only reason for an increase in support for right-wing violence. Other reasons include sudden changes in society and value systems,
insecurity of employment, and changes in family life, all of which have occurred in eastern Germany (Malarski 1993a:19–24 and 1993b).

1.2 Age profiles in east and west

Two members of the K. family no longer live in Rostock. One, the youngest brother, Karsten K., together with his wife Viola and two children, left
the GDR for the FRG in January 1990. They belong to the one million
former GDR citizens who have gone westwards since the opening of the
Berlin Wall. Karsten's mother and her partner had received permission to
leave for West Germany in 1988. Both are old-age pensioners and glad
that they moved since they are financially much better off than they would
have been if they had stayed in East Germany.

   As a result of unification it is likely that senior citizens in east and west
Germany will constitute heterogeneous social groups for years to come.
Significant differences will persist in incomes, quality of accommodation,
leisure pursuits, personal needs and expectations, and in political attitudes
(Schwitzer 1993). For example, old-age pensions in the five new states are
only 66% of those in the west; at the time of unification 60% of flats occupied by senior citizens in the east lacked basic amenities such as a bath-
room, toilet, hot water, and central heating; this was true of 40% of flats in
the west. There are still fewer homes for the elderly in east Germany and
even fewer community centres, which have been axed alongside facilities
for youth.

   Many older people in the GDR continued working beyond the official
retirement age. That is no longer the case. Indeed, old-age pensioners have
been joined by an army of younger people forced into early retirement. In
east and west Germany the number of retired people is increasing both in
absolute numbers and as a percentage of the total population. In 1979 20%
of the entire German population was over sixty; the figure is expected to
rise to 30% by the year 2030. The shift in the national age profile will not
only create problems for governmental budgets, it also means that the political influence of senior citizens, specifically in terms of their voting preferences, will grow. At present, every third voter for the CDU/CSU is over

sixty. Other parties have become keenly aware of the political potential of pensioners (for an overview of the current situation see Bischof 1993).

1.3 Conclusion: changing attitudes

Social changes inevitably generate shifts in attitudes, especially where political perceptions are concerned. The only member of the K. family to have identified himself wholeheartedly with unification and the new political establishment is Detlef. Many others in his family feel that they have been cast out, left behind, or even betrayed by unification. Such experiences are bound to undermine loyalty to the prevailing political system. There is also evidence that social concerns in the wake of unification have significantly altered traditional voting patterns.

A comparison between voting behaviour in 1990 and 1993 in east and west yielded startling results. In 1990 the CDU/CSU attracted predominantly older voters in both west and east. While support for the SPD and the FDP was not particularly age-related, the Greens counted most of their voters among the young, and adherents to the PDS (the successor party of the SED) belonged mainly to the older generation. By 1993 this pattern had changed. The vote for the CDU/CSU, although still mainly age-related, declined markedly in east and west, with substantial losses among young voters. Support for the SPD increased but showed no particular age focus. The vote for both FDP and the Greens did not change significantly. The right-wing Republicans, on the other hand, began to attract support, especially among younger and, to a lesser extent, older voters. By 1993 the PDS was strongly represented in the east among young people and those over fifty (Gluchowski and Mnich 1993). These figures indicate not only a shift of voting attitudes with regard to age but also a turning away from the established parties of government. They further show how particular social changes have affected the more marginalized groups of society in the wake of unification.

The disillusionment with the establishment which these voting patterns reflect is also evident in public perceptions of democratic institutions such as the Basic Law, Parliament, the law courts, government, trade unions, television, the press, and the police. Between 1990 and 1993 clear differences emerged between east and west Germans, with easterners enjoying far less confidence in such bodies than westerners (Gabriel 1993).

Hans Modrow provided a scathing criticism of the unification process and a gloomy assessment of the current social situation:

The Germans in the west [...] feel disappointed, angry, and thank-lessly misused. The frustrated hopes on both sides are leading to in-difference, intolerance, and a growing antipathy. The cleavages, not just between east and west Germany, but also between the poor and rich [...] are growing wider. Germany has become a disunited rather than a united fatherland. (Modrow 1993)

Modrow's assessment cannot simply be dismissed as political propaganda for the PDS. The experiences of the K. family support his view. A different question is whether the citizens of the new states would actually wish to return to the days before the autumn of 1989. To answer this it is necessary to provide a broader picture of the feelings of east Germans.

In a number of recent opinion polls east Germans were asked whether they believed that the decision for speedy unification in 1990 had been cor-rect. In October 1992, 69% replied in the affirmative; by October 1993 the figure had risen to 75%. The same poll asked east and west Germans what they felt were their most worrying and pressing problems: 68% of eastern-ers ranked unemployment in first place; the corresponding figure for west-erners was 48%. In second place for easterners were criminality, and law and order; in the west it was asylum policies and problems associated with foreigners (*Europäische Zeitung*, No. 44, November 1993:10). Despite their concerns, the overwhelming majority of easterners did not wish to return to pre-1989 days, nor did they want to change the unification process.

More information emerged from a major opinion poll conducted in Sep-tember 1993 (Hilmer and Müller-Hilmer 1993). While those interviewed declared overwhelming support for unification, they also displayed both disappointment and realism. Two-thirds of east Germans questioned do not expect the social and economic imbalances between east and west to dis-appear before the year 2000. They also believed that the generation that succeeded them would be the first to benefit from unification. Half be-lieved that unification came too late for them. Of these, 41% were in their thirties. Such pessimism in a relatively young age group is a dangerous source of potential social discontent for the new Germany. At the same time, 58% of those interviewed felt, like Detlef K., that they had gained personally from unification. Four out of ten citizens were disappointed about the changes, among them many who had lost their jobs. One in seven would now like to turn the clock back to before 1989. Most disturbing is the fact that 82% regretted the fact that nothing remains of the GDR's achievements, of which they had been rightly proud. This was a view also strongly held by the female members of the K. family.

According to the poll 27% of the population were still finding it hard to adjust to the new situation. This was particularly true of those aged over forty and is confirmed by the experiences of the women in the K. family. The numbers of people taking a pessimistic view of the future rose from 23% in 1991 to 33% in 1993. Again, the pessimistic outlook prevailed among the over forties. Women, the unemployed, and the early retired were particularly affected by feelings of frustration, insecurity, and resignation. Some 35% believed that they had become *Absteiger*, that is, their social status had declined; this group included mainly women, those over forty, former managers, and the unemployed. Only 13% felt that they were *Aufsteiger*, that is, their status had risen, whilst 52% saw their status as unchanged. The small group of *Aufsteiger* consisted principally of men, young people, and those with an income of over 3,500 DM a month (about 12% of all households).

The survey reveals that much of the aura of the 'golden west' has disappeared and that a more realistic view prevails. The new realism is not based solely on individuals' assessments of their economic situation. Some 95% of the interviewees declared that altogether too much value was attached to money. 86% felt that the new Germany was not a fair society. There is a discernible trend to romanticize certain aspects of the former GDR. This applies particularly to work, personal security, and social justice.

Political attitudes were also tested. In the general election of December 1990 the CDU and its allies received 54% of the vote. The survey indicated that if elections had been held in September 1993 the CDU would have received 21%, the FDP 9%, the SPD 38% (up from 24% in 1990), the Greens/Alliance 90 13% (up from 6% in 1990), the PDS 13%, and the Republicans 4%. A quarter of the interviewees held no voting views or were simply not interested in politics (for an analysis of the results of the national elections held in December 1994 see Chapter 5, Section 5.2.3).

To sum up: social changes in the new federal states have made east Germans far more realistic about unification than they were in 1989–90. For many, euphoria has given way to frustration and disillusionment, and there is a widespread belief that they have lost the revolution. Consequently, east Germans are increasingly opting out of civic life and the processes of political participation. Such alienation threatens to endanger democracy in the east, especially since the integration of the new states may not be complete until the next century. Accounts of the local elections held in Brandenburg in December 1993 confirmed the disturbing picture. Apathy prevailed not only among the voters but also within the parties, who had enormous difficulties finding enough supporters to stand as mayors and councillors. Just one month before the elections there were no candidates for 300 positions of mayor in the towns and villages of Brandenburg. At the same time the SPD could not find candidates for seats on two-thirds of the state's 1,700 local councils; election meetings were so poorly attended that they were cancelled (Paterson 1993a). The SPD election manager and General Secretary Günter Verheugen was profoundly discouraged by the political apathy that he encountered:

> It is very difficult to know what to say to the east Germans I meet who keep telling me that all politicians are useless and that they are to blame for everything. I must say I am very concerned. Disappointment, anger and bitterness run deep. (Paterson 1993c)

The truth of this statement is confirmed elsewhere. An opinion poll conducted in eastern Germany in 1993 showed that 72% of east Germans believed that they could exert little or no influence over important political, economic, and social developments in Germany. Some 61% thought that east Germans were once again turning their backs on politics and retreating into their own private worlds (Paterson 1993b). As FDP General Secretary for Mecklenburg-West Pomerania, Detlef K. foresaw a situation in which his party would soon be a party without members.

At the time the results of the local elections in Brandenburg on 5 December 1993 did not augur well for the national and European elections that were held in Germany in 1994. In the October 1990 state elections the SPD had polled 38·3% of the votes; in December 1993 the vote had fallen to 36%. The CDU had obtained 29·4% in 1990; it now achieved only 20% and limped into third place behind the PDS, who gained 22% (13·4% in 1990). The FDP and Green vote remained largely unchanged, and the neo-Nazi Republicans failed to make significant inroads. Although local elections are often influenced by local issues, it was clear that *Parteienverdrossenheit* (disillusionment with the established parties) was widespread. Although more marked in eastern Germany, *Parteienverdrossenheit* is currently also a phenomenon in western Germany. In 1993 Günter Verheugen warned: 'We are heading into an enormous political vacuum which none of the parties can fill and which will be occupied by calls for a strong man' (Paterson 1993c).

Social changes and shifts in political attitudes will not affect one part of Germany in isolation, or for that matter, only a part of Europe. Germany has to become a more united country. It must develop a clear identity for all its citizens and encourage them towards active participation in civic life and in national political institutions. Helmut Schmidt makes the following plea:

Until the end of this century and beyond, the most important thing
for our people, for our society, and for our state is brotherliness and
mutual solidarity. The German people has long understood that we
endanger the freedom of every individual and the freedom and happiness of our children if we ignore the commandment to show brotherliness and if we allow ourselves to slip back into an elbow-society
where egoism and ruthlessness triumph. (Schmidt 1993:242)

Further reading

Apart from works mentioned in the text, Hanesch (1994), Falter (1994),
and Anderson (1993) are recommended as introductions to the social
issues confronting contemporary Germany.

2
Views of the *Wende*

GERALD OPIE

2.1 Introduction

In the autumn of 1989 East Germans turned out in their hundreds of thousands in the major cities of the GDR to produce one of the most extraordinary events in the history of the twentieth century: the *Wende*, or turning-point, which led to the downfall of the ruling Communist regime. This chapter presents a perspective on these events, not in retrospect, but from the viewpoint of the people who were experiencing them. As is always the case with historical situations, one is tempted with hindsight to see the course of events as natural and inevitable, and to wonder at the blindness of those commentators who failed to predict the way that things would develop. Surely, we now assume, in the autumn of 1989 it must have been clear that the GDR could not continue and that Germany would become a united country. But while they were happening, events appeared to have the potential of developing in any number of ways, and what is in retrospect an obvious analysis would in the context of the time have seemed a bold, even a rash, prophecy. This chapter aims to convey, as far as possible, a sense of being there, with all the uncertainty and confusion, and fear, that the participants and observers experienced. The account draws on various sources representing different levels of society. These sources fall broadly into three groups: politicians, the press, and the ordinary people. The time-span covered is from early September 1989, when the Hungarian border with Austria was opened to the West, to the fall of the Berlin Wall on 9 November 1989. These were the months of political crisis that culminated in the first change of power in the GDR, and as such they represent the most critical period for observers and participants alike.

2.2 The period immediately before the *Wende*

There was always a discrepancy between the official GDR view of itself as propounded by government propaganda and the reality of life in so-called 'real existing socialism'. By the late 1980s, despite the censorship exercised by the regime, pressure to express the experience of that reality had increased to a point where a more truthful account of conditions in the GDR could be published in the country itself.

In 1988 a stir was caused by the publication of a volume of reportage by the journalist Landolf Scherzer (Scherzer 1988). In this study the author shadows Hans-Dieter Fritschler, the First Secretary of the SED for the area of Bad Salzungen in Thuringia, giving an honest impression of the everyday problems, economic, social, and personal, faced by a government official. The picture that emerges stands as a testimony to the state of the GDR in the period immediately before the *Wende*—a run-down society struggling to survive against all the odds and dependent on the commitment and self-sacrifice of a few overworked and demoralized idealists. The feeling that pervades the report is of a society that has lost its way and is nearing the end of its course, but unknowingly so. Not that Scherzer intended to create such an impression; and indeed the East German critic Helmut Hauptmann, reviewing the book in February 1989, praises the author for a responsible socialist criticism of the state of the nation (Hauptmann 1989). Yet one now senses that this is a last-ditch defence. Fritschler may be intended as a socialist 'positive hero', and he comes across as sincere, even heroic in his own way, but from today's vantage point the reader realizes that his heroism has little chance of being crowned with success. The heroism is more tragic than positive.

West German journalists visiting the GDR in the late 1980s also note a new openness, at least in private conversations, and a willingness on the part of some officials to admit that the reality of socialism is less than perfect. For instance, Hermann Rudolph, writing in the *Süddeutsche Zeitung* on 2 September 1987, talks of their admission that the prefabricated high-rise blocks of the Marzahn district of East Berlin are hideous. However, such openness comes in small doses. The general impression is that to get on in the GDR it was necessary to subscribe, or at least pay lip service to, the utopian fictions, the *So-soll-es-sein-Ideologie* ('the "this is the way it is supposed to be"-ideology'), as he calls it. Rudolph obviously feels that the *gute alte Funktionärs-DDR* ('the good old GDR of the party functionary') is on the way out. Others paint an even darker picture. Wolfgang Kramer, writing in April 1989, notes the general apathy of the population, its acceptance of the dirt, the crumbling buildings, the eternal shortages, the *Duckmäusertum* ('cringing attitude') of cowed people who have lost hope and self-respect; and this, he reflects bitterly, is happening in Thuringia, with its historical associations with the free spirit of Martin Luther (Kramer 1989). In the same month Heinz Verfürth sees little sign in the GDR of the spirit of *glasnost* and *perestroika* that is overtaking the rest of Eastern

Europe. He finds that the party functionaries pride themselves on the GDR's economic achievements and that they are condescending towards the Soviet Union. On the eve of revolution there is no sign of repentance amongst the higher echelons of the SED. His objections to the one-party state are met by the standard argument that the GDR has a plurality of political parties and by a spirited defence of the election procedures for the forthcoming, notoriously rigged, local elections on 7 May 1989 which were later to prove such a thorn in the flesh for Egon Krenz (Verfürth 1990).

The feelings of the average citizen immediately before the *Wende* are also ambivalent and, as might be expected, differ according to individual circumstances. Clearly the SED enjoyed a measure of support from the population: over two million were party members. This is not to say that party members were uncritical of the actions of their leaders. While the extent of disaffection is difficult to gauge, reports demonstrate that it did exist, particularly within the East German 'Conservative' party, the CDU. Jochen Steinmayr tells, for instance, of a local CDU meeting in Leipzig which he attended on 26 September and at which party members voiced criticisms so strong that the chairman felt constrained to put an end to the meeting before things got totally out of hand:

> A construction worker says, 'This party has been nothing more than a puppet of the SED for forty years,' and adds, 'I'm ashamed to have been part of it since 1948.' [...] It is amazing what those present dared to say. The few old people there launched an avalanche of resentment: 'We don't even get told when our head of state is ill. [...] Our CDU Minister of Post banned the Soviet journal *Sputnik.* [...] Of course young people are escaping, like monkeys out of a cage. [...] The whole of the leadership has got to go.' (Steinmayr 1989)

Steinmayr contrasts this mood with the picture of the CDU leader, Gerald Götting. Götting is portrayed as a complacent man, comfortably placed and on good terms with Erich Honecker, whom he addresses in the familiar *du*-person (*den er duzt*). Götting happily accepts the journalist's information that the grass roots of his party find his leadership ineffectual and asserts vaguely that he plans to change things. The gap between the leader and the led is all too apparent, and this in a party that theoretically stands in opposition to the SED. Steinmayr clearly feels that a revolution from above cannot be expected in the GDR. Any change must come from below or at least from outside the existing political parties.

Such a development, however, cannot be anticipated. In the last week of September Steinmayr paints a picture of a demoralized land whose citizens are emigrating in droves since Hungary opened its Western border in September 1989. His article is preceded by a photograph of a demonstration in front of the St Nicholas Church in Leipzig, but there are no signs of an impending uprising, and the caption reads: 'Hands raised in a victory salute. The only courageous demonstrations occurred in front of the Church of St Nicholas in Leipzig, but the majority of citizens of the GDR remained silent and resigned.' (Steinmayr 1989). The reporter finds a land 'in deep resignation and apathy'. He quotes a retired professor who declares that he expects little from the ranks of the dissidents because the SED has recruited all the country's political talent. Generally there is little political vision or sense of purpose, which is why so many want to leave:

> The supply situation is not so very bad [...] but people are leaving now for psychological reasons. They are seized by a strange kind of agoraphobia, and are unable to see a future because they are never told the truth, because they have long since stopped believing propaganda statements, imbibing their reality like a blue haze from the television. (Steinmayr 1989)

The proximity of the prosperous West German neighbour is a potent factor in luring away those who have no motivation beyond material gain. This Western orientation is expressed forcefully by an engineer and his doctor wife whom Steinmayr encounters in Schwerin. When he tells them that he is deliberately not watching West German television so that he will see things from only a GDR perspective, they are amused and suggest that he is the only one in the GDR doing this: everyone else is following events on the West German channels ARD and ZDF. Yet this couple also raise the vexed question of GDR identity by contradicting the thesis that the GDR commands no loyalty: they have after all just returned from Hungary and evidently declined to join the trail of refugees. They justify their action by saying that the GDR is where their jobs and their duty are.

The West German reporter Irmela Hannover, writing on 23 September 1989, discovers similarly ambivalent attitudes in her East German hosts in East Berlin. Journalists in their forties, they are very critical of the government, particularly of its pandering to the consumerist ideals represented by the FRG. They regard this policy as a serious mistake. Instead of taking up the unequal struggle for material prosperity with the West, the GDR should be concentrating on developing its own special identity, and turning its economic weakness into a moral strength by stressing the ecological ethic; by producing fewer unnecessary luxuries, the GDR is making a positive contribution to the future of the planet. Yet when they travel in the couple's Trabi to their weekend retreat in Mecklenburg, Thomas loudly curses the car and is embarrassed by the contrast with the Western vehicles they encounter along the way. The consumer paradise to the west is a perpetual irritant, even to these intellectuals with their progressive and fashionable views. However, they do not take the opportunity to leave the GDR. Despite the reporter's conclusion that the GDR's fundamental problem is that it has failed to create a sense of national pride in the forty years of its existence, the reactions of the East German couple are strangely mixed when they see the refugees on the television news. Uli regards the refugees as dupes of the FRG and victims of the GDR media's foolish propaganda. Instead of trying to put the audience off with horror stories of how a family with nine children has to struggle in Hamburg, East German journalists should interview a successful defector, say a wealthy dentist, about his deeper feelings and thus expose the shame he experiences at betraying his country. Hannover comments: 'I am surprised by my friend Uli's sudden fighting spirit—at last a little pride instead of the constant self-pity' (Golombeck and Ratzke 1990:69).

The American Robert Darnton offers the following first-hand account of the asylum-seekers in Prague:

> A couple of Czech police stood across from the building at a discreet distance, watching but not interfering. Every few minutes some East Germans, easily recognizable from their haircuts and their clothes, would walk up to the door, ring the bell, and disappear inside. Many had crammed their favorite possessions into a few suitcases and had driven to Prague in the most valuable possession of all, their Trabi, the product of years of saving and waiting. They usually left it on a side street, unlocked and with the key in the ignition, and walked the last few hundred yards. Those must have been the longest yards they had ever walked, for they left almost everything behind—not just the Trabi, but family, friends, a whole way of life. You could see the sense of loss mixed with hope in their faces as they arrived. Some smiled, some wept, some clenched their jaws and looked ahead. None of them stepped lightly over the threshold. (Darnton 1991: 71–72)

This account illustrates the patronizing tone that coloured Western sympathy for the refugees; when compared with the East German reaction, it appears sentimental in its concentration on the pathos of the scene. This is the reaction of someone not personally involved or in any way threatened by what he sees, an outsider who can afford the luxury of self-indulgent emotion. It also typifies the non-German, Western black-on-white attitude towards the mass exodus from the GDR. The notion that the refugees could be viewed as deserters is raised rhetorically, but the implied answer is that no-one who has seen the extent of their suffering could have the heart to denounce them in that way. Such a response fails to appreciate the divisiveness of the issue in the GDR and the profound effect on national self-confidence. This is not to say that there was no sympathy within the GDR for the refugees. Erich Honecker's remark that no-one should shed a tear for them was by no means universally applauded by those who remained behind. In an address given in the Gethsemane Church in East Berlin on 5 October, Bernd Albani speaks for many when he says of the refugees: 'Yes, I shed a tear for them, because they are young people living here in this country and wanting to work. Young people who had no hopes of this country because nothing is moving, everything is frozen rigid' (Ebert 1989:19).

The response within the GDR to the flood of refugees was much more complex and differentiated than the reaction abroad. In its harping on Honecker's ill-judged statement, Albani's address is clearly calculated to arouse sympathy for the refugees outside the German-speaking world. But they are more than victims of the Cold War. They are citizens of a state that has failed to fulfil an obligation to offer them the opportunity of a worthwhile life, members of a nation that can ill afford to lose them, and witnesses against a regime that has forfeited the right to rule. Again one senses too a certain pride in GDR nationhood which gives the lie to the thesis that the GDR failed to create any such feeling.

2.3 The protest demonstrations

A number of those interviewed by the West German writer Helga Königsdorf for her volume *Adieu DDR* refer to the existence of a separate East German identity (Königsdorf 1990b). The interviews make it clear that many of the demonstrators who took to the streets of the major East German cities in the autumn of 1989 were far from radical opponents of the GDR. The fortieth anniversary celebration of the founding of the GDR on 7 October was marked in Berlin by a counter-demonstration. However, although there was a high degree of frustration and anger with the prevailing social, economic and political conditions, not all the participants wanted to see the immediate fall of the state, and at least some were attracted out of curiosity alone. It is difficult to find representative reports of the motivation of the demonstrators, but first-hand accounts do exist. One of Königsdorf's interviewees, a young female student of journalism in her first year of study in Leipzig at the time of the mass demonstrations, begins as follows:

In the evenings we sat in front of the television, and we saw pictures of ordinary young men in leather jackets jumping into the crowds and tearing down banners. We asked what was going on. There were several people from Leipzig present, who said, 'Don't you know? It's been like that since February.' But we had not the faintest idea. (Königsdorf 1990b:71)

Out of curiosity and against the express orders of her teachers she attends one of the Monday evening demonstrations:

It was quite incredible. I had never seen anything like it, except at the Gethsemane Church after the election, but that was very quiet. But in Leipzig they assembled on the dot of five o'clock, more and more of them. [...] The police were there with their dogs and the crowd stood there crammed into the streets, singing the *Internationale*. And you thought to yourself that something really important was happening. (Königsdorf 1990b:72)

She is totally caught up in the mood of the situation:

I took part in the first great march at the end of September. [...] The crowds were standing all the way from the Opera to the Gewand-haus, I've never seen so many people at an informal demonstration. We marched down to the railway station in a state of total euphoria. (Königsdorf 1990b:72)

The interviewee is by no means a dissident but she is obviously deeply affected by the power of the mass, as were many others. She makes no mention of any complaint she may harbour against GDR society. The demonstration's strength is based on the feeling of integration and solidarity that comes from standing together rather than from any rational grounds. This feeling communicates itself to someone who is not participating from any sense of commitment to a common cause. Indeed, disappointingly for her interviewer, she misses the crucial confrontative demonstration of 9 October 'because of fear, I say that in all honesty'. She recounts her participation in a pro-GDR demonstration at a later date, where she is subjected to abuse from onlookers as a *Bonzenkind* ('bigwig's child'), a '*Stasi*-brat':

Somebody behind me shouted, 'Rather dead as red.' I said to him, 'It's "than", not "as".' He got furious and shouted, 'I couldn't care less'! I replied, 'If you think you're a German, speak German properly.' That was risky, I know, but he probably didn't dare do anything about it. We really were running the gauntlet. To left and right you could see wide open mouths bawling at you. So we said we had better leave it, it wouldn't achieve anything. (Königsdorf 1990b: 72–73)

The striking thing here is the intensity of the antagonisms that emerged when the solidarity of the earlier demonstrations gave way to more partisan protests as people sought a new sense of direction.

A different account of participation in a demonstration, this time in Berlin, is given by a teenage contributor to a volume which presents the responses of children and young people to what was happening around them (Leidecker 1991). The item is a diary entry for Tuesday 24 October 1989, shortly after Erich Honecker resigns. Having heard from his mother where the planned demonstration is to take place, the teenager turns up at the television tower on the Alexanderplatz at 5 p.m. He has no clear idea why he has come. About 2,000 people are there, standing around in groups, talking. He speaks to a bystander and gets drawn into the group:

> I ask some people near me a few questions and get talking to them, we get to know one another. I find in this group an atmosphere of togetherness such as I have never experienced before in a crowd. I feel really safe and secure here, everyone is friendly and open, I can have a marvellous conversation with everybody I meet. (Leidecker 1991:64)

When the march begins he continues talking to his neighbour because he does not want to march alone. Communication between the marchers, though they are total strangers, is most important to create the sense of belonging to the group. He is appalled by his neighbour's experiences: the man participated in the march of 7 October, which was brutally broken up by the security forces; he was arrested and held in police custody with several others, during which time he was subjected to humiliation and violence. The man's account impresses and disturbs the boy. At this moment the progress of the march distracts his attention, which he rather welcomes. As the march continues, the number of marchers swells and the boy is carried along as much by the feeling of identity with them as by any rational insights or reflections. He considers leaving to go home as it is getting late:

> I found that I could not leave the march. My neighbour found the same thing. This wasn't because the crush made it impossible to get out, but because we had the feeling that to leave the march would be like abandoning a close friend. We simply had to keep going. This

'feeling' stopped me several times from leaving. (Leidecker 1991:70–71)

The feeling of identity is sufficient to keep him with the marchers despite his awareness that things could go badly wrong at any moment. This almost happens as the marchers are going from Französische Strasse towards Unter den Linden and a voice suddenly shouts, 'Off we go to the Brandenburg Gate'. The boy instinctively realizes the danger and he is relieved when the suggestion is shouted down as an unnecessary provocation. Any fear he may feel is removed by the sense of security in the crowd and the support of bystanders:

> I was especially impressed by the reactions of the passengers on the underground. Several of them went so far as to show their sympathy for the demonstration by clapping or waving. I felt better than I had ever done at any public event. I had a real sense of security. (Leidecker 1991:71–72)

He is confident that a few rabble-rousers, whom he dubs *Chaoten* ('chaos merchants'), will fail in their efforts to incite the crowd to violence. When the march eventually reaches the Gethsemane Church he is impressed by the candles burning at the permanent vigil for political prisoners:

> The numerous candles at the entrance to the Gethsemane Church made an idyllic, magical impression on me; although that was not of course their purpose, all the little lights in the darkness of the night looked indescribably fairy-like. It was a terrific sight. (Leidecker 1991:73)

He also describes the numerous candles in windows along the way as 'giving an extraordinary boost to [his] self-confidence'. He joins in the chanting, the shouts of *'Egon Krenz—wir sind die Konkurrenz'* ('Egon Krenz—we are the competition'), and in the marchers' calls to bystanders and drinkers in the public houses along the route to join them: *'Bürger laßt das Saufen sein, kommt heraus und reiht euch ein'* ('Stop boozing, citizens, come out and join our ranks'). After four hours the march terminates at the Alexanderplatz and the boy goes home, reflecting on an unforgettable experience.

This report from a boy of fourteen inevitably does not afford much insight into the grievances of the demonstrators. However, despite its naive style and remarkably cool and detached tone, the passage does convey something of how it felt to be one of the Berlin marchers. The perspective is limited but this in itself provides a salutary corrective to the assumption that all the demonstrators had a panoramic view of events and a clear sense of political purpose. For many participants these early demonstrations were simply an expression of their frustration, nothing more. What impresses the reader in this account is the crowd dynamism that holds the participants together. A powerful magnetism also attracts many to the ranks of the marchers as they progress through the city. All the more impressive and unexplained is the tacit assent to non-violence, which wards off the risk of brutal repression: this was indeed the most extraordinary feature of these demonstrations. The only political observation that the boy makes is to express his disappointment that the Party leaders do not emerge from the Central Committee building as the marchers pass by. The demonstrators see only faces peering occasionally from behind heavy curtains:

> I wondered how the Party hoped to regain trust by such behaviour, and I was very disappointed. I was not the only one, as was shown by the occasional shouts of 'Shame on you!' and 'Cowards!' (Leidecker 1991:70)

Such are the sentiments, rather than violent anger and aggression, that animate the demonstrators and ultimately shame the SED into action.

A more sophisticated perspective on the demonstrations in Berlin is offered by Jens Reich, one of the founder members of the dissident group New Forum, in a short essay written in October 1990. On the evening of Monday 9 October 1989 Reich and his wife drove to Schönhauser Allee in search of their daughter Steffi, who is taking part in a protest march, as they fear for her safety. On arrival they are confronted by a police barrier, with lorries and water-cannon, blocking the entrance to Stargarder Strasse. Their daughter is somewhere inside the barrier with the demonstrators. At first the couple want to give up and go instead to the Grand Hotel, to a meeting with *Newsweek* journalists that they had intended to miss; but they are too agitated to settle, and they are disturbed by the absurd contrast between the elegant hotel interior and the thought of what is going on outside. They return to the Prenzlauer Berg and this time get through to the 'front', as they term it, at Pappelallee, where police and demonstrators face one another across the street. Suddenly, with the arrival of two busloads of *Stasi*, the nature of the confrontation changes. The security police brutally attack the demonstrators and load them into a bus:

> Eva could hardly contain her anger and wanted to intervene. Another middle-aged woman started speaking to the policemen in green, her voice getting louder and louder, until finally it became a shriek. She

was appealing to their conscience, saying that she might be their mother and asking whether they were not ashamed of themselves for beating up people like this. Several policemen did indeed look ashamed of themselves. Many of them were army recruits who had been detailed. Our own son could have been amongst them. (Reich 1991:175–76)

In the Gethsemane Church the mood is quiet and sombre. Noting the candles, the hunger-strikers, and their placards, Reich likens the atmosphere to 'the deeply moving stillness of a catacomb'. The dominant emotion is fear and occasionally the tension erupts:

As always on such occasions there were some who became hysterical. One of them accused everyone present of promoting counter-revolution, saying that it was all set up. A young girl approached us to ask for protection on her way home. We offered to give her a lift in our car. That made her think we were state security. Panic fear of the *Stasi* kept many people terrified. (Reich 1991:176)

Yet what stays above all in Reich's mind is the passive heroism of the protesters, their stoical apathy, and their disregard for personal safety. They were willing to risk everything rather than submit further to oppression:

Young people scorned suffering [...] They were no longer afraid, but they did not overcome their fear through heroism—it was simply that they did not care what happened. They just wanted to see an end of oppression. (Reich 1991:176)

The absolute passivity is what so impresses Reich, affecting him so much that he too feels that he acts spontaneously, without regard to the consequences, as though in a trance. Despite the differences between his account and the others discussed here, the uniting factor is the sense of euphoria or, more negatively, weird unreality experienced by the participants. They all feel as though drugged and liberated from the usual inhibitions. Although aggressive feelings are aroused, as in the case of Reich's wife Eva, these do not take the form of physical aggression against the authorities. Perhaps the awareness of state power and the memory of the recent Tiananmen Square massacre convinces the participants that physical confrontation is impossible and might provoke a 'Chinese solution'.

As outsiders West German correspondents provide an alternative view of the atmosphere immediately before the change of leadership. Kurt Köhler reports on 13 October 1989 on the mood in Dresden. The regime is uncertain whether to clamp down or hold back. The riot of the previous week, when the transit trains carrying the asylum-seekers from Prague passed through Dresden, is over, and clearly the authorities want to eradicate all traces of it: the smashed windows have been quickly replaced. However, the mood remains unpleasant, and the reporter feels that it will not take much to spark off another open conflict. The city appears to be in a state of siege, with armed riot police much in evidence and *Stasi* men in plain clothes mingling with the crowd. Two of the *Stasi* grab a demonstrator, who is too surprised to resist. The onlookers do not react:

> Bystanders want to help, but think better of it. Their faces betray their thoughts: it's still possible to intervene, there are only two security police, but we may get arrested, even beaten up, better leave it. (Köhler 1989)

The population has had recent experience of the indiscriminate brutality of police methods:

> Who is just walking about, who is just watching, who is a demonstrator? The police couldn't tell—or didn't want to. Eye witnesses say that when they cleared the street [...] they hit out indiscriminately. They are said even to have kicked prams and pushed them down steps. (Köhler 1989)

One unfortunate man, hurrying for his train, is beaten and taken away. The demonstrators remain calm and light a candle at the place where he is arrested.

Köhler describes the demonstrators as a 'cross-section of the population', with many young people from a variety of social backgrounds:

> [...] workers with large hands and weary faces, gentlemen in suit and tie, long-haired students with wire glasses à la Trotski, young women in mini-skirts, trainers and black stockings, punks with orange hair and parachutists' boots. (Köhler 1989)

In the afternoon Köhler sees some of the demonstrators attending a service in the cathedral. Evidently he does not rate the influence of the Church very highly, as he refers to the proceedings as running their usual course without much acknowledgement of the presence of the young people:

> The church, quite unlike in the West, was full of young people in jeans. Some seemed to be wanting a rest after three nights of demonstrating and were dozing with eyes half shut. Others were looking

expectantly at the clergyman. Would he speak about the current situation? In fact he kept to the scriptural text, and not even at the words 'Give strength to the faint and hope to the discouraged' did he come close enough to the microphone for his voice to sound louder. (Köhler 1989)

Like the politician quoted later who expects any change to come from the top, the Church in Köhler's view underestimates the young demonstrators; it offers them asylum but no moral leadership. Köhler portrays them as a loose, disparate group. Although suspicious at first of talking to him, they eventually articulate their ideas about the reforms they want to see. But Köhler's presentation of the march through Dresden reminds the reader more of a 'lads' night out' than of any organized political protest. He points out that there are no *Einpeitscher* (cheer-leaders) prompting them with slogans. After an interlude the evening ends in an ice-cream parlour with the march petering out in the early hours of the morning on the Leningrader Strasse; one of the protesters calls to a passing motorist from the West to make sure he spreads the word about what he has seen. The journalist draws no firm conclusions, preferring to allow the situation to speak for itself, but one senses that the general confusion makes it difficult for him to make sense of what is happening. The situation is tense but at this point no-one has a clear idea of how it will develop.

In other parts of the GDR the protests were slower to get going, but the atmosphere was extremely tense. On 20 October Carl-Christian Kaiser reports from Magdeburg. Although published just after Honecker's resignation, the material must have been assembled and the report written beforehand. Under the title *Die Ruhe täuscht* ('a deceptive calm') Kaiser tries to convey his sense of a community on the verge of disintegration. He relates how Werner Eberlein, Politburo member and First Secretary of the SED in Magdeburg, is confronted by steelworkers demanding freedom to travel, newspapers that tell the truth, protection for the environment, and wages based on performance. He comments: 'This seemingly well-ordered socialist city is cracking and crumbling at several points' (Kaiser 1989:5).

Like Kaiser, Eberlein clearly does not expect much to emerge from the efforts of the dissidents and he is particularly disappointed by the attitudes he encounters amongst members of the establishment, especially the Church. Admittedly the cathedral has posters just inside the main door advertising the views of the opposition groups, an exhibition of photographs of the demonstrations round the St Nicholas Church in Leipzig, and a large book in which visitors may sign their names as a mark of solidarity with the protesters, but the reception Kaiser receives from a vicar and his wife contradicts the view that the Church is solidly on the side of the people.

His hosts are *Parteipfarrer* ('Party priests'), and resent the presence of a Western investigative reporter. Their attitude is repeated by the former Bishop of Magdeburg, Werner Krusche, who compares the events with the Workers' Uprising of June 1953:

> This could lead only to new repressive measures, whereas what was needed was a considered, thoughtful, and discriminating dialogue. Moreover, this cathedral and the churches as a whole must once again become a place of prayer, however necessary it was to give shelter to the reform groups. (Kaiser 1989)

His caution shows the dilemma of the Churches, sympathizing with the reformers, but fearing to provoke a government backlash. Kaiser meets similar caution among members of the GDR's CDU. They call for patience on the part of the Western media, whose gloating is considered counterproductive. The GDR should be allowed to sort out its own problems, and it may take some time.

Reporting from Dresden, the novelist Martin Walser expresses similar discomfort with Western triumphalism. He feels strongly that the GDR must be left to decide its own fate: 'The word reunification is a term of Adenauer's, and we can forget it. The people of the GDR alone have the right to decide what happens to them' (1989a:68). Walser does not so much fear that Western attention will provoke a tough counter-reaction within the GDR. Indeed his description of the people's mood suggests that they are well able to look after themselves. Attending a première of Beethoven's opera *Fidelio* at the Semper Opera on 7 October, he finds himself caught up in a demonstration, with the Opera House sealed off by police:

> A young woman with her husband and child was trying to get from our side through the line of police to the demonstration. Who makes the law, asked the woman in a manner so agitated that the police officer simply let her through, and her husband and child too. The police had finally lost their authority. (Walser 1989a:67)

The woman's victory over the wavering forces of law and order betokens the impending collapse of the state, as does the enthusiastic mood of the opera audience as it responds to the obvious contemporary relevance of *Fidelio*. Two days later, after a performance of Heiner Müller's version of *Titus Andronicus*, the reading of a citizens' charter by one of the actresses is received rapturously by the audience. There is no doubt that in Dresden change is very much in the air and that the pressure for reform will prove irresistible. What concerns Walser is the Western response, which he finds both arrogant and complacent. The West and especially the FRG must understand that the GDR is the product of a historical situation for which the whole of Germany was responsible and to which the whole of Germany will need to find a solution. At this early stage in the *Wende* he is already looking towards the setting up of a new German federation, perhaps with Weimar as its centre. He is one of many who will not have been happy with the outcome.

The Western press was quick to raise the question of reunification, although usually noting that it was too early to think about it. But as the atmosphere in the GDR changed, reports from journalists on the spot began to reflect the growing confidence of the population. The replacement of Honecker by Krenz on 18 October 1989 marked the actual turning-point, as it demonstrated to the people that the old guard could be removed, even if there was considerable scepticism about what degree of change would result. After all, Krenz had the reputation of being a hardliner, despite the affable manner that he cultivated and the toothy grin which provoked a celebrated banner likening him to Red Riding Hood's grandmother.

A new mood was established by a massive demonstration on the Alexanderplatz in Berlin on 4 November. A number of prominent individuals addressed the rally. They included the writers Christoph Hein, Stefan Heym, and Christa Wolf, and also the ex-*Stasi* general Markus Wolf. In his memoirs Wolf points out that no-one expected the dramatic opening of the border within five days. In retrospect this demonstration, attended by some half a million people, represents a caesura in what is for him the tragic development of the revolution:

> On 4 November on the Alexanderplatz the call for a united German fatherland was not contained in any of the speeches and seen on none of the placards, nor was it heard from the crowd. It was a socialist protest demonstration calling for freedom of speech and opinion and freedom of the press, it was a settling of accounts with the past [...] and with those responsible for it. And despite the wave of emotions and differences in political and moral attitudes and values, the organizers, speakers, and many of the crowd shared an optimistic sense of a new beginning. What was on the agenda was our country, the German Democratic Republic, and its future. (Wolf 1991:227–28)

2.4 The opening of the border

The feeling of optimism surrounding the rally of 4 November 1989 on the Alexanderplatz is well captured in a report by the West German journalist

Marlies Menge. She conveys the feeling of excitement that animates the people as they anticipate the great gathering. They feel that this is no ordinary protest, one likely to fizzle out into nothing. Already, in the background, things are happening, as she finds when she visits a group of students in their run-down flat in Prenzlauer Berg, where they are planning an independent and democratic student organization. What they lack in experience they make up for in enthusiasm. Just how short they are of ideas is shown by the case of the student who on the morning of the rally has got no further with his speech than the words 'The Free German Youth ...' Yet the mood is positive. There are fears about the stance of the academic authorities and some students think that their careers may suffer from their involvement in the reform movement; nevertheless they are prepared to go ahead, for this is the culmination of years of waiting and frustration:

> The whole of East Berlin seems to be on the move. From all directions they come together, children, young people, those in their forties and fifties, the elderly. People display their opinions on banners freely in witty, critical terms. It is as though they had been waiting for forty years to devise and express their sentiments. (Menge 1989a)

Christa Wolf expresses the people's vision in her address to the rally: 'Imagine there was socialism and nobody ran away!' (James and Stone 1992:129). It is a time for dreams of utopian socialism, and there is a general sense of liberation and a new start. Yet Menge strikes a cautionary note: she tells of an old lady, a pensioner, who travels regularly to West Berlin and is struck by the sudden rise in demand for East German currency. Already the speculators are gathering, ready to move in and buy up the GDR.

Robert Leicht takes up the question of the psychological state of the nation:

> We in the West see the new beginning, add up the sensational changes, and think that the process of reform in the GDR therefore cannot be stopped. People over there are clearly far from feeling so optimistic. (Leicht 1989)

In the East there is fear of the future and distrust of the government and its apparent reforms: 'One woman sums up her experiences in a single sentence: "From day to day I get increasingly suspicious of what is being offered to us"' (Leicht 1989). Many people know that the leopard cannot change its spots; furthermore they hanker for the security of the past, which, if unpleasant, was known and at least calculable. Now they feel that they are living in a strange, unreal world with no clear direction and an uneasy sense of disaster just round the corner. The root of the problem is the lack of confidence and self-esteem arising from years of enforced tutelage. Certainly the population is suffering from a deep sense of inferiority *vis à vis* the West, as is apparent in the reply of a young girl who, when asked by the clergyman of her Church if she had ever felt pride, answers that she had been proud on holiday in Hungary to be taken for a West German. The enforced schizophrenia, as Leicht calls it, of having to pretend loyalty to the state in public whilst feeling quite differently in private has undermined the trust of the younger generation and undermined its education. He even suggests that those who have not joined the asylum-seekers are ashamed of remaining in the GDR since it was the risk taken by the refugees that initially triggered the revolution. If reform is to be undertaken it is difficult to see where leadership will come from in a society that is psychologically so deeply damaged. There is no clear programme of action, there are only vague calls for a better form of socialism. However, Leicht understands that the East Germans need to seek their own solution if they are to retain their self-respect: they cannot be expected simply to welcome a Western takeover. He is not sanguine about the prospects, counterbalancing Menge's enthusiastic account; he does not rule out violent clashes if the SED clings to power. At this point the course of events still remains uncertain, and, despite the sense of optimism felt by many, it is possible to envisage bloody revolution.

Leicht's reading of the situation soon proved to be unduly pessimistic, for the SED was in no mood for confrontation. In his memoirs Egon Krenz describes his mood in the days before the opening of the border on 9 November 1989. He seeks to persuade the reader that contrition rather than aggression was what motivated him to support reform. He claims to have been moved and encouraged to act by the appeal by Christa Wolf and other writers and artists published on the front page of *Neues Deutschland* on 8 November. He also describes the protests that were reaching him from all sectors of the population. At the time many observers saw the concessions as no more than a desperate attempt by the SED to retain power. Whatever trust one may place in Krenz's claims, he argues that the opening of the border was a deliberate effort to ease the situation for the population and to promote his programme of liberal reform. Although he repudiates the charge that the whole affair was bungled, he admits that it was not intended to open the border until 10 November. All that went wrong, he claims, was that Günter Schabowski, answering a journalist's question at the evening press conference on 9 November, made the mistake of saying that the new travel regulations were to come into force immediately rather than on the following day. Schabowski, for his part, denies any mistake. At all events the announcement took the world by surprise. Krenz, who was at a session of the SED's Central Committee at the time, describes the scene as follows:

> The journalists were taken by surprise and it was a few seconds before they realized what had been said. It was a few minutes after 7 p.m. Then they set to work with the satisfied feeling that they were dictating a sensation into their machines. The world learned what it was not supposed to know until the following day. GDR citizens watching television could not believe their ears. Almost immediately the unforeseen happened. Berliners, still incredulous, set off for the Wall. Soon there was a build up of traffic travelling west on the autobahns. The pent-up desire to travel that had been repressed for so many years was suddenly released on this one night. (Krenz 1990:182)

A more authentic reaction comes from Angelika Unterlauf, the newsreader who announced the event on GDR television:

> I read it without having seen it in advance, it arrived on my desk when the cameras were already rolling. My whole body began to shake. It only slowly began to sink in as I was on my way home after midnight. I stopped my Lada at Warschauer Platz. Some people came towards me shouting exultantly. They were all on their way to the West. What was it I read, I thought. When I got home my daughters were sitting in bed discussing what had happened with Peter. 'Mummy, shall we go now?' urged France. It was an emotional moment. That night the whole of my life passed before me. Moments of fear and repression. For weeks past I had been feeling wretched. I doubted every word I had to read. (*Berliner Illustrierte Zeitung*, 26 November 1989)

This account is a salutary corrective to the many Western reports of universal jubilation amongst East Berliners and to the media pictures of celebration, although of course such scenes took place. Unterlauf, whose career had followed a conventional course through the ranks of the FDJ and the SED, feels that her whole life is collapsing round her. Although relieved that the old order with its fear and repression is over, she is also in a state of shock and hardly able to assimilate the enormity of what has happened. This is very different from the standard Western response typified by the reaction of Walter Momper, Mayor of West Berlin:

People were beside themselves with joy. I saw one woman, as she crossed the white line slowly and unsteadily, uncontrollably burst into tears. Someone embraced her. At that moment I thought to myself how much suffering the Wall has caused, and that on this night the Germans were the happiest nation in the world. (Momper 1991:147–48)

Momper makes no mention of the psychological effects of the opening of the border. He is worried that the East German government will repeal the concession, or that a member of the GDR border guard will lose his nerve and start shooting. There is no appreciation of the complexity of the repercussions beyond the political practicalities.

A more differentiated reaction is offered by East and West Germans interviewed for a West Berlin newspaper. On the one hand there is the predictable anger of Helga Meerbusch, a journalist, who cannot forgive the regime for 'kicking everyone in the stomach'. Describing her feelings as she watches the Wall being demolished, she hints at the strength of her hatred for Honecker, whom she holds personally responsible:

The architect is lying in his bed somewhere gasping for air. I take a deep breath. Over there is the S-Bahn [the railway connecting East and West Berlin]. Tomorrow I shall be sitting in it. Or in that aeroplane up there. So that's what freedom feels like. (*Berliner Illustrierte Zeitung*, 19 November 1989)

Her amazement at her new-found freedom of movement is soured by anger and also by a need to justify herself and her compatriots: 'Anyone who asks why it lasted so long has no knowledge of that system of artificially induced fear, armed power, deliberately fostered weakness, and state-promoted lethargy' (*Berliner Illustrierte Zeitung*, 19 November 1989). On the positive side there is also pride in having achieved emancipation, a new 'upright stance' (a phrase which echoes the lyricist Volker Braun, 1979).

This contrasts strikingly with the impressions given by a West Berlin journalist, Bernd Philipp, who points out sardonically that he knows Florida and California better than he knows the eastern half of his home town. He feels resentful because he sees East Berlin as having been stolen from him by the GDR regime. For him the opening of the border amounts to the restoration of a birthright and he seems disappointed, even annoyed, at the casual manner in which it has been handled by the television: 'We are, I suppose, a nation of viewers. Our television presents us with the start of a revolution during the half-time interval of a football match. First half, revolution, second half' (*Berliner Illustrierte Zeitung*, 19 November

1989). He is aware of watching history in the making, and the event out-shines everything else that he has ever experienced: '[...] now the pulse of history is beating, and beating quickly; and I can be there'. This elated op-timism so characteristic of the Western response is typified by the interna-tionally celebrated musician Yehudi Menuhin. These days in Berlin are for him 'the greatest turning-point in the whole of human history'; they have 'symbolic significance' and show that 'the human race will no longer tol-erate wars and walls' (*Berliner Morgenpost*, 17 November 1989).

Members of the Ludwig family from East Berlin are less hyperbolic in their assessment, but they express a measured optimism. Their nineteen year-old daughter Anke, an apprentice tailoress at the opera house, thinks that she will leave, but her parents, who work in theatre and film, want to stay in the East. They agree that things have changed irreversibly and they are generally happy at the turn of events. They regret the loss of friends and colleagues who have left for the West, but there is not the expected euphoria. Christian, a production director at East Berlin's Maxim Gorki Theatre, declares:

> The time of cheap bread rolls and cheap rents has gone for us. [...]
> That frightens a lot of people. But we can have a better life now than
> before because a lot of things that distressed us have been cleared
> up. Whether we get a currency reform or ration cards, people will
> come out of their corners and become more crafty. Either way, it's
> all just beginning. (*Berliner Illustrierte Zeitung*, 19 November 1989)

Some were much less optimistic than this. Robert Darnton tells of visiting a friend in East Berlin soon after the border was opened. The friend reacts strongly against the idea that the Wall should be removed: 'Do not pull down the Wall. We need it for protection. It should be permeable but should remain standing' (Darnton 1991:77). For many East Germans the removal of the Wall was accompanied by profound fear and uncertainty.

2.5 After the Wall

With the breaching of the Berlin Wall the nature of the revolution changes, and the *Wende,* originally interpreted by Krenz to mean a process of in-ternal reform within the SED, assumes a new character. It becomes in-creasingly apparent that the forces working to reform the GDR and at the same time to preserve it as a separate state are doomed to failure. In a sense it can be argued the *Wende* was completed the moment the Wall came down. The writer Peter Schneider tells how a West German acquaintance of his attributed the reunification directly to his experience of the night of 9 November: 'To think that people who had been shut in for so long could suddenly get out. The look on their faces when they came out! It was stunning! If you ask me, reunification began on 9 November' (Schneider 1990:21). The journalist Roger de Weck writes on 24 November of 'a democratic primeval event' *(ein demokratisches Ur-Ereignis)* that is on a par with the French Revolution, England's Glorious Revolution of 1688, and the Italian Risorgimento. For him the breaching of the Wall will inevitably bring the two parts of Germany closer together: 'on 9 November at the latest both German republics entered a new era; their childhood days are over'. Speculation, he maintains, will cease and be replaced by plans of action: '[...] the period of prognoses is giving way to the period of manifestos (Weck 1989).

At this stage commentators are still misjudging the pace of change and speculating on the form of political system that will emerge in the GDR. Erhard Eppler answers the question 'Can the GDR be saved?' by a tentative affirmative. At the same time he knows he may be indulging in wishful thinking: '[...] anyone who is today seriously committed to the continuing existence of two German states could find himself at odds with reality' (Eppler 1989). The future is uncertain and no-one can predict how the GDR will look in a year's time. One thing, however, is certain: 'Reunification? So far as the people are concerned it has already taken place on the weekend of 10 to 12 November' (Eppler 1989). Wolf Jobst Siedler feels able to discuss the future status of Berlin, although he sees the city not as the national capital but as one important regional centre among many in a new, united Germany. For him the GDR ceased to exist with Honecker's resignation and the opening of the Wall (Siedler 1989).

After 9 November the citizens of the GDR knew that a radical change was coming and that it could be of a nature that they had not bargained for. Perhaps the last word should go to one of them, Friedemann Ehrig, an engineer and a member of the opposition group Democratic Awakening:

We are in danger of losing our liberation from the dictatorship of a political party to the dictatorship of finance. Is our democratic awareness strong enough to withstand the temptations of consumerism? What we need is a process of legal and political assimilation to progressive European norms. We should take this path autonomously and accept well-intentioned help without unnecessary pride. The aim should be equal partnership in a regionalized Europe. (Menge 1989b)

He was destined to be disappointed.

3
The GDR
Wende and Legacy

DEREK LEWIS

3.1 The *Wende* as starting-point

'Once upon a time there was a Germany of the East and one of the West. Then at midnight Cinderella was taken over by the ball.' This caption to a cartoon which appeared in the Italian daily *L'Unità* on the day of German unification (reproduced in James and Stone 1992:282) sums up the story of Germany from division in 1949 to unification in 1990. After forty years of separation, the impoverished sister (the GDR) was seduced by the rich and handsome prince (the FRG). At the time, few doubted West Germany's ability to sustain the economic fairy tale, and in the euphoria of unification everyone was expected to live happily ever after. Admittedly, by 1991 it was clear that the economic and financial demands of unification had been seriously underestimated. But at the time of the *Wende* nobody could deny either the eagerness of the majority of GDR citizens for unification or the hopes shared by the majority of Germans for a positive future in a spirit of national unity. The glass slipper seemed to fit perfectly.

This chapter reviews the pre-*Wende* period in East Germany before 1989, focusing on the institutions of the GDR and the conditions which led to its collapse. After summarizing the course of the *Wende* and assessing the East Germans' own contribution to the process of democratic renewal, the chapter considers how the GDR came to be seen as a fundamentally unjust, even criminal regime. Finally, it describes the measures which the Federal Government has adopted in response to the legacy of injustices which the Communist state bequeathed to the new Germany.

3.2 The institutions and power structures of the GDR

Outwardly the GDR had many of the features of a Western multi-party democracy. It possessed a constitution which nominally guaranteed basic rights, including the right of freedom of speech and assembly. Unlike the

Soviet Union, a single-party state, the GDR tolerated a number of political parties alongside the ruling SED; local and national elections were also held regularly. But behind the façade of pluralism the SED, the product of an enforced merger in 1946 between the German Communist Party and the SPD, exercised universal control. The SED's monopoly was enshrined in the first article of the revised Constitution of 1968: proclaiming that the GDR was 'under the leadership of the working class and its Marxist-Leninist Party', this article in effect made opposition to the SED a treasonable offence. All other political parties and mass organizations were obliged to acknowledge the SED's leadership role and were organized in Parliament as members of a block of puppet institutions called 'the National Front of the GDR' (otherwise known as the 'Block'). The function of the minor parties was not to oppose the SED but to act as vehicles of transmission, that is, to win over to Marxism-Leninism specific groups within the population. Thus the GDR-CDU appealed to a conservative Christian tradition, the LDPD to small tradesmen and the remains of the liberal bourgeoisie, the NDPD to nationalist elements, and the DBD to landworkers. So-called mass organizations targeted young people (FDJ), women (DFD), trade unionists (FDGB), artists (KB), and others (for an explanation of acronyms see the Glossary on page 329).

The SED employed a number of techniques of political control originally developed in the Soviet Union. The crudest technique was the straightforward party directive. Although directives could be implemented immediately they were normally translated into laws for nominal approval by Parliament; the possibility of Parliament challenging or even seriously debating directives did not arise in practice. The second technique involved placing SED functionaries in senior positions in non-party organizations, such as the trade unions or the youth movement. The third technique was based on very close co-ordination (officially called 'co-operation') between the Party and the civil service. Finally, the Party set up official control bodies to monitor key areas such as industrial production and farming.

With over 2·3 million members in 1984, the SED was nominally a party of the masses. In reality it was a rigidly authoritarian and hierarchical organization: decisions reached at a higher level could not be questioned lower down in the Party. The SED saw itself as a disciplined *avant-garde* for the working class, whose members it led in tutelage. Factions were not tolerated and setting up a separate lobby group within the Party invited severe punishment. During the 1950s and 1960s in particular the Party leadership instigated numerous purges in order to tighten its control. The SED was widely regarded as Stalinist, both because of its cult of the Party leader and, in later years, on account of the bureaucratic apparatus of totalitarian control that it maintained. One tool of control was the nomenclature, a register of key posts in the GDR whose functions and incumbents were closely monitored by the SED. An altogether more fearsome tool was the secret police, or *Stasi*, which is discussed below.

The SED maintained an extensive Party apparatus and organization. A large and carefully stage-managed Party Congress of delegates (over 2,500) met every five years to elect a Central Committee (222 members in 1986), from which in turn was constituted the Politburo (twenty-five members). Chaired by the Party leader (Erich Honecker from 1971), the Politburo was the real centre of political decision-making in the GDR. Second in rank to the Politburo, the Central Committee managed a vast bureaucracy of over 2,000 staff in forty departments. It ensured that the Politburo's decisions were implemented and supervised the theoretically non-party institutions of democratic government. These institutions included the People's Chamber, the Council of State, and the Council of Ministers. The People's Chamber, or Parliament, comprised 500 members from the political parties and mass organizations of the GDR. All the members and organizations in the Chamber were approved by the SED and formally acknowledged its leadership role. Parliament met only four or five times a year in order to rubber-stamp SED directives: it was therefore an acclamatory body, not a genuine forum for debate or legislation. The Council of State combined the functions of the Ministry of Foreign Affairs and the Ministry of Defence; it also administered elections and the legal system. The Council of Ministers functioned as the cabinet and represented the main organ of state government. The point to note is that all of these bodies were shadowed, staffed, and monitored by the SED. Thus, the outwardly democratic institutions of the GDR provided a façade for single-party control.

The most feared mechanism of control was the *Stasi*. Established in 1950, the *Stasi* became infamous during the 1950s for abducting former GDR citizens who had fled to West Germany. Branded as traitors, these unfortunates were usually executed or they perished in prison. Apart from organizing espionage activities, principally against the FRG, the *Stasi* had by 1989 established a vast network of full-time employees (85,000) and also unofficial informants (108,000) who were cajoled, blackmailed, or paid to spy on their fellow citizens.

The *Stasi*'s role was not defined in law or subject to parliamentary control: the organization was effectively an instrument of the SED, the Party's 'sword and shield'. Its prime targets were perceived enemies of the Party, although it emerged after the *Wende* that even Politburo members were routinely bugged (Schabowski 1991:45). During the early stages of the *Wende*, *Stasi* members attempted to destroy compromising evidence of the service's operations, including its huge archive of files on individuals. Citizens' committees sprang up throughout the GDR to thwart this action, and on 15 January 1990 protesters invaded the Normannenstrasse headquarters in Berlin, forcing the People's Chamber to set up a national committee to disband the organization once and for all. While the apparatus of the SED itself swiftly disintegrated, the *Stasi*'s files remained powerful symbols of Communist oppression; the right of access to the archives and the status of their contents continue to be important issues in post-*Wende* Germany.

3.3 The economy of the GDR

The economy of the GDR was centrally planned. The principle feature of the system was state ownership and management of land, agriculture, industry, and financial institutions. A small private sector was tolerated, notably in areas where the state failed to satisfy important needs, such as food distribution and small trades, but it never engaged more than 2% of the working population. Centrally devised plans regulated broad areas of development, investment, and pricing, and covered all areas of life in the GDR, including education, culture, and the media. A national plan would be announced for, say, the following five years; this was then broken down into shorter sub-plans for each sector of the economy and, finally, into very short planning periods for individual factories or concerns.

During its forty-year history the GDR experimented with various methods of economic control, although the principles of public ownership and medium-term national plans remained unchanged. Three phases have been distinguished (Cornelsen 1989:258).

During the first phase, from 1949 to 1962, the apparatus and mechanisms of central control were introduced. At a time when the post-war economy was attempting to recover from post-war devastation and the Soviet Union was insisting on reparations (these were halted only in 1953), the GDR strategically planned for maximum growth in its steel and heavy industry, at the expense of consumer goods. Major industrial centres were established to produce steel, chemicals, and lignite, and production targets were set centrally. Factories nominally met targets by concentrating on crude volume production or manipulating returns (for example, by including products which had not yet been manufactured from stockpiled materials). Although accounting mechanisms eventually became more sophisticated and factories gained some measure of independence, the main performance indicator remained the fulfilment of a centrally determined plan. In 1952 the government adopted its so-called New Course, switching investment to housing, light industry, and the food industry. But shortfalls in materials led to serious production bottlenecks, and many building and construction projects had to be abandoned. Shortages in consumer goods and food supplies, exacerbated by the enforced collectivization of agriculture from 1957, and a falling standard of living relative to the FRG resulted in large-scale emigration to the West. The Berlin Wall was erected in 1961 precisely to stem this outflow.

The second phase, between 1962 and 1970, saw the introduction of the New Economic System, a package of reforms which gave concerns greater local flexibility and material incentives. Factories were allowed to retain and reinvest their returns. Prices of materials, which were still fixed at 1944 levels, were updated, and science and technology were promoted in an effort to narrow the gap with West Germany. After a promising start the reforms failed through inadequate resources, supply bottlenecks, and the poor transport and energy system. When Erich Honecker replaced Walter Ulbricht as national leader in 1970, the reforms were abruptly abandoned.

Under Honecker (1971–89) central control of the economy was re-inforced. Factories were merged into large combines in order to co-ordinate and centralize research, development, and production. New methods of accounting and pricing were introduced and efforts were made to exploit energy resources more efficiently, especially after the sharp increase in oil costs from 1973. In order to reflect world prices and improve returns, the principle of fixed prices for consumer goods was relaxed in 1979 for the first time: while prices for basic items remained low, more sophisticated articles, such as electrical goods, became more expensive. Investment was targeted at key technologies, notably microelectronics and robotics. Despite these adjustments, a complex system of centrally determined subsidies continued to cushion loss-making concerns. Up to 1985 mounting foreign debts were contained by drastically reducing imports and increasing exports. But the chronic problems of supply bottlenecks and outdated, inefficient plant continued to retard growth and technological progress; only basic consumer needs were satisfied. An ambitious plan to solve the housing crisis was launched in 1973 with the aim of building or renovating up to three million homes by 1990. In 1988 the plan was declared a resounding success but in reality the statistics were faked. In October 1989 it was officially acknowledged that the scheme had failed and that the stock of old housing was deteriorating faster than it could be replaced (Weber 1991:201).

The GDR claimed to be among the ten leading industrial nations of the world, although this was questioned in the West (Schwartau and Vortmann 1989:306). It was estimated that the average working day for the East German was 10% longer than in the FRG. Industrial productivity in the GDR was only 50% of that of West Germany and even lower for agriculture. East German incomes were likewise between 60% and 70% of West

German levels and lower for pensioners (Leptin 1991:659–60). Although living costs were 5% lower in the East, goods and services were seldom available at their official prices. The demands of the military, the Party, and the state bureaucracy consumed a large portion of manufactured wealth.

The state traditionally proclaimed the advantages of the centrally planned economy to be stable prices for basic commodities, security of employment, universal welfare provision, and a fair distribution of wealth. The unstated drawbacks were industrial inefficiency, a heavily polluted environment, and the inability to innovate and to provide a range of luxury goods at affordable prices. The political élite decreed at the micro-economic level what goods should be available to which individuals. This meant, for example, that citizens could not indulge in private motoring on a significant scale, that telephones remained a restricted commodity, and that the fabric of buildings decayed. Such planning was not only economically unbalanced, it also required strict political controls in all areas of life and singularly failed to produce levels of prosperity comparable to Western countries.

3.4 Everyday life in the GDR

The experiences of everyday life under Communism are the most important personal legacy of the GDR state to its seventeen million citizens. They also constitute the main reason why the East German people embraced unification so readily. The following section will describe a number of areas representative of daily life for ordinary GDR citizens before unification—work, shopping, family life, and leisure.

Everyday life in the GDR was more strongly dominated by the work-place than is generally true in Western countries. Most factories had excel-lent nursery provision organized around workshifts so that parents could work without worrying about child-care. Factories usually provided meals for their workers (including the retired), who preferred to eat at their workplace than queue for basic foodstuffs at the state-run supermarket. Eating out at one of the few restaurants was not an attractive alternative: customers queued for tables, waited for indifferent food, and endured grudging service.

In the factory, workers were organized in collectives, called brigades. Common drawbacks at the workplace included overmanning (especially in administration), inefficient work practices, outdated machinery, and altern-ation between enforced idleness (caused by interruptions in supplies) and bursts of hectic pressure (to make up the lost production). The manufactured goods were often of poor quality. Workers could not take grievances to independent trade unions; unions in the GDR were closely identified with the state and existed primarily to stimulate production and meet planning quotas. Their welfare role extended to organizing subsidized holidays in the GDR and in other socialist states. A system of 'socialist competition' tried to motivate workers and stimulate competition through bonuses, exhortation, and official honours. Since the right to work was enshrined in the Constitution, workers could not easily be dismissed, even for inefficiency. Without the sanction of dismissal or the material incentives of a consumer market, Brigade leaders needed considerable personal skills in order to motivate their workforce. Though modest, incomes were adequate to meet the cost of food, rent, clothing, and local transport, whose prices were pegged artificially low. The programmed shortage of consumer and luxury goods meant that families accumulated large savings accounts: there was simply no market to absorb money earned.

Leisure facilities were organized by the state for young people. Activities centred on sport and culture invariably had a political flavour in that they were intended to foster loyalty to the state and stressed the benefits of socialism. Most schoolchildren spent part of their vacation in camps run by the factories where their parents worked. The daily routine was organized along paramilitary lines (early morning parade followed by sport). There were occasional discos and dances where youngsters queued for hours to listen to a mixture of Western and East German popular music provided by state-approved disc jockeys. Cinemas were few and poorly patronized, except when films from the West were shown. Life outside the cities could be particularly tedious for younger people. As for holidays, most people went camping within the GDR since hotels were not available to the casual tourist. A visit to a Western country required a visa and was out of the question for most people. Although during the 1980s more citizens were granted permission to visit close relatives in the FRG, travel restrictions remained a principal source of discontent.

When not procuring much-needed goods, queuing at shops, or waiting in official buildings, GDR citizens spent their leisure time at home with the family. Building a small country dacha for weekend visits or tending an allotment were popular outdoor pastimes. But as a rule East Germans developed remarkably private lives within the confines of their own homes. Here they would watch (West German) television or meet in small groups of close friends who would drop in unannounced (few had a telephone). The cultivation of the private sphere was a reaction both to the material drabness of life in the GDR and to the unremitting demands of political conformity in public. Moreover, only very close friends could be trusted not to be in the service of the *Stasi* who recruited citizens to inform on the views and behaviour of colleagues, fellow students, neighbours, and even relatives. It was a form of inner emigration, neatly termed the 'niche society' (Gaus 1983:156). After unification many felt that the one thing which East Germans could contribute to the new Germany was their appreciation of personal friendships and the solidarity born of material deprivation. Others have maintained that these virtues were never so deeply established as some Westerners claimed and predicted that they would not survive the new economic conditions (Reinschke 1991:48). There is now evidence that widespread gratuitous aggressiveness existed in the former GDR. The phenomenon is explained as a reaction to the need to kowtow to the political élite—'traces of the poison which everyone had to swallow' (Bobach 1993:9).

3.5 Why the GDR collapsed

Despite the accelerating pace of reform in Eastern Europe and widespread discontent in East Germany itself, the sudden collapse of the GDR surprised East Germans and foreign observers alike. Until the *Wende* many held East Germany to be the most stable of the Communist countries in Europe. After all it had the highest productivity and relative standard of living, and its rulers seemed to be firmly in control; there had been no organized national opposition since the Workers' Uprising of 1953.

Historians and sociologists offer various explanations for the fall of the GDR (Joas and Kohli 1993:12–26). One answer concentrates on the psychological disposition of the East German people. The argument concludes that, after years of conformity and an unhealthy absence of civic opposition to the regime, the frustration of the people grew too strong to contain. Certainly the scale of mass emigration during the summer of 1989 revealed just how unpopular the Communist system had become. Evidence supporting this view emerged from surveys of so-called 'subjective factors' conducted in the GDR between 1977 and early 1989 (Gensicke 1992). The surveys show how positive and loyal attitudes gave way over a ten-year period to pessimism about the state of the environment and the lack of consumer goods. Faced with industrial decline on the one hand and increased work pressure on the other, interviewees saw little hope for the future. This discontent may have occasioned the extreme disillusionment that set in at the end of 1989 when GDR citizens were brutally confronted in the public media with the failure of their political order, the corruption of their leaders, and predictions of imminent economic collapse.

Another view stresses the progressive loss of public legitimacy suffered by the SED. In the immediate post-war period the SED presented itself convincingly as the party of anti-fascism, a self-perception reinforced by the Nazis' vigorous persecution of the Communists. At first most people accepted the Communists' anti-Nazi credentials, enabling the SED to command considerable loyalty. In the longer run these credentials proved insufficient. The population needed more positive reasons for supporting the SED; these took the form of promises of social progress and higher living standards. Unable to fulfil these commitments, the SED finally sought to justify itself by resorting to the notion of peaceful co-existence with the West and by propagating the benefits of 'real existing socialism', an ambiguous formula which was intended to highlight the achievements of the socialist state but managed to suggest that the Party had abandoned its original vision of creating a prosperous, egalitarian utopia.

A third answer emphasizes the strength of the East European protest movements, which spearheaded the attack on Communism in Poland and Czechoslovakia and fuelled discontent in East Germany. An alliance of 'voice' (dissidents actively campaigning for reform within the GDR) and 'exit' (those merely wanting to leave) forged early in 1988 in Leipzig was instrumental in fostering the city's role as a centre of opposition to the regime (Joppke 1993). Although the citizens' groups played a key political role after the fall of the SED, those dissidents embodying 'voice' and campaigning for internal reform were, at least before 1989, small in number and poorly organized; 'exit' was the more representative mode of opposition. It is therefore hard to argue that a coherent opposition precipitated the regime's fall, as happened in Poland. More significant were weaknesses in the Communist system itself that prevented the state from responding positively to any form of opposition, regardless of its strength or origins.

The most serious shortcomings of the GDR stemmed from the long-standing domination by the SED and its monolithic, all-pervasive bureaucracy. It is possible to see elements of a feudalistic society in such a system, especially in the way a ruling caste enjoyed exceptional power and privilege. The parallel goes only so far, however, for a true caste society is based on tradition and inherited power. Not only were there opportunities in East Germany to rise in the hierarchy, the state was also committed to various forms of social progress, including womens' rights and education for all citizens. While some advances were made in these areas, it is true that far-reaching social and economic progress in the GDR was constrained by a party apparatus incapable of change and self-innovation.

Allied to the political stagnation were the economic failures documented earlier. Although there was no serious poverty or mass unemployment in the GDR, the standard of comparison for East Germans remained the FRG.

Since many had relatives in the FRG and watched Western television, they were acutely aware of better material conditions over the border.

Finally, external factors, notably *glasnost* and *perestroika* in the USSR, and the international peace process, were decisive in the collapse of the GDR. Little would have changed without Mikhail Gorbachev's reforms and the loosening of the Soviet grip on its satellite states. During the mass demonstrations of 1989 the Soviet authorities refused to commit their troops to support the SED. Hungary's willingness to allow East Germans to pass through to the West and ultimately the agreement of the Four Powers to German unification also contributed to the internal collapse.

Although both the time and fact of the GDR's collapse were unforeseen, the country was evidently in long-term decline. That this was not recognized sooner was because its rigid structures were able to conceal fatal defects. In the case of the GDR Western observers failed to recognize not just the scale of economic decline (the debt-ridden economy of the 1980s would probably have collapsed during the following decade) but also the internal weaknesses of the political fabric. Western ignorance about the extensive spying network maintained by the *Stasi* is one example of how little was known about life in the GDR. The true depth of popular discontent about the system is another. It is clear that that the GDR was vulnerable at many points. A product of the post-war division between East and West, the GDR was founded and sustained by an external power, the USSR; in the eyes of its own people it never acquired the the same claim to national legitimacy as its larger, wealthier, and more democratic neighbour, the FRG. But above all (and this aspect was consistently underestimated), GDR society suffered from serious system-immanent weaknesses which were camouflaged by its outwardly ordered and stable political structures.

3.6 The road to unification: treaties and events

Although it is difficult to set a precise date for the beginning of the *Wende* in the GDR, it had become clear by the early summer of 1989 that the SED was facing serious problems: opposition groups were in open protest; increasing numbers of citizens wished to emigrate; and Communism was retreating throughout Eastern Europe.

A key date for the *Wende* was 7 May 1989. On this day opposition groups in the GDR organized themselves nationally to monitor the local elections. In a bold demonstration of dissent the groups attempted to register publicly evidence that the official results, which claimed a 98·85% victory for the SED-dominated National Front, were falsified. One hundred and twenty protesters were arrested. Even more significant than actions by small opposition groups was the fact that people were queuing for exit visas for West Germany. This 'exit' form of opposition indicated a long-standing discontent in the population. A record 40,900 were permitted to leave during 1984, but the tide continued; by 1989 the backlog of emigration requests had reached 1·5 million, nearly 10% of the population. Finally, the decline of Communism in Eastern Bloc countries meant that the GDR was isolated internationally. The process began in 1985 when Gorbachev came to power in the USSR with an agenda of liberalization and reform. By 1989 reformist movements in Poland, Hungary, and Czechoslovakia had achieved progress towards free elections and multi-party systems. When Hungary dismantled its frontier with Austria in May it was clear that the era of the Iron Curtain was over.

In so far as it responded at all to these events, the SED on the one hand employed threats and on the other stuck its head in the sand, refusing to see the need for reform. In the People's Chamber on 8 June 1989 the Party declared its support for the massacre of dissidents in Tiananmen Square as the justified 'suppression of a counter-revolution'—a clear signal that the SED envisaged a violent 'Chinese solution' to the mounting opposition. As late as October 1989 the SED was concentrating on celebrating the fortieth anniversary of the GDR's foundation, claiming that a fully 'functioning, effective, socialist system' remained in place (*Einheit* 5 September 1989:1).

The dam burst in summer 1989. Over 1,000 East Germans, wishing to emigrate to West Germany, occupied West German embassies and missions in Prague, Warsaw, Budapest, and East Berlin. When, in defiance of a treaty with the GDR, Hungary opened its borders with Austria on 11 September, over 25,000 East Germans left for the FRG. Simultaneously, large demonstrations took place in most East German cities. People now demanded not only the right to leave the country but also political reform and free elections. Peaceful mass-protests began on 5 October in Magdeburg and Dresden and spread to other cities. The authorities reacted with brutality and arrests. Visiting East Berlin on 6 and 7 October to commemorate the fortieth anniversary of the GDR, Gorbachev publicly warned the SED of the need for reform. Honecker ignored his advice.

The protests reached a climax on 16 October with a demonstration of over 120,000 in Leipzig. This time the security forces did not intervene. The following day Honecker resigned from the Politburo after losing a vote of confidence. His successor, Egon Krenz, was still closely associated with the old guard and had long been regarded as Honecker's natural heir to power. As the exodus from the GDR and the demonstrations continued, the entire Politburo resigned (8 November) and the Berlin Wall was opened (9 November). On 18 November the People's Chamber, discovering its parliamentary role, agreed to form a provisional cabinet under Hans Modrow, a reformist regional SED leader. One of the first acts of the new Parliament was to commit the country to free elections. By early December the SED had abandoned its constitutional claim to a monopoly of power, disbanded its Politburo and Central Committee, and, at a crisis congress, replaced Krenz with a new leader, Gregor Gysi. Gysi, who had distinguished himself as a reform-minded lawyer representing dissidents during the 1970s, initiated investigations into corruption and misuse of office within the SED.

On 6 December the West German Chancellor Helmut Kohl announced a ten-point plan for unification. Soon after, on a visit to Dresden, Kohl was mobbed by East Germans clamouring for unity and chanting 'Germany, Germany!'. Economic stagnation and the popular mood drove the Modrow government, which had wanted to preserve the independence of the GDR, relentlessly towards unification. In a major shift in Soviet attitudes Gorbachev conceded on 30 January 1990 the likelihood of German unification. Faced with the collapse of the GDR's economy, the lack of confidence in its currency, and the unrelenting emigration to the West (about 3,000 a day), Kohl and Modrow set up a commission of experts on 13 February to prepare for monetary and economic union with the FRG. Introducing the West German mark in the East would, it was hoped, encourage East Germans to stay in the GDR.

At the first free elections in the GDR on 18 March 1990 the Conservative Alliance for Germany, which had campaigned for monetary union and swift unification, won a landslide victory. A non-Communist coalition government was formed under Lothar de Maizière (GDR-CDU), a lawyer and senior Church official in the GDR. The government's principal mandate was to negotiate reunification with the FRG. Economic and currency union was agreed in April and embodied in the State Treaty on the Creation of Monetary, Economic and Social Union, which took effect from 1 July. The treaty amounted to a takeover by the FRG. It provided for the replacement of the GDR mark by the West German mark and for the introduction of a free market economy in the East; social union meant adopting the FRG's welfare system based on employers' and workers' contributions.

At local elections on 14 October five provincial states or *Länder* were established after the West German model. These superseded the fifteen *Bezirke* (regions) which the SED had established in 1952 to reinforce central control from Berlin. All-German elections were set for 2 December. Already in early July, East–West German negotiations had begun on a treaty for full political union, the Treaty of Unification. This complex treaty placed the constitutional seal on union. It specified that the new Germany would be governed under the Federal German Basic Law, to which the five

GDR *Länder* would accede under Article 23. FRG law would apply throughout Germany, with transitional arrangements for a number of issues, such as abortion and property rights. The treaty established a Unity Fund to finance the needs of the new *Länder* and heralded changes in public administration, employment law, health, the environment, culture, education, and broadcasting in the East. Unification was set for midnight 2–3 October 1990.

Unification also required the agreement of the allied powers of the Second World War, the USSR, USA, Britain, and France. The resulting Treaty on the Final Settlement on Germany settled all external aspects of union. Germany would be a sovereign and united nation from 3 October, when residual allied rights would end. It would remain within NATO (the size of its army was set at 370,000) and maintain its commitment to European integration.

While the treaties were being worked out, events inside Germany moved swiftly. Despite pressure from a disintegrating GDR for even earlier union and all-German elections, the timetable for these was maintained. The election returned a clear victory for Chancellor Kohl, who had spearheaded the drive to unification. From the protests of May 1989 to unification, barely fifteen months had passed.

3.7 The transition to democracy

The Western takeover of the GDR necessarily cast East Germans in a passive role as they subsumed their constitutional identity into that of the FRG. Such a perspective, however, belies the personal courage displayed by opposition groups and demonstrators who challenged the regime at a time when it was still dangerous to do so. The *Wende* also saw unprecedented political activity in the GDR as new political models were evolved to effect the transition to democracy. The courage of individuals and the activity during the *Wende* provides some evidence that forty years of SED rule did not entirely destroy a democratic political culture east of the Elbe.

When considering opposition to the SED it is worth noting that reformist elements were present within the Party itself. Notably the SED's regional and middle-ranking leaders refused to use force against the demonstrators (Friedheim 1993). There were also last-minute attempts by individual groups within the SED to rescue the Party and to maintain national influence during the early *Wende*. However, the small number of Party reformists who had distanced themselves from Stalinism over several decades were unable to co-ordinate their efforts in time. After years of control and surveillance they did not even know how to contact each other. Other reformists were too slow to realize that the Party needed more than minor modifications, and there was also the genuine fear that the leadership would resort to violence (Falkner 1990:1755–57). Nevertheless, a reformist Communist-dominated government was the first to emerge from the collapse of the old regime: sixteen of the twenty-eight ministers of Modrow's interim cabinet were SED members, including Modrow himself, who had been First Secretary of the Dresden region since 1973.

The first national democratic forum to appear during the *Wende* was the Round Table, a platform for dialogue between opposition groups and government that had been used in other countries emerging from state Communism. Chaired by the Protestant Church, it met sixteen times between December 1989 and March 1990. The opposition groups originated in the international peace movement of the 1980s, when they led a clandestine existence under the protection of the Church. Rejecting violence, they envisaged a reformed GDR which would adopt a middle road between Stalinism and Western capitalism. Their ideal was a democracy involving maximum participation by the citizens. They differed about whether to adopt a planned or free market economy, about Western investment, and the scale of industrialization (Templin 1990:77–79).

The Round Table demanded free and secret elections, a new constitution, and the disbanding of the *Stasi*. After helping to dismantle the SED's hold on power, the opposition groups joined Modrow's coalition in early 1990 to form a government of national responsibility. Their motive was not to participate in power but to persuade East Germans that it was worthwhile staying in the GDR. The spirit of cooperation among members of the Round Table broke down with the approach of the national elections in March 1990. While the citizens' groups were prepared to assist the government, the organized political parties sensed electoral advantage in campaigning from opposition, and they effectively left the Table in early 1990. The forum's non-confrontational style, cultivated by the churchmen who chaired it, was unsuited to electioneering. During its final weeks the Round Table helped formulate the electoral law for the March national elections and advocated a variety of social measures. It also worked on a new constitution for the GDR, but this was obviated by the adoption of the Basic Law.

It would be easy to dismiss the Round Table as a talking shop. But after years without opportunity for open debate, this is precisely what it intended to be. The public and media attention which the forum attracted was out of proportion to its political influence, and it was associated with the small opposition groups rather than the mainstream parties. Despite its commitment to citizens' rights, the East German people abandoned the

Round Table because they wanted rapid unification. They had no time for a handful of clerics and intellectuals busy constructing visions of a separate GDR state.

The role of the four Block Parties (CDU, LDPD, NPDP, DBD) during the *Wende* illustrates the populist nature of the East German revolution. Their existence before 1989 meant that, unlike the one-party states of other Communist countries, a multi-party tradition was nominally in place when socialism collapsed. After Honecker's fall the members of the puppet parties pressed their leaders to break away from the Block. The two parties with a pre-GDR and pre-Nazi tradition, the CDU and the LDPD, quickly developed a new profile. In late 1989 the CDU, for example, acknowledged its co-responsibility for the Honecker period and affirmed its commitment to Christian and humanistic ideals, a social market economy, and reunification. The DBD, whose members were known as the 'green comrades', had most in common with the SED and, despite supporting political union and a free market economy, wished to keep the agricultural collectives.

Particular mention should be made of the Social Democratic Party. Forcibly merged with the KPD in 1946, the original SPD had been eliminated in the GDR. On 7 October 1989 and under the hostile eyes of the *Stasi*, a courageous group of fifty met in a pastor's house near Berlin to reconstitute the party. The GDR-SPD was initially a party of priests and intellectuals and had more in common with the human rights groups of the Round Table than with the pre-war SPD of the working classes. By early 1990 its membership had soared to 30,000. It proved especially attractive to the thousands deserting the SED. Under its leader and co-founder, Ibrahim Böhme, the Party affirmed its hostility to the SED and demanded the return of assets confiscated in 1946. The new party drew upon a historical tradition of social democracy which was rooted in the nineteenth century but had been significantly modified by the Godesberg Programme of 1959, when the (West) German party formally rejected Marxism and embraced free market economics. The GDR-SPD supported unification and, despite a desperate shortage of resources and experience, was expected to do well in the national election (Fink 1990).

In the prelude to the March elections the GDR's indigenous parties had little time to develop separate profiles. The main groupings were dominated by their partners in the FRG and the campaign became in effect an extension of the West German political party system. Although all major parties were committed to unification, East Germans regarded the West German Chancellor as the most likely politician to deliver it and supported the CDU-dominated Alliance for Germany. The SPD obtained a disappointing 22% of the seats. The PDS (the renamed SED) gained 16% and the Alliance 90, a union of citizens' groups, just 3%. Only the PDS and citizens' groups were committed to preserving the GDR, but in the first free national election in the East since 1933 the people voted decisively against maintaining the East German state (Winters 1990a, Dennis 1993).

Between April and October 1990 the inexperienced members of the People's Chamber enacted a vast amount of legislation. They processed and passed the complex treaties of unification, sometimes only seeing the drafts the day before. As unification approached, most parties merged with their West German counterparts. As a result their eastern identity was subsumed within the traditional Conservative, Liberal, and Social Democratic divisions of the West. The two-thirds parliamentary majority required for accession to the FRG was reached at a special meeting of the People's Chamber in August 1990. Both German parliaments approved the Unification Treaty on 20 September.

The consensus on unification concealed intense differences between the main parties in both East and West Germany which are too complex to discuss here. At one point both Liberals and Social Democrats left the GDR national coalition; the GDR-SPD claimed that the terms of the Unification Treaty ignored the interests of the GDR and that they condemned the country to economic servitude to the West. In the all-German election of December 1990 the electorates in both states strongly endorsed unification, dealing the fringe parties who had wanted to impede the pace of unification a crushing blow. Political commentators were especially harsh on the SPD, which they accused of conducting a negative campaign; the party was plunged into a leadership crisis (Winters 1990b).

The pattern of voting was similar in East and West, apparently confirming the absence of an independent political culture in the GDR. The fate of the Round Table and the verdict of the East German electorate indicated not only popular support for unification, but also a readiness to surrender whatever national identity the GDR had possessed. But these attitudes were an inevitable consequence of the vacuum left by the SED's collapse. The prestige of the West German political model and the sophistication of its electoral machine meant that neither reform Communists nor opposition groups had the time, credibility, or resources to establish a viable framework for maintaining the GDR as a separate entity. The positive aspect of the political manoeuvering between April and December 1990 was that East Germans took to multi-party politics with remarkable speed and were ready to turn the Block Parties into actively democratic institutions once they had cast off SED control. And even the PDS, whose disappearance was widely predicted after 1990, enjoyed a resurgence in the national elections of December 1994 as voters in the eastern states expressed their disillusionment with the course of unification.

3.8 Post-unification: the GDR as a criminal regime

On 20 December 1991 the Federal German Parliament passed a law which was seen as a necessary condition for overcoming the legacy of Communist dictatorship in the former GDR. The law placed management of the *Stasi*'s archives in the hands of a specially established authority, commonly known as the Gauck Office (its head, Joachim Gauck, had been co-founder of the citizens' rights group New Forum which played a leading role in the transition to democracy). In accordance with the Unification Treaty the *Stasi* files were distributed among fourteen regional archives within the former GDR, with the administrative centre in Berlin. The volume of files is enormous, comprising six million dossiers and extending for 200 kilometers. Individuals may consult the archives to discover who spied on them and to obtain evidence for the rehabilitation of victims of persecution. Public, political, and commercial organizations can also ask the Office to examine the files in order to establish whether their employees had worked for the *Stasi*. Public interest in the archives proved immediate and intense. In February 1993 Gauck reported that his staff of 3,000 were handling over three million requests for information, from both individuals and institutions, including the regional press and local government in the new federal states. Businesses were less interested, placing an employee's personal efficiency above *Stasi*-involvement.

A case which illustrates the problems surrounding revelations of the contents of the *Stasi* archives is that of Manfred Stolpe. Stolpe, a senior Protestant Church official in the GDR, became Minister President of the new federal state of Brandenburg after unification. In 1990 the West German newspaper *Die Welt* published rumours that Stolpe had acted as an informant for the *Stasi* on Church affairs. Between 1990 and 1992 allegations were made that he had passed to the authorities information about conversations with senior West German politicians, that he had played a role in the detention of dissidents, and that the *Stasi* had awarded him a medal for his services. In February 1992 the state of Brandenburg set up a committee of enquiry to investigate the allegations. Stolpe himself claimed that his contacts with the *Stasi* and SED were known to senior churchmen and that they extended only to practical, humanitarian objectives (such as persuading the authorities to issue exit permits, reunite families, and release dissidents). At one stage Stolpe was incriminated by the Gauck Office but conceded only that he may have been an unwitting informant. The debate raised several questions. Was it possible for someone not to know he was acting as an informant? Are the *Stasi* files reliable as a source of information? Is it safe to judge someone's integrity on the basis of reports and post-*Wende* statements by former *Stasi* officers?

The Stolpe affair also led to a reassessment of the role of the Protestant Church in the GDR. While it was no secret that the Church did not directly oppose the SED, the question now raised was whether the compromise had gone too far. Or was Stolpe merely a convenient scapegoat for the whole Church, which was merely achieving what it could against the resources of a powerful state? In stoutly defending his political and moral position, Stolpe became a symbol of eastern defiance against what was seen as a spirit of judgemental retribution conducted with the benefit of hindsight.

The role of the *Stasi* clearly illustrates the moral bankrupty of the GDR regime. The handling of this legacy has proved a divisive issue for Germans since unification. From the late 1960s the FRG had cultivated a practical working relationship with the GDR. Its aims in this relationship had been to promote inter-German trade, to alleviate the persecution of dissidents, and to halt the shoot-to-kill policy at the border. At no time was it suggested that the GDR leadership should stand trial as criminals, even if the opportunity arose. Indeed, in September 1987, Honecker received a positive reception on the first ever state visit to West Germany by an East German head of state. After unification this policy changed dramatically and the phrase *Regierungskriminalität* ('government criminality') came to be widely applied to the GDR regime. The change of approach was brought about by a number of factors, but principally by revelations about the methods practised by the *Stasi*, the scale of high-level corruption in the SED, and evidence of long-suppressed personal injustices.

After unification, the government responded to the notion of the GDR as a criminal state in a number of ways. First, it placed individuals on public trial. Second, it established parliamentary commissions of enquiry. Third, it provided legal means for compensating individuals for personal injustices.

The legal basis for placing citizens of the former GDR on trial is the inter-German Treaty of Unification. The treaty gave primacy to FRG law after 3 October 1990, although GDR law applied to crimes in the East committed before this date. The first to be tried were border guards who had shot and killed those attempting to escape to the West. Prosecutions began in September 1991 when the Berlin judiciary accused four guards of killing twenty-year-old Chris Gueffroy as he attempted to flee to West Berlin on 6 February 1989 (Gueffroy was the last of over 600 victims who died at the Berlin Wall). Two of the accused were found guilty and received up to three years imprisonment, which was seen as an unexpectedly severe sentence. The judges decided not only that the shoot-to-kill policy infringed East German law (the policy existed only in the form of secret military directives) but also that 'what is law is not always right', effectively asserting the primacy of international standards of human rights over the law of a sovereign state.

Placing senior leaders of the former GDR on trial proved to be more complex, partly because of their age and fragile health. In summer 1992 six persons, including the eighty-year-old Honecker, were accused of complicity in the killing or attempted killing of over seventy-five escapees. Although Honecker was charged with manslaughter, many observers regarded his crime as murder (Blumenwitz 1992:578). To expedite proceedings, the case against the ailing Honecker continued separately and the number of charges was reduced to the twelve most serious. The trial raised a number of questions. Can a state's right to secure its border by whatever means be the subject of legal proceedings? If so, is it possible to assign individual guilt? And since GDR law legalized the use of weapons at the border after 1982, under what law could the leadership be tried? These issues were shelved when the Federal Constitutional Court eventually decided that Honecker's prolonged detention amounted to an infringement of human rights. On 13 January 1993 he was released and granted asylum in Chile, where he died on 29 May 1994. Of the remaining defendants, Willi Stoph (formerly chairman of the Council of Ministers) and Erich Mielke (Security Minister and head of the *Stasi*) were released on grounds of ill-health (Mielke was later sentenced to six years for the murder in 1931 of two Berlin policemen, committed when he was a young Communist). On 19 September 1993 the three remaining senior party figures received sentences of up to seven and a half years. Although the court accepted that they were not directly involved in the killings, it judged that they were important links in the chain of command and were aware of the injustice of killing their own citizens at the border. That the shoot-to-kill policy was not officially acknowledged showed that its initiators were aware of its fundamentally criminal nature.

In view of the large number of projected trials Chancellor Kohl announced in March 1993 the appointment of a central commission to deal with official and government criminality in the GDR. In one notable trial in September 1993 Manfred Berghofer, the former Mayor of Dresden, received a suspended prison sentence of one year for falsifying election results. The judgement is an example of how GDR law has been applied retrospectively to the crimes of East German leaders; in law, GDR elections have been deemed to be subject to similar standards of probity as in West Germany. Prosecutions have also been brought against a number of former East German judges and lawyers for perverting the course of justice, as was laid down in GDR law but abused by the SED.

A controversial trial which took place in 1993 confused many observers by apparently applying West German law retrospectively: the trial was that of Markus Wolf, the GDR's former spymaster. Accusing Wolf of treason and bribery, the prosecutors maintained that spying for East Germany was answerable as an offence even after unification. The justification for the charge was that, unlike its West German counterpart, the GDR's secret service was part of a repressive system. It was even suggested that East Germans were still responsible to West Germany as the legal successor to the Third Reich and were therefore subject to the FRG's law of treason. Wolf was found guilty and sentenced to six years, although the court acknowledged that unification had influenced its deliberations. Wolf himself claimed he was a scapegoat for a discredited system, especially since Western agents were not similarly criminalized. Noting the asymmetry of treating East and West German spies differently, an appeal court overturned Wolf's sentence in May 1995. As for ordinary eastern Germans, many viewed the crimes of Mielke, who was closely identified with the universally loathed system of internal oppression, in a different light to the technical achievements of Wolf, whom they admired for his penetration of Western security.

Objectors to the trials highlighted several issues. First, they argued that it was unjust to pursue individual GDR leaders simply because they had maintained a border that both NATO and the Soviet Union had tacitly accepted. Second, they criticized the invoking of the imprecise concept of 'natural justice' to secure convictions not possible under existing law. Finally, the combing of archives to establish links between killings at the border and decisions reached by politicians in committee smacked of finding a crime to fit the criminal. Legal issues apart, the new rulers of the eastern states tended to exploit the trials to bolster their own political credibility in the face of mounting economic and social problems. While Germany has avoided overtly political show-trials, it has proved easier in practice to convict lesser figures than the ageing leaders who carried the greater responsibility.

Apart from trials in courts of law, the Federal Government has made extensive use of commissions of enquiry to uncover clandestine criminal activities. In June 1991 the Schalck-Commission began investigating the secret activities of former State Secretary Alexander Schalck-Golodkowski. As head of an innocuously named Department of Commercial Co-ordination, Schalck-Golodkowski provided foreign currency for the GDR, ran a network of firms in West Germany (these were disposed of to friends and colleagues in suspicious circumstances during the *Wende*), and managed a variety of secret accounts and currency transfers. The organization's turnover has been estimated at 50,000 million DM.

Another body, the Commission for the Assessment of the History and Consequences of the SED-Dictatorship in Germany, was given a wider brief. Announced in March 1992 and chaired by Rainer Eppelmann, cofounder of the civil rights group Democratic Awakening and a minister in de Maizière's government, the Commission comprised sixteen parliamentarians and eleven co-opted experts. It was charged with promoting understanding between east and west Germans, contributing to the rehabilitation of victims of persecution, and advising the Federal Parliament on what measures and political initiatives should be taken to overcome the legacy of the SED years. The Commission set up research projects and conducted dialogues with ordinary citizens and public forum debates. By the time the final report was submitted in June 1994, forty-four hearings had been held on issues such as government criminality, the *Stasi*, the role of the Church in the GDR, and the economy as an instrument of the SED.

In fulfillment of the terms of the Unification Treaty, the German government has also acknowledged the principle of compensation for injustices suffered under the SED. In June 1992 it introduced a law entitling former political detainees to 300 DM compensation for each month of imprisonment. Although criticized as half of what a West German would receive for unjust detention, the sum was defended by the government as reasonable within budgetary constraints. A more controversial form of compensation involved returning land and property to former GDR citizens who had been dispossessed by the state. Wherever possible the government has applied the principle that claimants should regain title to their land rather than be compensated financially, which would require enormous sums. At the same time, existing tenants and rights of usage were protected. Processing the huge number of claims has proved time-consuming. It has been estimated that it would require ten years to process the 1·2 million claims that were lodged by 1992. Naturally the delays have acted as a severe brake on investment, especially in run-down city centres while developers await the outcome of land disputes. Fast track procedures giving preference to investors have had limited success (Piazolo 1992).

Clearly the workings of the property law highlight the difficulties which Germany is encountering in integrating the eastern states. First, it is taking time to establish the administrative machinery to fill the vacuum left by the old regime. Second, it is essential to act quickly to promote economic confidence without simultaneously incurring huge costs. Third, there is the need to balance the interests of eastern Germans against those of western incomers. Finally, while the legal mechanisms are coming to grips with the legacy of one-party rule, complex moral and political questions arise from their operation.

Further reading

For the directions which research into the GDR took between 1950 and 1990, see Pollack (1993). Weidenfeld and Zimmermann (1989) contains comparative studies of all aspects of the FRG and the GDR from 1949 to 1989. Weber (1991) provides a general history of the GDR, while Joas and Kohli (1993) focus on explanations for the collapse. The course of unification is discussed in Glaeßner (1992). For studies of the opposition and its decline during the *Wende*, see Dennis (1993). Hancock and Welsh (1994) discuss economic and political aspects of unification. A useful reference handbook on German unity is Weidenfeld and Korte (1991). Hickel (1993) provides a non-technical summary of the economic issues thrown up by the integration process. German and foreign contemporary reactions to unification are collected in James and Stone (1992). For information about the *Stasi* see Fricke (1991), Gill and Schröter (1993), and (in English) Popplewell (1992). Richter (1993) gives a critical account of the trial of Erich Honecker. The journals *Deutschland Archiv* and *German Politics* contain useful documentary material and analysis.

Part II

The Political, Social and Economic Challenges

4
Germany as a European Power

MARK BLACKSELL

4.1 Introduction

The essential status of Germany as a European power is defined by the interplay of its geography, size, history, and culture. All have combined in the course of the twentieth century to produce at times a highly volatile mix that has done much to dictate the pattern of political events in the continent as a whole. The rise and fall of Bismarck's Second Reich, the impoverished aftermath of the First World War, the rapacious expansionism and brutality of the Third Reich, and after the Second World War the division of Germany into the FRG and the GDR along the fault line of the Iron Curtain (a division which separated the predominantly democratic and economically market-orientated West from the totalitarian and Communist East) are all key elements for an understanding of the nature of contemporary Europe.

The unification of Germany on 3 October 1990 has not obliterated this legacy but it has redefined its significance and heralded the beginning of a radically new phase in the country's history. The geopolitics of central Europe have been transformed: two key states at the forefront of the Cold War divide, the status and legitimacy of which had been widely disputed internationally, were merged in less than a year. The borders of the new state are now internationally recognized and undisputed, the sovereignty of the government is accepted, and a distinctive international role within the context of the European Union (EU) and NATO is beginning to emerge.

This chapter examines Germany's credentials as a European power in the light of unification, concentrating on the country's new political geography. Unification has not only redrawn and affirmed Germany's external borders. Its internal structure and governance have also been substantially reordered so as to accommodate two hitherto separate states within a single political and administrative framework. The consequences of these changes are far-reaching, leading to new political and economic alliances, and to substantially different patterns of trade and communication.

4.2 The geographical context

The new united Germany dominates the political map of central Europe, stretching over 500 km west to east from the River Rhine to the River Oder, and over 800 km north to south from the Baltic and the North Sea to the Alps. Although smaller in area at 356,755 sq km than either France or Spain, it occupies once again a focal position within the continent and is therefore a fundamental element in any strategic equation, a fact that has been demonstrated repeatedly in the course of the past century (Murphy 1991; Wanklyn 1941).

The new state is less than 70% of the size of Wilhelmine Germany which during the period of the Second Reich (1871–1918) extended east to include much of present-day Poland and further along the Baltic coast into what is now Lithuania. The loss of this territory has changed but not necessarily diminished Germany's position (Blacksell 1994). Germany has retained borders with nine other European states: Austria, Switzerland, France, Luxemburg, Belgium, the Netherlands, Denmark, Poland, and the Czech Republic. In some cases Germany shares a common language with its immediate neighbours: Austria is almost entirely German-speaking, Switzerland has a German-speaking majority, and the Czech Republic and Poland have significant German-speaking minorities; German is the third official language of Belgium, and Letzebuergesch, a German dialect, is, with French, one of the two official languages of Luxemburg (Figure 4.1). For reasons of geographical propinquity alone, the direction of both foreign and domestic policy in Germany is of immediate importance to other European states in a way that has no parallel elsewhere in the continent.

4.2.1 *The boundary question*

The physical geography of Europe sat uneasily with the division into two international power blocks after the Second World War. Indeed, in retrospect, one of the surprises of the second half of the twentieth century is that the Iron Curtain endured and proved to be such an effective political frontier for so long (Blacksell 1981). Previously the strategic importance of *Mitteleuropa* (Central Europe) with Germany at its core had defined the political and economic shape of the continent (Sinnhuber 1954). It is a measure of the power of this concept that, when attempting to summarize the changes to the political map after 1945, the American geographer Eric Fischer stated simply that *Mitteleuropa* had shrunk to a single line (Fischer 1956:60). Without further elaboration the metaphor made it clear that the dynamic heartland of Central Europe had disappeared, to be replaced by a boundary line between two competing political and military systems (NATO and the Warsaw Pact), each of which had its main power-base outside Europe.

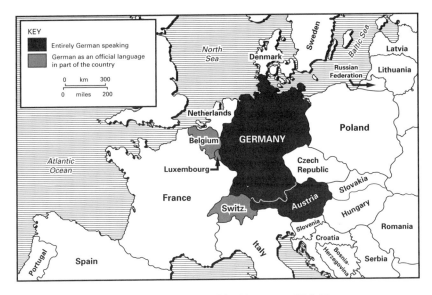

Figure 4.1   Germany and its European Neighbours

In 1989, however, these post-war certainties began to crumble throughout Eastern Europe and the Soviet Union. The previously virtually impenetrable barrier of the Iron Curtain became increasingly permeable, with ever larger numbers of people migrating to the West. The political changes in Germany were a crucial part of this process; indeed, one of the most pressing aspects of unification was the need to broker an international agreement that defined the borders of the new state, particularly in the east.

At the height of its power in 1939, the Third Reich had occupied 114,548 sq km to the east of the former GDR. Most of this territory is now in Poland, but it also included parts of the former Soviet Union: the area around Königsberg (Kalingrad) was placed under Soviet administration in 1945 and has subsequently become the independent state of Lithuania. In the absence of a final and comprehensive post-war settlement, the 1949 Constitution of the FRG, the Basic Law, left open the possibility, albeit in the vaguest of terms, that this territory might be included in a future reunified Germany. As the final status of the eastern border had never been properly clarified, these territorial aspirations, however unrealistic, became a major source of political tension.

When in the latter part of 1989 the collapse of Communist regimes in the GDR and in Eastern Europe was well advanced, the political process of resolving such a crucial area of uncertainty was surprisingly hesitant. After the breaching of the Berlin Wall on 9 November the Federal German Chancellor, Helmut Kohl, put forward a ten-point plan to deal with the German Question. Kohl's plan envisaged the two Germanies gradually merging as members of a confederation. Significantly the plan made no reference to German borders. The omission created the impression that unification would re-open the territorial issue, a view reinforced by the Chancellor's subsequent official visit to Poland where he received a rapturous welcome from the ethnic Germans living in the country's western areas which adjoin Germany (Kaiser 1990/91).

Since it became immediately apparent that the lack of sensitivity with which the border issue was being handled would jeopardize any permanent political solution in Central Europe, it was quickly included in the discussions. On 21 June 1990 the Federal Parliament in the FRG and the People's Chamber in the GDR simultaneously agreed to renounce any claims to lands east of the rivers Oder and Neisse, the boundary between the GDR and Poland. This statement of intent did much to relieve the tension and paved the way for a comprehensive treaty.

On 17 July 1990 the two Germanies and Poland formally accepted the existing boundary as permanent; they agreed that it should be underwritten by the four Second World War allies (France, the Soviet Union, the UK, and the USA) because of their legal responsibilities as former occupying powers in Germany. The Treaty on the Final Settlement on Germany formally ended the state of war that had existed since 1939; also known as the Two-plus-Four Treaty, it was signed on 12 September. The treaty defined the reunified Germany unequivocally as incorporating the territories of the FRG and the GDR together with the whole of Berlin. The agreement also required Germany and Poland to sign a treaty as soon as possible after unification confirming the *de facto* boundary between them as *de jure*; and it further required Germany to renounce all territorial claims. The final stage came after unification itself had taken place, with the signing of the German–Polish Treaty on 14 November. This treaty gave the legal seal of both countries to the Oder–Neisse frontier.

Now that the territorial extent of Germany was universally accepted, the new state could begin to secure its political position and to normalize relations with Poland and its other European neighbours. Undoubtedly, one of the consequences of this process has been to revive the geographical reality of *Mitteleuropa*. It is encouraging to note that, for the most part, this has not been viewed at the turn of the twenty-first century as a threat to stability elsewhere in the continent in the way that it was at the turn of the twentieth century.

4.2.2 *The demographic mix*

The significance of Germany's geographical position in Europe is re-inforced by the sheer size of its population. With some eighty million in-habitants it has the largest population in Europe, over 30% larger than France, Italy, or the UK. This fact gives the country substantial additional economic and political clout, but numbers alone provide only a part of the explanation for the influence that its people exert.

Several features of the composition of the population of Germany have deeply influenced the policies of the state. In 1989, before unification, the FRG had sixty million inhabitants of whom 2·3 million were German im-migrants who had left their homes in the East since 1949. In this context 'the East' refers to all the territory of the former Third Reich lying outside the FRG, for many Germans still had family and friends living in the GDR, Poland, and even parts of the former Soviet Union. Under Article 116 of the Basic Law anyone living within the boundaries of Germany on 31 De-cember 1937, or the child of anyone living in Germany at that date, has an unrestricted right to German citizenship. The Basic Law also extends the same right to anyone forced to leave Germany during the period of the Third Reich (from 30 January 1933 to 8 May 1945). Before 1990 these immigrants formed a large but well-integrated minority who had a strong vested interest in seeing the unification of the two Germanies brought about on terms that ensured the demise of the totalitarian Communist re-gime in the East and the primacy of the Basic Law of the FRG. The im-migrants formed pressure groups which did much to ensure that the goal of eventual unification remained on the political agenda in the FRG, and their influence was crucial in determining the speed with which the opportunity was seized in 1989–90. Now that unification has occurred, it will be inter-esting to see whether their aspirations have been fully satisfied. Despite the treaties discussed above, there are still many German families whose roots are in a Germany that extended beyond the boundaries of the new unified state.

Another important facet of unification is that it did not simply remove a frontier and allow two artificially separated groups of Germans to resume life together in a single country. Throughout their forty-year history the FRG and the GDR had been largely independent of each other and had de-veloped sharply contrasting societies. The population of the FRG had more in common with Austria and Switzerland than with the GDR. In turn, life for East Germans shared greater similarities with conditions in Poland and what was then Czechoslovakia than with West Germany. In both Germanies the majority of the population had been born and entirely brought up in their respective countries. On being thrown together, many Germans found that they had little in common and were divided by a daunting economic gulf. After the initial euphoria a considerable animosity developed between *Ossis* and *Wessis*. This has become a persistent source of social and economic discrimination and, it is estimated, will take at least a generation to disappear (Fulbrook 1991).

Alongside these internal tensions Germany, like most other industrial countries in Western Europe, has had to accommodate substantial numbers of foreigners in its society. These include 4·3 million *Gastarbeiter* (guestworkers) and their families, who originate mainly from Eastern Mediterranean countries (Italy, Greece, Turkey, and the republics of the former Yugoslavia). Initially, they came on a temporary basis to bolster the labour force, but many now have a permanent right of residence and have chosen to stay permanently. Also, over one million asylum-seekers from throughout the world have taken advantage of Germany's formerly relatively liberal constitution in order to gain a residence permit. In recent years Germany has admitted far more asylum-seekers than any other country in Western Europe. Between 1983 and 1991 the figure stood at 959,000. This was 41·9% of the total number of asylum-seekers entering Western Europe, more than three times the number entering France (297,000), the next most popular country of entry (King 1994). There has been a growing political debate in Germany about the disproportionate share of asylum-seekers it has accepted, and one of the main objectives of its six-month presidency of the EU in the second half of 1994 was to see this burden shared more equitably amongst its fellow member states (*Guardian*, 5 July 1994:11).

Germany is not alone amongst European countries in having become a multi-cultural and multi-ethnic society with sharp economic disparities between rich and poor. Where it differs is in the depth of the divisions arising from the process of unification and in the large volume of newcomers admitted during the past decade. As a result, there is a rawness in relations between the various groups that, though visible, is less threatening elsewhere in Western Europe.

4.2.3 *The changing pattern of economic well-being*

Unification has fundamentally altered the economic map of Germany by introducing into the well-ordered and generally prosperous FRG five new federal states (Brandenburg, Mecklenburg-West Pomerania, Saxony, Sax-ony-Anhalt, Thuringia) together with the capital of East Berlin, all of which are substantially poorer in economic terms than western Germany. It has also changed the pattern of regional deprivation in the territories of both the former FRG and the erstwhile GDR. What had been a border zone (the *Zonenrandgebiet*) on the margins of the economy in both countries, sup-ported by a whole gamut of regional economic aids, has been transformed into an area of economic opportunity at the heart of the nation's economic space—*eine neue Mitte* (Wild and Jones 1993).

Not only have new markets been opened up on both sides of the inner-German frontier, the huge public investment by the FRG in the former GDR, estimated to be 150 billion DM by the end of the century, will of it-self generate enormous economic opportunities. The first priority of the in-vestment programme is a total overhaul of the communications and transport systems. Throughout the new federal states this involves the in-stallation of expensive new telecommunications systems, the relaying of electricity mains, and a massive road-building programme. The most ambi-tious and costly of all infrastructural programmes is the 56 billion DM *Verkehrsprojekte 'Deutsche Einheit'* (VPDE, Transport Projects for Ger-man Unity). This aims to bring Germany's east–west transport links, which at the height of the Cold War were for the most part dismantled and closed on the GDR's side of the frontier, into line with the requirements of the post-unification age. Scheduled for completion in 1997 the VPDE pro-gramme includes the modernization and, in some stretches, construction, of eight east–west trunk railway routes, the restoration of the disused section of the Mittelland Canal in the new federal states, the upgrading of three existing *Autobahn* links, and the building of five new west–east *Auto-bahnen* (Lübeck-Rostock-Schwedt, Göttingen-Halle, Kassel-Eisenach, Schweinfurt-Erfurt, and Bamberg-Suhl) (Wild and Jones 1994). Figures 4.2 and 4.3 illustrate the extensions to the road and rail network.

Nevertheless, even massive public investment cannot hide the larger-scale regional economic discrepancies in the country. Nor can it prevent jobs and workers from moving westwards. Since unification the redistribu-tion of population away from the east and north and towards the south and west has continued on a scale equalled in recent times only during the im-mediate aftermath of the Second World War. In the first three months after unification nearly one million people changed their place of residence, a third of them moving to a different federal state. There has been a marked haemorrhage from the east, most notably from the industrial region around the cities of Dresden, Leipzig, and Halle, to the states of Baden-Württemberg and Bavaria in the south, where the growth in new employment is strongest. But there has also been a strong movement from

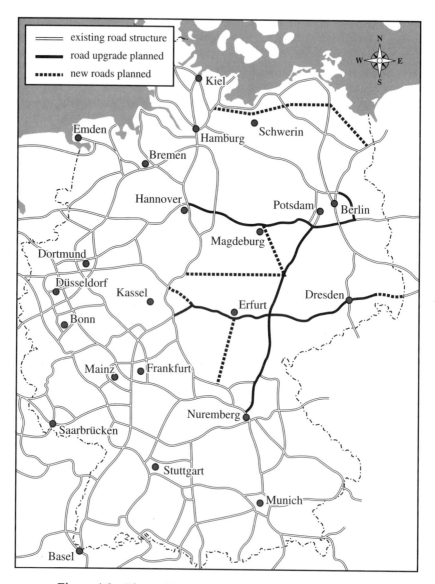

Figure 4.2   Planned Extensions to the Motorway Network

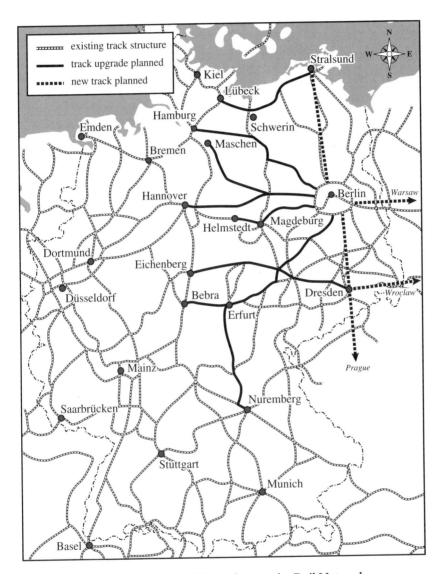

Figure 4.3 Planned Extensions to the Rail Network

north to south, especially from Schleswig-Holstein and Lower Saxony to Hesse and Baden-Württemberg. This movement long pre-dates unification and reflects a fundamental redistribution in the focus of economic activity in the FRG away from older industrial areas like the Ruhr and towards new centres that have no equivalent industrial tradition.

It remains to be seen whether such trends in the distribution of economic activity will be reversed by the longer-term effects of unification. The relentless centralization of economic activity along the Rhine-Rhône axis has been a dominant feature in the economic geography of Europe in the final quarter of the twentieth century. But a new industrial heartland for the twenty-first century could be in the process of being forged in Central Europe as the effects of the huge investment and restructuring programmes begin to take real effect. At such an early stage in the process it is impossible to predict the outcome with any confidence. At the same time it is irrefutable that the political and economic programmes intended to revitalize the eastern federal states and reshape Germany are much more than mere tokenism, as some political commentators have maintained. The decision to move the German capital from Bonn to Berlin by the turn of the century is indicative of the political determination behind the restructuring programme (Smith 1992).

4.2.4 The nature of unification

In some respects the term unification is a misnomer. For all practical purposes what occurred was a takeover: the extension of the political and economic system of the FRG to the whole of the former GDR. The Communist regime in the East, which had so flamboyantly and with such apparent confidence celebrated its fortieth anniversary in October 1989, simply imploded in less than a year. Its demise was part of the wider collapse of the constellation of republics that constituted the Soviet Union, including the political infrastructure that underpinned them.

The GDR was in every sense a client state, created in 1949 at the behest of the Soviet Union. Without the economic backing and military 'support' of its superpower protector, it was stripped of national credibility and of its political and economic coherence. In one important respect the GDR was different from all the other Warsaw Pact states in Eastern Europe: it had no deeper historical roots to which it could return when the Communist political and economic system disintegrated. Even though *de facto* acceptance of the GDR as a state had gradually gained ground in the FRG over the preceding two decades as part of the *Ostpolitik* initiated by the former SPD

Chancellor, Willy Brandt, one can say with hindsight that unification on the terms offered was almost certainly the only realistic option.

If unification was inevitable, the process by which it should be achieved was far from certain in early 1990. Despite somewhat misty-eyed references to the 'German twins' at the time (Link 1993), no part of the political, social, and economic infrastructure of the GDR was congruent with that of the FRG. At the same time the speed of political events in 1989 and 1990 meant that decisions about the nature of the future state had to be made almost instantaneously. Such decisions also had to be acceptable both to the German people on either side of the political divide and to the wider international community.

4.2.5 *The structure of local government*

The FRG is a federal state: a substantial devolution of political power to the individual states, the *Länder*, is unambiguously written into Article 23 of the Basic Law. The GDR, on the other hand, was a highly centralized state, which in 1952 had consciously rejected the existing administrative structure based on *Länder* in favour of fourteen much less independent and less powerful regions, or *Bezirke*. Given the way in which unification proceeded, it was inevitable that the *Länder* system of the FRG would be extended to the former GDR, not least because the Basic Law made specific provision for accommodating an enlargement of Germany in this way. The advantages of this path were its speed and the adoption of the tried-and-tested Basic Law; alternative methods would have taken longer and would have required major constitutional changes. On the other hand, it did not necessarily follow that the pre-1949 pattern of *Länder* would be reinstated. In theory the opportunity could have been taken to review the whole of the *Länder* structure and to introduce a more rational and efficient system throughout Germany (Rutz 1991).

In the event such a comprehensive overhaul was thought to be impractical in the time available. The speed of the unification and the inability of the GDR government in the first half of 1990 to do anything but react to the dictates of public demand rendered the imposition of a new order in the East (one that could easily be assimilated into the FRG) inevitable (Roberts 1991). Equally, the trauma experienced by the FRG in incorporating the GDR and the consequential readjustment meant that there was little time and energy for implementing wider administrative reform in the country as a whole.

The pre-1952 order of five *Länder* was, therefore, reinstated with little debate or controversy, despite the fact that most of the population directly

affected was completely unfamiliar with the shape or the function of the
new units, not to mention with the civil servants who were supposed to
administer them. Although the creation of five new federal states was the
pragmatic solution and one that emphasized historical continuity, it did
little to ease the transition for the former citizens of the GDR. They were
denied even the concession of a familiar administrative map in the head-
long rush to ensure that unification was completed at the earliest possible
opportunity. The way in which this and other aspects of unification were
handled provoked substantial retrospective criticism and charges of political irresponsibility, though in some instances there is more than a whiff of
party political point-scoring in such accusations (Schmidt 1993a).

4.2.6 *The introduction of a market economy*

By far the most difficult aspect of unification has been the transformation
necessary to enable the GDR's command economy to conform with the
capitalist market-orientated model (Bryson 1992). The transformation
meant that the entrenched élite of the GDR and its powerful national
bureaucracy for economic planning had to be replaced by a system based
on private capital and open competition. In turn, this meant that the population at large of the new federal states had to learn how markets function,
not to mention how the economic and legal institutions that underpin the
market system work in practice. The need for reform reflected the inherent
inefficiencies of the command economy, inefficiencies that are unsustain-
able in a true market economy.

The introduction of a market system in eastern Germany demanded first
and foremost that assets be transferred from the public to the private sector. The instrument charged with this huge undertaking in the former GDR
was the Trust Agency, which was established by the outgoing East German administration in 1990 and confirmed by the terms of the Unification
Treaty. The Agency's role was to transfer public assets to the private sector. Once this task was completed, it would close itself down. The Agency
was granted initial powers to provide up to 25 billion DM in loans which
were to be repaid by the end of 1995. Although there was never any
expectation that the Agency would be profit-making, the scale of the task
which it faced vastly exceeded all expectations and the majority of holdings were disposed of with little or no financial return. As a result, by the
time it was wound up in 1994, the Agency had not only accumulated substantial debts, it had also come to be seen by the population of the new
federal states, however unfairly, as no more than a mechanism for dispos-

ing of their jobs and livelihoods rather than, as originally intended, the gateway to a new economic future.

Privatization was, however, only one aspect of the process of change. A key feature of the GDR was its monolithic socio-economic structure based on large organizations such as collective farms and multi-facetted industrial combines. When they were established, these organizations were seen as entities that could be more easily accommodated within the integrated socialist economic planning system. They turned out to be a serious impediment to any form of competition and, therefore, to the whole process of unification. Privatization had to be accompanied by a dismantling and disaggregation of the existing economic framework if the conditions for market competition were to be put in place. Furthermore, laws had be enacted and institutions created that would underpin a competitive environment. In practice, the main problem lay not in identifying what measures were necessary, but in acting quickly enough to prevent people from suffering unduly during the transition.

The scale of the adjustment is well illustrated by the changes that had to be made to the legal system after unification. Even though the nature and role of the law in the GDR had been completely different from that in the FRG, federal jurisdiction was extended to all the new *Länder* with immediate effect on 3 October 1990, with only a few transitional exceptions. The difficulties inherent in such a speedy change were compounded by the lack of suitably trained lawyers and professional legal staff. Not only were practising lawyers few in number, much of the work performed by the legal profession in the old FRG had in the GDR been undertaken within the framework of the Communist Party bureaucracy. To make matters worse, more than 20% of lawyers who had been practising in the GDR were deemed to be tainted by their association with the regime and were declared unfit to practice after unification (Blacksell 1995).

The relatively small number of professional east German lawyers who remained in office had to cope not only with civil and criminal codes with which they were largely unfamiliar but also with a totally unmanageable work-load. The solution which was adopted was to encourage lawyers from the west to move east. But this was far from ideal because the newcomers had no knowledge of the system that had existed before unification and they found it difficult to empathize with the needs of the population of the former GDR. Initially there was considerable resentment of the relative affluence of the newcomers and a degree of suspicion of their motives for moving east, though such feelings waned as the crucial importance of their legal expertise became apparent.

The success of economic unification was predicated, of course, on there being a single, internationally convertible currency for the whole of the newly enlarged Germany. But although the force of the argument for a single currency was clear in principle, there were serious misgivings: opening up the former GDR economy to the full force of competitive pressures from the West by adopting the West German mark (DM) might well induce economic collapse in the new federal states (Bryson 1992). In the event the speed at which unification proceeded in the course of 1990, coupled with political disintegration in the GDR, left little room for manoeuvre. Despite the misgivings of many economists, the West German mark became the official national currency on 2 July 1990. GDR citizens were allowed to convert East German marks, including a limited amount of their savings, on a 1:1 basis.

The currency union imposed severe pressures on the economy in the new federal states. To minimize the adverse effects, a Fund for German Unity was set up. This provided for a total of 115 billion DM to be invested in the east by the end of 1994. Investment by the Fund has generated a huge volume of public works. The Fund has played a key role in the urgent task of renewing (and to some extent creating) the transport, communications, and service infrastructure in eastern Germany with the aim of bringing it up to the standards of the rest of Western Europe. Although supplemented by a further 24 billion DM through the creation in March 1992 of the two-year Upswing East programme, the worry was that the renewal would not be complete by the time the Fund was wound up at the end of 1994 and that there would be insufficient private capital to fill the gap. It has been a source of great concern that so much of the industry in the former GDR has not survived the transition to the private sector and, as a result, is still not in a position to contribute to tax revenue. The difficulties have been further compounded by the fact that the economy in the former FRG has been in the doldrums since the early 1990s, partly as a result of the global recession, and partly because of the higher domestic taxes that have had to be imposed to pay for the Unity Fund. The overall result has been an insufficient level of private investment to meet the demands of economic reconstruction in the new federal states.

When the process of economic transformation began in 1990 it was confidently predicted that it would take about a decade to complete. But this timescale soon appeared optimistic; a generation would now seem to be more realistic. The main reason for the miscalculation was the parallel collapse of the GDR's former partners in the Council for Mutual Economic Assistance (COMECON), the trading block of East European socialist states set up in 1949. Since the GDR was the largest single trading partner of the Soviet Union within COMECON, the demise of the USSR has destroyed a crucially important market, one for which it has proved almost impossible to find an alternative. The generally poor quality of goods produced in the former GDR meant that they were unable to compete with those from the West, at least until production and working practices could be brought up to Western standards. This only began to happen in 1994.

4.3 Germany and the European Union

From the outset the FRG has been closely involved with European integration. Indeed, the initial driving force behind economic integration in Western Europe in the early 1950s was a desire to see German mining and heavy industry drawn back into the mainstream of economic activity after the Second World War. Over the years, however, the European Union (EU) has changed its form and function dramatically. The first stage was the establishment of the European Coal and Steel Community in 1952. In 1958 the European Economic Community (EEC) and Euratom were created. Thereafter, the member states gradually merged into a single European Community (EC), resulting in the formation of the EU in 1993. At the same time, membership has expanded. The original six (Belgium, France, Germany, Italy, Luxembourg, and the Netherlands) were joined by Denmark, Ireland, and the UK in 1973, by Greece in 1981, by Portugal and Spain in 1986, and by Austria, Finland, and Sweden in 1995.

German unification marked an important step in the process of enlargement. For the first time it brought a former Communist state, albeit a rather unusual one, into the EU. This forced the EU, and with it Germany, to consider whether it should remain a Western economic organization, or whether it should broaden its regional scope and become embroiled in the political changes occurring in Eastern Europe. The decision is a difficult one, but it cannot be avoided, especially since Germany has been pitched during the course of the debate from a position on the periphery of Western Europe during the Cold War to one at the heart of a wider Europe, a Europe seeking to fill the vacuum left by the collapse of the Soviet Union and by the military retrenchment of the USA (Figure 4.4).

In the 1950s the FRG saw the political momentum towards economic and political integration in Western Europe as a means for re-establishing its credentials as an independent state in the international community. The then Chancellor, Konrad Adenauer, made it his prime concern to ensure that the FRG played a full part in the process, and he relegated the emotional and politically sensitive issues of the future unification of Germany to a secondary position: the attainment of international acceptability was his paramount concern (Korka 1990). The policy was demonstrably successful, not least because of the close personal rapport that developed between Adenauer and the French President, Charles de Gaulle. The relation-

Figure 4.4   Germany and the European Union

ship was based on a strong sense of mutual advantage: while Adenauer wanted to make the fledgling FRG internationally acceptable, de Gaulle saw a Franco–German alliance as a way of resisting what he termed 'Anglo-Saxon' domination of a politically and economically united Europe.

The political manoeuvering was quickly reinforced by the success of the FRG's economy, which became heavily reliant on the evolving open market within the EU, Germany's major trading partner. Economic growth was reflected, in turn, by the strength of the West German mark. In the 1960s the role of the US dollar as the main international trading currency began to be challenged, and in Western Europe the mark became its main competitor. Various attempts were made to link the currencies of other Community members to the value of the mark and, although these were not notably successful, unified economic management, including managed exchange-rates and even a single currency, became a prime objective of Community policy. In 1979 the FRG Chancellor, Helmut Schmidt, and the French President, Valérie Giscard d'Estaing, joined forces to set up the European Monetary System (EMS); the initiative, logical in economic terms, broke the political mould. Since then, the German mark has become increasingly powerful; it has now virtually achieved the status of an unofficial reserve currency to the extent that the health and management of the FRG economy dictate monetary policy throughout the EU.

Yet German economic dominance has to be viewed against the changing geographical size and shape of the Community/EU. The first enlargement in 1973 coincided with a period of economic and political paralysis in Western Europe, induced largely by events elsewhere in the world, notably the successive oil crises that destabilized much of Western trade. When stability returned towards the end of the decade it was clear that the FRG's position within the Community had been strengthened rather than weakened by the addition of the three new member states (UK, Denmark, and Ireland). The crucial element in this increase of German strength was the UK, a country with an economy of similar size to those of France, Germany, and Italy (Denmark and Ireland were too small to effect any major change on their own). The UK saw membership as an opportunity to reorientate its trade towards Europe, but the unintended result was that it became tied ever more closely to German economic decision-making, thus enhancing the economic and political dominance of the FRG within the Community.

The Mediterranean enlargement in the 1980s confirmed the *status quo* of German predominance: Greece and Portugal were too small to affect materially the overall economic balance, while Spain's principal objective was to integrate itself more securely in the established mainstream of Western European trade. On the other hand this enlargement substantially widened the economic gap between the member states. All three Mediterranean states were relatively poor, and their accession meant that the nature and extent of the regional problem within the Community had to be redefined. From Germany's point of view, it made much more urgent the whole question of how to finance transfers between rich and poor countries and regions.

Since 1989 both the collapse of the Soviet Union (and of the client Communist states it supported in Eastern Europe) and the unification of Germany have redefined yet again the future of the EU and of Germany's position within it. In general terms, the debate has centred on two related issues. The first issue is whether it is more important for the EU to deepen and strengthen the existing economic and political links between members, or to widen the membership to include as many European states as possible. The second issue is that of 'variable geometry': broadly, this means abandoning the concept of equality of status between the EU's member states and substituting different levels of membership and participation according to such variables as size and economic well-being.

Predictably perhaps, the way forward appears to be a mixture of approaches. With the accession of Austria, Finland, and Sweden the membership has been widened. These are wealthy countries, already closely allied to the Western European economic system. They are expected to make net contributions to the EU budget and to help finance the necessary transfer of resources to the poorest regions in the south and west and to the new federal German states. In a sense, this process can also be seen as a deepening, because the accession will spread the economic burden within the existing structure of the EU and reinforce the interdependence of the member states. A similar assessment, although at a far less significant level, would apply if either Cyprus or Malta succeeded with their applications to join the Union.

In many respects variable geometry is already a reality in the EU. As the central institutions (the Council of Ministers, the Commission, the Parliament, and the Court of Justice) have gradually become more powerful, so national hegemony has progressively declined. Symptomatic of this trend has been the growth of qualified majority voting since the Treaty of Rome was modified by the Single European Act in 1987. This arrangement allocates votes to states roughly on the basis of their size, which means that Germany's dominance has been formalized in the political decision-making structure. Subsequently, the scope of qualified majority voting has been steadily extended, both by mutual agreement and by the implementation of the Treaty on European Union in 1993. As a result, the existing hierarchy of states has been further reinforced.

Officially, what has not been sanctioned is multi-tiered membership, though in practice this already exists. For example, new states have been admitted with transitional periods of up to ten years before they become fully integrated economically into the union. Obviously, this concept could be extended to accommodate the needs of the former Communist states in Eastern Europe that are now queuing up to join. Poland, the Czech Republic, Slovakia, Hungary, Romania, Bulgaria, Slovenia, and Croatia have all firmly indicated their desire to become members, and variable transitional arrangements, appropriate to their particular circumstances, would seem to be the obvious way to proceed.

As far as Germany is concerned the agreed prospective expansion seems certain to alter fundamentally its position within the EU. Self-evidently Germany will become a central rather than a peripheral European state and will seek to reopen many of the historic economic links that were firmly established in Central Europe before the Second World War. This means that Germany will also inevitably play an even more influential economic and political role. The German mark will dominate inter-union trade to an even greater degree than before, and the sheer size of the united country's population of eighty million will ensure that Germany acquires a political and economic standing that other member states will find hard to match.

4.4 External relations and the emergence of a German foreign policy

Unification has been a liberating experience for Germany because it has ended more than forty years of dispute about German national identity and the political legitimacy of the German state. It has also enabled Germany to develop its own foreign policy unencumbered by the shadow of division, by the possibility of future unification, and by unfinished business arising out of the absence of a peace treaty at the end of the Second World War.

From its creation in 1949 the FRG was always seen, even by itself, as a temporary expedient, a stepping stone towards a permanent political solution that would eventually incorporate a new Germany into Central Europe. The Basic Law recognized this in various ways, notably in its specific provision for incorporating new *Länder* into the Federation (Article 23), and in the strictly limited defensive role accorded to Germany's military forces (Article 87). While not sharing this view of its provisional role, the GDR could not fail to be influenced by the position taken by its larger Western neighbour (Blacksell 1982). In practice, neither state accepted the legitimacy of the other, and third-party states were divided over which manifestation of Germany they supported.

Despite this uncertainty both states were incorporated into the international community, though on a restricted basis. Some six years after NATO was founded, the FRG became a member (in 1955). This was a momentous decision for the FRG and the Western Alliance in that it extended the concept of a purely national defensive role for German military forces to the whole of the Atlantic north of the Tropic of Capricorn and to most of Western Europe and North America. Nevertheless, it is important to stress that the scope of West Germany's role in NATO was still restricted and could not be extended without an amendment to the Basic Law. The Warsaw Pact responded promptly to the NATO initiative by admitting the GDR as a member later in the same year, thus bringing it into the rival military alliance of the Cold War.

Membership of military alliances was not just a symbol of recognition for the two German states; they each used it as a political weapon to further their respective views of one another. This was particularly important for the FRG, which used membership of NATO to proclaim itself as the only legitimate German state and with a duty to represent all Germans. In 1955 the FRG government embraced what became known as the Hallstein Doctrine (named after Walter Hallstein, a senior official in the Foreign Office), whereby it refused to maintain diplomatic relations with any state that recognized the GDR. The success of the ensuing campaign to enforce the doctrine was remarkable. No NATO members and only a handful of non-Communist states world-wide afforded recognition, thus effectively isolating the GDR. The only state that recognized the GDR and was also recognized by the FRG was the Soviet Union; this exception was made in the interests of the German prisoners of war still held in that country in the 1950s. The GDR had no wish to pursue a similar policy but found itself forced to live with the boycott and largely unable to operate beyond the confines of the Communist world.

The FRG's policy of non-recognition of the GDR survived for more than a decade until the change in foreign policy introduced when the Social Democrats (SPD) wrested control of the government from the Christian Democrats (CDU) in 1969. The new Chancellor, Willy Brandt, began to replace the exclusionary policies of the Hallstein Doctrine by what became known as *Ostpolitik*. The new policy was based on rapprochement with the GDR and with Communist Eastern Europe generally. *Ostpolitik* aimed to achieve a gradual normalization of diplomatic relations between the two Germanies, though the policy never went as far as according the GDR formal diplomatic recognition. The result was the widespread recognition of the GDR elsewhere in the non-Communist world and a substantial general legitimization of both German states. The problem with *Ostpolitik* was its relative lack of tangible results in normalizing relations between the

FRG and the GDR (Blacksell and Brown 1983). Communication between the two countries remained tightly controlled and strictly limited in extent. Only as the political collapse in the late 1980s gathered pace did a genuine change occur.

The speed of events in the lead-up to unification has already been discussed, but it is also important to underline the ease with which apparently intractable military issues were overcome (Harris 1991). In 1989 at least half a million Warsaw Pact troops, drawn mainly from the Soviet Union, were stationed in the GDR. By the middle of 1990 agreement had been reached on a phased withdrawal of them all, and the Soviet Union no longer objected to the unified Germany joining NATO. The only condition laid down by the USSR was an undertaking that no NATO troops would be stationed in the new federal states until 1995, coupled with the promise of substantial financial credits to compensate the Soviet Union for the costs of running down its garrison in the former GDR. Subsequently, with the dissolution of the Warsaw Pact in 1992, the question of membership of military alliances became little more than academic.

Unification together with the break-up of the Soviet Union has profoundly altered the strategic position of Germany both in Europe and the world at large. The ending of the Cold War has not as yet resulted in a formal increase in the number of states in NATO, but under the Partnership for Peace agreement of 1994, twenty-one states in Eastern Europe and Asia (all, with the exception of Sweden and Finland, formerly under Communist control) have signalled their desire to join (Figure 4.5). Just as Germany occupies a pivotal position in the EU, it also finds itself potentially at the hub of NATO rather than on the front line of a global military confrontation. These new circumstances demand a complete reassessment of Germany's military role. For Germans to try to assume overt military leadership in Europe would still prove controversial, both at home and abroad, but the very limited defensive role set out in the Basic Law is equally unrealistic for a fully fledged state. The situation persuaded the German Federal Constitutional Court to rule in July 1994 that it was permissible for German forces to assume a wider military role within the framework of NATO, if called upon to do so. The full meaning and significance of this development is yet to be tested, but it clearly provides the opportunity for Germany to assume an equal responsibility with other NATO states for maintaining peace across a much more fragmented political map of Europe.

Figure 4.5 Germany and the Partnership for Peace

4.5 Conclusion

As the twentieth century draws to a close it is fascinating to reflect on the way in which the geopolitical world order has changed and to speculate how it might develop in the twenty-first century. A hundred years ago a small group of European states, including Germany, was consolidating world-wide colonial empires and Kaiser Wilhelm II was proclaiming that Germany should pursue a policy of *Weltpolitik* (Taylor 1993a). Europe was still at the heart of events and the coming rise of the American and Soviet empires was almost entirely unpredicted (Mackinder 1904). Now the Soviet Empire has come and gone and the USA is retreating from many of the global commitments that it assumed at the end of the Second World War. Europe is once again a cohesive force in its own right; but it is also much more introspective than a century ago and is concerned primarily with securing its internal regional stability.

For Germany the new order, with its emphasis on co-operation and integration rather than on national competition, is salutary. The distinguishing characteristic of German foreign policy is membership of Western, free market, international organizations such as the EU and NATO, and on using these as a platform for shaping the direction of economic, military, and political events rather than on seeking to dominate in its own right. There remains the persistent danger that regional conflicts in the Balkans and the Caucasus may once again ignite a wider European war. But perhaps the most surprising fact is that, after political humiliation and military defeat fifty years ago, a unified Germany is now not only at the heart of events in Europe but is also widely viewed as a key contributor to maintaining the peace.

Further reading

Recommending up-to-date further reading on unified Germany is very difficult: there is a plethora of speculative comment about the potential effects of unification but very little authoritative analysis of the actual long-term impact. For the most part, the events of 1990 are still too recent for any such evaluation to be meaningful. Nevertheless, Jones (1994) gives a useful overview and the following provide more detail about the major themes addressed in this chapter.

Kaiser (1990/1) gives an excellent analysis of the political events leading up to unification, while Schmidt (1993a) provides a broader overall critique, if somewhat partisan. Two very good studies written by geographers at the time are to be found in Harris (1991) and Murphy (1991).

Blacksell (1994) provides a more recent assessment. The economic aspects of unification are exhaustively dealt with in Bryson (1992), while the social implications are eloquently discussed in Fulbrook (1991). The missed opportunities for administrative reform are considered in Rutz (1991). Finally, there is a trio of research papers by Jones and Wild, which provide a fascinating insight into the spatial changes that have occurred in the border zone between the two former Germanies since unification (Wild and Jones 1993, 1994; Jones and Wild 1994).

5

The Changing Framework of German Politics since Unification

CHARLES JEFFERY

5.1 Introduction

The process of German unification—the incorporation of the former German Democratic Republic (GDR) into the Federal Republic of Germany (FRG)—was completed in a legal sense on the *Tag der Einheit*, the 'day of unity' at midnight on 2–3 October 1990. In a more practical sense, though, the *Tag der Einheit* marked only the start of a much longer process, that of the 'great social experiment' of 'putting Germany back together again' (Conradt 1993:1). The two German states had developed separately and on opposed ideological foundations in the intervening forty-one years since their division in 1949: the eastern GDR had come to form a key part of the Soviet-led Communist bloc in Eastern Europe, while the western FRG had developed a stable, liberal democratic political system and one of the world's strongest capitalist economies, and had emerged as a key partner in West European integration and the Atlantic security alliance.

The task of integrating two such divergent entities into a coherent whole has inevitably brought with it immense political difficulties. The euphoria and optimism which abounded in Germany during 1990 rapidly gave way in the face of those difficulties to a widespread sense of pessimism and disorientation. Unification posed unexpectedly severe problems in rebuilding the decrepit economy in the former GDR, problems worsened by the effects in both east and west of the international recession of the early 1990s. The economic problems of unification have also, through their differential impact on eastern and western Germans, sharpened the lingering social division which distinguishes and divides easterner from westerner, *Ossi* from *Wessi*. These problems of internal adjustment to unification have, moreover, taken place amid the wider processes of change in European and world politics ushered in originally in the Gorbachev years. The 'new' Germany also, therefore, faces the additional problem of considering and defining the international role it wishes to play in the 'new world order'.

Altogether, these difficulties pose unusually far-reaching challenges for German politics in the 1990s, especially since the political framework within which those challenges are being confronted is essentially that of the old West Germany. The formal process of unification during 1990 saw the existing structures and traditions of West German politics for the most part simply extended to incorporate the former GDR and thus to create a new and territorially expanded version of the 'old' Federal Republic. The leading West German parties, for example, quickly established themselves during 1990 as the leading parties in the east as well. In the economic sphere the Treaty on the Creation of Monetary, Economic and Social Union of 1 July 1990 introduced the West German mark and the social market economy to the east. And the Treaty of Unification that came into force on 3 October 1990 extended the ambit of an only marginally modified West German Constitution, the Basic Law, to cover the territory of the former GDR and formally to create the new, expanded Federal Republic of Germany. Finally, a series of discussions with Germany's major foreign partners—most importantly with the four victorious allies of the Second World War (the USA, the USSR, the UK, and France) and with the European Communities—were held during 1990 to discuss the international implications of unification. These discussions were successfully concluded by the autumn of 1990 on the implicit assumption that the foreign policy of unified Germany would not deviate markedly from the established principles which had shaped West German foreign policy before unification.

The question this chapter addresses is the extent to which, or indeed whether, the political framework bequeathed by West Germany can flex and adjust effectively to meet the immense challenges set in train by unification. In a chapter of this length it is impossible to give a comprehensive account of the various problems of unification and their impact on German politics. The approach taken here is therefore to present case studies of key aspects of post-unification politics in Germany. These have been chosen both to illuminate some of the problem fields identified above and also to demonstrate the effects of unification from different perspectives of political analysis. The following section casts light on popular input into politics by examining the significance of the differing interests of east and west Germans for relationships between voters and parties in the unified Germany. There is then a discussion of the impact of unification and its problems on Germany's institutions of government, focusing on the implications that the economic differences between east and west have begun to have for the functioning of the German federal system. The final section discusses the problem of reassessing Germany's role in the international arena, drawing in particular on the example of German European integration policy since unification.

5.2 Unification and the German party system

Much has been written since unification about *die Mauer im Kopf*, the 'wall in the head' which separates westerner from easterner in united Germany, an ironic analogy to the physical walls which used to divide the West and East German states. This 'wall' has both historical and contemporary 'brickwork'. On a general level, forty-one years of separate development in ideologically opposed states have imbued easterners and westerners with differing sets of political and social values (Fulbrook 1991). That historically based cleavage between east and west has subsequently been sharpened since 1990 by some of the practical problems thrown up by unification. Eastern Germans have become increasingly disillusioned by the collapse and subsequent stagnation of their economy since 1990, especially when they compare their economic situation with the generally far higher levels of prosperity which exist in the west. They have also had to confront demoralizing revelations of widespread complicity in the activities of the former GDR's internal intelligence service (the *Stasi*) and the need—in part related and similarly demoralizing—to 'import' untainted and experienced westerners to shape and build up public services in the east (Conradt 1993:4–7). In the west, on the other hand, a growing disaffection has emerged over the material burdens imposed by the cost of financing social security and economic reconstruction in the east, especially since the wider international recession slowed down the western economy in 1992–93. These differences in experience and perspective have led to an ongoing sense of irritation and tension between easterners and westerners (Hahn 1993).

As the current German Chancellor Helmut Kohl has noted, one of the great tasks of German politics in the 1990s is that of social integration, of 'bringing them [easterners and westerners] together again, bridging the gulf which separates those minds' (Kohl 1991). Traditionally, political parties have played a key role in West European democracies in helping to bridge such differences of background and interest in society. Typically, political parties emerged in Western Europe as representatives of the interests of particular social groups or collections of groups (for example, groups based on class/occupation, religious affiliation, regional identity, and so on). And by pressing—in electoral competition with other party/group interests—for such interests to be met by the institutions of government in the state concerned, they have tended to secure for themselves the continued support and loyalty of those groups. By providing in this way stable and reliable channels for the expression of different, competing group interests and for the incorporation of at least some of those interests in government policy, parties have generally played an important role in bridging and managing social divisions (Padgett 1993a:1–3).

The aim of this section is to examine the extent to which political parties are capable of performing this bridging role in the context of a unified Germany. This question is all the more interesting in view of the fact that, as was noted above, the party system of unified Germany is essentially that of the old West Germany. Can a party system that emerged out of the differences of interest in West German society bridge the differences of interest which now exist between the western and eastern German electorates?

5.2.1 *The elections of 1990*

The immediate experience of the elections of the unification year of 1990 would suggest that it is indeed possible for the party system of the pre-unification Federal Republic to span the interests of the electorates in east and west. Following the collapse of Communist authority in the GDR in the autumn of 1989, the major West German parties—the Christian Democratic Union (CDU) (supported by its Bavarian counterpart, the Christian Social Union, or CSU), the Social Democratic Party (SPD), and the liberal Free Democratic Party (FDP)—sponsored and later merged with likeminded counterparts in the east. These eastern incarnations of the western parties won over two-thirds of the vote in the GDR parliamentary (People's Chamber) election of 18 March 1990 (Table 5.1), a position they consolidated after their mergers with the western parties in the all-German parliamentary (*Bundestag*) election of 2 December 1990 (Table 5.2). As a result the CDU/CSU and FDP were able to renew their previously West German coalition government after the December election, and the SPD equally renewed its previous West German role as the leading opposition party of united Germany. Only two indigenous eastern parties succeeded in gathering a significant share of the eastern vote in the 1990 elections: the Party of Democratic Socialism (PDS), the reincarnation of the former East German Communist Party (SED) under a new name, and the Alliance 90, a combination of several of the civil rights groups which had played a prominent role in anti-Communist opposition in autumn 1989 and which joined forces with the emergent eastern Greens in December 1990.

The electoral landscape which emerged in the united Germany by the end of 1990 therefore seemed to herald a notable triumph for the capacity of the established West German parties to spread their appeal to the eastern electorate. On closer examination, though, this triumph of the established western parties rested on unstable and impermanent foundations.

Table 5.1 The Election to the People's Chamber (GDR) 18 March 1990

Party/Party Alliance	%
Alliance for Germany (Christian Democrat)	48·0
SPD	21·9
League of Free Democratic Democrats	5·3
PDS	16·4
Alliance 90	2·9
Others	5·5

Table 5.2 The *Bundestag* Election of 2 December 1990

Party	West %	East %	Germany % overall
CDU	35·5	41·8	36·7
CSU	8·8	–	7·1
SPD	35·7	24·3	33·5
FDP	10·6	12·9	11·0
Greens (west)	4·8	0·1	3·9
Alliance 90/Greens (east)	–	6·0	1·2
PDS	0·3	11·1	2·4
Others	4·3	3·8	4·2

Most importantly, the votes won by CDU, SPD, and FDP in the east in 1990 did not and could not reflect any stable and enduringly loyal basis of support in a part of the country which had not experienced genuinely competitive party politics for almost sixty years. The votes they received in 1990 therefore reflected much more the *short-term* judgements of eastern voters on their current policy positions on the issue of unification rather than any *longer-term* sense of loyalty to the parties' identities and traditions (Jeffery 1992:121–26). Such short-term, issue-based judgements are, of course, unreliable and subject to change as the major issues of the day themselves change, and could not as such be seen as a stable electoral basis. It had also become clear by the early 1990s that the position of the major parties in their western heartlands was less than wholly secure. Throughout the 1980s a growing body of evidence pointed to the erosion of long-term party loyalties built up since the foundation of the Federal Republic in 1949. Especially significant here were growing tendencies to floating-voting and non-voting, and the emergence of new party-political forces capable of siphoning votes from the major parties on both their left (the Greens) and right (the Republicans) flanks (Jeffery 1992:116–21).

5.2.2 *The record of the parties since 1990*

The short-termism of the eastern electorate and the erosion of long-term party loyalties in the west posed a two-fold challenge for the established western parties in the Federal Republic of the 1990s. They needed to develop a more stable and reliable basis of support in the eastern electorate and (at least in the case of the CDU/CSU and SPD) to shore up an eroding electoral base in the west.

This balancing act did not prove easy. The CDU/CSU, SPD, and FDP all conducted (often rather subterranean) strategy debates after 1990, yet none succeeded in conjuring up a focused and credible all-German strategic vision. This was in particular true of the FDP. Christian Søe aptly summed up the problem in a play on the title of Hans Fallada's novel, *Little Man, What Now?* by asking 'little party, what now?' (Søe 1993). Despite achieving one of its best ever results in 1990, the FDP has since shown scant sense of purpose beyond remaining in government. Its problems were compounded by the retirement from the party leadership of the enduringly popular former Foreign Minister, Hans-Dietrich Genscher, and his replacement by the low-profile and often lacklustre figure of Klaus Kinkel. The situation has not proved much better for the SDP or the CDU/CSU. Under the pragmatic leadership of Rudolf Scharping, the SPD seemed to become mired in a *Vermittlungsausschusspolitik*, a rather faceless politics focused on the Mediation Committee of the *Bundestag* and the *Bundesrat* (the second chamber in which Germany's *Land* governments are represented). Scharping sought to use the SPD's *Bundesrat* majority to tinker at the margins with legislation passed by the government majority in the *Bundestag* at the expense of defining a clear alternative strategy. At the same time the Christian Democrats seemed to run out of ideas amid the unexpectedly difficult post-unity problems of policy management, in particular regarding economic reconstruction in the east (Flockton 1993). Gunter Hofmann and Werner Perger wrote, for example, of the search in vain for issues to develop in the election campaigns of 1994 which led a leading CDU figure, Heiner Geisser, to suggest that 'we try to focus on foreign policy, because we have lost our competence in economic policy and we have got nothing of significance to present in domestic politics' (Hofmann and Perger 1994).

Geisser's candid admission of programmatic bankruptcy neatly summed up the inability of the three established parties to define a clear all-German vision to present to the electorate. In consequence they tended to take what one might call a 'lowest common denominator' approach, attempting to be as inoffensive as possible to as many as possible in east and west. This, of course, was a recipe for blandness which was not well-suited to their need to establish a strong and stable basis of support in the east or to halt the erosion of loyalties in the west. The absence of a clear message and direction was reflected in a growing sense of detachment of voters from the established parties and a concomitant willingness to consider alternatives and 'float' from one party to another. This was illustrated quite starkly in the run of *Land* elections held between the *Bundestag* elections of 1990 and 1994. These showed the electoral base of the two largest parties, the Christian Democrats and the Social Democrats, to be highly volatile and vulnerable to erosion in part by one another, but increasingly by Germany's minor parties: in the west the Greens, the far right, and in Hamburg, the remarkable *Stattpartei* ('Instead-of-a-Party'!); and in the east the PDS, capitalizing on the disillusionment caused by the difficulties of the eastern reconstruction process. The problems of the FDP proved to be even more dramatic at the *Land* level. From April 1992 through to January 1995 it endured a run of nine consecutive *Land* elections in which it failed to obtain the 5% of the vote necessary to secure representation in the *Land* parliaments.

5.2.3 *The 1994* Bundestag *election*

The volatility of voter–party relationships revealed in this pattern of *Land* election results provided an important background to the national-level opinion trends which shaped the 1994 *Bundestag* election campaign. It emphasized the failure of the major parties to stabilize their bases of support in east and west, and confirmed a growing preparedness of voters in both parts of the country to change their party allegiances at short notice, often under the impression of the major political issues of the day. The short-termism and issue-sensitivity of the German electorate was illustrated most clearly in the changing fortunes experienced by the CDU/CSU and the SPD in the year preceding the 1994 election.

During most of 1993 and into the first months of 1994, the SPD had a clear and, at times, overwhelming lead over the CDU/CSU. But this reflected less any deeply felt attachment to the Social Democrats and more the unpopularity of the CDU/CSU-led government presiding over a recession whose effects had been exacerbated by the sluggish recovery of the eastern economy. However, the situation changed radically in the spring of 1994. A combination of emerging signs of recovery from the recession and the inept presentation of tax proposals by the SPD produced a dramatic mood-swing in favour of the CDU/CSU. After being some eighteen points behind the SPD in both east and west in March 1994 (according to the regular opinion polls conducted by the Mannheim Forschungsgruppe Wahlen) the CDU/CSU had pulled level by May/June. Buoyed by an unexpectedly strong showing in the June 1994 Euro-election and by the CSU's success in winning the September Bavarian *Land* election by its customary wide margin (and thus in ending the run of poor results the Christian Democrats had been recording at the *Land* level), the CDU/CSU moved into a clear poll lead in midsummer which it held through to the election in October (Table 5.3).

Table 5.3 The *Bundestag* Election of 16 October 1994

Party	Seats	Germany		West		East	
		%	±%	%	±%	%	±%
CDU/CSU	294	41·5	-2·3	42·2	-1·9	38·5	-4·1
CDU	244	34·2	-2·5	33·0	-2·0	38·5	-4·1
CSU	50	7·3	+0·2	9·2	+0·1	–	–
Alliance 90/Greens	49	7·3	+2·3	7·8	+3·1	5·3	-0·9
FDP	47	6·9	-4·1	7·7	-2·9	4·0	-8·5
PDS	30	4·4	+2·0	0·9	+0·6	17·6	+7·7
Others	0	3·5	-0·7	3·8	-0·6	2·7	-1·1

Two factors were especially important in sustaining this lead. The first was Helmut Kohl. Kohl's personal popularity has undergone something of a rollercoaster-ride in recent years. Prior to 1990 he was widely lampooned as a bumbling, gaffe-prone, and insensitive figure lacking in communication skills, only to emerge during 1990 as the *Kanzler der Einheit*, the 'Chancellor of German Unity', whose vision and managerial skill dominated the unification process and secured the CDU/CSU victory in the 1990 election. After 1990 Kohl's popularity dipped sharply again amid the economic problems of the post-unification 'hangover'. Yet again, though, he bounced back. He was able to offer, it seems, an image of strength, security and maturity with which neither the younger, more technocratic image of Rudolf Scharping nor the SPD's more combative and forceful 'team' of Oskar Lafontaine and Gerhard Schröder could compete. Interestingly, the CDU's ubiquitous election poster featured just a close-up of Kohl, surrounded by supporters, on which the party logo was conspicuously absent. To all intents and purposes Kohl was the CDU's election campaign.

Indeed, it was Kohl who played the key role in the second factor which maintained the CDU/CSU lead over the SPD in the run-up to the 1994 election: the 'red socks' campaign. The 'red socks' were a reference to the 'toleration' an SPD-Green coalition had extended to the ex-Communist PDS to secure a workable majority in the eastern *Land* of Saxony-Anhalt after elections there in June 1994. The accusation of over-hasty collaboration with a party linked to the unhappy memory of East German Communism—and condemned by Kohl as 'red-painted fascists'—struck a chord in western Germany at least, where the PDS was widely seen as an extremist party, well beyond the pale of normal democratic politics. It was less effective as a campaign issue in the east, where the PDS was much more widely seen as a legitimate political force pushing for otherwise unrepresented eastern concerns. But, as the CDU campaign managers undoubtedly reckoned, less than a quarter of the all-German electorate was located in the east, close to those concerns.

A conspicuous feature of the election campaign in 1994—reflective of the 'lowest common denominator' approach of the major parties—was the absence of clear, future-oriented policy prescriptions. This was by and large an *inhaltlos* campaign, one which lacked substantial policy content and discussion. Nowhere was this more true than in the case of the FDP, which rather lamely argued that an electorate faced by a rash of local, *Land*, and European elections during 1994 was too 'fatigued' to bear a policy-driven campaign for the *Bundestag*. As a result it ran what it called a purely 'functional' campaign, the function of which was to buck its disappointing trend of *Land* election results and secure the 5% needed nationally to remain in the *Bundestag* and in government.

In the end the FDP crossed the 5% hurdle quite comfortably, aided by tactical voting by CDU/CSU supporters. The FDP vote—and to a lesser extent that of the CDU/CSU, which recorded its worst result since 1949—was, though, down significantly on 1990 (compare Tables 5.1 and 5.3), cutting the governing coalition's majority severely from 134 to just 10. Never before in the Federal Republic had a sitting government come so close to being voted out of office. Previous changes of government (in 1966, 1969, and 1982) had all come about as a result of changes in the composition of governing coalitions rather than as the direct result of elections. Chastened by this unenthusiastic endorsement by the electorate,

Kohl's renewed government emerged from the electoral fray to face a new and pugnacious combination of opposition forces. The PDS retained and strengthened its representation in the *Bundestag*, winning enough constituency seats (four in total) to bypass the 5% hurdle normally required for proportional representation in the *Bundestag*. It immediately promised to use its strengthened position to push for the interests of its primarily eastern supporters, most of whom are disillusioned with their experience so far of unified Germany. The Greens, now projecting a more moderate and pragmatic image than in the 1980s, recovered well to score their second best ever result. And finally the SPD, despite squandering the opinion poll lead it enjoyed during 1993, succeeded in stopping the rot of electoral decline it had experienced in every election since 1980, gaining nearly 3% compared to the 1990 election, and announcing, like the Greens, a policy of constructive and consistent opposition through to the next election in 1998.

5.2.4 *Looking ahead*

In conclusion, perhaps the most significant aspect of the 1994 election results was the performance of the FDP. Although the Free Democrats did succeed, against many predictions, in surmounting the 5% hurdle, they did so in a way (through the 'loaned' votes of, according to some estimates, over one and a half million Christian Democratic voters) which hardly suggested any real recovery from the directionless drift which plunged it into trouble in the first place. This continuing weakness of the FDP may come to play a decisive role in shaping the course of German politics over the next four years. Put bluntly, the party faces extinction unless it can rediscover a sense of purpose which, after thirteen years of unbroken coalition government, can demarcate it clearly from the Christian Democrats. Many have posed the question '*wozu die FDP?*'—what is the point of the FDP? If the party does not find a clear answer soon, it may opt to break the coalition and return to opposition in order to renew itself more thoroughly away from the constraints of government. This possibility has led some to dub the present government a 'lame duck' (Thies 1994:222). This description is all the more apt since the SPD commands a clear majority of votes in the *Bundesrat*, in which most government-introduced legislation needs assent. The SPD's *Bundesrat* majority presages a continuation of Scharping's *Vermittlungsausschusspolitik* and will serve to draw the SPD yet more firmly into the legislative process despite its numerical inferiority in the *Bundestag*. Some have dubbed this situation with some justification as an 'informal Grand Coalition' of CDU/CSU and SPD (*Der Spiegel*, 17

October 1994:19–10). Some in the SPD, notably Gerhard Schröder, would not be averse to seeing a Grand Coalition put on a formal footing if the current coalition did break up. This may be a sound tactical vision for a party which has been out of power for thirteen years in a country which has never rejected a sitting government at the polls. It recalls the Grand Coalition of 1966–69 which was formed when the FDP quitted a CDU/CSU-led coalition and which paved the way for an era of SPD-led government with a revitalised FDP as the junior partner. If a similar pattern of events evolves over the next couple of years, though, one thing is certain: the SPD will be looking to the new-look, pragmatic Greens, not the FDP, as its favoured coalition partner. Red-Green in 1998?

5.3 Unification and the federal system

Under the terms of the Treaty of Unification the territory of the former GDR formally joined and therefore enlarged the FRG on 3 October 1990. On joining the FRG that territory automatically fell under the jurisdiction of the Basic Law (with the exception of a number of transitional arrangements set out in the Treaty of Unification; see *Bundeszentrale für politische Bildung* 1990:43). Most of the Basic Law, first drawn up in 1949 and amended several times since then, is concerned with describing the organization and responsibilities of the FRG's institutions of government. Unification thus saw the extension of the remit of those institutions of government to the territory of the former GDR.

In other words, a system of government designed for and refined in a West German context now has to address and manage the problems which the former GDR has brought into the new Germany. One of the most interesting tasks currently facing observers of German politics is to assess how much the system of government that used to work in the old FRG will change and adapt itself to the new circumstances of unification. Since a full examination of all Germany's political institutions (legislative, executive and judicial, national, regional and local) would extend far beyond the scope of this chapter, this section can offer only a partial insight into this question. This it does by focusing on the impact of unification on arguably the most important feature of government in Germany, the federal system.

5.3.1 *The new* Länder *and the old federal system*

The Basic Law was drawn up in 1949 against the background of the National Socialist dictatorship in Germany between 1933 and 1945. With the brutality and criminality of Nazism in mind, one of its principal aims was to erect barriers to the abuse of governmental powers. This it did above all by dispersing powers and responsibilities among different institutions of government so that they would counterbalance one another and thus prevent any one dominant power centre from emerging. The federal system of the FRG was an essential part of this strategy. A federal system consists of two levels of government, national and regional, each of which is given a sphere of constitutional responsibilities of its own, along with the financial resources to carry out those responsibilities (Watts 1991:28). The creation of such a federal system in the Basic Law was intended above all to restrict and counterbalance national government power by entrenching important governmental responsibilities and resources in the German regional states, the *Länder*.

The 'old', western FRG had ten *Länder*: Baden-Württemberg, Bavaria, Bremen, Hamburg, Hesse, Lower Saxony, North Rhine-Westphalia, Rhineland-Palatinate, Saarland, and Schleswig-Holstein. In addition, West Berlin, although formally still under the authority of the four victorious Western powers of the Second World War (USA, USSR, UK, and France), to all intents and purposes formed an eleventh *Land*. The nature of the division of powers between these *Länder* and the national level, or Federation (*Bund*), is important to note. Federal systems elsewhere, for example in the USA or Canada, tend to give the national and regional levels a separate and independent power in different policy fields to make laws and put them into practice. The two levels of government in such systems tend to work *independently* of each other. In the 'old' FRG the tendency was, however, much more for the two levels of government to exercise different kinds of power within the same policy fields. This created a relationship of *interdependence* between the two levels of government. This interdependent relationship had a number of foundations. First, over time and for a number of different reasons (Bulmer 1989a:45–47), the Federation came to be responsible for making laws in most fields of policy. As a result the *Länder*, by the 1980s, made few laws of their own. However, the responsibility for administering and implementing these federal laws was normally exercised by the *Länder*. The *Länder* thus controlled the lion's share of administrative experience and resources in the old FRG. Third, the role of the *Länder* was further buttressed by the powers of the *Bundesrat*, an institution which consists of representatives of the various *Länder* governments, and which stands alongside the directly elected *Bundestag* as the second chamber of the FRG's Parliament. The most important of these powers is its right to veto and reject any federal laws which are deemed to affect the interests of the *Länder*, a right which was applicable to over half of federal laws by the 1980s.

The powers of the *Länder* in implementing federal legislation and the veto powers of the *Bundesrat* together gave the *Länder* 'resources' that were indispensable to the making of federal legislation (Bulmer 1989c). As a result they were increasingly drawn in to help in the formulation of federal legislation in consultation with the Federation (on the assumption that they might otherwise have prevented the effective implementation of that legislation or have vetoed it in the *Bundesrat*). This process became known as 'co-operative federalism'. The relationship between the federal and the *Länder* levels of government was one of interdependence and was based on compromise and negotiation in the framing of national level laws.

The aim of this section is to examine what effect unification is likely to have on co-operative federalism in Germany. Can the established practices of (West) German federalism survive the challenges posed by unification? Unification added five new *Länder*—Brandenburg, Mecklenburg-West Pomerania, Saxony, Saxony-Anhalt, and Thuringia—to the federal system and gave full *Land* status to the now unified city of Berlin. These new *Länder* were, to put it mildly, thrown in at the deep end in October 1990: aside from certain exceptional transitional arrangements they were expected in theory to assume the full range of responsibilities already performed by the old, western *Länder*. They lacked not just the administrative experience to perform this tremendous catching-up process (a problem which has partly been dealt with by importing *Wessi* civil servants) but also, and much more importantly, the tax revenues to finance it. The scale of tax revenues raised depends mainly on the level of economic performance, and, as has already been noted, the eastern economy entered a nosedive after unification which was swift and devastating. The subsequent depression has proved to be stubbornly long-lasting. As a result the new *Länder* raise less than half the tax income per capita of their western counterparts. At the same time they face, as a by-product of economic collapse, extraordinarily high expenditure burdens in the fields of social security and economic reconstruction (Jeffery 1993:14–15). Low income and high expenditure together create extreme financial weakness in the eastern *Länder*. This weakness, for reasons that can best be illustrated with a brief examination of some of the emerging problems of co-operative federalism in the 'old' FRG in the 1980s, poses a severe threat to the continued operation of co-operative federalism in unified Germany.

5.3.2 *Problems of co-operative federalism*

Co-operative federalism requires compromises not only between Federation and *Länder* but also, crucially, between the *Länder* themselves. To make an effective input into federal policy-making the *Länder* need a certain level of compromise and solidarity among themselves so that a single, collective *Länder*-front can be maintained in dealings with the Federation. The capacity for generating and asserting this collective voice began to decline in the 1980s as the established spirit of co-operation among the *Länder* showed signs of breaking down.

The key problem was an increasing divergence of economic performance among the *Länder*. A number of them, particularly Bremen, Saarland, and Lower Saxony, had seen some of their major industries enter serious decline just as others, notably Baden-Württemberg and Hesse, had begun to exploit the potential of new, hi-tech, high growth sectors. The resultant widening of economic disparities led to serious tensions between the *Länder*. These tensions arose over the distribution of financial resources among the *Länder*. The FRG had evolved a complex system of financial equalization which was designed to redistribute tax income from the more prosperous *Länder* to their poorer counterparts so that all ended up with roughly the same level of income per capita to fulfil their various responsibilities (Jeffery 1993:8–10). But widening economic disparities led to a growing resentment among the higher income *Länder* of Baden-Württemberg and Hesse: in their view they were being penalized for their success by being forced to devote increasing sums to bailing out 'unsuccessful', financially weaker *Länder*. At the same time some of the low-income *Länder* held the opposite belief: they felt that they were not receiving enough from the equalization process. The financial equalization system was geared to reducing differences in *Länder* income but took little account of the expenditure needs specific to any one *Land*. *Länder* affected by industrial decline not only had falling incomes but also faced the increasing expenditure caused by the effects of economic weakness (for example on social security and investment in new industries). These *Länder* thus felt that the income-equalizing effects of the system were increasingly inadequate to meet their growing expenditure needs.

By the end of the 1980s this emerging fault-line between richer and poorer *Länder* showed signs of hardening into permanency. Some of the richer *Länder*, especially Baden-Württemberg, Bavaria, and North Rhine-Westphalia, began to turn away from their previous commitment to their weaker counterparts and to place a new emphasis on devoting their greater resources to independent policies within their territories, notably in the field of regional economic development (Allen 1989). The weaker *Länder* showed on the other hand an increased tendency to seek extra financial assistance from the Federation despite the fact that this would in return imply greater federal influence over their affairs (Exler 1992:25–26).

This growing divergence of *Länder* self-interests around a rich–poor fault-line had severe implications for the federal system. It pointed to a scenario in which the sense of collective interest on which co-operative federalism had been based could fall apart: a group of richer *Länder* would be tempted to 'go their own way', leaving the rest to fall into increasing dependence on and subordination to a Federation with the power to pull their financial strings. The overall result of such a scenario would be to remove the main way in which the *Länder* have been able to offer a counterbalance to the Federation, leading effectively to a greater concentration of power at the federal level.

The potential dangers inherent in this scenario were made all the more acute with the addition of the new *Länder* to the federal system in 1990. Their extreme financial weakness immediately widened the gap between rich and poor in the *Länder* community and superimposed a new east–west dimension on top of the existing poor–rich fault-line which had begun to disrupt co-operative federalism in the 1980s. If co-operative federalism—and through it an effective, collective *Länder* counterbalance to the Federation—was to survive in the 'new' FRG, it was imperative that old and new *Länder* together found a basis on which to bridge their differing financial interests and to present a united front against the Federation. Otherwise, as Heidrun Abromeit has warned (1992:81–120), a 'two-class' federal system could emerge, with the eastern *Länder* (and most likely some of their poorer western counterparts) becoming financially dependent on the Federation and the richer western *Länder* making their own way as best they can, feeding their greater resources into their own, independent policy initiatives.

5.3.3 Towards a 'two-class' federal system?

Although it is still too early to reach any definitive conclusions, developments in the politics of the federal system since unification certainly seem to vindicate Abromeit's warning. Even before the new *Länder* were formally incorporated on 3 October 1990, the old *Länder* had demonstrated an attitude which suggested that they viewed the new *Länder* less as prospective partners and more as threats to their existing interests. One indication of this attitude was given in negotiations between the western *Länder* and the Federal Government during 1990 on the most suitable means of financing the responsibilities of the new *Länder* in the years immediately after unification. These negotiations (Klatt 1992:7–10; Exler 1992:27–37) created a special German Unity Fund to finance the eastern *Länder* until their planned incorporation into the system of financial

equalization alongside the western *Länder* from the start of 1995. The remarkable feature of those negotiations was the way the western *Länder*
consistently attempted to pass onto the federal level as large a share as
possible of the financial burdens that would be imposed by the incorporation of the new *Länder*. In terms of financial self-interest this was an understandable reaction but it hardly augured well for any future financial
solidarity between old and new *Länder* (Sturm and Jeffery 1992:171). It
seemed that the priority of the old *Länder* was one of damage limitation
rather than the creation of an east–west *Länder* partnership capable of
holding the Federation in check.

   This essentially negative attitude was further demonstrated in an
amendment to the Basic Law introduced in the Treaty of Unification concerning the number of *Bundesrat* seats allocated to each of the *Länder*.
Traditionally the number of seats given to each *Land* was weighted ap-
proximately in relation to population size. The amendment introduced in
the Treaty of Unification slightly changed this weighting so that the 'big
four' *Länder* (Baden-Württemberg, Bavaria, Lower Saxony, and North
Rhine-Westphalia) controlled over a third of the total number of votes, as
they had done before unification. The amendment, pushed for strongly by
the big four, was a flagrant exercise in damage limitation. It gave them
enough seats in the new *Bundesrat* to block potential constitutional
changes (which require a two-thirds majority in the *Bundesrat*) and simultaneously prevented the new *Länder* together from having enough seats to
do the same. The motivation here was, again, primarily financial self-interest: to enable the big four to block any unwelcome future changes in the
rules of financial equalization that might favour the new *Länder* and to
prevent the new *Länder* vetoing changes that might benefit the big four in
the west (Sturm 1992a:126–27).

   Confronted by these negative attitudes, it is not surprising that the new
Länder placed more emphasis on working together to pursue their specifically east German interests than on trying to work in concert with the western *Länder*. They have in some cases, notably in education policy, pursued
a policy agenda clearly different from that of the western *Länder* (see
Chapter 7). They have also shown themselves willing to accept a high degree of federal influence over their affairs in return for extra financial assistance from the Federation (Sturm 1992b:122–24; Klatt 1992:10–11).

   In other words, neither the western nor the eastern *Länder* showed
themselves to be capable of compromising, or indeed of trying to compromise, over the interests which divide them. They were, however, provided with an opportunity to bridge their differences in Article 5 of the
Treaty of Unification. The article required discussions on constitutional reform to be conducted directly after unification; such discussions would aim

to propose and formulate any constitutional changes deemed necessary as a result of unification, including changes in the relationships between Federation and *Länder* (*Bundeszentrale für politische Bildung* 1990:45). A *Bundesrat* Commission on Constitutional Reform was created in March 1991 and fed proposals into a Joint Constitutional Commission of *Bundestag* and *Bundesrat*; the Commission submitted a final report on proposed constitutional changes in the summer of 1993. At the same time separate discussions were held on reforming the system of financial equalization in a way capable of meeting the needs of the new and old *Länder* from the start of 1995 (when the German Unity Fund was scheduled to be shut down).

These various discussions provided a clear opportunity to rethink the needs of the much more diverse, post-unification *Länder* community and to reshape the powers, responsibilities, and resource base of the *Länder* in a way that would enable them to retain their role as a counterbalance to the Federation in the future. But that opportunity was not taken. Broadly speaking, the more affluent western *Länder* were concerned to gain more independent policy powers and to protect their higher levels of income so that they could exercise such powers effectively. The eastern *Länder* and the poorer western *Länder* were much less interested in gaining additional powers and far more concerned to secure enough income to carry out their existing responsibilities, either through transfers from the richer *Länder*, or if need be through direct subsidy by the Federation (Jeffery 1993:22–38). The outcome, predictably, was a fudge of the differing perspectives which left the existing characteristics of the federal system by and large intact.

5.3.4 *Looking ahead*

In short the West German *status quo* of the 1980s has been reproduced in only marginally amended form for the united Germany. As shown above, this *status quo* proved to be increasingly inadequate in maintaining the balance between Federation and *Länder* in the old FRG as economic differences widened within the western *Länder* community. It would now seem even less capable of doing so in view of the far wider economic differences between east and west in the new FRG. Unless eastern and western *Länder* suddenly discover a capacity for compromising over their different interests (a prospect which seems to be highly improbable), the federal system of the future will consist of the fractured and weakened, two-class *Länder* community predicted by Abromeit, ranged against a much strengthened federal level.

This conclusion has a resonance which extends beyond the federal system and which will undoubtedly have an impact on the other institutions of government in Germany. These institutions are rooted in an exclusively pre-1990, West German context. They now have to transform themselves into institutions of all-German government. The process of transformation will inevitably modify the way in which these institutions of government interact with each other and the functions they perform. So far the effects of transformation have perhaps been illustrated most clearly within the federal system, where west meets east in a concrete and direct way within the *Länder* community. The problems thrown up by west meeting east are, however, also being experienced and addressed at least indirectly throughout the German system of government. This meeting of west and east will, over time and inevitably, leave a distinctive and enduring mark on the way that all of the components of that system work.

5.4 Unification and foreign policy

This final section moves away from the domestic politics of unification and examines some of the implications unification has had for Germany's external role. One of the key questions any state has to confront is how to shape its relations with its neighbours. This question has long been a controversial, even fateful one for both Germany and for the rest of Europe, partly because of Germany's inherent economic strength and its strategic position at the centre of Europe but above all because of the experience of the two world wars, when vast areas of Europe fell under German military domination. The aim of this section is to examine how smoothly the answers that were developed for this 'German Question' in West Germany before 1990 have been adapted to the new situation since unification. The section will pay particular attention to the impact unification has had on Germany's policy on European integration.

5.4.1 *The West German foreign policy style*

Carl Cavanagh Hodge described the West German foreign policy style as one of 'ostentatious modesty' (Hodge 1992:224). Hodge was pointing to the tendency of successive West German governments to avoid embarking on unilateral and assertive foreign policy initiatives and to work, wherever possible, on a low-key, multilateral basis in concert with their international partners. This restrained, multilateral approach has a number of origins which stretch back to the 1940s and 1950s and which were partly imposed from without and partly accepted and developed from within the Federal Republic.

The international politics of the years following the Second World War were dominated initially by the experiences and memories of Nazism and then increasingly by the effects of the emerging Cold War which by 1949 had divided both Germany and Europe into two hostile blocs. The memory of Nazism left a lingering suspicion and fear among West Germany's neighbours of the potential economic and military power of West Germany. Their concern was, as a result, to place restrictions on West Germany's ability to redevelop that power. Increasingly, though, the confrontations and tensions of the Cold War demanded that West Germany's economic and military potential be harnessed to the American/West European commitment to containing the influence of the Soviet-led Communist bloc. These essentially contradictory expectations of the FRG were reconciled during the 1950s in a series of measures designed to facilitate West German economic and military reconstruction within a framework of constraints which as far as possible were designed to prevent West Germany from using its power independently.

Accordingly, West German rearmament was conducted from the mid-1950s wholly within the framework of NATO. All West German forces were subordinated to the NATO command structure, were allowed to participate only in defensive operations within NATO territory, and were therefore prevented from pursuing independent military operations. Further constraints included a ban on West German forces using weapons of mass destruction (nuclear, chemical, or biological), and the continued stationing of forces from other NATO member states in West Germany. A similar if less overt process in the field of economic reconstruction was also under way in the 1950s, when West Germany was admitted as one of the founder members of the early institutions of West European economic integration, which were later to develop into the European Union (EU) of today. The assumption here, particularly in the eyes of France, was that the pooling of economic policy sovereignty in European-level institutions would effectively give West Germany's neighbours a veto over how West German economic power could be used. An international framework of restrictions was thus imposed over economic and military affairs in West Germany, leading it, in the memorable analogy of Bulmer and Paterson (1989), to resemble the plight of Jonathan Swift's Gulliver during his captivity in Lilliput: a colossus bound and restrained by its smaller and weaker counterparts.

When discussing Germany's 'plight' it should, however, be stressed that this framework of constraints was freely accepted and confirmed by the CDU/CSU-led governments of the era and, by the late 1950s, by all the other major forces in West German politics. Playing a constructive role in international organizations brought with it, after all, considerable benefits. It helped to remove the lingering stigmas bequeathed by the Third Reich and to rehabilitate West Germany as a reliable partner in international affairs. The emergence of West Germany as a trustworthy international partner also provided economic benefits in the form of increased trade flows, in particular through the institutions of West European integration. This was especially important for West Germany, whose industries were (and still are) heavily geared towards export markets in Western Europe.

These benefits helped to institutionalize multilateralism, that is, working in co-operation with fellow member states of international organizations, as the keystone of West Germany's approach to foreign affairs. The commitment to multilateralism was strengthened further by what William Paterson (1993:10) has called West Germany's 'leadership avoidance reflex'. This reflex, an aversion to taking an assertive lead role in foreign policy initiatives, was rooted in memories of the aggressive foreign policy of the Third Reich and acted as a psychological constraint on West German foreign policy-makers. The tendency not to play a strong lead role was underlined in a more concrete sense by the domestic structure of foreign policy-making in West Germany. As noted in the previous section, the Basic Law tends to disperse powers and responsibilities among different institutions of government. This has helped to prevent any one centre of power in West German politics from defining and promoting an over-arching grand design in foreign affairs, just as it does in domestic policy (Bulmer 1989c). This inbuilt protection against strong leadership has been especially evident in foreign policy in the field of European integration (Bulmer and Paterson 1987:25–84).

5.4.2 *After unification: the breakdown of consensus*

As shown earlier, the external constraints imposed on West German foreign policy in the 1950s were confirmed and supplemented in various ways within the FRG itself. As a result a policy of restrained multilateralism in foreign relations was perpetuated right through to German unification in 1990. Moreover, as noted in the introduction to this chapter, the international discussions which ran in parallel with the internal German debates on unification in 1990 were concluded on the assumption that a united Germany would continue to follow the established foreign policy orientation of West Germany. The question this section addresses is the extent to which that assumption is likely to be borne out. After all, German foreign policy now serves a very different domestic political context. It is not inconceivable that the domestic problems and tensions caused by the integration of the former GDR will produce new and different foreign policy priorities. It should also be remembered that German unification has taken place alongside other far-reaching changes in European politics, above all the renewed attempt to force along the process of West European integration in the early 1990s and the collapse of Communism in Eastern Europe and in the former Soviet Union. Again, it is possible that these wider changes in European politics will cause the traditions of the old West German foreign policy to be modified. Will, or can, united Germany continue in the face of these changed domestic and international circumstances to adhere to the 'culture of reticence' (Asmus 1993:143) which lay behind West Germany's restrained multilateralism? Or will changed circumstances lead to changes in Germany's role in Europe, perhaps in the direction of a greater foreign policy assertiveness?

These and related questions have provoked an intense debate among academics, journalists, and politicians, both within and outside Germany. Many have pointed to an implicit or explicit threat of a greater German assertiveness in the post-unification era, even to the extent of asking the question: 'Should Europe fear the Germans?' (Markovits and Reich 1993). In response a number of writers have gone to some length to explain why Europe 'should not fear the Germans' (Goldberger 1993; Paterson 1993). The debate on both sides has often adopted a rather skewed and loaded approach, which probably says more about the historical prejudices of the authors concerned than about current German foreign policy. There certainly seems to be little convincing evidence that German policy has suddenly become a threat to be feared. The predominant feature of German foreign policy since unification has, on the contrary, been its hesitancy and uncertainty. It has become beset by a sense of disorientation which, while not departing from multilateralism, has found it difficult to adjust the traditional multilateralist approach to a new environment.

It has, in other words, not proved possible to adapt the previous guiding principles of (West German) foreign policy seamlessly and smoothly to the new situation of the 1990s. As a result a number of foreign policy issues that have arisen since unification have not been met with clear answers. One example is the dispute surrounding a so-called 'out-of-area' role for the Federal German Army, the *Bundeswehr*. Following the Gulf War of early 1991 there was a protracted debate about changing the rules of engagement of the *Bundeswehr* which were inherited from West Germany. The *Bundeswehr* had traditionally worked on the assumption that it was restricted to defensive operations within the area comprised by NATO's member states. A number of issues that emerged after unification pointed, though, to a need to reconsider that assumption and to develop an out-of-area role for the *Bundeswehr*. These included: requests for German assist-ance in the United Nations-sanctioned anti-Iraqi coalition in the Gulf War; the possibility of German participation in UN or NATO intervention in former Yugoslavia; and wider calls for Germany to take on a role in United Nations peacekeeping and peacemaking operations. Progress in changing *Bundeswehr* rules of engagement was, though, made only fitfully and in the face of considerable domestic opposition (Kamp 1993). Only in July 1994 was the issue resolved in a judgement of the Federal Constitutional Court which ruled that there were no constitutional obstacles in the way of out-of-area operations under a UN flag.

The main change to note in the out-of-area debate was not that there was any radical departure from established foreign policy traditions. The out-of-area operations so far undertaken or discussed have been firmly embedded in the *multilateral* contexts of the UN or NATO. The most sig-nificant change concerns rather the breakdown of domestic consensus on a major foreign policy issue. Foreign policy in the (West German) past was with few exceptions (for example, the mid-1950s rearmament debate and the disputes surrounding the deployment of a new range of US nuclear missiles in the early 1980s) not normally controversial at the popular level. However, the out-of-area debate split public opinion down the middle, with eastern Germans less in favour of an out-of-area role for the *Bundes-wehr* than western Germans and supporters of left-wing parties less in fa-vour than those of the parties of the right (Gibowski 1993b).

This new fractiousness of public opinion has important implications in a state in which policy-making powers are dispersed among different polit-ical institutions: it enables those institutions to appeal to and also to claim to represent different constituencies. This can lead to uncertainty and stag-nation in policy-making if, as a result of being buffeted by a capricious public opinion, the various centres of political power pull in different dir-ections. This has certainly been the case with regard to out-of-area opera-tions, with the Federal Government pushing for change and the SPD using its powers in opposition to slow and to block that change. It has also been the case in other fields of German policy, notably on the conflicts in former Yugoslavia (Heuven 1993) and on controlling the (in part related) in-creased flows of refugees into Germany from instability in Eastern Europe (Drummond 1993). This new pattern of division in public opinion since unification, ranged alongside and in part reinforcing institutional conflict in policy-making, has also been clearly illustrated in the case of European integration policy.

5.4.3 *Unified Germany and European union*

Prior to unification West Germany had long been one of the member states of the European Community most consistently committed to deepening the process of European integration on the road to a full-blown federal union of European states. This commitment was based on the view of successive governments, strongly supported by public opinion, that a European union was the best way of guaranteeing peace, stability, and prosperity on the European continent (Bulmer and Paterson 1987:1–14; Kohl 1993:6). West Germany had accordingly played a key role—in multilateral co-operation with all of its partners, and especially France (Bulmer and Paterson 1987:225–31)—in shaping some of the major steps in the evolving integration process: for example, the creation of the European Monetary System (EMS) in 1978, and the preparations for the Single European Act in the mid-1980s. This commitment to deepening integration was apparently left untouched by unification, with the now unified Germany equally prominent in pushing forward the negotiations which led to the Maastricht Treaty on European Union of December 1991.

The emergence of the Maastricht Treaty on European Union was very closely linked to German unification. Many of (West) Germany's partners in the European Community (EC) had expressed concern in 1989–90 that unification would confront them with a stronger and more assertive Germany. These concerns were used by Helmut Kohl and his then Foreign Minister, Hans-Dietrich Genscher (working in tacit alliance with the President of the EC Commission, Jacques Delors), as a catalyst to increase the pace of European integration. A more deeply integrated EC was seen by some of the concerned member states as a means of binding a unified Germany, Gulliver-like, 'into a framework of checks and balances to its potential hegemony'. The German view was that, if this were so, 'we should exploit their fear before it diminishes' and use it to press for advances on the road to the long-standing German aim of full-scale union (Spence 1991:6,8). Kohl's government, presenting German unification and European union as intrinsically interlinked, accordingly played a key role in the negotiations that led to and shaped the Maastricht Treaty. This treaty set out preconditions for the establishment of a European Economic and Monetary Union (EMU), made some limited moves towards a European Political Union, and more generally spurred on the integration process in a number of policy fields (Wistrich 1994:7–10).

One might deduce from the above a smooth and straightforward extension of pre-unification European policy traditions to post-unification Germany. This has not, however, proved to be the case. After being one of the strongest advocates of the Maastricht Treaty, Germany was, embarrassingly, the last of the member states of what is now the European Union to ratify it (in October 1993), finally enabling the Union to come into force (on 1 November 1993). The intervening period of almost two years proved unexpectedly difficult for Kohl's government, as it was forced to confront new institutional obstacles in European policy and a breakdown of previously high levels of public support for the integration process.

The Federal Government was, at the institutional level, forced to confront worries in both the *Bundestag* and *Bundesrat* about the implications the Maastricht Treaty had for their own powers and responsibilities. Both, as a result, won significant concessions from the Federal Government as a *quid pro quo* for their ratification of the Maastricht Treaty. At the insistence of the SPD the *Bundestag* won for itself a right to veto Germany's participation in future steps towards EMU (Harmon and Heisenberg 1993:43) and the *Bundesrat* won for itself and for the *Länder* it represents a whole series of new and important rights in the shaping of future European integration policies (Leonardy 1992). Significantly, both sets of concessions have in effect led to a further dispersal of policy powers in European integration policy between the various German institutions of government. As a result it may in future be yet harder for the Federal Government to secure domestic institutional agreement on future developments in European integration.

The problems a dispersal of power can bring were given clear illustration in two other Maastricht-related issues in the period 1991–93. First, there emerged (and remains) a simmering disagreement between the Federal Government and the *Bundesbank* (the powerful, independent German Central Bank) over both the principle and the means of moving towards EMU. This disagreement at least partly underlay the EC exchange-rate crisis of September 1992 and helped to sour relations between Germany and a number of its European partners (Harmon and Heisenberg 1993:41–43). Second, the Federal Government was forced to wait anxiously in the autumn of 1993 for the Constitutional Court to make a ruling on the Maastricht Treaty before Germany could formally ratify the treaty. The Constitutional Court has, if requested to do so, the right to examine the compatibility with the Basic Law of any treaty Germany plans to sign. It was only when the Court finally gave a (somewhat qualified) go-ahead in October 1993 that Germany could finally complete the ratification process (Laux 1993).

All these domestic obstacles to the smooth development of the Federal Government's European integration policy reflect, at least in part, a growing and unprecedented sense of unease in German public opinion about European integration. This unease has a number of sources. Most generally, there are concerns, as in other EU member states, about the limited accountability, the 'democratic deficit', of European-level decision-making (Reif 1993). There is also a growing belief that Germany needs to devote more energy and above all more resources to its domestic problems than to the project of deepening European integration, especially where the latter imposes financial burdens on Germany (Kirchner 1994). Most importantly, though, there exists a deep aversion to giving up the German mark in a European EMU. This is one of the few issues on which the vast majority of eastern and western Germans are in agreement (Gibowski 1993a); it provides a rare link of common interest and purpose between east and west, but, unfortunately for the Federal Government, runs counter to official German policy.

German policy-makers can therefore no longer rely on a strong public consensus that a commitment to deeper European integration is necessarily in Germany's interests. This has been reflected in the emergence of the institutional obstacles encountered by the Federal Government in the field of integration policy since Maastricht, with the *Bundestag, Bundesrat, Bundesbank,* and Constitutional Court each giving voice to at least some elements of this new Euro-scepticism in Germany. With this post-Maastricht experience in mind it seems unlikely that the united Germany will act in the future as such a driving force in deepening the European integration process as West Germany did in the past.

5.5 Conclusions

The conclusion reached in the previous section is not intended to imply that Germany will turn its back on the EU (and on more than forty-five years of European integration history) and concentrate separately and independently on its own affairs and interests. Germany will remain committed, as in other foreign policy fields, to a multilateral approach to solving what are, in today's interdependent world, common problems of economic management, political stability, and military security. Germany is, though, likely to play a more circumspect role than hitherto, as changing trends in public opinion and the institutional complexities of foreign policy-making limit its room for manoeuvre.

In other words the political inheritance from West Germany's foreign policy traditions is being and will continue to be redefined and reshaped to address the very different problems and needs of a united Germany. The earlier sections of this chapter showed that a similar process of adaptation and change has also been taking place in the electoral and institutional arenas of domestic politics. Like the 'old' foreign policy, neither the 'old' party system nor the 'old' federal system have emerged unscathed from the attempt to integrate the East into a Western framework. The scale of the various changes to the inherited framework of West German politics which unification has produced has not always been fully expected or adequately predicted. They should not, though, be seen as especially unusual, since, as Gerald Kleinfeld has pointed out: 'In domestic as in foreign policy, the programs and goals of yesterday's Germany are not easily adaptable to the problems of today and tomorrow.' The resultant 'clashes between the assumptions of yesterday and the challenges of today' (Kleinfeld 1993:49) will continue to be the trademark of German politics for the foreseeable future.

Further reading

The scope of the literature on German politics after unification is huge and ever-expanding. For follow-up reading on public opinion and parties after unification see Dalton (1993), Padgett (1993), and the special issue of *German Politics* on the 1994 *Bundestag* election (Vol. 4, No. 2, 1995). The most up-to-date survey of the federal system after unification is given in the special issue of *German Politics* (Vol. 1, No. 3, 1992) entitled 'Federalism, Unification and European Integration'. Broader introductions to Germany's political institutions in general are given in Smith (1992), Sturm (1992b), and Schmidt (1992). Geipel (1993) is a useful set of contributions on German foreign and European policy and, alongside Huelshoff, Markovits, and Reich (1993) and Goldberger (1993), provides an introduction to the debate about Germany's international role. James and Stone (1992) provide a collection of reactions of politicians and journalists to German unification. More broadly, Smith, Paterson, Merkl, and Padgett (1992) present a comprehensive survey of issues in post-unification politics. The journal *German Politics* has three numbers per year dedicated mainly to current political issues and problems.

6

The German Economy
Decline or Stability?

KARL KOCH

6.1 Introduction

One of the characteristics of post-war West Germany has been its astonishingly successful economic performance over a long period. From its foundation in 1949 until unification in 1990 the FRG displayed annual growth rates of remarkable consistency. It is true that Germany has experienced economic reverses: these include the recession of 1965–66, the aftermath of the oil crisis in 1974, and the slowing of growth at the beginning of the 1980s. But in each case the government of the day was able to resolve the problems by applying appropriate policies within the framework of the social market economy.

It was this background of economic strength, achieved and sustained on the basis of the social market model, which underpinned the belief at the time of unification that West Germany commanded the resources to incorporate and regenerate the eastern federal states. In the euphoric months after the fall of the Berlin Wall Chancellor Helmut Kohl was convinced of the ability of the social market system to absorb the economic demands of unification. On the day of monetary union (1 July 1990) Kohl assured East Germans that nobody would be worse off than before and that many would be better off. To West Germans he promised that unification would take nothing away from their current prosperity, indeed there would be wealth for everybody in the coming years (Priewe and Hickel 1991:86). The Chancellor repeatedly stressed, especially in the run-up to the national election of December 1990, his vision of the prosperity that lay ahead. This faith in the inherent superiority of the social market economy was severely tested by subsequent events. Although western Germany enjoyed a short-term internal boom during the immediate post-unification period, this was soon followed by recession and the economy faced an almost catastrophic decline in activity during 1993. At this point economists began to analyse the German economy more critically and to identify its underlying problems.

This chapter begins by outlining the principles of the social market model, demonstrating how this formed the basis for West German economic success after 1949. The major developments that took place in the economy up until 1989 are briefly reviewed. With unification in October 1990 came the unique challenge of transforming the centralized system of the former GDR into a viable Western-type economy. After examining the spectacular downturn of 1993 and the implications which this had for industrial relations, the chapter assesses whether the FRG has sufficient resilience to overcome the setbacks that have accompanied unification.

6.1.1   *The social market economy: the foundation of economic achievement*

The social market economy is regarded as the pillar that has sustained West German prosperity and economic dominance within Europe throughout the post-war era. On 15 July 1949, two months before the founding of the FRG, the Conservative CDU adopted in its Düsseldorf Guidelines the principles of the social market as the basis for economic reconstruction after the devastation of the Second World War. Ten years later, in its Godesberg Programme, the SPD cast off the historical mantle of a Marxist party committed to a centrally planned economy and embraced a policy of achieving social reform within the framework of the free market. Since 1959 the two main political parties in Germany have thus maintained a consensus on the efficacy of the social market as the basis for developing and managing the national economy.

The principal architects of the post-war German economic miracle were Ludwig Erhard, the first Economics Minister of the FRG, and Alfred Müller-Armack, professor at the University of Münster, who advocated as early as 1946 the need for a social market orientation. Erhard and Müller-Armack built on theoretical foundations established by a group of scholars working in Freiburg during the 1930s under the leadership of Walther Eucken. Known as the Freiburg School, this group developed a model of economic policy that could counter the contemporary trend towards greater state intervention. Although they advocated the creation of a free-market mechanism that would give primacy to private competition, they rejected the archaic *laissez-faire* approach of nineteenth-century capitalism. But while they believed that government intervention was necessary to ensure social justice, they were convinced that the level of intervention should be held to a minimum. The social market concept was conceived as a model that combined freedom of initiative for the individual with the principle of social progress. For the western zones of Germany before 1949 the ideas of the Freiburg School played a key role in the debate about the best way to regenerate economic activity and regain prosperity.

Erhard and Müller-Armack set clear objectives for the social market economy. First, it was to bring about a high and sustained level of economic prosperity through competition, growth, the encouragement of foreign trade, and full employment; these were fundamental Keynesian targets. Second, an independent Central Bank was to be created in order to achieve price stability, balance-of-payment equilibrium, and a viable monetary system. Finally, a system of social security, social justice, and social progress would be maintained through economic growth and judicious state intervention. The object of such intervention would be to sustain a fair relationship between income and the distribution of capital within German society. The essential feature of the social market model was, therefore, a balance between social and purely economic interests. Although the model required state intervention, such intervention would conform to market principles: that is, there would be no interference with the fundamental mechanism of free competition.

During the post-war years the economic theory underlying the social market model was only one side of the coin. As the political differences between the USSR and USA intensified between 1945 and 1948 the concept of the social market economy became linked to the ideological differences between East and West. The successful reconstruction of the economy of the western German zones, which began in June 1948 with the currency reform, was soon seen as a vindication of Western ideology over the Communist regimes that were establishing themselves in Eastern Europe. The currency reform, which gave birth to the West German mark (DM), produced a stable money supply, which in turn promoted psychological confidence and provided a solid foundation for the implementation of the market economy. In addition the European Recovery Programme (otherwise known as the Marshall Plan after US Secretary of State George Marshall, who initiated the programme for financing economic revival in Western Europe in 1947) supplied cheap investment credit, which acted as a priming pump for recovery.

With the founding of the Federal Republic in September 1949 the economic system in the western zones of occupied Germany acquired a solid national and political basis. In order to compete internationally German industry was compelled to modernize itself after the war years. Two factors helped in this process. First, the influx of refugees and expellees from the east ensured that wage rates in the labour market remained low. Second, the first West German government adopted tax and credit policies which favoured the producer. But it was the Korean War from 1950 to 1953 which provided the motor for the real 'economic miracle'. During this period industrial production rose rapidly and the basis for the ascendancy of the German export industry was established. In particular West Germany was able to meet world demand for machinery, engineering products, chemicals, and heavy industrial equipment. The reservoir of cheap labour created by the internal migration from the east and a general shift from agricultural to manufacturing employment supplied the necessary manpower. The result of these developments was an extraordinarily high growth rate of gross domestic product (GDP) between 1951 and 1956, which in 1955–56 reached a peak of over 11%.

The West German economy received a further boost on 25 March 1957 with the signing of the Treaty of Rome, which established the European Economic Community (EEC). Apart from providing Germany with a road back to political respectability after the Second World War, the gradual abolition of customs constraints within the EEC promoted the expansion of exports and imports between member states, from which West Germany benefited considerably.

6.1.2 Economic trends from 1960 to 1980

If the 1950s were years of post-war recovery and rapid boom, providing economic and political stability, then the 1960s saw West Germany's integration into the global economic framework. German growth rates of 1959 and 1960 no longer reached the high levels of earlier years, and with the economic crisis of 1966–68 the golden years of post-war economic growth came to an end. The recession had profound political and economic effects. It led to the formation of a Grand Coalition of the major political parties, CDU/CSU, SPD, and FDP, marking the end of almost twenty years of CDU/CSU domination of post-war Germany. It also resulted in a programme of major economic reforms designed to combat the crisis.

The first measure was the Stability and Growth Act, initiated by the SPD Economics Minister Karl Schiller and passed by Parliament in June 1967. The Act provided a series of policy instruments for regulating the excessive swings in the cyclical pattern that had hitherto characterized the German economy. Four economic cycles occurred between 1950 and 1967: 1950–54, 1955–58, 1959–63, and 1964–67. Each cycle began with an initial surge in demand, resulting in higher inflation and rapid wage increases, after which there was a period of growth. The Act hoped to control these fluctuations by introducing new elements of planning: these included fine tuning the economy through the use of fiscal indicators (such as taxation and investment levels) and synchronizing policy decisions at federal, *Land,* and local level.

Clearly the Stability Act represented a modification of the social market economy as originally conceived. The best illustration of this modification was Schiller's programme of Concerted Action (*Konzertierte Aktion*), which brought together leaders of industry, trade unions, government, and the banks in annual meetings to agree guidelines for national economic policy. Although the state had little influence on the levels at which wage levels were set, the Concerted Action forum was responsible for introducing the FRG's first ever incomes policy, albeit in an informal and weak form. The mechanism worked as follows: together with the Council of Economic Experts (a panel of five independent experts established by law in 1963 to provide data and advice for the government in assessing the state of the German economy), the Concerted Action group first established what wage levels might be compatible for the macro-economy and then proposed them to the government for implementation. The forum remained in existence until 1976, when the trade unions left it in protest against employers' opposition to the Co-determination Act, which increased participation by workers in the supervisory boards of companies employing over 2,000 people. Co-determination, the net of legislative provisions allowing employees various rights in the decision-making process at company and plant level, remains to this day a central issue in German industrial relations.

From 1969 to 1982 the FRG was governed by an SPD-FDP coalition, first under the Chancellorship of Willy Brandt (1969–74) and subsequently under Helmut Schmidt. Responding to the problems of the 1960s, German industry implemented drastic programmes of rationalization and automation. As a result of these measures and also of mergers, industry became more productive. An export-led upswing occurred in 1969, with German goods benefiting from a high global demand. However, activity during the 1970s was severely affected by the oil price strategy of the Organization of Petroleum Exporting Countries (OPEC), which raised the price of crude oil from $3 to over $30 a barrel. The increased cost of energy contributed towards a growing economic instability in West Germany and highlighted its dependence on international trade. Most significantly, unemployment rose; this would prove to be an ongoing problem for the government.

Despite these difficulties the German economy continued to perform well: between 1974 and 1980 gross national product (GNP) increased by 19% per capita. Significantly, however, foreign trade surpluses, which reached a record second highest level in 1978, began to decline. The year 1979–80 saw the surplus in the balance of trade fall to less than half that of the previous year so that it no longer covered the deficit in the balance of services and transfer payments. At the end of 1980 the balance of current transactions showed a deficit of around 28 billion DM; this, after more than a decade of trade surpluses, represented a severe psychological blow for the Germans. Coupled with the apprehension with which Germans traditionally view any movement towards inflation, it was no surprise that the Social-Liberal coalition of Helmut Schmidt came under strong criticism. In October 1982 Schmidt's government paid the penalty for not reducing budget deficits, and Helmut Kohl (CDU) formed a new government coalition with the FDP.

6.1.3 *The German economy in the 1980s*

Kohl's government decided on a fundamental redirection of policy, an economic *Wende*. The 1980s presented the West German economy with a series of problems: the oil increases of 1973–74 and 1979–80 had eroded GNP by about 2%; export markets had become much more competitive; and unemployment had also increased, fluctuating between 5% and 9%. The first problem was the uncertainty triggered by the decline of the dollar, which lost over half its value between 1984 and 1987. The decline was especially worrying because German economic success since 1949 had been based on export-led investment. The fall in the dollar acted as a spur to the independent German Federal Bank to apply a firm monetaristic policy in the form of tight control over interest rates and the total money supply. The second problem also came from overseas: Japan's growing export industry began to threaten the crucial mechanical engineering sector in Germany, which currently employs over one million people. Finally Germany saw it as an urgent priority to complete the single integrated market of the European Community (EC): the political negotiations promised to be complex and the economic costs high.

Until the 1980s Germany had served as an economic and social model for the rest of the world (*Modell Deutschland*). Protected from direct politicization through a rational framework of policy formulation, Germany's massive and prosperous economy supported a stable national political culture without deep social disparities. The problems outlined above now led economists to question the viability of the model. In particular it seemed no longer possible to sustain the core of the model, the magic Keynesian quadrilateral of stable prices, economic growth, full employment, and a balance of payments equilibrium.

During the 1980s the FRG diverged from the model as it applied radical measures to resolve its problems. A major priority of the Federal Government was to reduce budgetary deficits and government spending, but it was hampered in this aim by the traditional autonomy of the federal states. Although the Kohl administration succeeded by 1985 in reducing the federal deficit to one of the lowest of the decade, the deficit rose again in the following years and it became a persistent problem after unification. Chancellor Kohl's government based its national economic policy on neo-classical principles: it wanted to reduce state involvement and to provide greater freedoms for market forces through deregulation; it also aimed for a more flexible labour market.

Table 6.1 GNP and Productivity in the FRG (Percentage Annual Change)

Year	GNP	Productivity
1984	2·8	2·9
1985	2·0	2·0
1986	2·3	2·2
1987	1·8	1·8
1988	3·7	3·1
1989	3·4	3·4
1990	3·5	3·5

Source: Calculated from *Sachverständigenrat*, 1990–91

As Table 6.1 shows, GNP and productivity improved after 1986 although unemployment continued at around 8%. The upturn was weak and it failed to address either the fundamental issues of industrial restructuring or the urgent need for innovation in new technologies. Chancellor Kohl's economic *Wende* proved to be a long way from being a major turning-point. Nevertheless at the beginning of 1989 inflation was under control and there was a balance of payments surplus. Furthermore the EC, by taking just over 50% of all exports, had in effect become a home market for Germany's output. On the eve of the momentous changes that were to explode in Eastern Europe at the end of 1989 the West German economy was secure and stable: continuity and consensus were still the mainstays of national policy.

6.2 The German economy in transition

The revolution of 1989 and the speed at which events unfolded in the GDR caught political and economic policy-makers in the two Germanies quite unprepared. Chancellor Kohl's strategy towards East Germany was uncertain at the time the Berlin Wall came down, but the rapid disintegration of the GDR soon propelled him towards achieving rapid unification, which was formally concluded on 2–3 October 1990. The swiftness of the political changes meant that economic policies for the new Germany had to be worked out at breakneck speed. As a result the transformation of East Germany from a centrally planned economy to a free market system was carried out with almost brutal haste.

The transformation began with the Treaty on the Creation of a Monetary, Economic, and Social Union. Signed on 18 May 1990 after a mere six weeks of negotiations between the FRG and the GDR, the treaty provided for the introduction of a common economic area from 1 July 1990. The treaty was the product of political and social pressures, arising in particular from the continuing westward exodus of East Germans who could see no future for their former country. The effects of the treaty on the GDR's economy were catastrophic. The main provision was the introduction of the West German social market economy, together with the appropriate institutions and policy instruments. But its most controversial aspect was the currency union (more precisely: the replacement of the East German mark by the West German mark), in particular the conversion rate (the ratio at which East Germans would be able to convert their old currency to the new one). The issue provoked bitter conflict between politicians and economists, and the influential Council of Economic Experts openly declared their concern in a letter to Chancellor Kohl (9 February 1990):

> It is unavoidable that currency union and the introduction of the DM will give the population of the GDR the illusion that they have achieved parity with the living standard of the FRG. That cannot be: income is bound to productivity, and productivity in the GDR is way behind that of the FRG. The expectation that productivity and, at the same time, wages and pensions will rise substantially is correct, but the economic preconditions for this will have to be created first. Currency union cannot do this.

This view was to be fully vindicated. The aggregated conversion rate that was adopted—1 FRG mark to 1·81 GDR mark—meant that the GDR mark was artificially overvalued. The aggregate was made of a 2:1 conversion rate for most assets, liabilities, and contracts, and a 1:1 rate for savings up to 6,000 GDR marks held by each person aged over sixty-five (2,000 GDR marks for those under fourteen and 4,000 GDR marks for the age group in-between). The conversion immediately generated 140 billion DM in cash and savings deposits at the disposal of East Germans.

The importation of the West German mark into the GDR economy was instantaneous and disastrous, exposing the underlying and long-standing structural deficiencies of the command economy. First, it effectively severed trade relations with the former countries in COMECON (the trading block maintained by the Soviet Union and its former satellites) and exposed the reliance of East German exports on an over-protected foreign market. Although the GDR's trade with COMECON had declined marginally from almost 70% in the 1960s, it still stood at around 64% before unification. Inevitably currency union instantly cut off export outlets for East German concerns: in the clothing industry, for example, 90% of output had gone to COMECON markets. Second, currency union starkly exposed the extent of mismanagement and the archaic industrial structure of the GDR's economy. Although in international comparisons the East German economy had appeared to show consistent growth during the 1970s and early 1980s, there was no clear understanding of its true condition. Much of the claimed expansion was due to internal rises in national income. More seriously, the performance of key sectors (for example, high technology industries) that were not in fact growing was simply omitted from official statistics. Furthermore a chronic lack of investment over the years had produced a steady decline in plant and equipment. In general East German industry was structurally orientated towards the energy-producing and basic 'dirty' industries, such as chemicals, coal, and iron; after unification Germany is still grappling with the legacy of environmental pollution which these industries have left behind.

By the late 1980s the cumbersome and autarkic economic decision-making apparatus of the GDR could no longer respond to the demands of open world markets. Decisions reached by the central State Planning Commission were relayed to a rigid and hierarchical structure of industrial management in which companies, plants, and suppliers were vertically integrated into enormous industrial combines (*Kombinate*). Furthermore, by fixing unrealistic prices for raw materials and capital and consumer goods, and by strictly controlling policies on external trade and currency exchanges, the state made reforms difficult, if not impossible.

Reforms were attempted at various times during the history of the GDR but none of them succeeded in producing a viable economy. For example, the New Economic System of 1963 went some way towards using 'economic levers' such as wages and prices as a means of giving institutions greater flexibility. However, as the dissident Rudolf Bahro demonstrated in his famous critique of East German industrial society (Bahro 1977), the system failed through lack of internal communication and because its out-of-date management was unable to deal with the demands of a modern, sophisticated, and technology-based industry. The economy of the GDR progressively stagnated and for all sections of GDR society the gap between expectations and economic reality widened: it was this gap which fuelled the peaceful revolution of 1989.

6.3 Economic transformation after unification

Once the decision had been made to unite Germany it was clear that the GDR economy had to be transformed as swiftly as possible in order to stem the internal migration from east to west. Economists proposed two models for the harmonization of eastern Germany with the west. The optimistic model was based on a new 'economic miracle', such as had occurred after the Second World War in West Germany. This view assumed that investment and demand in eastern Germany would be very high and that a transformed infrastructure and a revitalized industry would trigger an economic 'take-off'. The alternative scenario, the Mezzogiorno model, assumed that internal labour migration from the disadvantaged eastern region to the more prosperous west, coupled with a programme of subsidies, would eventually eradicate economic imbalances. Whichever model was adopted it was clear that transfer payments from west to east would play a crucial role in the transformation process. On 8 September 1992 Chancellor Kohl informed the Federal Parliament that annual transfers of 150,000 million DM would be required for the foreseeable future. Transfer payments indeed proved essential in sustaining the eastern economy immediately after unification.

There was pressure, especially from trade unions and from workers in the east, to harmonize collective bargaining structures and equalize wage levels. The pressure was increased by the continuing internal labour migration during the first phase of unification. The setting of wage levels in the light of east–west differences became a central issue in the economic and political transformation of eastern Germany, the more so when it emerged that industrial productivity in the former GDR had been seriously miscalculated. While estimates at the end of 1989 placed GDR productivity at between 30% to 80% of West German levels, it soon became apparent that the true level was only 30%. In early 1992 productivity in the new federal states remained at 40% while unit labour costs were a staggering 172% of western levels. Within two years unit labour costs had increased by 55%.

The low levels of productivity combined with demands for wage equalization created an insurmountable dilemma for the German economy. First, earned incomes needed to rise in order to cover increases in living costs in the east; but in some cases incomes actually fell as subsidies were discontinued at the end of 1991. Second, income differentials between east and west heightened social tensions and feelings of resentment in the eastern states. While wages remained lower in the east, there was little prospect of halting the internal migration westwards. Faced with low productivity and insufficient markets for their products, eastern industries could not afford to raise unit labour costs through wage increases.

Table 6.2 GNP and Inflation Indicator in Western and Eastern Germany (Percentage Annual Change)

Years	Western Germany		Eastern Germany	
	1990	1991	1990	1991
GDP	4·5	3·6	-14·4	-30·3
Inflation	2·6	3·6	0·2	13·6

Source: Calculated from *Deutsche Bundesbank Monatsberichte*, 1991

Table 6.2 shows how quickly key economic indicators began to diverge between west and east Germany after unification. From July 1990 the new federal states experienced a steep fall in industrial output, accompanied by a catastrophic decline in employment. In 1989 the labour force in the GDR stood at ten million; this dropped to 4·4 million in early 1993, 40% less than in early 1990. Unemployment rose from 9·5% in 1991 (842,000) to 15·5% (1·1 million) in mid-1993.

6.4 The privatization progamme

A key instrument in the transformation of the economy in the east was the Trust Agency, which was created by legislation passed by the People's Chamber of the GDR on 17 June 1990 and confirmed in the inter-German Unification Treaty. The Agency was assigned two specific objectives: to privatize production units and assets, and to dismantle the system of public ownership and state entrepreneurship in the former GDR. Its task was to create as many competitive enterprises as possible in order to stimulate investment and preserve employment; it was also responsible for restoring property to private owners. The Agency faced an enormous challenge: it had not only to sell over 10,000 former state-owned enterprises but also to secure employment and develop job creation programmes. Between June 1990 and May 1993 it succeeded in privatizing around 12,300 production units, realizing 42·5 billion DM from these sales. The cost of the Trust Agency was high. In 1994 its annual budget was 45 billion DM, most of which was spent in providing investment for plants, jobs, and environ-mental control and improvements.

The policies of the Trust Agency proved controversial from the very beginning. Official guidelines encouraged the development of small and medium-sized companies, which Detlev Karsten Rohwedder, the Agency's first president, saw as essential for the success of a fully functioning, com-petition-orientated market economy. The difficulty was that east Germans had no experience of managing industrial plants under free market condi-tions, a fact which led Rohwedder's successor, Birgit Breuel, to appoint western-trained management personnel to the supervisory boards of newly formed companies. While this move may have been economically neces-sary, it reinforced the subordinate role into which east Germans now see themselves as cast. Whatever easterners may have achieved within the confines of the socialist system appears to have little value in the rush to-wards a market economy.

Although it undoubtedly acted as a catalyst in transforming the eco-nomic landscape of eastern Germany, the Agency attracted strong criti-cism. Most seriously, its adherence to a strict policy of privatization has been held at least partly responsible for the deindustrialization of eastern Germany. Many plants could not be privatized and had to go into liquida-tion: 2,650 concerns had suffered this fate by May 1993 and the figure rose to 3,500 at the end of 1994. In 1993 most of the companies still waiting to be privatized were small: 70% of these employed fewer than one hundred employees and only 25% had a workforce of over one thousand; a relat-ively small number of workplaces (100,000) was involved overall. While the Agency was always obliged to ensure that such companies were capable of being privatized, it is fair to point out that it targeted a great deal of expenditure at sustaining the labour market. Apart from helping small craft-based and co-operative ventures to get off the ground, it pro-vided redundancy support for weak companies to the tune of 6,200 DM per employee.

The main constraint facing the Trust Agency was the slow pace of in-vestment in the new federal states. This was exacerbated by the 1992–93 recession. Although the Agency was wound up at the end of 1994 and its activities either redefined or subsumed in the responsibilities of the Federal Government, its task was far from completed. Many companies which had undertaken to invest and to provide secure jobs in the east had declined to honour agreements: by July 1993 50% of contracts were being renegoti-ated and only 852,000 out of the total number of agreements providing 1·45 million jobs were contractually secured. This amounts to a guaranteed investment of 88·2 billion DM out of a potential total of 179 billion DM. Foreign investment in eastern Germany has also been disappointing: in

1993 only three Japanese firms (Nippon Sanso, Asahi Glass, and Mitsubishi Motors) took up offers of investment arranged by the Agency.

6.5 Problems of the labour market

The challenge of absorbing an inefficient and strongly centralized command economy into the free market system has presented particular problems for the German labour market, especially at a time of recession. The following section will consider labour market policies in the new Germany, in particular developments in industrial relations and in the collective bargaining system. There has also been a marked trend towards decentralization in wage agreements and labour relations policy, which will be examined in some detail.

6.5.1 *Industrial relations and collective bargaining*

Before 1989 the economic prosperity of the FRG was due in no small measure to the uniquely co-operative nature of the German industrial relations system. Four years after unification the question arises of how this German model of 'social partnership' has reacted to the strains of integrating the former GDR.

The eastern states rapidly adopted western German collective bargaining arrangements and immediately ran into problems. The East German Trade Union Federation (FDGB) of the former GDR had acted as a compliant mass organization, serving the needs of the SED, who used it as an instrument of political and social control. The FDGB had no experience of the particular skills that are required in a pluralist society to resolve industrial conflicts. For its part the West German trade union movement found itself overtaken by the pace of events. The FRG-based unions failed at first to appreciate the urgency of organizing labour in the east along western lines; when they did so, they transferred their existing structures eastwards, but hastily and without adequate preparation. As one analyst commented:

> By late March 1990 the pace of the takeover strategy being pursued by Bonn began to accelerate rapidly, and the unions faced the choice of either mounting a breakneck effort at organizational expansion or watching the former GDR territory join the Federal Republic virtually devoid of functioning unions. Within only a few months, essentially from March to September 1990, the unions threw all their resources into creating an organizational basis that could fulfil the

need of East German employees to have democratic unions operating at their place of work. (Fichter 1993:25)

In 1990 the immediate and overriding concerns of ordinary trade union members in eastern Germany were standards of living, unemployment, and wage levels. From the outset the unions pressed for eastern wages to be brought up to western levels within three to five years. At the same time the speed of the unification process brought other important issues to the fore. When collective bargaining under market economy conditions began in East Germany in summer 1990, fears over higher prices and taxation, not to mention other costs, placed concerns about vocational qualifications, industrial rationalization, and reductions in the working week high on the unions' agenda. Nevertheless the overriding demand of the unions during this early phase remained the closing of the east–west wage differential. Before 1 July 1990, eastern wage levels were between 30% and 35% of western levels. By the time agreement between employers and unions was reached during the initial stage of collective bargaining in late 1990, they had risen to between 40% and 50%.

During the second round of collective bargaining, agreements were concluded to bring work grades and broad-band categories of wages and salaries into line with those in the west. Far more difficult and controversial was the third stage. From early 1991 onwards the trade unions' principle goal was to attain full wage parity between the old and the new federal states. The first collective agreement on a plan for achieving a phased harmonization of wages was signed on 1 March 1991: it applied to the metal-working and electrical industries in Mecklenburg-West Pomerania. A similar pilot agreement for Saxony, the industrial heartland of eastern Germany, provided for a series of gradual increases in wages and salaries. These were to be between 69% and 71% from 1 April 1992, between 80% and 82% from the 1 April 1993, and up to the full 100% of west German levels from 1 April 1994. The agreement also set targets for reducing the working week to thirty-nine hours from April 1994 and to thirty-eight hours from April 1996.

The Saxony agreement was accepted by the entire east German metal-working industry, and it also acted as a model for other sectors. Initially both the employers' associations and trade unions welcomed the harmonization of wages in phases: it allowed the unions time to consolidate their organizations in the new federal states and it afforded the employers a solid basis for long-term planning. However, as the prospects for the national economy worsened, the agreement came under harsh criticism from politicians, economists, and entrepreneurs alike. When the internally generated boom of 1991 in west Germany evaporated, and the east German economy moved into deep depression, employers revised their view of the phased wage harmonization agreement. For their part the unions were forced to reconsider their wages policy in the light of unacceptably high labour unit costs and persistently high unemployment levels.

The issue that brought wage harmonization back on the agenda was a revision clause that had been inserted in the collective agreements after they had been originally signed in March 1991. The clause allowed for revisions to be made to the phased wage harmonization agreement should the economy find itself under severe stress. Amidst intense controversy the employers invoked this clause at the beginning of 1993 and offered the trade unions a wage rise of only 9% in place of the increases agreed earlier. Furthermore the employers argued for the inclusion of an additional clause which would allow firms that were unable to meet the collectively agreed wage increases to negotiate separate agreements. Unions regarded the employers' move to cancel existing contractual arrangements as undermining the *Tarifautonomie* (the 'tariff system' by which wage agreements in Germany are reached independently by employers and unions and are legally binding on both partners) and the principles which had upheld the co-operative collective bargaining relationship for so long.

The ensuing dispute led to a short strike and was eventually taken to arbitration before the Metal Workers' Trade Union (*IG-Metall*) and the Federation of Metal and Electrical Industry Employers' Associations (*Gesamtmetall*) agreed to extend the phased wage harmonization agreement to 1996. As a result of the conflict metal industry workers in the east achieved a 26% wage increase. They also demonstrated that, even with a third of the labour force unemployed, they were not prepared to surrender their demands for wage parity. The unions did make one important concession: a clause was inserted into the agreement which made it possible for companies that could not afford to meet the collectively agreed wage increases to pay below the tariff rate.

6.5.2 *The challenge of decentralization*

The unique economic circumstances of the new federal states have opened the door to a reappraisal of established collective bargaining practices throughout Germany. Before 1989–90 the trend towards decentralization in collective bargaining had already emerged. This has now been reinforced by unification. In Germany industrial relations at plant or factory level are governed by the Works Constitution Act of 1971 which sets out standard procedures regulating the relationship between Works Councils and managements. The parameters of collective bargaining in Germany, which has always been conducted through the Works Councils at plant level, are clearly circumscribed and are legally defined.

Works Councils enjoy a series of statutory rights ranging from co-determination and consultation to the right to information. Co-determination rights can be legally enforced (through compulsory arbitration if necessary) and apply to working times, payment methods, bonusses and performance-related pay, holiday schedules, and to company policy on recruitment and dismissal. For those areas to which co-determination specifically applies, management and Works Councils are required by law to reach agreement through negotiation at plant level. Rights to information and consultation in other areas are not so strictly enforced, but in 1989 they were extended to include the introduction of new technology. Through its economic committee the Works Council also exerts a limited influence on the company's financial affairs, although it has no direct say in the financial policy of management.

A Works Council is subject to two constraints. First, it cannot negotiate over issues which are currently the object of collective bargaining between employers and trade unions. It is merely charged with ensuring that collective agreements signed by these parties are implemented and upheld at plant level. Second, the Works Constitution Act specifically requires management and the Council to work for the common good of the company: conflict of any type is prohibited by law.

It is clear from the above rights and constraints that a highly complex relationship exists between different levels of bargaining (that is, local and collective) and between the agents involved in industrial negotations. During the 1980s Works Councils in West Germany saw their role as the employees' negotiating representative increase: central to this development was the unions' recognition that Councils were essential to the system of employee participation and that they had to learn to co-exist with them. The metal-working industry, which employs 3·7 million, illustrates the importance of the Councils for the unions. In the 1990 Works Council elections the metal-workers voted 64,962 members into office in about 10,000 plants; 82% of these councillors belonged to the Metal Workers' Union. In practice Works Councils in large companies are dominated by the trade union for that industry.

Despite the domination of industries by large unions Germany has seen a shift since 1984 from bargaining at the level of industry and region towards negotiations at individual plants. The shift was foreshadowed by innovations in technology which were already being introduced in the 1970s and have been gaining pace ever since. As one commentator put it: 'Labour law must become more flexible: we must move away from (comparatively) rigid regulations governing a whole industry in favour of "made-to-measure" solutions for individual plants' (Hoyningen-Heune and Meier-Krenz 1988:294). The argument for moving away from inflexible, industry-wide labour laws that were no longer appropriate to the working conditions imposed by new technologies was reinforced by events that took place in 1984 when the Metal Workers' Union initiated a co-ordinated national campaign for a thirty-five hour working week. This led to the greatest industrial conflict in German post-war history and was re-solved only after Georg Leber, a former SPD government minister, per-suaded the parties to accept an award through arbitration. The so-called 'Leber Compromise' proved to be a crucial ruling for industrial relations, for it included the provision that the details of the nationally agreed work-ing week of 38·5 hours could now be implemented through local factory agreements. This 'opening clause' in the collective agreement represented a significant move towards the decentralization of industrial bargaining: vital negotations would now take place at plant level and a variety of dif-ferent working conditions would be created throughout the same industry.

The 'opening clause' has caused considerable friction, particularly among west German employers who until now have maintained a tradi-tional solidarity. Large companies have been able to extend their plant op-erating time through shift work, but the *Mittelstand,* the all-important small and medium-sized company sector accounting for over one-third of GDP and two-thirds of the workforce, has found itself at a disadvantage. In these firms, where single shift production is the rule, plant operating hours and working times have declined. Unhappy about the high level of recent wage agreements (on average 6·5% in 1991), more and more *Mittelstand* companies are calling for greater decentralization of collective bargaining. Employers' associations and trade unions, however, remain firmly commit-ted to the principles of collective bargaining and to sectoral or industry-wide agreements.

In eastern Germany the call for decentralized bargaining has come as a response to the disastrous economic performance there. But the structures required for effective bargaining are rudimentary in the eastern states. Works Councils, for instance, are essential bargaining agents at local plant level. In what was still the GDR, Works Councils were constituted be-tween December 1989 and April 1990: their legal basis was the short-lived Trade Union Law of the GDR and the various agreements that were worked out individually between factories and the Councils. After the Monetary, Economic, and Social Union of 1 July 1990, the Federal Ger-man Works Constitution Act (1971) came into force, displacing the earlier provision. The Act introduced a significant change in the relationship be-tween the nascent Works Councils and company managements. Companies, for their part, faced increasing pressure from the Trust Agency, competition from the west, and a deteriorating economic situation.

By spring 1991 the Works Constitution Act formed the basis of all elected Works Councils in east Germany. In many cases the 1991 Act signified a retreat from the (for the workforce) more favourable agreements which had been worked out earlier between individual councils and employers. Increasing tensions between the Works Councils and managements were exacerbated by the rapidly increasing unemployment figures after mid-1991. At first Works Councils were acquiescent about unemployment but their attitudes changed as joblessness became a permanent feature of the east German economy. From 1992 onwards Works Councils pressed for a more active trade union presence at plant level and for the creation of representative bodies which would not be fettered by the obligation of the Works Constitution Act to avoid conflict. In fact it has been shown that trade union representation at plant level in east Germany is marginal; in many small and medium-sized companies it is absent altogether (Ermischer and Preusche 1992:22).

Although trade union presence in local factories is weak, east German union members regard the role of organized labour at regional and federal level as vital. Such strong support stems from the perception by rank-and-file members that trade unions, at these higher levels, are the appropriate mechanism for achieving rapid wage increases. But the German system of collective bargaining depends in no small measure on a linkage between Works Councils and union organization at both regional and local branch level. In western Germany unions have integrated Works Council members into their regional bargaining machinery; here they act as a moderating influence. They try to avoid problems at plant level and have called in recent years for greater elasticity in negotiations in individual factories. Such flexibility has been seen as a stabilizing factor: 'In the "Germanic" countries the lower levels were anticipated, even shaped, by union leaderships, employers, and/or the law. Indeed, rather than representing oppositional forces they have often been focuses for inserting a concern for the fate of individual companies into union calculations' (Crouch 1993:287).

Currently in eastern Germany the link between plant level Works Councils and branch and regional level union organization has become dislocated. An effective strategy for collective bargaining is needed to overcome this. Despite the severe economic constraints in the eastern states Works Councils there do not accept that real wages must fall in order to reduce the rising level of structural unemployment. This attitude implies a shift away from sectoral level bargaining strategies, where the unions and employers understand the need for drastic changes in wage policies if the economy is to return to previous growth rates.

6.6 Economic development in the 1990s

The western German economy experienced a sharp recession at the turn of 1992–93. By the end of 1993 almost 500,000 jobs had been lost in the west; inflation was 4%; exports fell by 6%; and GDP contracted by 1·7%. German industry continued to face difficulties in international markets. Downswings in the economies of major European trading partners together with the appreciation of the German mark held export activity at a sluggish level. The vital machine tool industry was seriously affected: production fell 29% from the previous year to 10 billion DM, and the workforce shed 14,000 jobs. In 1993 Germany's share of the global export market for machine tools declined by 4% to 23%, and its former position as the leading exporter was lost to Japanese competitors, who improved their market share by 5% to 25%.

There were signs by the end of 1993 that the west German economy was stabilizing and would show a marginal increase in growth. On the supply side, conditions for stimulating investment in western Germany improved. Wage settlements were moderate and companies had rationalized production. Some sectors, such as housing construction, were buoyant. But the all-important labour market did not improve. In November 1993 the number of unemployed rose by 525,000 compared with the same month in the previous year; the total jobless was 2·49 million.

In contrast to western Germany the eastern states showed an upturn in economic activity during 1993. Since unification western Germany has earmarked huge financial transfers from the public purse in order to cushion the effects of adjusting to market conditions, to restructure industry, and to develop the infrastructure. In 1993 it became clear that east German industry was gathering momentum as new products emerged and manufacturing processes got under way. The manufacturing sector increased its output by 15% at the end of 1993 and there were signs that the economic recovery would encompass other sectors too. The weak point of east German industry remained exports: loss of the former eastern and central European markets had not been compensated by an expansion into western Europe.

Despite the increased level of economic activity the labour market in eastern Germany actually declined during 1993. To some extent the loss of jobs in manufacturing was balanced by expansion in the construction and the services sector. But the figure of 1·5 million unemployed in eastern

Germany in November 1993 was 65,000 higher than for the corresponding period of the previous year, an unemployment rate of 15·1%. Particularly worrying was the high percentage of unemployed women: their share of the jobless total reached a staggering 65%.

From mid-1993 onwards public sector finances throughout Germany deteriorated, with *Bund, Land,* and local authorities running substantial levels of debt. Although 1994 saw signs of an upswing in economic activity the public sector debt is an underlying problem that will not be resolved in the short term. Much of the debt can be ascribed to the crippling costs of unification, but the 1993 recession also had a major impact. At the end of 1993 there were almost four million unemployed, and a further two million people were on retraining, job creation, and early retirement schemes, all of which were federally financed. The total cost of welfare benefits and employment-related schemes amounted to 140 billion DM, the largest single item in the FRG's labour and social budget for 1994. In all, government expenditure increased by 6% to 54% of GDP in 1993; despite increases in VAT and personal income tax, total revenue increased by only 2·3%. In the current economic climate it is difficult to see how such a large public sector debt can be reduced.

6.7 Conclusion and outlook

While the processes of division and unification are not new to German history, each period has had its own set of political, social, and economic problems. As far as unification is concerned, these problems emerged after a period (from 1983 to 1990) of robust economic growth in the FRG, a growth shared by most Western industrial countries. But the era of uninterrupted economic prosperity that the FRG enjoyed after its foundation is past. Since 1992 the global and domestic economic environment on which the new united Germany depends has become less propitious. In such a climate the economic costs of unification, which are in any case much higher than expected, are proving difficult to bear. The post-unification transformation process has effectively created a dual economy within Germany: on the one hand a wealthy and relatively productive western half; on the other a much poorer eastern half which is struggling to overcome the legacy of a failed system of central planning.

The strains of integration are especially evident in the sphere of industrial relations. The restructuring of the east, high levels of unemployment, and increasing social tensions are pushing the existing system of collective bargaining to its limits. East–west wage differentials have led to an increase in plant-specific wage agreements which are not readily compatible with traditional collective bargaining arrangements based on centrally determined and legally binding contracts. Not all the pressure for change arises from unification: new technologies were already beginning to influence working practices in West Germany before the Berlin Wall came down. Nevertheless it is true that unification has acted as a catalyst for more rapid change than might otherwise have occurred. If Germany is to retain its neo-corporatist industrial relations institutions, these will have to adapt themselves to the post-unification situation.

German economists greeted the beginning of 1994 with optimism. They predicted an upswing in GDP, with industry about to increase its investments in plant and equipment. Manufacturing output and private consumption were, it was suggested, set to rise. German industry may indeed come out of the 1993 recession slimmer, more efficient and productive, and prepared for a 'lean production' style of manufacturing. But the signs are that further corrections and adjustments to the economy are needed. Certain problems, of which unemployment is one, will continue, while others, such as the public sector deficit, will require several years to eliminate. The recession forced Germany to ask some searching questions about its economic system. The answers exposed some glaring weaknesses, for example inefficient management practices, sagging productivity, and inflexible labour relations. However, the economic transformation process appears to have left the basic economic structures of the FRG intact, which suggests that stabilization at some point in the future is possible.

Further reading

A good historical introduction to the West German economy up to the mid-1960s is Stolper (1967). The succinct study by Abelshauser (1983) completes the picture to 1980. For detailed data on this period, Glastetter and others (1991) is indispensable. For a useful overview of the German economy since unification see Smyser (1992); more detailed discussions can be found in Priewe and Hickel (1991) and Hickel and Priewe (1994). An informative and erudite chapter on German industrial relations since 1990 is Jacobi (1992). The *Monthly Report of the Deutsche Bundesbank*, which includes statistical supplements, is a useful source of information and data on current developments.

7

Education in the New Germany

EDWARD NEATHER

7.1 Introduction

After the collapse of the Third Reich in 1945 the two German states developed quite distinct educational systems. The FRG sought to restore the traditional shape of the German school system with its selective *Gymnasien* and *Realschulen* (for explanations of school types see Appendix 7.1). The GDR rejected what it saw as bourgeois traditionalism and developed a system of comprehensive, polytechnical education, drawing largely on Soviet models. The separate development of the systems over a period of forty years was brought to a close by the events of 1989 and subsequent unification. Before charting the process of change within the former GDR since the collapse of the Berlin Wall, this chapter outlines the school system as it developed in the FRG.

7.2 Education in the FRG

The Basic Law of 1949 demonstrated a resolution to exclude from education in the FRG any possibility of the re-emergence of a centralized tyranny akin to the Nazi state. Responsibility for educational policy-making was widely distributed, leaving the federal states with sole responsibility for educational matters within their boundaries. This concern for decentralization, the so-called 'cultural sovereignty' (*Kulturhoheit*), produced significant variations in educational policy among the individual states. As a result, a number of bodies were set up in the FRG to provide a measure of co-ordination and joint planning. The most significant of these is the Standing Conference of State Ministers of Education, the *Kultusminister-konferenz* (KMK).

Because of the differences between the federal states, generalizations about education in Germany must be viewed with care. Nevertheless, the commonly adopted pattern of schooling after 1949 was the traditional one of *Volksschule* for the majority, with selection for *Realschule* or *Gym-*

nasium for the minority. Created largely in its present form by the Prussian statesman and thinker Wilhelm von Humboldt in 1808, the *Gymnasium* represents in many ways the kernel of traditional German educational philosophy. Humboldt was concerned with the value of general education, which, he felt, should aim at individual self-fulfilment regardless of vocational considerations. The *Volksschule* (comparable to the English elementary school) was concerned to meet the more narrowly vocational needs of the majority of citizens. The *Realschule* was seen as occupying a middle position. Founded in the nineteenth century to reflect the needs of a growing commercial class, it aimed to produce what would now be called 'middle-management' in industry. Developments after the national Educational Plan of 1959 divided the *Volksschule* into a primary school (*Grundschule*) and a secondary school (*Hauptschule*), so that all pupils attended a *Grundschule* before a decision was taken as to the most suitable schooling from the age of eleven.

Together with the provisions for vocational education discussed below, the above pattern of schooling has remained largely intact, despite various attempts at reform. In the early 1960s in particular, there was a growing awareness of the need for the system to adapt to changing circumstances. Georg Picht's influential book highlighting the 'catastrophe of German education' appeared in 1964 (Picht 1964). Five years later, an important article drew attention to research findings showing that 'certain groups, notably industrial and agricultural labourers, [are] grossly underrepresented in intermediate and secondary schools' (Robinsohn and Kuhlmann 1969:313). A series of plans was proposed to enable schools to postpone premature decisions about selection by introducing an orientation stage between primary school and selective secondary schools. A number of states went further and introduced *Gesamtschulen* (comprehensive schools), usually as pilot schools. Such developments depended heavily on the political complexion of the federal state (Bavaria, for example, has two *Gesamtschulen* compared with sixty-five in Hesse.) But comprehensive schools have remained controversial. None has been founded in Hesse since 1974, and CDU-controlled states have always strongly supported the traditional framework, including the selective *Gymnasium*. The tendency to label 'comprehensive' as 'Communist' has not always been avoided. This became very clear in the referendum held in North Rhine-Westphalia in 1978, when the 'Stop-Co-op' movement frightened voters with a campaign claiming that 'co-operative' (comprehensive) schools were a backdoor to a socialist education system.

One area of schooling where reforms were achieved was the *Oberstufe*, the equivalent of the English sixth form. The heart of the reform, decided by the KMK in 1972, was the abolition of the class as the basic unit of teaching and organization, and its replacement by a flexible system of course modules, each lasting for one semester and organized into groups of main and subsidiary options. Traditional assessment was replaced by a points system; the points gained formed part of an element of continuous assessment contributing to the final examination, the *Abitur* (Neather 1993).

This, in outline, is the West German school system which provided the alternative educational model for the new federal states after the collapse of the GDR. The way in which that model has replaced the Marxist system since 1989 is the subject of the rest of this chapter.

7.3 Education in the 'other' Germany

Education was one apparent success story of the 'other' Germany. Of course, within the political culture of the GDR, the primary purpose of education was to establish in the pupil's mind a 'socialist consciousness'. Not only the obvious subjects of politics, citizenship, and Marxism-Leninism served this overriding political objective; all school subjects and all vocational training shared the same aim. The traditional German inter-dependence of *Erziehung* (education of the whole person) and *Bildung* (education in terms of knowledge and subject study) was distorted by the dominance of the concept of the 'socialist personality' as the true objective of *Erziehung*. Choice of educational content and method were thus sub-jected to the over-arching educational mission of a socialist state. The dogmatism that drove the decision-makers of the GDR led them to dis-regard the frustrations of teachers and others who supported the principles of the system and the ideal of the unitary comprehensive school, the *Ein-heitsschule* or *Polytechnische Oberschule* (see Appendices 7.1 and 7.3), but at the same time deplored the way in which ideological principle be-came a reason for the state's failure to take note of differences in individ-ual achievements, interests, and personal development. These detractors felt that 'comprehensive education for all pupils' (*Einheitsschule für alle*) paradoxically failed to promote the equality of opportunity which was its primary purpose. By the time of the IX Pedagogical Congress of the GDR in June 1989, a significant number of participants in the education system were hoping for new thinking. Instead, the Congress produced, unbe-lievably when one considers that only six months later the whole society had collapsed, a euphoric account of achievement and success and a promise to continue in the same vein.

But the ideological bankruptcy of the ruling faction and its inability to listen to reasoned argument and constructive criticism from its own sup-

porters should not hide the fact that the educational system of the GDR
had significant achievements to its credit. Western commentators had
written about them in glowing terms:

> Beyond our borders exists an educational system which [...] has al-
> ready achieved many of those educational aims about which we have
> almost given up dreaming; a universal, horizontally structured edu-
> cational system with a ten-year comprehensive basic education for
> all; a consistent, scientifically based approach to teaching; a firmly
> established link between work and learning in the form of polytech-
> nic education, and much more besides. (Brämer 1981:87)

There is no simple answer to the question of what the educational system of the GDR achieved. During the *Wende* internal critics of the system
felt very strongly that here at last was the chance to reassert the principles
of a just and fair comprehensive system, allowing individual talents to be
developed. For some months writers were optimistic about the opportunity
for a new beginning based, this time, on a genuinely socialist school system. The first all-German elections of 2 December 1990 removed any such
possibility: the election of Conservative (CDU) Parliaments in all but one
of the new states ensured that the most significant change to the education
system would be the importation of federal German structures. To what
extent any part of the GDR education system has been preserved and to
what extent federal German patterns have been adopted will be examined
later. First, this chapter explores the resurgence of more democratic socialist ideas as an alternative to the centralist policies of the preceding years.
Second, that debate is set against the background of events and of political
necessities as they emerged. Finally, the most recent developments in the
new federal states are analysed.

7.4 Hopes for a new socialist future

The period before the *Wende* saw a debate unfold in East German society
in which groups were prepared to speak out against the barrenness and ri-
gidity of existing structures. Groups of frustrated teachers and lecturers
raised issues concerning the democratization of their schools, and there
was a real hope that the IX Pedagogical Congress of June 1989 would initiate significant changes to the system. These hopes were dashed and observers were left with the feeling that the system was incapable of reform:
'For many educationalists in the GDR the bitter truth was all too evident,
that the school together with the theoretical model of education which it

represented had reached a dead end' (Hage 1990:20). At the root of problems in the GDR's education system was an excess of political ideology. This had stifled individualism, democratic processes, and dialogue. To move forward would have meant abandoning this ideology, but that was not possible within such a rigidly structured and autocratic state.

In the last days of the GDR the gap between the claims that had been made for education and the reality that was obvious to all had produced a form of public hypocrisy which manifested itself in paying lip-service to a system in which nobody believed any longer. Such *Doppelzüngigkeit* ('speaking with two tongues') was symptomatic of a serious collapse of social values (Wirth 1990:73).

The debate on education which took place in the months following the regime's collapse was in many ways a continuation of the discussion which had already started and been stifled. The main difference was that the debate was now encouraged and had a real hope of achieving vital changes. Much of what was written between November 1989 and May 1990 shows that individuals were convinced that they had at last genuine freedom to influence the course of events. Many commentators were looking for ways of renewing socialism by adopting a more open and democratic model (for example, Land 1990). Only later did it become clear that reunification would entail the adoption of existing West German patterns of educational provision. Looking back to this period, a visiting professor from the University of California sees it as a time of great volatility and excitement:

> Parents and pupils achieved great freedom of action in these months. The conditions arose for a radical transformation of school and education. Thus the first months of 1990 became one of the most fruitful periods in educational renewal. [...] For this period one can rightly claim that the political and pedagogical liberties in the schools of East Germany were entirely the work of the East Germans themselves. (Rust 1992:3).

At the forefront of the concerns and hopes expressed during this period of renewal stood the notion of a truly democratic education which would allow pupils to grow and develop creatively and without the imposition of forms of thought and behaviour derived from a sterile ideology. One writer, A. Hoffmann, expresses the hopes of that time, demanding that individuality be cherished and education cultivate tolerance towards alternative ways of thought. Hoffmann summarizes his hopes and recommendations under three headings: democratization, individualization, and creativity. Democratization is essential because pupils need to participate in the decisions being made about their lives: 'The authoritarian school failed, for the most part, to develop the need of young people to strive for autonomy; it often blocked self-sufficiency and independence in thinking and in forming judgments' (Hoffmann 1990:9–10). Young people, he says, need to broaden their horizons, seek experience, and see the world. It is clear from his proposals that Hoffmann sought to meet the specific criticisms which had been levelled at the East German school system and at the attitudes of young people that prevailed before the *Wende*. Now that the shackles were removed it was necessary for schools to overcome 'indifference, an unwillingness to speak out, and a lack of social commitment'. The only way to meet these problems was to make schools more democratic.

Approaching the question of individualization, Hoffmann again starts from criticisms of the existing structures. The GDR version of the *Einheitsschule* had reached a dead-end because its insistence on producing stereotypes precluded dynamic change: 'It becomes more and more obvious that the stereotyping and the mediocre thought-processes which it produces are an obstacle to economic, political, and social development'. Hoffmann sees individual thought and initiative as the only way in which solutions will be found to the great problems facing the world. So the *Einheitsschule*, which had once been seen as one of the achievements of GDR education, is now summed up in the telling sentence: 'It is clearer than ever that what was supposedly suitable for everybody has the great disadvantage that it wasn't really suitable for anybody' (Hoffmann 1990:12–13).

Finally Hoffmann considers creativity, claiming: 'In the schools of the GDR, nimbleness of mind plays a subordinate role.' Although the standards of the weaker pupils had been raised by the strategy of 'nobody gets left behind', and the effects of 'levelling down' had been to 'level down to a relatively high plateau', there had been a failure to meet the needs of more gifted pupils, particularly of independent thinkers. Teaching methods were notoriously unimaginative: teachers had been wary even of using creative and gaming techniques for fear of not being thought serious.

Hoffmann's study is valuable in two ways. First, it isolates a number of the most commonly repeated criticisms of the achievement of the *Einheitsschule*. Second, it makes proposals for change at a time when freedom of movement for future developments seemed possible. The claims for freedom and creativity which Hoffmann articulates also reflect the renewed interest in forms of free and alternative schools that emerged during the *Wende*. Such schools had been banned under Communism (Paetz and Pilarczyk 1990). Much of the debate was carried on in local working groups made up of teachers and other interested individuals. After considering the need to introduce a humanistic and liberating form of education, one such group in Dresden concluded: 'For the city of Dresden, this can mean [...] reviving the traditions of Waldorf pedagogy which was destroyed by the Nazi regime after 1933 and was again liquidated by Stalinism after 1949' (*Arbeitsgruppe Bildung und Erziehung* 1989:3). In retrospect it is hard to imagine the ferment of ideas and opinions that materialized in those heady times when a myriad of working groups was set up in every town and community to reshape the structures of society and daily life. There emerged a powerful reaction against the old structures, often expressed in terms reminiscent of the idealism and optimism of Rousseau or Pestalozzi:

> Education in our society must make an effective contribution, both today and in the future, to the development of independently thinking and acting human beings who have been educated in the traditions of humanism and who will be able and willing to take independent and responsible decisions and to transform the conditions of their own lives. (*Arbeitsgruppe Bildung und Erziehung* 1989:3)

For every aspect of education from kindergarten to university these working groups produced papers, discussed reforms, and rejected views of education which were too narrowly focused, too ideological, or too lacking in concern for individual growth. It cannot be said that such discussions had no purpose. They were part of a vast renewal of humanistic thought, a chance to revisit ideas and visions which had been hitherto forbidden territory. What now lends the documents a special poignancy is the knowledge that in the event the renewal of GDR schools largely assumed the form of a takeover of Western German educational principles and structures. Although the changes would bring a new freedom of thought and opinion and a more open curriculum, the hoped-for new socialism in a new society was not to be:

> The question, which is fully justified, should now be asked: what became of all these dreams, expectations and efforts? [...] In a historically almost unique process the entire education system of the GDR was dismantled. Kindergartens and after-school groups were abandoned; almost 6,000 polytechnic and Sixth Form Schools were closed and transformed into schools in a selective system with totally different conditions for their structures, their personnel, and the content of the curriculum. (Döbert 1993:1)

Indeed, even as the parents, teachers, and students were having their discussions, politicians were working towards other objectives. As early as

February 1990 Jürgen Möllemann, the FRG Minister of Education, was talking of 'a step-by-step integration of the educational systems in a future German Republic':

> Central to much of the debate about school reform were the twin principles of the *Einheitsschule* and polytechnic education. These principles had been the foundation of the GDR's comprehensive school, the POS, even if the reality had disappointed the hopes. (*Die Welt*, 14 February 1990)

During this period articles in the *Deutsche Lehrerzeitung*, the professional journal for teachers in Germany, offered a week-by-week picture of the argument about the virtues or vices of the *Einheitsschule*. For example:

> What, then, does the future hold for the GDR school? Can we speak only of failures? Or are there features which could be retained in a European Germany? [...] Conservatives in the GDR are fighting for us to adopt the school system of the Federal Republic with its selective schools. [...] The comprehensive school is to be cast aside. [...] Instead of retaining the progressive framework of the comprehensive school so that a thorough reform and new structures can evolve from within, many need only to hear the word *Einheitsschule* to make them see red. (Futasz 1990:3)

The opposite point of view, however, was frequently stated:

> A society based on achievement urgently needs schools based on achievement and on providing the maximum opportunity to develop all talents. What we need is [...] a selective school system. (Müller and others 1990:4)

Polytechnic education was also at the forefront of the debate:

> In the process of fundamental social restructuring which has now begun in the GDR there is clearly a need for discussions about the educational system, in particular, about the extent to which all the goals, programmes, and methods of polytechnic education may still meet social conditions and requirements. (Erbrecht and Klein 1990:67)

The to and fro in the debate about what should be imported from the FRG and what should be retained from the GDR was an essential part of the process of coming to terms with the sudden and violent changes that were sweeping through the established system. In reality the possibilities for freedom of action and choice were strictly limited. After the elections of 18 March 1990 preparations for reunification proceeded apace and it became increasingly clear that the predominant pattern of education in the new federal states would be firmly based on West German models. The following section examines what these patterns were and assesses the scope for variation and adaptation provided within the terms of the Hamburg Agreement which was reached by the federal states of the FRG in 1964.

7.5 Educational developments during the *Wende*

In its efforts to meet the demands of swiftly changing circumstances after the fall of the Berlin Wall, the SED hastily published an action programme that included proposals for reforms in education. While admitting the need for reform, the document was encumbered by the phraseology of the old regime: 'The new youth policy of the Party must contribute to the process whereby young, confident citizens grow up to commit themselves actively to a modern socialism in their homeland [...]' (*Neues Deutschland*, 11–12 November 1989). The tone clearly fails to address the needs of the situation. The document proposes the abolition of military training (*Wehrunterricht*) from the curriculum and from apprenticeships. It declares that examinations must be changed so that they record real achievement. Students are to be given the chance to participate in decisions about educational reform.

Soon after he became Prime Minister on 13 November 1989, Hans Modrow (SED) included a major statement on the future of education in an address to the People's Chamber (Anweiler 1990:100–2). Modrow declared that his government would initiate a wide-ranging debate leading to a new Education Law. His speech expresses the wish that positive elements from the past be retained but accepts the widespread criticism that the East German system had encouraged conformity and discouraged individual thinking and diversity of opinion.

After the GDR elections of 18 March 1990 a new Ministry of Education and Science was created under the prime-ministership of Lothar de Maizière (CDU). Intended as a transitional body it replaced the two ministries hitherto responsible for schools and higher education. The transitional ministry remained the highest authority for education until unification on 2–3 October. In the meantime the Law for the Introduction of Federal States of 22 July 1990 was passed; this ensured that education would eventually become the responsibility of the states, as in the FRG. A first move towards adopting this structure was a decree of the Council of

Ministers which established local authorities (*Landesschulämter*) as provisional bodies alongside the district authorities (*Kreisschulämter*) that were currently administering local education. A further decree of 30 May 1990 set up new consultative structures at the level of school administration. The core of these arrangements was the School Conference (*Schulkonferenz*) for each school. This was a forum of teachers, parents, pupils (in a ratio of 2:1:1), and representatives of the community. At the level of federal state (*Land*) and district (*Kreis*) advisory committees (*Landesschulbeiräte* and *Kreisschulbeiräte*) and bodies analogous to the School Conference were established (*Landesschulkonferenz* and *Kreisschulkonferenz*). All existing headteachers were dismissed and their jobs redefined. They could then reapply for their posts and indeed a good many were reappointed. These appointments were decided by district school inspectors (*Kreisschulräte*) or, in the case of schools teaching to *Abitur* level, by regional inspectors (*Landesschulräte*) after hearing the views of the School Conference.

7.5.1 *Private schools*

On 22 July 1990 the People's Chamber passed a law allowing the introduction of private schools. The law also recognized church schools (*Pro- und Oberseminare*). These had existed under the Communist regime, though their leaving examinations were not acknowledged by the state and they could therefore train only church workers. The new law recognized the Waldorf schools, which were already being established, and opened the way for other forms of private and experimental schools.

The collapse of the monolithic centralized education system had brought about a renewed interest in a variety of types of schools (Paetz and Pilarczyk 1990) and the law on private schools was a first response to parents' demands for alternatives to state schooling. The law approximated to the FRG's provision on private schools. According to this the state agreed to provide 70–90% of finance, while the schools fulfilled specified obligations regarding school attendance and leaving certificates.

7.5.2 *The ten-year* Polytechnische Oberschule (POS)

In the first phase of post-*Wende* restructuring the core of the ten-year POS was not touched. However, by establishing sets by ability (*Leistungsklassen*) in years nine to ten (ages fifteen to sixteen) the reformers took a first step towards differentiation by ability, as is customary in the FRG. *Leistungsklassen* for years nine to ten were also established in the sixth-form *Erweiterte Oberschule* (EOS) which had previously taken pupils from year eleven. In this way the EOSs extended their intake downwards and prepared to become *Gymnasien* at a later date. Similarly, *Leistungsklassen* in existing ten-year POSs extended their provision upwards to include years eleven to twelve, thereby moving closer towards either a selective *Gymnasium* or a comprehensive *Gesamtschule* with sixth-form intake (*Oberstufe*). For the school year 1990–91 the new classes were established at 250 EOSs and 550 POSs. The main criticism levelled at the POS during the *Wende* was the lack of differentiation between pupils of varying ability. The uniformity of its curriculum and its failure to make demands on able pupils were held responsible for what was generally agreed to be mediocrity of achievement. While holding, at least during this transitional stage, to the principle of the ten-year comprehensive school, proposals for reforming the POS crystallized around ideas for introducing flexibility: these included differentiating by ability and allowing pupils to transfer between schools.

As for the curriculum, the study of Russian became an option alongside other languages instead of a compulsory first foreign language for all. The rush to adopt English as the principal language option exposed an acute shortage of teachers for this subject. There were also problems over the provision of Latin if the subject were to achieve the same high status as in the FRG. An important part of the POS timetable under the old regime had been work experience (*polytechnischer Unterricht*). After the *Wende*, however, many firms rushed to get rid of their obligations to provide pupils with productive work, which was seen as an extra cost in already difficult circumstances. Hitherto work experience had required the pupil to spend one morning every fortnight in a factory or in some other productive environment. In 1990–91 this system was replaced by a new subject, *Technik*, which approximated more closely to FRG notions of work experience (*Arbeitslehre*). It was claimed that, instead of the narrow concentration on production, the whole area of technical and industrial work experience should enter the curriculum. Information technology would also be taught earlier. A ministerial decision of 6 June 1990 established that firms could not unilaterally break their existing agreements. At the same time, arrangements were introduced to provide financial support for such schemes. As a temporary measure many schemes were transferred to the district (*Kreis*) for administration and financing. The subject of *Staatsbürgerkunde* (essentially Marxism-Leninism) was replaced by western *Gesellschafts-kunde* (social studies). Textbooks were retained for the time being in certain politically neutral subjects, but in subjects such as foreign languages and social studies there was a large input of books from west German publishers (offered free of charge in the first year).

7.5.3 *The* Erweiterte Oberschule (EOS)

The main criticism levelled at the EOS concerned the element of selectivity for entry into year eleven. In the old GDR entry numbers depended on economic planning figures; political criteria also played a role in the selection process. This selectivity, particularly the exclusion of pupils on political grounds, was seen as wholly contrary to the newly formulated right to education. Also, the two years of the EOS were seen as inadequate preparation for higher education, especially when compared with the *Abitur* course in the FRG which normally lasts three years. The reform process first removed entry quotas. Entry to the *Abitur* course could now be decided by individual performance and parental choice. As a result the number of pupils entering the 1990–91 school year doubled. As explained earlier, preparatory courses for the *Abitur* were also established by introducing years nine and ten as *Leistungsklassen*. This meant that the EOS became virtually a four-year *Abitur* course. A full six-year *Gymnasium* would then be established by allowing transfer to the *Abitur* after year six. The élite special schools of the former GDR could be brought into the system as *Gymnasien* with special subject profiles (west Germans had expressed interest in keeping the special schools for music and sport).

As for evaluation there was particular urgency that the *Abitur* in the new federal states should reach parity with that in the FRG. The KMK had made a commitment to achieve this by 1994. Only if this target was met was the KMK ready to allow the existing GDR *Abitur* to be accepted as an entry qualification for the universities of the FRG.

7.5.4 *Vocational education*

The main problem about vocational education in the east was that firms could no longer support the financial burdens of training now that they were exposed to the cost-cutting and competitive disciplines of the market economy. Various models of reform were tried, only to be overtaken by a new government ruling. The currency union of 1 July 1990 obliged the GDR 'to seek to achieve the legal framework and career structure of vocational education in the FRG'. With this aim in mind the People's Chamber passed a special law on 19 July 1990, preparing the way for the adoption of the FRG's Laws on Vocational Education from 1 September. This meant that the GDR took over the West German dual system and that Works Training Schools (*Betriebsberufsschulen*), which had been a feature of industrial plants in the GDR, were replaced by Vocational Schools (*Berufsschulen*) under the authority of the local district. The GDR also adopted the classification of trades and professions laid down by the Law on Vocational Training of 1969, including all appropriate regulations and curricula. A special case was the vocational course leading to the award of the *Abitur*, which had existed in the GDR. Many in the former GDR wished to retain the vocational *Abitur* but West German authorities were opposed to continuing with a qualification of this kind alongside the traditional *Abitur* and it was eventually discarded.

7.5.5 *Higher education and teacher training*

The first demand after the *Wende* was to reintroduce the traditional independence and autonomy of universities in the GDR. An independent Conference of Rectors of the GDR was swiftly established, but dissolved in the summer of 1990. Institutions of higher education had been organized on the Soviet model in separate subject areas (*Sektionen*), which were now abolished in favour of a return to a traditional faculty structure. In the Provisional Higher Education Law of 28 September 1990 the faculty structure was established in accordance with the Framework Law of 1976, which laid down the framework for the whole of higher education in the FRG. Just as the Hamburg Agreement set out the organizational structure for schools in the new federal states (see Section 7.5.6), so did the Framework Law become the basis for reforming the universities of the former GDR. And just as federal German administrators were drafted in to set up the new school systems, west German professors were appointed to faculties as Foundation Deans with similar powers for universities. Besides the restoration of autonomy to the institutions, there were important questions of academic freedom and course content to consider. These included how to encourage respect for independent study and critical freedom on the part of students. Students also needed to learn how to make their own course decisions and to choose study options.

Basic studies in Marxism-Leninism, which had formed part of every student's course, were scrapped. The demise of what was a major element in higher education studies highlighted a particular problem in the integration of the two systems, namely staffing. The ratio of staff to students in the GDR was 1:5 and in the FRG 1:20; lecturers had much lighter teaching loads in the East. On 3 October 1990 the universities received the right to dismiss lecturers. The grounds for dismissal were either inadequate professional qualification or personal unsuitability. This ruling was aimed in part at lecturers who owed theirs jobs solely to their activity in the SED. Evidence of *Stasi* involvement led to immediate dismissal. Some institutions with a strongly ideological bent were dissolved and occasionally reconstituted with new staff. As with other aspects of education policy, the attempt was made to fill the gap between unification and the eventual passing of laws by the new federal states.

As for initial teacher training, the most pressing need was to require teachers of primary age children to qualify to university level. In the GDR trainees for primary education had been accepted at the age of sixteen and given a four-year training course in a Teacher Training College (*Institut für Lehrerbildung*). They could then teach in years one to three (*Unterstufe*) of a ten-year POS. Secondary level teachers who had not attended either a Pedagogical University (*Pädagogische Hochschule*, PH) or a university department would now all undergo university training; the PH would be incorporated into the universities, as had happened in most states in the old FRG. For teachers from class four onwards (*Mittelstufe*), two subjects were to be studied at university, but with a free choice, which had not been available previously. Studies for teachers of classes four to ten were to last four years. For *Abitur* level and vocational education, training would last five years. After a two-year period of foundation study (*Grundstudium*), a decision could be taken about which school type the prospective teacher should prepare for. Thus teacher training, which had been shaped to meet the demands of a largely comprehensive secondary education, started to adapt to school type, with length of training the decisive factor in subsequent status and salary. Another new element was the introduction of the two-phase teacher training model from the FRG. This required the candidate, after university studies, to complete a school-based training period of eighteen to twenty-four months (*Referendariat*) under the authority of the federal state.

7.5.6 From Wende *to unification: challenges for the new federal states*

The early period of educational change shows how eastern Germany increasingly adopted significant elements of the educational system of the FRG. In the final sitting of the Inter-German Education Commission on 26 September 1990 this process received inter-governmental approval; the meeting also recommended harmonizing the school year and the holidays for 1990–91. It was stressed that 'the principle of cultural sovereignty of the federal states is of fundamental significance in the process of integration of the educational systems'. This appeared to offer the new states some room for manoeuvre to maintain positive elements of their past system if they so wished. But paragraph 37.4 of the Unification Treaty stated that the new states must base their education systems on the Hamburg Agreement of the KMK. How could the new states balance the requirements of the Agreement with the principle of cultural sovereignty? The following section considers in detail the systems that have been developed by the new states.

7.6 The school system in the new states

Section 7.4 discussed aspects of the debate which took place in the GDR when it was still assumed that there was a possibility of forging new institutions of education. But it soon became clear that the agenda for change would take the form of introducing significant elements of the educational system of the FRG. Paragraph 37.4 of the Unification Treaty put the matter beyond further debate by stating that the eastern states must base their education systems on the Hamburg Agreement of the KMK.

7.6.1 *The Hamburg Agreement*

The Hamburg Agreement of 1964 is the most important regulation governing aspects of common policy and practice in the education systems of the original eleven states of the FRG (Staupe 1991:85–86). Its adoption by the new states in the Unification Treaty established that they would have the freedom of action allowed by the principle of cultural sovereignty; at the same time this freedom would effectively be curtailed by the basic terms of the agreement (Stamm 1991:188–91).

The Hamburg Agreement lays down such details as the length of compulsory schooling, the dates of the school-year, the duration of holidays, the recognition of leaving certificates, marking standards, and the starting age for learning foreign languages. It describes the permissible school types and specifies criteria for allowing pupils to move from one type to another. It lays down the *Grundschule* as the basic primary stage for all pupils. For secondary education it describes the *Hauptschule, Realschule, Gymnasium*, and, since the late 1960s and early 1970s, the *Gesamtschule* (Appendix 7.1). It also defines the appropriate leaving certificates and final examinations for each school type. To the Hamburg Agreement were added a number of subsequent decisions of the KMK, such as the regulations relating to the conduct of sixth-form education, dating from 1972 and 1988.

Apart from the provisions of the Hamburg Agreement there is also an important political dimension to education in the new Germany. In the first all-German elections of December 1990, only Brandenburg among the new federal states elected a Social Democratic (SPD) government. The CDU governments of the other eastern states were certain from the onset to be conservative in matters of education, in particular in the choice between a selective or a comprehensive system of schooling.

7.6.2 The School Laws of the new federal states

Space does not permit a detailed analysis of education in all the eastern states (for more information see: *Dokumentation der Schulgesetze der Länder*, KMK 1992). After providing a general summary this section considers in detail an aspect of educational provision in two of the new federal states: the Saxon proposal for a *Mittelschule* and the Brandenburg plans for vocational education.

During the transition to unification each new federal state was allocated a partner state from the old FRG. Administrators from the partner state were closely involved in every aspect of development in the east, and many now find themselves in permanent senior positions there. It comes as no surprise, therefore, that the structure, style, and wording of the new School Laws correspond closely to the laws which exist in West Germany.

The state that has most completely taken over the school structure of the highly conservative western model is Mecklenburg-West Pomerania, which has opted for the primary school to be followed by a three way division into *Gymnasium, Realschule,* and *Hauptschule*. In general the new states have not favoured the *Hauptschule*. They are aware of the criticisms aimed at this type of school in west Germany, and at the problems associated with it becoming a 'school for left-overs' (Rösner 1989:11). Elsewhere, Saxony, Thuringia, and Saxony-Anhalt have all proposed a two-way division after the primary school. Each has set up selective *Gymnasien*, not only because of the political imperatives of their CDU governments but also in response to the widespread sense of under-achievement in the GDR and to parental demands for selective schools promoting achievement. After the selection process for the *Gymnasium* has creamed off the best pupils, there is a single school for all those pupils not selected, a sort of 'skimmed' comprehensive school. This establishment goes by a number of names (in Saxony the *Mittelschule*, in Thuringia the *Regelschule*, and in Saxony-Anhalt the *Sekundarschule*). But the underlying philosophy is the same: to maintain at least an element of the *Einheitsschule* or comprehensive education, even though the system as a whole has become selective. In Brandenburg, the SPD government and the proximity to Berlin have ensured that there are no *Hauptschulen*, but there are a small number of *Realschulen* alongside the *Gymnasien* and *Gesamtschulen* which form the secondary school choice for the majority of pupils.

In all the eastern states restructuring of education has led on the one hand to the disappearance of the vocational and work experience arrangements which were generally reckoned to be a worthwhile feature of the GDR and on the other to the introduction of the traditional West German dual pattern of vocational and technical education. This aspect of the system is considered more closely below.

7.6.3 *The Saxon* Mittelschule

The Saxon *Mittelschule* is an example of one area in which the new federal states have chosen a path of their own. The *Mittelschule* teaches pupils from classes five to ten (ages ten to sixteen; see Appendix 7.4). Classes five and six are regarded as a period of observation and orientation to allow for transfers to the *Gymnasium* if it emerges that pupils have been wrongly placed. For this reason the curriculum for these two years is common to both *Mittelschule* and *Gymnasium* and pupils are taught in mixed ability classes rather than sets. From class seven there is setting by ability and aptitude, so that pupils follow what is effectively either a *Hauptschule* or a *Realschule* programme within a single establishment. Pupils choosing the *Hauptschule* programme may choose a specific core or profile of subjects relating either to technology or to domestic economy. Those taking the *Realschule* path may choose from a range of profiles, with a bias towards languages, economics, or technology. The teaching within the profile specialism takes up four hours each week alongside the rest of the general curriculum. The subjects outside the profile, such as German, maths, and sciences, are also taught in ability sets. Depending on the course followed pupils take the appropriate school leaving certificate, either *Hauptschulabschluß* in class nine or *Realschulabschluß* in year ten. As in the west German system these leaving certificates give the right to further education, either in vocational schools or in a *Gymnasium* providing courses that lead to the *Abitur*, if the pupil demonstrates sufficient ability.

It remains to be seen how the *Mittelschule* proves itself in the coming years. Fears that it will be *Hauptschule* in all but name are angrily rejected by Education Ministry officials, but the pressure from parents for places at the *Gymnasium* is considerable and English experience in areas where selective and non-selective schools operate together is not encouraging.

7.6.4 Vocational education and the Brandenburg model

Technical and vocational education enjoyed a high profile in the GDR. The whole system was strictly controlled from the centre to ensure that the output of trained workers matched the demands of central planning. According to the Constitution every young person had the right, on leaving school at sixteen, to learn a trade. Over two-thirds of apprentice entrants were trained at Works Training Schools; the remainder attended training schools run by the state at local level (*Kommunale Berufsschulen*). Although the system was successful in producing a high level of practical skills it could be criticized for failing to plan for the future: training was too closely integrated into existing work routines and was embedded into the patterns of an outdated economic structure.

As in all aspects of education in the eastern states a colossal reorganization has been necessary in vocational education. The West German dual system has been introduced for the lowest level of vocational education. In the old FRG some two-thirds of an age group entered the dual system either directly after the period of compulsory schooling or after further years of education. The basis of the dual system is part-time attendance until the age of eighteen at a vocational school (*Berufsschule*) where students receive theoretical instruction in the area of their chosen skills and an extension of general education; at the same time they are given practical skills training in a factory or other work centre. This vocational education is financed largely by the employers. The entire system requires a significant element of agreement and co-operation between all partners, including unions, employers organizations, and educational authorities. The *Berufsschule* forms the basis of a complex system of different types of vocational training schools: the *Berufsfachschule* requires at least one year's full-time study to prepare skilled craftsmen for certain professions; the *Fachoberschule* is a higher level vocational school which requires an entry qualification of at least the level of the *Realschule* leaving-certificate and leads to a technically based university entrance qualification; the *Fachschule* is intended for students who have finished their apprenticeship, have additional practical experience, and now wish to extend their qualifications.

A feature of vocational education in West Berlin since 1979 has been the *Oberstufenzentrum* (OFZ), a career-related school centre gathering together all the aforementioned institutions under one roof. This pattern is now being developed in Brandenburg. Although centred on vocational and technical education, the OFZ also encompasses in its most fully-developed form the sixth-form provision for the immediate geographical area. The OFZ is still to a large extent a principle of organization rather than a physical reality: Brandenburg has not yet had time to build centres such as those established in Berlin, but the concept is an interesting one. In 1994 some forty OFZs had been set up, providing about 154 training courses at the level of the *Berufsschule*. Almost 100% of students who are eligible complete the school part of their 'dual' course in the OFZ.

7.7 Current issues and concerns in the new federal states

Enough time has passed in the process of adapting the educational patterns of the FRG to the eastern states for it to be possible to draw some conclusions and to define the main problem areas (Weishaupt and Zedler 1994, Rolff and others 1994). These areas are to do with the popularity (or otherwise) of certain school types, regional disparities in educational provision, and the consequences of a dramatically falling birth-rate.

7.7.1 *Public perceptions of the* Hauptschule *and the* Gymnasium

Although only one eastern state has actually introduced the *Hauptschule*, schools such as the Saxon *Mittleschule* do have *Hauptschule* streams. However, whether viewed as separate schools or streams within a school, the *Hauptschule* is unpopular. In Saxony-Anhalt, for example, 63·3% of all children attend the *Sekundarschule* but only 9·5% of pupils are in the *Hauptschule* stream. Dissatisfaction with the comprehensive tradition of the former POS and the lack of job outlets for leaving certificates from the *Hauptschule* make it unlikely that this form of school will gain any popularity with parents.

Entry figures for the *Gymnasium* are very different. In 1992–93 some 30% of pupils entered a *Gymnasium* and it is highly likely that this percentage will rise. Despite the absence of a comparable school type in the GDR and the uncertainty of parents and teachers during the transition phase, the popularity of the *Gymnasium* seems to suggest some effort to return to an earlier German tradition in education. The figures also show that only 5% of pupils in the *Gymnasien* in the east had to repeat a class, which compares favourably with 4·3% in the old FRG.

7.7.2 *Regional disparities in school provision*

One of the striking characteristics of the restructuring of education in the new federal states is the very clear regional disparity in the choice of schools following primary school. Regional variations in available school places have already revealed some startling differences. For example, in the communities of Thuringia the proportion of pupils transferring to the *Gymnasium* varies between less than 10% and more than 60%. In the towns, similar variations have been recorded. In Erfurt the fluctuation is between 19% and 67%. Factors influencing such variations are not only the regional differences mentioned above but also the concentration of social classes in certain areas and the aspirations of parents. It seems likely that such regional disparities are likely to increase as the spread of a free housing market in the east leads to more social segregation in residential areas.

7.7.3 *The results of a falling birth-rate*

The sharply declining birth-rate in the east since the fall of the GDR is a potent factor in school reorganization. In Brandenburg, for example, the birth-rate has dropped by 65% (from 32,997 in 1989 to 11,669 in 1993). In every state of the former GDR the rate of fall is between 35% and 42%. These figures have had a marked effect on planning. There has been an attempt to ensure that primary schools can be maintained at one-form entry and that secondary schools can be at least a two-form entry. Other attempts are being made to integrate classes between various school types. The *Gymnasium* seems able to survive the fall in the birth-rate and is projected to achieve an average three-form entry. But many other schools are threatened with closure if the decline in the birth-rate continues. A survey in Mecklenburg-West Pomerania concludes that some 20% of *Grundschulen* will close if the principle of one class per year on entry is to be maintained (Baumbach and others 1994). The figure for the *Realschule* is 40%. The alternative to extensive school closures will be a full-scale review of the achievements and possibilities of small schools.

7.8 Conclusions

The educational changes in eastern Germany have had a mixed reception. The general opinion during the first phase of readjustment was that the new federal states should seek inner reform and not introduce an alien system. Surveys of teachers and parents carried out in 1993 in Thuringia show that scepticism about the imported system continues. A majority of teachers and parents claim that the primary stage of the old POS was superior to the new *Grundschule* and that the secondary stage was better than the new *Regelschule*. The figures show a strong feeling in favour of the *Gesamt-*

schule (although Thuringia has only three such schools altogether), particularly among parents and teachers of the *Grundschule*. Other findings make it clear that parents and teachers believe that significant elements of the old educational provision have been lost, notably, schools close to home, whole-day provision for pupils with working mothers, and sporting and leisure facilities.

The key question asked in the surveys was: 'Taking everything into consideration, do you think that the school system introduced in 1991 has brought advantages or disadvantages?' Teachers are the most positive in their responses, particularly those in *Gymnasien*. Among parents only 45% unambiguously see advantages; 18% see disadvantages and 38% are undecided. Many point to the lack of financial and material resources for the schools and, in particular, to limited co-operation with parents and restricted career advice for pupils.

The question that presents itself after this rather negative evaluation of the educational changes is whether the responses are part of the general disappointment at the failure of hopes to materialize after the *Wende* or whether they are more deeply rooted in the educational and social climate that had established itself in the GDR. At the moment of writing the external restructuring of the system has been completed and has required major efforts to solve the problems inevitable in such a massive task. Such problems include, for example, the reallocation of every single school building to its new function in the system, and the review of the whole teaching profession to exclude those with strong SED or *Stasi* connections. And all this has been carried out, not only at the level of the school (which has been the main focus of this chapter) but also in higher education, in the universities, and in teacher training. The process of change, in both schools and universities, has frequently been called 'historically unique'. The adjustments demanded of individuals in the education system are hard to imagine for outside observers: parents faced with a bewildering choice of new types of school for their children; students caught mid-way in their studies and finding themselves working in a different institution and confronted by a different ideology; teachers expected to change styles, methods, text-books, schools, and examinations. The new systems still face daunting problems, particularly in coping with a falling birth-rate, unemployment, political disappointments, and fundamental social changes. The process of change is far from complete, but the structures and staff are now in place and one may now hope for a period of stabilization and a more gradual process of adaptation.

Further reading

There are few available sources in English on the details of educational developments in the former GDR. Berlin is the only state to publish some of its information leaflets in English; these are updated quite regularly (an example is 'Schools in Berlin', available from the *Senatsverwaltung für Schule, Berufsbildung und Sport*, Bredtschneiderstraße 5, 1000 Berlin 42). Another resource in English is the periodical *Bildung und Wissenschaft/Education and Science*, published monthly and available free of charge from Inter Nationes, Kennedyallee 91–103, D–53175 Bonn; this publication frequently has articles on aspects of educational development in the new states. Copies of publications describing the educational systems can be obtained from the *Kultusministerium* of each of the states.

Appendix 7.1: School Types in the FRG and the Former GDR

The *Einheitsschule* does not refer to any existing school type, either in the former GDR or in the FRG. A general term designating an all-through comprehensive school, it dates from the 1920s, when it was used by the school reformer Paul Oestreich.

The *Gesamtschule* is the West German version of the comprehensive school, now found also in Berlin and Brandenburg.

The traditional three-phase German system selects children at the point of leaving the *Grundschule* (primary school) to determine whether they move on to the *Gymnasium* (grammar school), to the *Realschule*, or to the *Hauptschule*. The *Hauptschule* and the *Realschule* (both for years five to ten) prepare pupils for a leaving certificate (*Hauptschulabschluß, Realschulabschluß*); the *Hauptschule* is comparable to the old non-academic English secondary modern school; the *Realschule* prepares pupils for middle-management posts in industry and the public services; the *Gymnasium* prepares pupils for the *Abitur* or university entrance examination.

Some details about the terminology for technical and vocational schools are given in Section 7.6.4. Special schools for children with mental or physical disabilities are called *Sonderschulen* or *Förderschulen*.

In the former GDR the main school type was the ten-year *Allgemeinbildende Polytechnische Oberschule* (POS or APOS), which was divided into three stages: *Unterstufe* (primary); *Mittelstufe* (lower secondary); and *Oberstufe* (upper secondary) (see Appendix 7.2).

After completing the POS, selected pupils went on to the *Erweiterte Oberschule* (EOS) for a sixth-form education leading to the *Abitur* in two years.

Appendix 7.2: School Types in the New Federal States

Brandenburg
Grundschule (classes 1–6)
Gesamtschule (classes 7–13)
Gymnasium (classes 7–13)
Realschule (classes 7–10)

Berufsschule
Berufsfachschule
Fachoberschule
Fachschule

Förderschule

Mecklenburg-West Pomerania
Grundschule (classes 1–4)
Hauptschule (classes 5–9)
Realschule (classes 5–10)
Gymnasium (classes 5–13)

Berufsschule
Berufsfachschule
Fachoberschule
Fachgymnasium
Fachschule
Sonderschule

Saxony
Grundschule (classes 1–4)
Mittelschule (classes 5–10)
Gymnasium (classes 5–12)

Berufsschule
Berufsfachschule
Fachschule
Fachoberschule
Berufliches Gymnasium

Förderschule

Saxony-Anhalt
Grundschule (classes 1–4)
Sekundarschule (classes 5–9/10)
Gymnasium (classes 5–12)

Berufsschule
Berufsfachschule
Berufsaufbauschule
Fachschule
Fachoberschule
Fachgymnasium
Förderschule

Thuringia

Grundschule (classes 1–4)   *Berufsschule*   *Berufliches Gymnasium*
Regelschule (classes 5–9/10) *Berufsfachschule*   *Fachschule*
Gymnasium (classes 5–12)   *Berufsaufbauschule*
                               Fachoberschule

Appendix 7.3: Outline of Education in the GDR until 1989

EOS: *Erweiterte Oberschule*, sixth-form course leading to *Abitur*
FAA: *Facharbeiterausbildung*, craft training leading to work
FAA *mit Abitur:* craft training with *Abitur* leading to technical higher education
FSA: *Fachschulausbildung*, higher technical training leading to work
APOS: *Allgemeinbildende Polytechnische Oberschule*, the General Polytechnic Comprehensive School

AGE	YEAR	SCHOOL TYPE			
18	12	EOS	or FAA	or FSA	or FAA
17	11	(to *Abitur*)	(*mit Abitur*)		
16	10				
15	9	APOS			
14	8	(*Oberstufe*: upper secondary level)			
13	7				
12	6	APOS			
11	5	(*Mittelstufe*: lower secondary level)			
10	4				
9	3	APOS			
8	2	(*Unterstufe*: primary level)			
7	1				
6		*Kindergarten*			
5		(Not compulsory)			
4					
3		*Kinderkrippe*			
2		(Crèche: not compulsory)			
1					

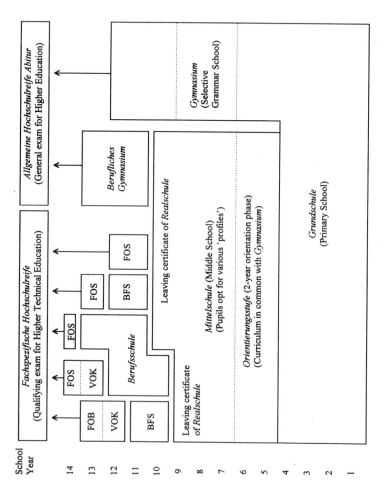

Appendix 7.4: The Education System in Saxony

8
Women in Germany from Division to Unification

INGRID SHARP and DAGMAR FLINSPACH

8.1 Introduction

Although the immediate post-war period brought the same problems for the whole of Germany, the changes in women's lives during the period 1949–90 must be looked at in the context of a divided Germany, since the development of a Western-style democracy in the FRG on the one hand and Soviet-style democratic centralism in the GDR on the other led to very different life experiences for the citizens of each state. Because the traditions of female emancipation that evolved in the two Germanies after 1949 diverged so radically, this chapter will begin with a review of the historical situation of women in each country; it will then consider the consequences that the collapse of the GDR and the unification of Germany have had for women since 1989–90.

8.2 The aftermath of war

At the end of the Second World War there were over seven million more women than men in Germany. In all four zones of occupation female labour proved essential in the task of reconstructing the fabric of a devastated society, and the picture of the *Trümmerfrauen* (literally 'rubble women') who rebuilt Germany brick by brick at the end of the war has become a familiar one. In 1945 the population of defeated Germany faced a seemingly insuperable problem of basic survival: nearly half of the pre-war accommodation stock had been destroyed or badly damaged; there was little food to be had, and the flood of refugees from the East aggravated an already acute situation.

In the private sphere the numerical imbalance between the sexes was also having its effect. As well as the war-widows there was a large number of single women, some with children, who could not expect to marry; all these women had to provide for themselves financially. Neither was life necessarily easier for married women whose husbands had returned from the war physically unharmed: the couples' different experiences of the war, their incompatible expectations of marriage and family life, and the fact that many women had rushed prematurely into marriage in the desperate climate of the war all contributed to produce extremely high divorce rates. The traditional family model, the wife at home with the children and the husband as sole provider, was no longer appropriate. The model applied neither in practical terms, as the exclusive provider was a scarce commodity, nor psychologically, as women had become used to fending for themselves and had gained in confidence and self-reliance through their war experiences.

8.3 The Federal Republic of Germany: the law

Article 3 of the Basic Law of 1948 states:

1. All persons are equal before the law.
2. Men and women have equal rights.
3. No-one may be disadvantaged or privileged because of their sex, descent, race, language, country of birth and origin, faith or religious beliefs or political opinions.

This article establishes the principle of equality for women in all areas of life. And yet, although such equality may seem self-evident today, it took a great deal of pressure from the handful of women involved in formulating the Basic Law, backed up both by others active in the post-war women's movement and by the weight of public opinion, to have this statement included at all. The first women's groups were founded in 1945 under the umbrella organization, the German Women's Council (Nave-Herz 1989:62–65). These groups argued that women had earned equal rights because of their services during the war and afterwards. In 1948 a Parliamentary Council was charged with the formulation of a provisional Constitution for the Western zones of occupation which would remain valid until a peace treaty had been signed. The Council included four women representatives, Friederike Nadig (SPD), Elisabeth Selbert (SPD), Helene Weber (CDU), and Helene Wessels (Centre). Elisabeth Selbert put forward a paragraph on equal rights for inclusion in the draft Constitution. Although this move was rejected at first, the pressure of women's groups and public opinion was enough to ensure that Article 3, Section 2 ('Men and women have equal rights') was passed at a second reading. To the present day the lines of battle drawn here (women and women's groups on one side, conservatives and the church on the other) continue to clash on issues affecting women. For example, during 1993–94 the two sides crossed swords over the reform of the abortion law following unification.

When the FRG was founded in 1949 the existing Civil Code needed extensive revision to bring it into line with the principle of sexual equality. However, the political will to bring about a speedy revision was lacking, particularly within the conservative, church-related parties, who wished to establish the traditional family at the heart of German society. Not until eight years later in 1957 was the Civil Code revised. Women had to wait until 1958 before they had equal access to family property or income, and until 1959 before a husband's right to the final decision in disputed areas of marriage and to the upbringing of the children was annulled. These early revisions, however, continued to define the *Hausfrauenehe* (literally: 'housewife-marriage') as the norm. The wife was expected to ensure that any other activities which she undertook were compatible with her primary responsibility to household, husband, and children. Even after the reform of family law in 1977, which was predicated on the idea that husband and wife were equal partners with joint responsibility for family life and parenthood, social attitudes lagged behind legislation and women continued to be seen first and foremost as housewives (Kolinsky 1993:49–54).

8.4 Women at work in the FRG

The founding years of the FRG were characterized by conservatism in the social as well as political spheres. With growing economic prosperity came a parallel stability in social life which was heavily influenced by the moral norms and family values of the church groups and conservative politicians. The popular television soap programme of the day was *Familie Saubermann* (The Cleanman Family), which showed the traditional role-division within a 'natural' hierarchy: the programme placed the man at the head of the household and portrayed the woman as the 'angel in the house', responsible for the smooth running of family life. Part of the mother's role was to mediate within the family unit to preserve harmony in relationships; she had also to provide emotional support for all the family members, especially the father. The family was placed at the heart of the West German state. Government policy was directed at supporting the traditional family, with the founding of the Ministry for the Family in 1953 and the reintroduction of child benefit in 1955.

Reality failed to match the prevailing ideal and women continued to work outside the home in steadily increasing numbers: in 1950 women made up 31·4% of the total workforce, in 1989 around 38% ; the number of working mothers with school-age children trebled between 1950 and 1962. Working mothers were seen as a serious social problem. They were accused of neglecting their children and of being motivated by selfishness and by a desire for material luxury. The term 'latch-key children' (*Schlüsselkinder*) was used to refer to the neglected and possibly delinquent offspring of these inadequate mothers. Although the term had first appeared in a World Health Organization study, the 'maternal deprivation' identified in the study was in fact used in connection with the child's experience of war and had nothing at all to do with working mothers (Schütze 1992).

Combining motherhood and paid employment produced serious problems for women. Women's primary responsibility for the family remained a major barrier to equality of opportunity, and the recognition of child-care as a social obligation rather than as a private issue for individual women to resolve was a key demand of the women's movement in the 1970s (Doormann 1990:257). Despite the need for female labour during the boom years of the economic miracle there was no public provision for child-care, and women continued to suffer discrimination in employment: they were consistently paid less than their male colleagues for the same work. Before 1955 women were paid on a different wage-scale from men. Even after such overt discrimination was forbidden by law in 1955, 'women's work' was re-categorized as 'light work' and paid accordingly. Underlying this decision was the assumption that work done by women was of less value than that done by men.

Marriage and children remained the accepted life-style for women, who were supported by the state through tax incentives and generous child benefit. For women who also wished to work the 'three-phase-model' was encouraged by the Conservative government of the 1960s and remains to the present day the ideal of the CDU/CSU. This model divides the woman's working life into three phases: (1) training or education, followed by a period of employment; (2) marriage and children, a period of ten to fifteen years when her career is suspended in favour of household and child-rearing; and (3) re-entry into employment while retaining primary responsibility for the household. This model reflects the reality for many German women, as the combination of motherhood and career is hampered by the shortness of the German school day and the lack of affordable and adequate child-care provision (Kolinsky 1993:154; Einhorn 1993:262). In a world of rapid technological advances the realities of re-entry into professional life after a break of ten to fifteen years mean that a woman's career development and earning capacity are bound to be adversely affected, with consequent reductions in the level of her pension on retirement (for recent figures throughout Europe see Merkel 1991).

8.5 The women's movement in the FRG

Towards the end of the 1960s the younger generation of women had begun to demand change. These women, often from the middle classes, had benefited from improved educational opportunities. Not only had they become acutely aware of the contradictions within society, they were inspired with a desire to do something about them. The first arena for women's activism was in the student movement that had spread from America and France. The student movement called established hierarchies and power structures into question but its male revolutionaries left unchallenged and indeed perpetuated the traditional gender hierarchies that discriminated against women. Women's councils were formed within the Federation of Socialist Students (SDS) and at the SDS conference in September 1968 Helke Sander spoke out forcefully against sexism within the movement. Speaking on behalf of a women's group from Berlin, the 'Action Committee for the Liberation of Women', Sander identified the double oppression of women under capitalism and in a patriarchal society. She argued that women had 'to perceive oppression in our private lives not as private but as politically and economically conditioned. We need to change the whole quality of personal life and to understand the process of change in terms of political action' (*Frauenjahrbuch* 1975, see Haug 1992:188). Sander reinforced her points by pelting male delegates with ripe tomatoes. The famous incident of the tomatoes marks the beginning of the new women's movement in West Germany. Women such as Sander had direct experience and an instinctive understanding of discrimination. This found a ready echo with many women outside the socialist revolutionary milieu of the universities. Women's groups inspired by the slogan 'the personal is political' sprang up throughout the FRG .

One of several campaigns which drew women together was the demand for the reform of the abortion law. The impetus came from the Social-Liberal coalition government which came to power in 1969 and proposed to reform paragraph 218 (usually written as §218) of the German penal code. Under this law an abortion had always been a criminal offence in Germany. It soon became clear that women's groups would not be satisfied with the mere reform of §218. They aimed at its complete abolition and mounted a public campaign to achieve this.

In 1971 the national weekly magazine *Stern* published the 'confessions' of 374 women, some of them public figures, who had had abortions and who supported the campaign for the repeal of §218. First used in the French campaign for the legalization of abortion, this spectacular tactic was now adopted by Alice Schwarzer, one of the most influential figures in the German feminist movement. Thousands of women signed petitions against §218; a number of men, including many from the medical profession, also declared their support.

The following year saw the blossoming of women's centres throughout Germany. These were places where women could meet, exchange experiences, and receive information. Many centres contributed actively to the anti-§218 campaign and organized buses to take women over the border for safe abortions in Dutch clinics. In March 1972 the first national Women's Conference was held and considered a great success. The publicity surrounding the campaign to decriminalize §218 attracted broad support from women of all ages and social backgrounds. But it also made women activists aware of the extent of their powerlessness: not only was political and legal power concentrated in male hands, but the medical profession was also dominated by men. Members of the women's movement developed an understanding of their situation through feminist writings from America and later through German texts by women such as Alice Schwarzer, Ursula Krechel, Jutta Menschik, and Marie-Louise Janssen-Jureit. These writers and their supporters did not build on the bourgeois-liberal traditions of nineteenth-century feminism which had tried to achieve its aims in co-operation with men and male institutions. Aiming to expose and challenge the patriarchal structure of society, they specifically excluded men from participation in the movement's activities. In their rejection of male power structures they turned away from a hierarchical structure, favouring instead a loose, democratic organization without recognized leaders or programmes.

In 1975, the International Year of the Woman, the Federal Constitutional Court rejected the draft law on abortion: which had been passed by Parliament, as incompatible with the Basic Law. The law proposed that abortion should be legally permitted up to the twelfth week of pregnancy; at the same time the woman should receive compulsory counselling to persuade her to continue with the pregnancy. The Court ruled that the draft law offered insufficient protection to the life of the unborn child, which the Basic Law also guaranteed. In 1993 the same argument defeated a similar draft law passed by Parliament after unification had brought the issue into the centre of political debate. To the campaigners' frustration the women's movement had once again lost the battle against §218 (Prützel-Thomas 1993).

Although the publicity generated by the campaign attracted large numbers of women, the movement itself, now deprived of a unifying cause, lost the impetus for political action and split into smaller groups. These concerned themselves more with individual reflection, the exchange of personal experiences, and feminist theory. Central issues were questions of sexuality, life-style, self-awareness, and the creation of a feminist counter-culture through the encouragement of literary, cultural, and artistic activities. Women's festivals and theatre groups were organized. The Women's Diary (*Frauenkalender*), listing useful addresses and feminist activities for the coming year, has appeared since 1975. In 1976 the feminist magazine *Courage* was founded, followed in 1977 by *Emma*. Women's presses were set up which published and distributed feminist literature and advice for women. These initiatives were so successful that mainstream commercial publishers set up their own women's lists, much to the disgust of the movement. Frigga Haug has identified a 'reading cult' based on key texts adopted by the women's movement. These texts became the focus of discussion groups and had enormous significance for women (Haug 1992:200). Texts which achieved cult status in Germany included Verena Stefan's *Häutungen* (Shedding, 1975) and Svende Merian's *Der Tod des Märchenprinzen* (Death of Prince Charming, 1980). Alice Schwarzer's *Der 'kleine Unterschied' und seine großen Folgen* (The 'Little Difference' and its Large Consequences, 1975) became an immediate best-seller and attracted an unprecedented storm of abuse, largely from male readers. Ironically, the need for a women's movement was illustrated by the deeply misogynistic tone adopted by some critics (for examples of readers' responses see Wiggershaus 1979:123).

Parallel to this development, local projects were mounted to improve the lives of women in specific areas. The most important of these projects was the establishment of women's refuges, the first of which was founded in Berlin in 1976. As elements of feminist ideas and activities became incorporated into the mainstream of cultural life, radical feminists looking for a fundamental change in society no longer felt represented by the women's movement. Some moved into alternative culture while others attempted to change the political and social institutions from within. Indeed, women made great strides in moving into positions and areas previously reserved for men.

Culturally the 1980s were associated with the New Age movement. For the women's movement this meant a retreat from political activism into a new cult of womanhood with an emphasis on mysticism and spirituality. Because they were considered to be expressions of masculine structures of thought, rationality and science were rejected in favour of a more intuitive grasp of the world. The view that women are linked directly with the natural world produced an increased interest in alternative medicine. This is reminiscent of the 'wise woman' tradition that had largely been destroyed by the persecution of witches in the sixteenth and seventeenth centuries. A new cult of motherhood sprang up, celebrating pregnancy and childbirth as the most important physical and psychological experiences of a woman's life. The emphasis on the polarity of masculine and feminine natures appears to some to come dangerously close to the traditional, conservative view of women.

Within the context of the new mother-cult, the *Lohn für Hausarbeit* ('wages for housework') campaign was revived in the latter half of the 1980s. The aim was not simply to gain social recognition for the work that women do in the home but also to provide financial support for widowed housewives. Widows receive only 60% of their husband's pension and housewives have no pension in their own right, leading to much female poverty in old age. The majority of feminists reject the demand for wages for housework as they see it tying women even more securely to the home.

In 1979 a new phase of political activism began in response to a rightward shift in German politics and to increasing international military tensions. An escalating arms race was being funded at the expense of the welfare state and swingeing cuts were taking place in those very areas which affected women most: child benefit, education and training, crèche and nursery-school places, women's refuges, and care for the sick and elderly. Women were expected to step in and fill the gaps in social provision. At the same time there was a move to draw women into the military process: in the name of equal opportunities, women were encouraged to volunteer for military service. In response a women's peace movement emerged, protesting against the proliferation of nuclear weapons and the arms race, the destruction of the environment, and the reduction in welfare state spending.

The women's peace movement brought together in protest actions various autonomous groups and organizations affiliated to political parties and trade unions. One such action was the women's March for Peace from Dortmund to Brussels in 1983. Women also co-operated with other peace initiatives, as shown in the human chain from Stuttgart to Neu-Ulm in October 1983. Despite the breadth of the movement irreconcilable differences within the feminist ranks emerged over the issue of peace. L. Doormann identifies three strands of thought. The first was represented by *Emma* and welcomed the possibility of military service for women. This group opposed the identification of peace as a specifically female concern. The second, more widely-held view was that war was an extension of patriarchal power relations and that, while women were directly affected by war, they had no place in the military decision-making process. This group appealed across ideological lines and aimed to link women in East and West in common protest against the inhumanity of war. The third group did not believe that women's issues could be isolated from general political questions, and saw peace as an area in which women had a direct political interest. Women sought peace, not because they were by nature any more peace-loving than men, but because they were already adversely affected by the arms race and would necessarily be involved in the event of war (Doormann 1990:286–87).

As the peace issue clearly shows, opinions differed widely within feminist circles and it is no longer possible at this stage to speak of a 'women's movement' held together by common views. A further illustation of this is the anti-pornography campaign of the late 1980s, which encountered its fiercest opposition from within the ranks of the women's movement. The campaign began in the 1970s when women protested against the screening of the pornographic film *Die Geschichte von O* (The Story of O) in 1975. Later, in 1977, *Emma* complained to the Press Council about a magazine cover picture which degraded women. *Emma* complained again in 1978, this time about the cover pictures of *Stern* magazine, which portrayed women as sexual objects. Neither case was successful but the publicity generated served to raise public awareness of the issue. The pornography campaign of the late 1980s was a different matter. Again the impetus came from *Emma*, which published its own draft law to control pornography in response to the increased volume and violence of pornographic material. Accusations that the protesting feminists were being prudish and denying their own sexuality were once again levelled at the campaigners but this time much of the criticism came from other feminists. One of the major goals and achievements of the women's movement had been that women should accept and experience their own sexuality, whether lesbian or heterosexual; many women now demanded the right to their own erotic material and opposed any form of censorship. The debate centred on issues of censorship and definition and on how to establish the boundaries between the erotic and the pornographic.

Despite internal divisions the importance of the women's movement as a force for change should not be underestimated. During the 1970s it was undoubtedly responsible for pioneering work in bringing the continued discrimination against women into public consciousness. Frigga Haug describes the achievements of the women's movement as a 'victorious defeat' in that the state was forced to address the question of women's disadvantage on legal, economic, and social levels (Haug 1992:185). To some extent feminist ideas have been institutionalized in that the movement's demands have now been adopted by the state and absorbed into the manifestos of the main political parties. Women's disadvantage has been articulated and recognized as a political problem throughout Europe; current progress in closing the gender gap is being centrally monitored in the European Union.

In Germany the transforming effect of the entry of the Greens into Parliament in 1983 can be seen in the subsequent policies and statements of the SPD and the CDU/CSU. In terms of seats held, the parliamentary presence of women in the Green Party in 1987 amounted to 57% compared with only 16% for the SPD and 8% for the CDU/CSU. The latest figures show an overall upward trend from 15% in 1987 to 20% in 1990. The SPD committed itself to 40% female representation in Parliament by the 1990s. Even the CDU/CSU would like to see representation of women at all levels, in line with female party membership, although they have stopped short at committing themselves to quotas (for a detailed outline of the positions of the political parties see Kolinsky 1993:233–54).

In education women are closing the gap in qualification levels that has always existed in the FRG. In 1989 women constituted 42% of students, compared with only 19% in 1950. This figure is still surprisingly low, given that girls perform equally well at school and are as successful as their male counterparts in attaining university entrance qualifications. The proportion of female postgraduate students is even lower, with women gaining only 33% of master degrees and 24% of doctorates. Although 62% of students who gain a higher school-teaching qualification (*Staatsexamen*) are female, a pyramid effect can be observed whereby the higher the educational level, the smaller is the proportion of women. Thus, while 70% of primary school teachers are women, they make up only around 40% of grammar school teachers and only 3% of university professors (Kolinsky 1993:129,139; Haug 1992:215).

Working women in Germany still earn on average 30% less than men, a figure remarkably constant across Europe (Merkel 1991:2). They are still clustered at the lower end of pay scales and become more scarce the higher up one goes (Kolinsky 1993:187). In practice women have a much narrower range of jobs to choose from than men. They tend to be found in those professions which are an extension of the nurturing and service role they play in the family, such as education, clearing up after people and looking after the sick (in 1991 74% of working women throughout Europe were employed in service industries; see *Informationen Extra* 1991:2). The disproportionate representation of women in part-time and marginal employment makes them particularly vulnerable to dismissal, and female unemployment is indeed higher.

The achievements of feminism cannot simply be measured in terms of success or failure in removing the continued inequalities in politics, education, and employment. Haug argues that 'feminism has infiltrated at all levels of bourgeois culture. It has dissected its language, profaned its literature, ridiculed its sciences' (1992:215). Feminism as counter-culture has not only challenged the interpretation of history in the West, it has profoundly and permanently altered the prevailing cultural climate.

8.6 The German Democratic Republic: the law

Although sheer necessity motivated the *Trümmerfrauen* on either side of the ideological divide, for the leaders of the Soviet zone these women had taken the first step towards genuine equality. One of the official aims of the GDR government was the economic emancipation of women. This was in line with socialist theory and the Soviet model. For many Marxists, the problem of women's oppression would be solved once legal barriers to women's equality with men were removed. As early as 1946 the principle of equal pay for equal work was established in the trade union movement. In 1947 the German Democratic Women's Federation (DFD) was set up to represent women and lead them towards economic independence. In 1949, with the founding of the GDR, the equality of men and women was enshrined in the Constitution. Like the socialist system itself, the drive for women's emancipation was not the result of a grass roots movement, but was imposed from above. This is at the heart of later criticisms that the SED/Soviet government imposed its own version of emancipation on women, at no time consulting them as to what they themselves wanted. This is in obvious contrast to the development in the West, where the women's groups formed themselves independently of the government in order to campaign for rights that were in many cases granted automatically in the GDR.

The economy of the GDR developed on a totally different basis from that of West Germany. The GDR received no aid from the Marshall Plan, which provided American assistance for economic recovery in Europe, and it was forced to carry a heavy burden of war reparations. The East German 'economic miracle' consisted in first surviving and then in achieving a basic standard of living for its citizens. The major problem faced by industry in the GDR was a shortage of labour, necessitating the mobilization of all potential workers, including women. The official vision for women during the 1950s was based on integrating them into the workforce and into active political life. Women were encouraged to move into former male preserves, to educate themselves and to obtain qualifications. In the literature of this period women were typically depicted as struggling (with the support of an enlightened party official) to overcome old-fashioned notions about a woman's place. The GDR's Act for the Protection of Mother and Child and the Rights of Women (1950) laid the foundation for all subsequent laws in the GDR. Measures specified included the introduction of maternity benefits, paid maternity leave, and child allowance; there was also a commitment to providing crèche facilities and nursery schools.

Laws introduced during the 1960s addressed the issue of women's under-representation at decision-making levels. The right to work was no longer enough: the aim was to ensure that women had not only a legal right of access to managerial positions but also the necessary qualifications to take up such opportunities. Official 'measures for the advancement of women' amounted to positive discrimination designed to support women in their attempts to gain further qualifications. Women's committees were set up at the workplace to ensure that these measures were enacted. Paid work outside the home having been established as the norm for women, official policies were now directed towards ensuring that neither women's expectations of themselves nor the residual sexism of bourgeois consciousness would prevent women from assuming their proper place in society.

During this period it was recognized that women still suffered under the dual burden of career (or job) and family. More and more, women delayed having children because of the intolerable burden that this would place on them. As a result the birth-rate declined. Policy was therefore directed at the 'industrialization' of the household. The problems of feeding the family, washing the clothes, and taking care of the children were moved into the public domain, especially in the form of provision at school and workplace. Improved technology in household equipment was also designed to lighten the burden for women.

In 1971, three years after the incident of the flying tomatoes in West Germany, the leader of the SED, Erich Honecker, felt able to announce to the world that the problem of women's emancipation had been solved in the GDR. What justification did he have for making this claim?

After the VIII SED Party Conference in 1971 it was decreed that the legal and economic basis of equality between the sexes had been established. Subsequent policy now built on these achievements to ensure that girls and women enjoyed equality of opportunity in education and in society as well as compatibility of career and motherhood.

The aim within education was to give girls and women the same opportunities as boys and men. Figures show that the GDR was relatively successful in attracting girls into areas of study traditionally dominated by boys, notably sciences and industry. In 1989 48·6% of students in higher education were female; of these 73% were training to be teachers, 66·7% were studying economics, 55·2% were medical students, and 46% were engaged in maths and science (Einhorn 1992:126). It was recognized that education had an important part to play in changing the way women were perceived by society. The attitudes of very young children could be influenced more readily once a network of crèches, nursery schools, and school-based afternoon child-care for older children had been introduced. Care was taken that little boys and girls received exactly the same treatment and played with the same toys. Later the school system ensured that all pupils, regardless of gender, took the same subjects up to the age of sixteen, when compulsory schooling ceased. Students who wished to combine study with having a family were assisted by a range of measures. These included grants for students with children, guaranteed child-care facilities and the provision of suitable, cheap accommodation. Children over sixteen who were in full-time training or education received a grant of 200 marks a month, regardless of parental income.

8.7 Women at work in the GDR

The view of the woman as a worker was largely accepted in GDR society. A survey conducted in 1990 found that, while 25% of West German women saw themselves as housewives, only 3% of GDR women wanted to take on this role (the results were published in the *Süddeutsche Zeitung* under the title: 'A housewife: a dream job for only three percent of women: most women want a career and a family'; 17 February 1991:5). The ability to combine motherhood with a career was also taken for granted, and women tended to start their families at a young age, usually in their early twenties. There were financial incentives for couples to marry and have children early. Interest-free loans of 7,000 marks were granted to couples under thirty for household equipment. The debt could be 'childrened off' (*abgekindert*), meaning that it was reduced at the birth of each child. If three children were born within the first eight years, the entire debt was cancelled. To ensure happy productive marriages, divorce was made simple and based on the principle of the irreparable breakdown of a marriage. As women were able to support themselves even as single parents, it was unusual for one partner to have to support the other after the divorce. The majority of divorces were sought by women: in 1989 women petitioned for 69% of all divorces (Winkler 1990:111). Child-care facilities and maternity benefits, coupled with the liberal laws on abortion (free and legal up to twelve weeks at the discretion of the woman concerned), gave women a real choice about when and whether to have children and enabled many women to combine motherhood with full employment. In 1989 91·2% of GDR women of working age were either in employment or in training and education, compared with 55% of West German women (Einhorn 1992:127).

Maternity leave was generous, comprising six months paid leave followed by release from work for up to twelve months for a first child and eighteen months for subsequent children. Pay during maternity leave was equivalent to sickness benefit. Single mothers could extend this period for up to three years if no crèche facilities were available. Pregnant women and women with children under one year (under three for single mothers) could not be sacked, and the workplace was obliged to offer a woman her job back at the end of the period of absence. State-run child-care facilities were generally available to all women who wanted them; they were free, with a nominal charge for lunch, and were open between six in the morning and seven in the evening. For women on shift work there were special crèches where the children boarded during the week and returned home only at weekends. In 1989 crèche facilities were used by 80% of children up to the age of three. Kindergartens were used by virtually all three- to six-year-olds, and the *Schulhort*, a day home which provided school-based supervision for children after the end of the school day, was attended by about 80% of all pupils aged between six and ten years (Kolinsky 1993:265).

What is striking about these measures is that they were directed almost exclusively at women and concentrated on women in their role as workers and mothers. Based on the belief that women's equality meant nothing more than full employment and economic independence, the SED's policy in this area was largely concerned with population growth and employment. Far from breaking down traditional attitudes, the measures that were designed to help women combine career and child-care served only to reinforce expectations on the part of both sexes that child-care and housework should remain the sole responsibility of the woman. Instead of recognizing that child-care is a social issue affecting more than simply the mother, the measures underlined the assumption that child-care was an individual, predominantly female responsibility. The advantages enjoyed by women at work led to their being treated as a 'problem' and were paradoxically a hindrance to their professional advancement. As seen from the mass dismissals of female workers in the transition to a market economy, their special treatment made them costly to employers and vulnerable during times of economic crisis.

An official role model for women was perpetuated in literature, reinforced by the media, and supported by legislation. It posited a woman who managed to combine the duties of a model wife and mother with a demanding job outside the home, while at the same time studying for further qualifications and enjoying all the cultural opportunities that were open to her. In addition to all this she was to be socially and politically active while remaining truly 'feminine': a creative home-maker, a sympathetic listener, a fun-loving companion, and a dynamic lover. After an eight-hour working shift and daily struggles with the defects of the economy, which made shopping and maintenance of the home an exhausting, time-consuming affair, women must have had little energy left over for their family, children, and for political activism, let alone for an imaginative and fulfilling sex-life. The effect of the 'superwoman' role model was oppressive and placed an additional burden on the individual psyche. Women were dissatisfied with their lives and plagued by feelings of guilt as they failed to live up to their own expectations. Inevitably they suffered enormous physical and psychological stress and felt less and less willing or able to take on additional responsibilities. Most positions of responsibility in the GDR were actually one-and-a-half or even two-person jobs and relied on the existence of a partner in the background. But women were expected to conform to the model of the male worker, who had traditionally been able to work unencumbered by household duties. Unacknowledged sexism at work meant that women had an overwhelming need to prove themselves to male colleagues, often at the expense of other important areas of life such as children, friendships, and relaxation. Problems associated with high-powered mothers were a common theme of children's literature.

Education was non-sexist to the extent that boys and girls followed the same curriculum but the norm was again the male, and the particular importance of the army in GDR society meant that girls had less value. While career advice helped to steer some girls into 'male' areas, no attempt was made to steer boys into 'female' jobs, with the result that the same concentration of women in certain jobs was found in the GDR as in the West. Studies reveal that women's work was less valued and certainly less well-paid (68–75% of men's wages), more monotonous, with less access to technology than men's work. Women were more often to be found working beneath their qualifications and were ghettoized in areas of the economy traditionally seen as 'women's work'. Some 75% of women fell into this category, which was largely a continuation of the nurturing or service role they played in the home (Nickel 1990:40).

The state's attempts to take over the service role traditionally fulfilled by women were largely unsuccessful. Women still had on average thirty-seven hours of housework to perform (not helped by the erratic supply of certain goods); men spent around eight hours a week on household chores, and even these were often restricted to certain tasks performed under instruction from the housewife. The advantages enjoyed by women in the workplace legitimized this blatantly unfair situation while allowing a negative role model to influence the division of labour between girls and boys in the household. Boys had more free time during the week than girls and were often not expected to play any part in the home. Not surprisingly most young men continued this pattern into their married lives, causing a great deal of disappointment to their wives and ultimately contributing to the high divorce figures.

The fact that children could be cared for round the clock undoubtedly enabled women to work long hours, but at great personal cost to themselves and often to their children too. The inflexibility of outside work, coupled with the disproportionate time required for necessary chores such as shopping, meant that extremely young children were forced to fit in with the pattern of a working day, often spending long hours away from home. The main source of child-care in West Germany was (and still is) the grandmother. But in the GDR, owing to the relatively young age at which women became mothers and the pattern of their working lives, the grandmothers were often still in full-time employment. Combining a career and a family was certainly possible and being a single parent did not mean a life of poverty and disadvantage, but questions about the quality of family life were not addressed. Although most commentators recognized that the basis for women's emancipation had been laid, there was much more work to be done before Honecker's 1971 statement could be said to be true, even in the limited sense in which he meant it.

8.8 Women's movements in the GDR

As mentioned earlier, the only officially permitted women's organization in the GDR was the DFD. The DFD did not make policy: it disseminated it. This is hardly surprising: the emancipation of women was organized from above, with the enlightened SED (female membership 33·5%) leading the way. Dismissed after the *Wende* of autumn 1989 as a 'crochet and knitting circle', the DFD had never been able to challenge the SED line. Honecker's premature claim in the 1970s that equality between the sexes had been achieved stifled further discussion of women's issues. As a result it was impossible to find a platform for alternative interpretations of what emancipation might mean, and the exploration of alternative models of society was restricted to tiny groups under the umbrella of the Protestant Church. There was no chance for a broadly based feminist consciousness to develop in the GDR. Lesbian groups, protected by the Church, began to meet in the early 1980s and the 'Women for Peace' movement was founded in 1982. Those active in such groups, such as Bärbel Bohley and Ulrike Poppe, suffered state harassment in the form of surveillance and, in some cases, imprisonment or expulsion from the GDR.

During the demonstrations of 1989, when the social order seemed open to renewal and old assumptions were being challenged, women too started to make themselves heard. Discussion about what constituted equality and emancipation for women was taken up again and brought into the public arena. At the beginning of November 1989 an open letter was published in the GDR's only women's magazine, *Für Dich* (Schwarz and Zenner 1990:7–9). Signed by prominent women academics, the letter called into question the claim of women's emancipation in the GDR and set out a programme of demands. In response to this letter, one month later on 3 December 1989, the Independent Women's Assocation (UFV), the first such organization in the GDR, was founded at a mass rally in Berlin attended by over 1,000 women. The UFV brought together the hundreds of individuals and small groups working in isolation. Its aim was to ensure that questions concerning women were not passed over or marginalized in favour of 'more important' areas of discussion, as had so often been the case in the past.

The newly founded women's movement in the GDR took as its starting-point the fact that, even though official policy had been directed at only a very narrow area of women's rights, the material base had been established on which a genuine liberation of all citizens could be achieved. It was important to ask questions about everyone's quality of life and to explore alternative life-styles to the family unit. The quality of child-care, the length of the working day, the introduction of quotas to break down the barriers between men's and women's work were all subjects for debate. Building on the important social network that had enabled women to combine motherhood with a career and kept them financially independent of men, the aim was to go further and challenge the official definition of emancipation. The movement criticized the official assumption that economic independence alone was a sufficient condition for women's equality: the reality for most women meant the freedom to work like a man and then the obligation to go home and work like a woman as well. Their demands were based on the assumption that women's rights in the GDR represented a point of departure and that they would be preserved. In fact, this was not to be the case.

The early days of the Modrow government, which was in power from December 1989 until March 1990, looked hopeful for women. Having gained access to the Round Table talks (see Chapter 3, Section 3.6), the UFV was able to ensure that issues affecting women were not marginalized or ignored. Together with the Round Table, the group worked on the formulation of a 'Social Charter' that demanded rights for all citizens and genuine equality of the sexes (Hampele 1993). In no other East European country were women able to gain such influence, albeit temporarily, over events.

The overwhelming vote for the CDU in the March elections was widely interpreted as a vote for unification by the most rapid route possible. As the date of unification approached, events exposed the vulnerability of women in the disintegrating society of the GDR. Women were the first to lose their jobs, with female unemployment rising twice as fast as that of men during 1990. Women also found it extremely hard to find another job, reaping the reward for the perception of the woman worker as a 'problem'. Single mothers were particularly vulnerable as the social network that had secured their existence crumbled. In the legislative vacuum that existed until FRG law replaced that of the GDR, pregnant women lost their jobs, women were no longer taken back after maternity leave, prices rose, and crèches came under threat. In addition many women experienced personal trauma as their partners unceremoniously left them to start afresh in the West. They were also frightened about dangers to their children, such as drug abuse and AIDS, and were concerned about the higher levels of crime and violence that might accompany the new society. Hitherto taboo subjects, such as incest and domestic violence, came out into the open, while new frustrations and feelings of helplessness and humiliation led to an increase in violence against women. The flood of pornographic videos, peep shows, and sex shops which poured into the GDR after the fall of the Berlin Wall was greeted by some women as a symbol of new-found freedom and liberation. But many felt threatened by the view of women perpetuated by western pornography and advertizing that used images of women as sexual objects (including beauty contests). Western marriage agencies praised the virtues of the feminine, hard-working and sexually liberated women of the GDR. In this maelstrom the achievements of socialism were eroded at frightening speed.

8.9 After unification

The term 'unification' suggests that the two systems merged, but in fact the GDR became a constituent part of West Germany under Article 23 of the Basic Law. The process entailed the adoption of West Germany's laws and Constitution, lock, stock and barrel. The contest between the political systems had clearly been decided in favour of the West, and even aspects of GDR life which were superior to provisions in West Germany, such as child-care and maternity benefits, were either dismissed as ideologically tainted and not worth saving, or they were considered too costly to implement. In many areas women of the former GDR lost benefits and rights which they had come to take for granted and for which West German feminists had been campaigning for years.

In the area of reproductive rights women in east Germany have lost access to free and legal abortion on demand up to twelve weeks after conception. Instead they are subject to the provisions of §218 as revised by the Federal Constitutional Court on 29 May 1993. Despite hopes that the

GDR model would be adopted in the united Germany, the ruling means that abortion continues to be a criminal act, although women who have abortions and doctors who perform them are immune from prosecution. In most cases abortion is no longer available free of charge and women are required to attend compulsory counselling. Although the new ruling represents some progress for women in western Germany, it is a setback for those in the east who see the compulsory counselling requirement as a sign that women cannot be trusted to make a responsible decision in an area which affects them so intimately.

In most cases the effect of the new laws was softened by delaying their implementation for a period after formal unification. Indeed the issue of abortion was so controversial that it threatened to block the entire merger process and a final joint ruling was postponed for two years after unification. East German mothers of babies born before 1 July 1991 could still draw GDR maternity benefits, while the GDR provision of up to six weeks paid leave to care for sick children under fourteen years of age was replaced by the West German entitlement of up to five days paid leave for the care of children under eight on 1 July 1991 (Berghahn 1992). Maternity benefits in the united Germany, although excellent by UK standards, are less generous than those of the former GDR and tend to make the woman more dependent on her partner, in that it is impossible to live on the amount of benefit paid. Since employers are liable to pay part of the maternity benefit, as opposed to the mother receiving social security funding for the whole amount, it is less attractive for them to employ young women.

Areas of female employment were the first to shed workers. Women's positions are vulnerable because of the widespread perception that women are primarily responsible for home and family. The expectations of west German employers setting up businesses in the east are determined by the standards which they bring with them from the former FRG: for them the 'three-phase model' is the accepted norm, so men are preferred for training and employment. Children, or the possibility of children, are seen as a factor reducing the productivity and reliability of female workers. The possibility of pregnancy is a powerful disincentive to train or employ younger women, and some western firms have been accused of making offers of employment conditional on a woman submitting to voluntary sterilization. For whatever reason there has been a dramatic drop in the birth-rate in the former GDR and a sharp rise in sterilization figures.

It is estimated that well over 50% of the unemployed in the former GDR are women; those in work are over-represented in temporary jobs. In some branches of industry, such as textiles, female unemployment has reached 80%. Despite these high levels of unemployment, women have taken up fewer places on government job creation schemes than men (Kolinsky 1993:280–82). Trapped in a vicious circle, women are also disappearing from the unemployment register. Without access to child-care they are deemed to be unavailable for work and so cannot count as unemployed. If they are out of work they either cannot afford or are refused child-care facilities. Reduction in child-care has in itself released thousands of women previously employed as nursery teachers or carers in crèches onto the labour market.

The effects of female unemployment include the de-skilling of women who are forced to accept poorly-paid, lower status work. This predestines them for poverty as they reach retirement age or are forced into early retirement. The age at which women are considered too old for employment is about forty; for men it is ten years later. The psychological effects of unemployment are well documented. Women who were used to defining themselves in terms of their jobs and felt they were making a contribution to society have to face the fact that they are no longer needed.

Despite these developments, feminist arguments and women's groups are not well received in the former GDR. The UFV, which at one time could mobilize 40,000 supporters for a single event, is now reduced to a small group of women, mainly academics. Together with the Greens it achieved only 2·6% of the vote and failed to get a single seat in the March 1990 elections, when women's overall representation in Parliament dropped from 35% to around 20% (Kolinsky 1993:289). Once unification became inevitable the role of the UFV had to undergo radical change. It could no longer aim to reconstruct GDR society and the organization lost a lot of support as a result of the internal difficulties which it experienced in deciding on its role (for a discussion of the UFV and other women's groups in the former GDR see Einhorn 1993:203–9).

Before unification meetings between women's groups in East and West were often characterized by incomprehension, suspicion, and disappointment. East German women felt that their own experiences were denigrated by Western feminists seeking to impose their own solutions. For their part Western women were disappointed that forty years of economic equality in the GDR had not proved to be as liberating as they hoped. While Western feminists at first expected a boost to the women's movement through collaboration, they soon began to fear that the movement would be weakened by GDR women's unfamiliarity with and hostility to feminist arguments and by their lack of feminist consciousness. Fruitless bickering about who was the more liberated, East German women with their experience of economic independence or Western women with their theoretical base, proved a further obstacle to co-operation. The division of Germany had produced very different traditions of self-perception. Even the common language proved to be a barrier to understanding since terms and concepts had developed different meanings and associations. Nanette Funk has argued that feminism in the West was predicated on individualism, while the underlying philosophy of Eastern Europe was 'holistic and collectivist, with no emphasis on the individual and her or his rights' (Funk and Mueller 1993:13). There is a long tradition in socialist feminism of transcending gender differences and fighting along class lines. East German women's remembered experiences of an oppressive regime have led them after unification to feel greater solidarity with east German men against the new oppressors (the west Germans and the exigencies of the market economy) than with members of their own sex in the west. Hostility to feminists from the west is often a spill-over from a more general hostility to patronizing *Wessis*, although it is also partly a result of the highly intellectual approach which western feminists often take. As it was used in the GDR, the term 'feminism' is imbued with negative images and there is widespread confusion about what the word really means. While the association of the concept of female emancipation with socialist ideology and policies makes some women shy away from it, others retreat because of a desire not to be associated with western ideas. Paradoxically, the very problems that should make women ripe for feminist analysis and action have made them less responsive. There is a feeling that existential problems preclude luxuries such as feminism and that to pursue women's interests separately would constitute a diversion from the main economic issues. The experience of unemployment does not mobilize women, rather it makes them depressed and incapable of action. Hildegard Nickel speaks of the 'frozen rabbit effect' (*Kannincheneffekt*), whereby women remain immobile in the face of danger, unable to fight or run (Nickel 1990:40).

To concentrate too strongly on the hostility towards feminism in the former GDR would be to imply that there is a flourishing women's movement in west Germany; this is far from true. Many see the women's movement as a spent force in a post-feminist society. The women's movement of the 1970s was born out of anger and a sense of outrage in the prevailing climate of protest and the questioning of old hierarchies. Following the collapse of Communism and the consequent disorientation experienced by leftist movements, the political context in 1993 is characterized by a general shift to the right in Western Europe and by the rise of nationalism and the Church in Eastern Europe. The trend is for women to be moved out of the public sphere, and this is often associated with increased value being placed on the woman's special role as mother. As noted earlier there is a striking overlap between certain groups within the women's movement and conservative forces in terms of their emphasis on the differences between the sexes. Any retreat from the public sphere by women, however it is packaged, must be seen as a dangerous step, for history has shown that if women do not represent their own interests, these will be overlooked.

In Western countries feminist demands have been to some extent incorporated into the state and this has opened up the world for women to such an extent that the younger generation of women cannot relate to stories of oppression and restrictions that they have not experienced themselves. In the popular mind feminism has become adversely associated with lesbianism, hatred of men, and a desire to achieve a position of unfair privilege. Such 'feminists' are caricatured as joyless, puritanical, and life-denying, and are characterized by imputed attitudes to make-up, fashion, and sex. While denying that they pursue equality, these women indeed take equality of opportunity for granted and have internalized feminist ideas. Apart from being associated with negative values in this way, feminism is being blamed quite unfairly for the frustrations of women's experience in both east and west (an issue discussed at length by Susan Faludi 1992). Because feminism is associated with the demand for the right to work and access to the same career opportunities as men, it is blamed for the painful reality experienced by many working mothers, a ceaseless round of 'obligations from which there is no reprieve' (Kaplan 1992:225). Because of low pay, inadequate child-care, the lack of emotional support at home, the continuing responsibility for household and family, the cost to women is often far greater than the compensations; the gloss of freedom and self-fulfilment which paid work was supposed to bring has become tarnished.

In this climate women and men start yearning nostalgically for a supposedly golden age where gender roles were fixed and women had the 'privilege' of staying at home. In discussions about the demise of the former GDR the high level of female employment is now seen as a symptom of the economic failings of the system, as a working man could not support his family on his wages alone. The idea of a return to the hearth and full-time motherhood is tempting to women who have been exhausted by the struggle with the inadequacies of the socialist system. The unique position of new Germany is that it is possible to see the effects of two very different traditions of emancipation and to arrive at a synthesis. The GDR experience teaches us that, although necessary, equality before the law and economic emancipation are not sufficient conditions for genuine equality. The swift erosion of women's rights during the unification process shows that so-called 'post-feminism' is nothing but a dangerous myth.

The women's movement can no longer afford to see itself as directed against men and the state. Women's emancipation cannot be measured simply by the extent to which women are able to assume male life-styles and career patterns that were originally predicated on a network of emotional support and service provided by a home-based wife. That path is not available to women. Nor is emancipation about cocooning women in a bond of babies and menstrual ritual that continues to exclude men. As Kaplan argues, once a particular group has been identified as the oppressor, the options are limited. If the revolution is to be successful the enemy must be killed, subjugated or re-educated:

> In all cases, power and control has to be taken away from them or the revolution has failed. As said before, women could not eradicate or overpower half of humanity. Familial, physical and sexual ties make this unthinkable and somewhat impractical. (Kaplan 1992:273)

Perhaps the women's movement has reached the stage of embarking on the ideological re-education of men. Such a stage could be signalled by the fact that in January 1993 *Emma*, the flagship of a major part of the new women's movement, changed its self-understanding from a magazine 'for women by women' to a magazine 'for people'.

The women's movement in the new Germany is characterized by pluralism. In place of a single 'feminism', there is a plurality of responses to a deeply complex issue. At the very least, the collapse of state socialism has served to discredit blanket solutions and has exposed the ultimate sterility of enforced orthodoxy, so the idea of a single organization which speaks for all women emerging at this stage is both unlikely and undesirable. For some time to come the activities of women's groups in the new Germany will continue to be fragmented and characterized by a multiplicity of motivations and actions. Whether these groups will come together to form anything like a coherent women's movement depends on their ability to combine passionate convictions with a mutual tolerance of diversity.

Further reading

For recent studies of the position of women in West Germany before 1990 see Frevert (1990), Haug (1992), Helwig (1987), Herve (1990), Kaplan (1992), and Schenk (1990). For the GDR see Corrin (1992), Einhorn (1993), Faber and Meyer (1992), Kahlau (1990), Schwarz and Zenner (1990), and Wander (1989). Recommended studies for the post-unification period include Dölling and others (1992), Einhorn (1993), McElvoy (1992), Funk and Mueller (1993), Geißler (1991), Kolinsky (1993), Mitscherlich and Burmeister (1991), Mudry (1991), Nickel (1990), and Süssmuth and Schubert (1990). The autumn 1991 issue of the *Feminist Review*, No. 38, is a special issue devoted to women in eastern Europe after the *Wende*; it contains articles by Dölling, Haug, and Einhorn.

Part III

The Cultural and Artistic Challenges

9

The German Media

JOHN SANDFORD

9.1 Introduction

Before unification the contrasting press and broadcasting systems in the two German states provided an exemplary paradigm for the sharply opposed notions of the functions of the media in Western and Soviet-style societies. In the old FRG the media were beholden to an ideal of press and broadcasting freedom based on the notion that there was a plurality of legitimate viewpoints. This freedom was enshrined in laws that were intended to place limits on the role of the state in the activities of the media. In the GDR on the other hand the media were seen as instruments of state control over society: their function was to establish and consolidate a particular world-view in the population as a whole through the careful and deliberate selection and presentation of information. The removal of Communist control in the GDR in the early months of 1990 and the subsequent unification of the two states led to the replacement of this ethos by western ideas. It also introduced a radical restructuring of press and broadcasting in the former GDR.

Like so many other changes that followed unification the restructuring of the media was almost exclusively one-sided: the fundamental changes to the media landscape in the five new federal states had no real echo in the west, where things carried on in their own way. However, the media structures that have emerged in eastern Germany are by no means an exact mirror-image of those in western Germany. The newspaper-buying habits of eastern Germans (and, to a lesser extent, their magazine-buying habits) have proved distinctly resistant to western patterns. As a result there are still two distinct Germanies as far as the press is concerned. The West German media did not represent some kind of static and fully-formed entity that could be simply extended eastwards. Indeed, at the moment of unification broadcasting in West Germany was undergoing a major shift away from its traditional norms of public-service provision based on terrestrial transmitters and moving towards a dual system of public and commercial programming in which cable and satellite technology were being increasingly used. These developments have continued apace since unification so that the unified broadcasting system now in place in both eastern and western Germany differs markedly from the one that operated in the FRG more or less unchanged until the early 1980s.

9.2 Pluralism and Communist Party control

Although the Constitutions of both the FRG and the GDR proclaimed freedom of the press, the practical implications for the media in the two countries were very different. The inclusion of these guarantees in the respective Constitutions is an indication of the status which the two states accorded to this freedom and to other civil rights. The Basic Law of the FRG begins with a lengthy catalogue of rights; it then describes the state system that is regarded as the framework within which they may best be realized. In the GDR's Constitution the proclamation of civil and social rights was preceded by articles stating the political and economic principles of the socialist state. The guarantees of freedom of opinion and of the press appear in Article 5 of the Basic Law. In the GDR's Constitution, such guarantees did not appear until Article 27. Whereas the Basic Law begins by declaring the 'dignity of the individual' as inviolable and asserts that it is the duty of the state to 'respect and protect' this dignity, the GDR Constitution opened with a proclamation of the leadership of the 'Marxist-Leninist Party' (that is, the SED). Thus, in theory at least, press freedom in the FRG is seen as one manifestation of the 'dignity of the individual' that it is the state's duty to preserve. In the GDR on the other hand the press (and all other public manifestations of opinion) were subordinate to whatever constraints the Party, which claimed to have privileged insight into the laws of social and historical development, judged to be appropriate to the well-being of the socialist state.

The West German principle of media freedom from state control has always been more clearly exemplified in the press than in broadcasting. Whereas newspapers and magazines in the FRG have always been concerns run ultimately according to criteria of commercial profitability, radio and television have, as in other European countries, traditionally been felt to require closer control and public accountability. In a landmark Television Verdict of February 1961 the Federal Constitutional Court, called upon to give a ruling on the admissibility of commercial television, declared that there was a fundamental difference between the press and broadcasting concerning their technical capacity to ensure the realization of Article 5 of the Basic Law. Whereas pluralism of opinion in the press was ensured by the sheer numbers (both actual and potential) of newspapers, the Court claimed that in broadcasting, and especially in television, the limited availability of frequencies and the high costs involved meant that a different regime had to apply. The Court maintained that, unless a better solution could be found, such a regime was best served by the existing arrangements in West Germany according to which broadcasting services were provided exclusively by non-commercial public corporations (Williams 1976:24–31, Sandford 1976:102–5).

Although it did not use the terms in its 1961 Television Verdict, the distinction that the Federal Constitutional Court was in effect making was that between 'external pluralism' and 'internal pluralism' (*Außenpluralismus* and *Binnenpluralismus*). These terms, introduced in subsequent rulings of the Court, have become key concepts in the wider debate about how broadcasting is to be organized and in court rulings and legal enactments at both federal and *Land* level in the 1980s and 1990s. 'Pluralism', the potential for providing a voice for the widest possible range of public opinion, was seen by the Court as the cornerstone of the free media. 'External pluralism' is exemplified by the free press, where, in theory at least, the broad spectrum of competing organs ensures that all significant opinions can find an outlet. But since the technical and financial constraints of broadcasting were considered to limit severely the potential for pluralism *between* the outlets, more deliberate arrangements had to be made to ensure pluralism *within* the electronic media. Pluralism, whether 'external' or 'internal', was definitely not considered a virtue in the GDR. Here the 'press freedom' 'under the leadership of the Marxist-Leninist Party' that the Constitution proclaimed was construed as the freedom to keep in step with the inevitable course of history; and since the most sophisticated awareness of what this meant lay with the Party it was ultimately the Party that determined both the organization and content of the media. Accordingly, the GDR media were not commercial operations and their structure and development were determined by political rather than economic considerations. In fact the landscape of the newspaper press and, to a slightly lesser extent, that of the magazine press, hardly changed at all between the 1950s and the demise of the state in 1990. For the greater part of its history there were some forty daily papers in the GDR, divided geographically between the seven Berlin-based central organs (including, most prominently, the SED's *Neues Deutschland*) and the local and regional papers. The regional newspapers with the largest circulation were the dailies that the SED produced for each of the country's fourteen administrative districts, the *Bezirke*. Politically, the GDR's daily press could be divided between the seventeen organs that belonged to the SED, and the remainder, which were published by the mass organizations and the Block Parties; but like the organizations that published them, all were ultimately beholden to the SED's version of Marxism-Leninism and any differences lay not in ideology but in their attempts to address different geographical and social interests in the population.

The GDR's newsstands presented a picture of utter conformity: all the papers on offer typically presenting the same front-page headlines, photographs, and stories. The conformity was ensured by the centralized provision of news (in particular by ADN, the country's only news agency for the domestic media) and by the daily, weekly, and longer-term directives on content and presentation that all editors were obliged to observe. Overarching control lay with the government's press office, which in turn was subordinate to the Central Committee and the Politburo of the SED. Indeed, so watertight was the system of co-ordination and control and so punctilious were editors and journalists in observing the Party line that the one feature so often popularly associated with totalitarian information systems, an office of censorship, did not exist as such in the GDR: the system worked perfectly well without it.

In one important area the ideal of a watertight media monopoly did not work, and that was in the sphere of broadcasting. Although Western newspapers and magazines were simply not available to the average GDR citizen, the authorities could do nothing to prevent the spillover (and also the deliberately boosted transmission) of radio and television programmes from West Germany and West Berlin into the East. Indeed, the small size of the GDR meant that there were few places (notable exceptions being the area around Dresden and the north-east corner of the country) where viewing West German television was not an almost universal habit. And by the 1980s at the latest, it was a habit the authorities did little to prevent. The response of the two channels of the GDR's own television service to this persistent ideological contamination was surprisingly wooden. Only in the field of entertainment was any serious attempt made to win back viewers. News and current affairs programmes, subject to the same mechanisms of Party control as the press, remained as unadventurous (and unwatched) as ever.

9.3 The 'unification' of the German media

For all its tradition of dour conformism GDR television transformed itself more rapidly than the other media when SED control collapsed in the autumn of 1989. Direct Party interference in programme content faded away almost as soon as Erich Honecker resigned in mid-October, and programmers and presenters quickly began to explore the limits of their new freedom. The following weeks turned out to be an interlude of undreamt-of liberation for the broadcasters, as the state, continuing despite its terminal disarray to provide the material wherewithal for radio and television, at the same time abandoned its role of controller and monitor of programme content. The effect on television news was especially dramatic and the new critical (and self-critical) tone won back audiences in such numbers that by the end of the year viewing figures for the East German news had increased ten-fold; in a complete reversal of the previous situation, far more viewers now regularly watched their own bulletins than those from West German stations.

A more critical approach and more open reporting also manifested themselves in the GDR press, but here the most dramatic development came with the opening of the frontiers on 9 November 1989. Now Western papers and magazines suddenly became available to East Germans, initially as souvenirs brought back from trips over the border and soon from enterprising vendors who brought them over by the van-load. It was not long before the newspaper companies themselves began exploiting the new market, and by the spring of 1990 several West German titles were already producing special editions for the GDR.

The early months of 1990 brought an unprecedented blossoming of the press in the GDR. Freed from Party control, the country's traditional publications were joined on the newsstands not only by the West German press but also by a range of new home-bred publications, often reflecting the visionary politics of the citizens' movements that had epitomized the early stages of the revolution. But these heady days did not last. Although the range of titles and overall circulation figures put the GDR proportionally ahead of the FRG for a while, the rapid erosion of the political idealism of the early weeks and more especially the harsh realities of newspaper publishing in the emerging market economy led to the collapse of the citizens' movement journals. As their initial curiosity value wore off, the sales of West German publications also declined steeply. The only real survivors of these hectic months were, curiously enough, the original East German titles. Now under Western ownership and practising Western-style 'non-ideological' journalism, the former SED district dailies (*Bezirkszeitungen*) turned out to be the only lasting success story in the new press landscape of East Germany.

Although the press was taking on a new shape as a result of market forces in a process that had already begun in the revolutionary autumn of 1989, the East German broadcasting system, consisting essentially of two television channels and three main domestic radio services, was in its external structures still unchanged at the moment of unification. Reflecting traditional assumptions about the differences between the two media, the Unification Treaty did not mention the press: it was implicitly classified as a commercial matter. Broadcasting, on the other hand, was seen as a public matter and the subject of a full and lengthy article. According to Article 36 of the Treaty, responsibility for radio and television in the former GDR was to be transferred to the competence of the federal states and thus brought into line with the West German system by the end of 1991. Until this process was completed the services were to be run as an independent public organization headed by a Broadcasting Commissioner.

The restructuring of East German broadcasting turned out to be one of the most contentious of the many upheavals that the five new states were to experience in the year or so following unification. The appointment of the forthright Broadcasting Commissioner, Rudolf Mühlfenzl, a member of the Bavarian Conservative establishment, was pushed through in a manner that seemed to bear little relation to the provisions of the Unification Treaty. Moreover, Mühlfenzl and his team of exclusively western advisors set about savagely reducing the staffing level to, by 1991, barely a third of that in GDR times. Many Germans in the east saw the whole operation as one of the most blatant examples of arrogant Western colonialism. This sentiment was reinforced by Mühlfenzl's refusal to allow the popular New-*Länder* Network, a newly-established third television channel that eastern Germans had come to regard as uniquely their own, to remain in operation after the year-end deadline. By early 1992 Mühlfenzl's task was complete and broadcasting in the former GDR had been fully restructured in accordance with the federal pattern.

9.4 The press today: daily papers

The peculiarities of a country often lie in the eye of the beholder, and this is certainly the case with the press. From a British perspective the German daily press is distinguished by the dominance of regional and local organs and by the lack of an equivalent of the London-based national dailies. Although this structure may not seem odd to, say, American or Italian observers, its roots lie deep in the history of German journalism and is explained above all by the lack of an obvious metropolitan centre in German public life comparable with London or Paris. In fact, if one excludes the financial daily *Handelsblatt* and the 'alternative' *tageszeitung*, only one German paper has a truly national circulation, and that is the sensationalist *Bild-Zeitung*, although even *Bild* appears in a number of distinct regional editions.

With a circulation of some four and a quarter million, *Bild* has long been a force to be reckoned with in German public life. Founded in 1952 by Axel Springer, its formula of aggressively bold headlines, garish layout, and brief, punchy articles quickly caught on with the public, and within a couple of years of its launch it became the country's biggest-selling paper. Indeed it was not long before it attained its present status as the best-selling daily in continental Europe. Its success with its readers has been matched by the decidedly low esteem in which it is held in polite society and by received opinion in cultural and intellectual circles. Part of this distaste is undoubtedly accounted for by the paper's unashamed brashness. But there have long been deeper concerns about the power that such a unique position in the country's press places in the hands of a paper's owners and editors (it is estimated that the paper reaches one-third of the adult population each day). Until his death in 1985 Springer used *Bild* as a platform for his right-wing political views, at times latching onto particular themes in concerted campaigns which the rebellious students of the 1960s, themselves repeatedly the object of particularly venomous headlines in *Bild*, described as opinion manipulation.

It is not simply anxiety about *Bild*'s power over public attitudes or dislike of its politics that has exercised its critics. There have also been concerns about its journalistic methods, brought to light above all by the investigative writer Günter Wallraff as a result of his experiences working incognito as a reporter for the paper in 1977 (Sandford 1990:1–35).

Bild has long been the exception that proves the rules of German journalism. Although some other papers have sought to emulate its sensationalist style, they are few in number, strictly local in distribution, and essentially restricted to a handful of big cities. For the rest, the German press presents a distinctly sober image. This is especially true of the so-called supra-regional dailies, papers which, like *Bild*, are available country-wide but which fall short of the status of national papers since they are rooted in particular regions where their sales are concentrated. The category of these 'supra-regional daily newspapers' (*überregionale Tageszeitungen*) is traditionally reckoned to include just four titles: the *Süddeutsche Zeitung*, published in Munich (circulation: 397,000); the Frankfurt-based *Frankfurter Allgemeine Zeitung* (394,000) and *Frankfurter Rundschau* (189,000); and *Die Welt* (208,000), which moved in 1975 from Hamburg to Bonn and, following unification, to Berlin.

Undoubtedly the best-known German papers abroad, these four differ in the degree of their attachment to their particular regions. While *Die Welt* and the *Frankfurter Allgemeine* (which designates itself in its masthead as a 'newspaper for Germany') tend to be less distinctly rooted in their places of publication and to enjoy a correspondingly wider distribution, the *Frankfurter Rundschau* carries a great deal of regional news and advertising. The content of the *Süddeutsche* also has a distinctly Bavarian flavour, although the paper introduced in 1992 a national edition in an attempt to give itself a keener edge in the competition for readership. There are also differences in the politics and the readership appeal of the four supra-regionals. Both *Die Welt*, the loss-making flagship of the Axel Springer concern, and the *Frankfurter Allgemeine* are politically Conservative. Whereas *Die Welt* is the most downmarket of the four, adopting a style that in British terms would lie somewhere between the *Daily Telegraph* and the *Daily Express*, the *Frankfurter Allgemeine*, very much the paper of the establishment, is the heavyweight of German journalism. Both *Frankfurter Rundschau* and *Süddeutsche*, on the other hand, are left-of-centre in their politics; this is especially true of the former with its appeal to the country's left-liberal intelligentsia.

For all their prominence at the national and international level the supra-regional dailies do not play anything like the role that even the serious national dailies play in Britain. By international standards their circulations are small. Although *Bild* sells over a million copies there are several regional papers with higher sales. In fact for most Germans *the* daily paper has always been a local or regional title; even those who take *Bild* or one of the supra-regionals also often subscribe to a local daily (a monthly or quarterly subscription is the normal way of buying a paper in Germany and accounts for two-thirds of sales). Unlike its British counterparts which are typically relatively lightweight evening papers with an emphasis on local news, the local and regional dailies in Germany usually appear in the morning, are sober and serious in their style and wide-ranging in their news coverage. In many of these papers the extent of international and national reporting, not to mention the coverage of such areas as the arts and the economy, is impressive. In some cases it is outstanding, so that many educated Germans are happy to make do with the one local paper where for comparable coverage their British counterparts would be obliged to take both a national daily and a local paper.

This traditional pattern of daily newspaper sales in West Germany has scarcely been touched by unification. In some respects the pattern that established itself in East Germany after the war has also shown itself to be remarkably resistant to change. Thus despite privatization and the removal of the centrally planned and controlled media system, the press in the east still retains structural peculiarities that were, in part at least, imposed in order to consolidate Communist control in the early days of the GDR. This is particularly true for the former *Bezirkszeitungen*. Although the *Bezirke* were largely artificial creations with little historical legitimacy, the papers that served them were, from the meagre range of titles available, the preferred reading of most East Germans, not least for their local coverage. With the collapse of Communism the *Bezirke* were abolished and many of their powers were taken over by the five new *Länder*. Meanwhile most

Bezirkszeitungen had entered into co-operation agreements with a range of western German papers. These agreements were soon to develop into outright takeovers as the Trust Agency sold off the eastern German papers to their western 'partners'. Now placed under new ownership but in many cases keeping their original titles, they have managed to a remarkable degree to retain their local readers' loyalties. As a result they enjoy today some of the highest circulations in the whole of Germany. Less than a year after unification no fewer than five of the ten best-selling dailies in Germany were former GDR *Bezirkszeitungen*: three of them, the *Freie Presse* (Chemnitz), the *Mitteldeutsche Zeitung* (Halle), and the *Sächsische Zeitung* (Dresden), achieved sales of over half a million.

The other two main categories of newspapers in the new federal states, the former Berlin-based dailies and new titles founded after the collapse of Communism, have not fared so well. It is undoubtedly an indication of the strength of the provincial tradition in German newspaper publishing that the GDR's national daily papers, the former central organs of the political parties and mass organizations, scarcely survived the transition to a market system. Their huge print-runs either shrank dramatically (from over a million each in the case of *Neues Deutschland* and the young people's daily *Junge Welt* to 85,000 and 64,000 respectively in 1993) or they disappeared altogether, as occurred with the former trade-union paper *Tribüne*, which enjoyed pre-1990 sales of around half a million, and *Der Morgen*, the paper of the former Liberal Democratic Party, the LDPD. In 1990 *Der Morgen* transformed itself very promisingly into a much-admired serious daily, but it too was unceremoniously buried a year later by its new western owners, the Axel Springer Verlag. Significantly, the only East Berlin-based papers to have survived tolerably well are essentially local ones, such as the *Berliner Zeitung* and the *Berliner Kurier* (formerly *BZ am Abend*, the most downmarket of the GDR's papers).

The new titles that appeared on the East German market in early 1990 were of two types, each addressing a specifically East German readership. In the first place there were the radical organs of the citizens' movements, some of which had already appeared as underground publications during, and in a few cases even before the 1989 revolution. Hardly any of these survived the rapid marginalization of the visionary politics they represented, though the weekly *Freitag*, created out of the former GDR cultural weekly *Sonntag*, still provides a flavour of what they stood for. The other new titles were brash, speculative commercial ventures, founded with an eye to the substantial share of the East German market taken by the West German *Bild-Zeitung*. The most successful of these was *Super!*, which mixed well-tried western techniques of scandalmongering and sensationalism with appeals to specifically East German feelings of *Ossi* solidarity and indignation about the western takover. For a while *Super!* managed to make major inroads into *Bild*'s eastern sales, but it too was closed down in July 1992, some fifteen months after its launch, when the Murdoch Corporation withdrew from the partnership with the West German Burda concern, under whose auspices it was published.

9.5 The press today: the weeklies

Inasmuch as there is a national press in Germany, it is to be found in the periodical press rather than in the daily newspapers. The serious weeklies in particular, most notably *Die Zeit* and *Der Spiegel*, help provide that sense of belonging to a national cultural and political community that in Britain tends to be the province of the daily newspapers. The lack of a developed Sunday newspaper tradition in Germany, where only the Sunday editions of *Bild* and *Die Welt* play a significant role in the market, contributes further to the comparatively high sales figures of the weeklies. For instance, *Die Zeit* alone has a circulation (490,000) well above even the combined figures for all the serious British weeklies, and the news magazine *Der Spiegel*, with sales of around one million, has no home-grown British equivalent.

Equally distinctive are the *Illustrierte,* non-specialist magazines with a popular appeal that cultivate a photo-journalism long since absent in Britain since the demise of *Illustrated, Picture Post* and *John Bull.* With the folding of *Quick* in August 1992 only three *Illustrierte* were left: *Stern, Neue Revue* and *Bunte* remain a prominent and familiar part of the German press scene. The range of more specialist magazines is particularly wide. Aimed specifically at women, men, and teenagers, as well as motorists, gardeners, anglers, and other hobby enthusiasts, these are not dissimilar to their counterparts in many other countries. By far the biggest circulation in Germany (over eleven and a half million) is that of *ADAC Motorwelt*, the membership journal of the country's major motoring organization, but if one leaves aside this rather special case, the highest sales figures are found, both individually and collectively, in the radio and television listings magazines, the *Programmzeitschriften*. Although weekly listings are also available in newspapers as well as in many other magazines and 'free papers' funded by advertising, the *Programmzeitschrift* category contains numerous titles, with three selling over two million copies each.

The effects of unification on the established weekly market have been muted. The increase in sales figures made possible by the new eastern German readership has been patchy and for the most part far from proportional to the additional potential market. In general the more serious weeklies have a much lower market penetration in eastern than in western Germany, whereas in a number of cases the popular end of the magazine market has achieved quite large sales increases. Even here there is clearly a niche for more modest formats targeted specifically at an eastern readership, as with the popular weekly *Super Illu*, which continues to practise the *Super!* formula in the shape of a downmarket general interest magazine. The re-emergence of the former GDR publication *Wochenpost* as a serious weekly has added another publication to the category of *Die Zeit* but it too has a predominantly eastern readership; together with its relatively modest size and circulation, it would appear to pose little threat to its western counterparts.

9.6 Broadcasting

The radio and television system established in West Germany after the Second World War was organized according to public service principles inspired by the BBC. The West German radio and television service was, moreover, regional in structure, a characteristic that accords with the constitutional principle that places legislative competence for such matters as education and the media in the hands of the individual *Länder* rather than with the Federal Parliament in Bonn. Although they are often referred to as the '*Land* Broadcasting Corporations', the principle of 'one *Land*, one broadcasting service' actually held true in only five of the ten *Länder* of the old FRG and West Berlin. Elsewhere the picture was more complicated: three *Länder* shared the *Norddeutscher Rundfunk* (NDR); in the south-west, the single *Land* of Baden-Württemberg was divided between the *Süddeutscher Rundfunk* (SDR) and the *Südwestfunk* (SWF), the latter also serving the adjacent *Land* of Rhineland Palatinate. Since unification and the Mühlfenzl interlude, two further corporations have been established in eastern Germany: the *Mitteldeutscher Rundfunk* (MDR) serves three *Länder*; the *Ostdeutscher Rundfunk Brandenburg* (ORB) serves one *Land*. East Berlin has come under the aegis of the original West Berlin service, the *Sender Freies Berlin* (SFB). The northern *Land* of Mecklenburg-West Pomerania has joined Schleswig-Holstein, Hamburg, and Lower Saxony as the fourth partner in the NDR. There are now eleven *Land* Broadcasting Corporations in all.

Although each corporation is subject to the Broadcasting Law of the *Land* or *Länder* it serves, the principles behind their organization and the structures derived from these principles are very similar. In keeping with the ideal of democratic accountability each broadcasting corporation is ultimately responsible to its Broadcasting Council (*Rundfunkrat*). The members of the Council represent a range of interest groups from within the region, including the political parties of the relevant *Land* parliaments, which are proportionally represented. Inevitably some feel excluded from the list of 'socially significant groups' that as of right have seats on the Broadcasting Councils. Nevertheless the range of inputs is broad, covering, for instance, employers, trade unions, the Churches, and educational, cultural, sporting, and press affiliations. In recent years there has been a tendency to greater flexibility, with seats created for minorities and other less specific groupings. Although the system is in principle far more open than that of the BBC, whose Board of Governors is appointed 'by the Queen in Council on the advice of the Prime Minister', there has long been a tendency, as in so much of German public life, to allow party-political considerations to play a significant role in the appointments and hence ultimately in programming policy too. As a result particular Broadcasting Councils are recognizably 'black' (CDU) or 'red' (SPD) in their party leanings. Whilst the Council is the body to which the broadcasters are ultimately accountable both for the financial management and for the programming policy of their corporation, day-to-day decisions are taken by the next level in the pyramid, the Administrative Council (*Verwaltungsrat*), and above all by the most powerful individual in the organization, the Director General (*Intendant*). Both of these are ultimately appointed by and accountable to the Broadcasting Council (for more details of the structure of the public broadcasting corporations see Williams 1976).

The principle that each region should have its own broadcasting corporation offering a full range of programmes was a token of the widespread determination in the early post-war years to break with the highly centralized system of media control that had been created by Joseph Goebbels, the Nazi propaganda minister, and to return in part to the structures that had existed in the Weimar Republic. In practice the principle is fully realized only in radio broadcasting, where each regional corporation does indeed provide its *Land* or *Länder* with at least three fully-fledged services. The much more expensive medium of television, on the other hand, has necessitated a greater pooling of resources.

In 1950 the newly-founded corporations set up an umbrella organization, the ARD, to co-ordinate many of their activities and to represent their common interests at home and abroad. Today the ARD is best known as the shorthand term for the First German Television Channel (*Erstes Deutsches Fernshen*, set up in 1953), though the overall remit of the organization covers much more, not least the redistribution of revenues from the larger, wealthier corporations to the smaller, poorer ones according to a formula originally agreed in 1958. A second television channel, the ZDF (*Zweites Deutsches Fernsehen*), was added in 1963 and was followed by a third set of channels. The third channels are the most truly regional of the FRG's television services: some of them serve just one *Land*, whilst others are run co-operatively by two or three adjacent corporations. At the other extreme the ZDF operates a single national service based in Mainz, although its legal basis, true to the principle of *Land* competence in broadcasting, lies not with the Federation but in an inter-*Land* treaty. The programming structure of the First Channel is more complex, being akin in some respects to that of ITV in Britain, with each region contributing an agreed share of programmes to the national network.

The public service principle and the broadcasting structures based on it that emerged in the first decade or so of the FRG's existence have proved remarkably resistant to change. The twin threats of state control and commercialization were apparently warded off successfully at the beginning of the 1960s, when the Federal Constitutional Court ruled against an attempt by the Adenauer government to establish a national commercial television channel. As a result the FRG kept its established broadcasting system more or less intact until well into the 1980s at a time when many other European countries were witnessing major changes in the provision of radio and television. However, in its judgement of 28 February 1961 the Court did not rule out for all time the possibility of commercial broadcasting but merely its admissibility in the prevailing circumstances. In passing it should be noted that the term 'commercial broadcasting' is slightly confusing in the German case as the public service corporations also broadcast commercials, although the bulk of their income comes from the licence fee paid by their audiences.

The 1961 Television Verdict turned out to be the first in a series of what, by the 1980s, were known as 'Broadcasting Verdicts', covering not only television also but radio and the 'new media' in a wider sense. At issue in all the Federal Constitutional Court's deliberations has been Article 5 of the Basic Law and its proclamation of freedom of opinion. Each successive Broadcasting Verdict (there had been seven by 1993) can be seen as a refinement in the light of developing technical, political, and economic circumstances of the principles set down in the 1961 ruling.

There had always been pressure from interested parties for the introduction of commercial television and radio in the FRG. By the end of the 1970s actual and anticipated developments in cable and satellite technologies were making the premises of the Court's 1961 ruling look increasingly out-of-date. Above all the political change of 1982 definitively opened the gates to the wholesale transformation of German broadcasting that took place during the rest of the decade. While Helmut Schmidt's SPD government had been decidedly wary about commercial broadcasting, the new CDU-led government of Helmut Kohl embraced the idea with gusto.

The introduction of private radio and television services has remained a convoluted and highly contentious matter, not least because the hallowed principle of *Land* responsibility for broadcasting has meant that the pace and nature of change differed from region to region depending on the political complexion of the *Land* government. This is despite the fact that radio and television signals are no respecters of *Land* boundaries, especially if they come from satellites, which is increasingly the case since the mid-1960s.

The new FRG has a very different broadcasting landscape from that of only a few years ago. But the change was not brought about by unification. In 1990 the new *Länder* were slotted into a system that was already transformed. The outward signs of change (the first commercial radio and television services began broadcasting in the mid-1980s) have been accompanied by an extraordinary proliferation of laws and institutions at the *Land*, inter-*Land*, federal, and European levels. Where formerly each *Land* simply had its own broadcasting law to regulate the operation of its public service broadcasting corporation (or an inter-*Land* treaty for a jointly-run corporation), these have now been supplemented by detailed media laws, one for each of the sixteen *Länder*. These laws cover the operation of commercial broadcasting services and the State Media Authorities (*Landesmedienanstalten*) that supervise their activities. To provide an overall framework, there is also a lengthy 'Inter-*Land* Treaty on Broadcasting in the United Germany' which came into force at the beginning of 1992, replacing an earlier inter-*Land* treaty of 1987.

Underpinning all of these legal arrangements are the successive Broadcasting Verdicts of the Federal Constitutional Court. In the course of the 1980s these verdicts laid down a series of markers for changes in radio and television. In so doing they established and refined the terminology of the debate about commercialization. In the first of its 1980s judgements the Third Television Verdict of 1981 (the Second Television Verdict was delivered in 1971), the Court declared that, while commercial broadcasting is not incompatible with the Basic Law, adequate guarantees of pluralism must be provided in law even when technical limitations on the number of programmes have been overcome; the free play of market forces cannot alone ensure such pluralism (*Media Perspektiven*, No. 6, 1981:421–43). In its verdict the Court introduced the important notions of 'external pluralism' and 'internal pluralism' mentioned earlier. The former is typified in the German press and the latter in German public service broadcasting, where the Broadcasting Council in particular is designed to ensure that a pluralism of views has access to the airwaves even though the broadcasting corporations themselves enjoy (or, at least, used to enjoy) a monopoly position in relation to their listeners and viewers. Both models, the Court now proclaimed, were acceptable ways of ensuring freedom of broadcasting. At the same time the Court made it clear that the press was still not the model for broadcasting: here legal provisions would continue to have to temper the free play of market forces in order to ensure genuine pluralism and freedom.

In the the Fourth Broadcasting Verdict (1986) the Court introduced two further important notions (*Media Perspektiven Dokumentation*, IV, 1986:213–47). First, it recognized that a 'dual order' had emerged in West German broadcasting, comprising the established public corporations and the new commercial services. Second, this meant that the public corporations were now entrusted with the 'essential basic provision': they had to provide the breadth, variety, and quality of programmes that could not be automatically expected of the commercial services. This crucial point made clear that the public service corporations could not be replaced by commercial operators; indeed, it made the continuing existence of the former a precondition for the admissibility of the latter. The point was affirmed and its practical implications clarified the following year in the Fifth Broadcasting Verdict (*Media Perspektiven Dokumentation*, III, 1987:145–68) when the Court declared that the public service corporations enjoy a 'guarantee of continued existence and development' and may not therefore be put at any disadvantage *vis-à-vis* the commercial channels. In practical terms this means that public service broadcasting must be adequately funded to enable it to keep up with technical and other developments that may affect its competitiveness.

Embedded in a huge web of legal enactments, the dual order of present-day German broadcasting is of bewildering complexity. Although the picture is for the most part not dissimilar in different parts of the country, there are still variations from *Land* to *Land* in the organizational principles governing, for instance, commercial radio. This is especially true in North Rhine-Westphalia, whose media law has prescribed a so-called 'two column model', which, along the lines that originally applied to Britain's Channel Four, attempts to free programme-making from commercial pressures by keeping it separate from revenue-generating activities. The North Rhine-Westphalia model represents a third way between private and public broadcasting and is as such unique in the FRG. Elsewhere the dividing lines between the two sectors are more distinct, with radio listeners having a choice between the three or four programmes provided by their public service corporation and by an increasing number of commercial stations typically on a region-wide basis, though sometimes with local opt-outs. These are mostly local stand-alones, though in some *Länder Land*-wide commercial stations also exist. In addition to these local and regional services, public service broadcasting at the national level has been provided since the beginning of 1994 under the joint umbrella of the ARD and the ZDF by the programmes of *DeutschlandRadio*, created out of the pre-viously-existing *Deutschlandfunk*, *RIAS-Berlin*, and *DS-Kultur* (the last of which had in turn been formed from the former East German *Deutschland-sender*).

As for television, the range of programmes available depends on whether a household has cable and/or satellite facilities. At the level of traditional over-air terrestrial reception the three original public service channels (ARD, ZDF, and the regional Third Channels) have been joined over much of the country by the two main commercial channels, RTL and Sat 1. By virtue of being the first to start operating when private television got underway in 1984 these two have been able to establish themselves as the uncontested leaders in the field; they were granted use of the few re-maining terrestrial frequencies as and when these were made available by the Federal Post Office.

Most other commercial channels are available only from cable or satel-lite, offering with a few notable exceptions a diet of entertainment pro-gramming; as cable television at least is much more developed in Germany than in, say, Britain, they still reach a large and growing number of house-holds. The cabling of West German towns in the 1980s was undertaken by the Kohl government deliberately to force the pace of change in broadcast-ing. It was a highly contentious measure which exploited the Federal Gov-ernment's constitutional competence in the field of telecommunications and faced the *Länder*, despite their responsibility for radio and television, with a *fait accompli* in the form of a sudden increase in the number of available channels waiting for broadcasters to occupy them. The aim of *Telekom* (the national telecommunications operator in the FRG) is to con-nect 80% of the country's households to the cable network by 1997, a fig-ure that is expected to be reached in the western half by 1995. Already virtually 100% availability has been achieved in some western cities, such as Hamburg and Bremen, though the actual take-up rate is lower: some 60% of households that can be connected have actually elected for a cable link. Rates in eastern Germany are much lower. In early 1993 only 4% of households in Saxony Anhalt were cabled although cabling there is now proceeding very rapidly and to a higher technical standard than in some of the older western systems (Zimmer 1993; Schmitt-Beck and Dietz 1993).

9.7 Prospects and problems

It has always been recognized in the FRG that the threat to press freedom is essentially two-fold: overweening state control and the concentration of economic power over the press in fewer and fewer hands. Germany has experienced both in extreme forms: the former in the Third Reich and in the GDR and the latter in the Weimar Republic in the shape of the Hugenberg press empire. Like all Western democracies the FRG interprets 'press freedom' not only as a 'freedom *from*' (that is, freedom from state interference) but also as a 'freedom *to*', namely, the economic right not only to set up newspapers and magazines but also the right to buy (and compete against) existing ones. The result is all too often press concentration, the negation of the very pluralism that freedom of the press is supposed to embody.

The tendency towards concentration has caused alarm in the FRG, in particular because of what has happened in the predominantly local and regional daily press. The national total of daily papers looks extremely healthy by British standards even though, until unification, it steadily declined almost every year since the 1950s. The generally accepted indicator of variety in the press is not the number of titles, as many of these are variants of a single paper, but the number of independent editorial units. In 1954 there were 225 such units. By the mid-1970s the figure had sunk to around 120 and it stayed at this level until unification. More important than the total of daily papers is the equally steady tendency to create local and regional monopolies, so-called 'one-paper districts'. These areas, where previously there may have been a number of competing local or regional dailies, now have only one. Since for most Germans *the* daily is the local one, living in these 'one-paper districts' means in effect having no choice. The process leading to this is the all-too-familiar one of bankruptcies, takeovers, mergers, and co-operation agreements, often thinly masked by the practice of retaining an old local title when in fact the paper has become identical in content to all the others in its new stable.

What has happened in the former GDR is a highly accelerated version of the process of press concentration that has been going on for over forty years in the old FRG. The initial blossoming of the East German press landscape (the transformation of the existing papers, the founding of dozens of new ones, and the advent of papers from West Germany) was already rapidly fading by the time of unification: several of the former GDR titles fell by the wayside, the new ventures shrank to almost nothing, and the sales of West German newspapers fell sharply once their curiosity value wore off. Today the degree of press concentration in eastern Germany exceeds that in the west. In a report submitted to the Federal Minister of the Interior one commentator has gone so far as to claim that it surpasses that of the old GDR (Schneider 1992:434).

The survival and success of the former SED regional papers, which now rank among the best-selling dailies in the whole of Germany, is striking.

Equally noteworthy is the fact that they and to all intents and purposes the rest of the eastern German press are now in western hands. The policy of the Trust Agency in disposing of existing titles has been much criticized. But given the perception of the press as a saleable commodity and the lack of capital among eastern Germans it was inevitable that titles would be bought up by westerners. Unification has thus increased the power of the western press concerns, for it is they who have been the main beneficiaries of the sell-off of the East German titles.

The coincidence of unification and the establishment of a growing commercial sector in German broadcasting has also consolidated a process that was already well underway in the West: the growing concentration of power in both the printed and the electronic media in the form of the 'media-multis'. The emergence of these organizations, with interests not only in newspapers, magazines, radio and television but also in book publishing, films, and music and video production, has been one of the most significant developments of the 1980s in the German media. Where concern was previously expressed about the power of the press, now it is directed increasingly at media power on a much wider scale.

Press power in the FRG used to be synonymous with the Springer organization. In some respects the growth of the Axel Springer Verlag has been untypical of the very German process of press concentration at the regional and local level. The status of the Springer Verlag as Germany's (and continental Europe's) biggest publisher of newspapers and magazines was largely achieved not through the acquisition of existing titles but by the creation of successful new ones, notably, of course, the *Bild-Zeitung*, the most *un*-local of all German papers. Nor did the Springer concern play much of a role in the scramble for the big East German titles: unlike its rivals it chose to invest in smaller publications, in the event unwisely. However, the Springer concern, which had always campaigned for commercial broadcasting, was quick off the mark in the 1980s to set up the second of the big two private television stations, Sat 1, in which it currently has a nominal 20% direct holding. In practice the Springer control over Sat 1 approaches 25% (on account of the company's 35% holding in the television news service *Aktuell Presse-Fernsehen*, which in its turn owns a further 20% of Sat 1). This is a symptom of the increasingly complex interlocking chains of interest and control that the media multis have established in recent years. And it is not simply a matter of ownership: the Springer company is adept, for instance, at promoting Sat 1 programmes in its own radio and television weeklies as well as in its daily papers.

The largest direct share in Sat 1 (43%) is in the hands of Leo Kirch. Particularly since his acquisition of a 35% holding in the Axel Springer Verlag, Kirch is undoubtedly the most powerful single figure in the German media. Born in 1926 Kirch began his media career in the mid-1950s by buying up films, an activity that was to repay him handsomely as his collection became increasingly indispensable with the growth of television in Germany. Today the television stations are singularly beholden to him for their film output: his holdings now total 15,000 titles, not to mention a further 50,000 hours of television programmes. A much more retiring figure than Axel Springer, Kirch has worked away at building up an empire that is concentrated in the production, distribution and exhibition of films, and in commercial television. Recently his activities in commercial television have begun to attract attention, not least because he has interests in no fewer than five different German channels. The fact that it is not entirely clear just what or how great all these interests are and how they relate to one another is another example of the increasing difficulty of unravelling the patterns of power that now exist in the German media (Dähnhardt 1992).

In a survey in 1992 eight organizations were identified as German media multis. These were Bertelsmann (the largest media conglomerate in Europe and, after Time-Warner, the second largest in the world), Springer, Kirch, Holtzbrinck, Bauer, Burda, Gong, and WAZ (Röper 1993). In itself the number of media multis is not excessive and suggests a degree of competition and pluralism that accords with the ideal of the free press. There are, however, less sanguine ways of viewing the situation. For a start not all of these groupings are entirely independent of each other, as the entanglements of Kirch and Springer illustrate. There is also the fact that certain media are more or less dominated by a much smaller number of groups. This is especially the case with commercial television, where the major channels fall into two main 'families'. The first is the Kirch/Springer grouping which dominates Sat 1, DSF, Pro 7, and the *Kabelkanal*. The second is the alliance between Bertelsmann and the CLT company, which has an 85% share in RTL, as well as holdings in RTL2 and Vox. Other multis have specialized in the print media, where some have achieved dominant positions in important markets. Nationally, for instance, the Burda-Verlag controls over a third of all magazine sales; in common with other publishers that previously specialized in magazines it has taken advantage of unification to branch out into the newspaper market in eastern Germany.

It is not only the power, potential or actual, of the media empires that interests observers of the German media scene. The intense debate about the arrival of the new media that was conducted in Germany in the late 1970s and early 1980s focused also on the question of quality (Sandford 1985). The claim that quality will suffer and standards will be dragged down as the stations try to maximize their advertising revenue by seeking

out large audiences through a policy of vulgarized lowest common denominator programming is often adduced when the introduction of commercial broadcasting is on the agenda. It is undeniably true that the overall
programming levels of the private television services in Germany are much
more down-market than those of the ARD and the ZDF, and the same goes
for commercial radio; even the Federal Constitutional Court has recognized
this as inherent in the nature of commercial broadcasting. The head of
RTL, Helmut Thoma, is in no doubt that the appeal of vulgarity is a cornerstone of commercial television. But more has not meant only worse:
even RTL has its serious programmes, such as Alexander Kluge's '*10 vor
11*' although, according to Thoma, 'hardly anyone watches, and if they do
it's only in order not to miss the sex show that follows it' (Thoma
1992:63). And not all the new channels have been quite so unashamedly
aimed at a mass market. It must, however, be said that the exceptions are
either non-commercial, like 3-Sat (a co-operative service of the German,
Austrian, and Swiss public service channels) and the Franco-German venture arte, or, like the news channel n-tv, they have failed to win more than
a minute share of the audience unless, like Vox, they quickly abandoned
their initial high ideals in the search for larger audiences.

Unification, which came at a critical moment in the development of the
German media, has been for them a mixed blessing. For the east Germans
it clearly brought liberation from what was generally recognized, even by
its own practitioners, to be a stultifyingly dysfunctional system. At the
same time there seems little doubt that problems that have traditionally beset the FRG's media have been exacerbated by unification with the result
that eastern Germans have not acquired quite such a shining example of
Western pluralist practice as the ideals of the Basic Law envisage.

Further reading

The texts of the Constitutions of the FRG and the GDR are in Schuster
(1978); for a comparison of the principles behind the two systems see
Sandford (1988). For the media in the GDR see Sandford (1976:184–209),
and Holzweißig (1989, 1991); on the role of Western television, see
Naftzinger (1994). A standard textbook on the contemporary media in the
FRG is Meyn (1992). For the most up-to-date survey in English with emphasis on the political and legal context in Germany see Humphreys
(1994). There are also detailed and lengthy entries on many aspects of the
media in Noelle-Neumann, Schulz, and Wilke (1989). Useful for up-to-
date information on developments in all the media, including documentation on relevant laws, is the monthly journal *Media Perspektiven*. The legal

context of the organization of German broadcasting is discussed in detail in Porter and Hasselbach (1991). Heigemann (1988) and Ernst (1992) also cover developments in the electronic media, although the pace of change is so rapid in this area that even these are already becoming dated. Developments in public-service broadcasting, including the texts of all relevant laws, are monitored in detail in the *ARD Jahrbuch*, the annual year-book of the ARD. For an overview of the GDR media before the *Wende* see Holzweißig (1989). Also recommended are the entries *Medienpolitik, Presse, Rundfunk*, and *Fernsehen*, including other relevant entries cross-referenced under these headings, in Zimmermann (1985). On developments in east Germany since unification see Baerns (1990), Streul (1991a, 1991b), and Sandford (1992, 1993); articles on this area appear occasionally in *Deutschland Archiv*. Circulation figures given in this chapter are taken from the *IVW-Auflagenliste* January 1994 and are rounded to the nearest thousand. Unless otherwise indicated, they refer to the number of copies sold per issue in the first quarter of 1994 (the author is grateful to Michael Schallmeyer of the *Informationsgemeinschaft zur Feststellung der Verbreitung von Werbeträgern e.V.* for supplying the data).

10
Writers in Transition
The End of East German Literature?

10.1 The position of writers in the GDR before 1985

Summing up the discussion on East German writers up to 1993, the West
German dramatist Ulrich Greiner had the following to say:

> The author as moral authority has been a common phenomenon in
> Germany. [...] The public role of the author achieved a unique late
> flowering in socialism, and particularly in the GDR. The author
> acted and wrote in the service of either the Party (as a Party writer)
> or else of the alluring project of true socialism (which in some cases
> could be directed against the Party). Those who did not do so dis-
> appeared into the underground or to the West. (Greiner 1993)

This west German view of the literary production of the GDR overstates
the case and generalizes in the interest of making a point. Nevertheless the
position of writers under the 'real existing socialism' of the GDR was very
different from the situation these writers faced after unification.

From its beginnings in the Soviet zone of occupation in 1945, GDR literature was seen by those in power and also by many of the authors who
produced it as a tool or weapon for changing attitudes and values and for
assisting in the development of the new socialist society. Literature's function was to advance the new enlightenment: this was shown by the importance the Soviet administration attached to the reopening of the theatres in
the ruined cities of their zone and specifically by their support for the production of Lessing's *Nathan der Weise* (Nathan the Wise) in the autumn of
1945, only a few months after the end of the war. Despite the many freezes
and thaws in East German cultural policy between 1945 and 1989 there
was never any fundamental questioning of the role of literature. Regardless
of how much their viewpoints might contrast in levels of differentiation,
cultural functionaries and writers both accepted the premise that literature
had an important part to play in achieving the ideals of socialism, however

defined. For the authors of the GDR this resulted on the one hand in material privileges and on the other in unwelcome direction from the state. Their situation before 1989 contrasts starkly both with the largely benevolent neglect of literature by the leading political and industrial circles in West Germany and with the very different criteria by which GDR authors, and to a lesser extent their literary works, have been judged since the *Wende*. In one sense East German literature has obviously ended; in another the literary harvest from these experiences is only beginning.

Like other groups in the GDR, authors had to be organized. Many were, of course, members of the SED and discussed literature within their Party groups. Membership of the Writers' Association of the GDR was essential for anyone wishing to have their work published in East Germany. The Writers' Association served a number of functions: it acted as a transmission belt for the Politburo's current cultural policy; it had a coercive role, with sanctions to keep authors in line, which ranged from friendly talkings-to up to expulsion (effectively a ban on publication); it also served simply as a club, ensuring that writers knew their colleagues more personally than in less organized societies. These features, together with the fact that the GDR was a small country, all contributed to make literary production within the GDR more homogeneous than in the West, so that GDR literature often appeared to be conducting an internal discussion on a current agenda.

The chief publishing houses in the GDR were state-owned and the main literary publisher, Aufbau, was under the direct control of the SED (a fact which emerged only in 1990). In any case the readers engaged by publishers had to ensure that a work was publishable. Publishable did not mean, as in the West, profitably marketable or in keeping with the publisher's house profile. A work was publishable in the GDR only if it received approval for printing (*Druckgenehmigung*) from the Ministry of Culture, that is, if it was in keeping with the current guidelines on cultural policy. Publication outside the GDR (and that meant principally in the FRG) of a work that could not appear in East Germany was regarded at least as an act of disloyalty and could have legal consequences: the author could be charged with the quasi-treasonable crime of bringing the state into public disrepute or with an offence against the currency laws. For these reasons much of the discussion of critical literature took place before publication between the publisher's reader and the author: it involved a calculation of how elastic the current official policy on literature might be and of what changes the author would accept. Since both author and publisher had a prime interest in getting books published there was an incentive to compromise rather than to risk printing approval being refused or the paper allocation being cut back.

In these circumstances most instances of censorship were acts of self-censorship by the authors, either at the suggestion of the publisher or at the initial stage of writing. Operating within the system, writers knew what they could say and how they could say it; the writing characterized as critical consisted for the most part in works which tried to push one or the other of these boundaries back a little. The deletion of calls for bilateral disarmament in the GDR edition of Christa Wolf's *Frankfurter Vorlesungen* (Frankfurt Lectures, 1983), explicitly indicated by omission marks in the text, was the exception. Normally censorship did not need to go that far.

Official propaganda always made much of the extent to which literature was read by large numbers of the population, contrasting it with the 'elitism' which (it was claimed) characterized the consumption of literature in the West. It is true that interest in literature was more widespread among the GDR population, but this was at least partly a result of the different position literature occupied within the general range of book, magazine and newspaper production there. As Christoph Hein remarked in his address to the Tenth Congress of the Writers' Association in 1987, the amount of information and discussion in the press was so small that the literature of some authors functioned as a replacement for the usual forums of critical debate; it was received less in terms of its specific role of literature than as an officially-tolerated expression of current problems (*Schriftsteller-verband* 1988). This role coincided with the perception some authors had of their mission in society. Christa Wolf's *Was bleibt* (What Remains, 1990b) provides a good illustration of how its narrator is regarded as a source of aid and guidance both by the young woman who visits her and by the audience at her literary reading. Additionally, GDR writers enjoyed an audience which read closely, critically, and with an ear for implied meaning. As the poet Kurt Drawert puts it: 'Where speaking freely is forbidden, words carry a greater weight than in a democracy where hardly anyone listens' (Drawert 1993).

Although the circumstances of literary production and reception in the GDR were quite different to those in the FRG, Britain, and the United States, it cannot be assumed that they totally precluded any diversity either in the kinds of literature produced or in authors' attitudes. Admittedly, the shelves of East German bookshops carried their share of uninspired or badly written books, the output of hack authors, but at times the GDR produced literary and dramatic works of international interest. The key words are 'at times', for this was dependent on political circumstances and on the current state of cultural policy. The expulsion of the singer-poet Wolf Biermann in 1976 initiated a cultural freeze, which lead to protests and exclusions from the Writers' Association and to the departure of a number of important writers for West Germany. The late 1970s were a period of cultural doldrums, exacerbated by the worsening economic situation.

The situation in the mid-1980s was changed by developments outside the GDR which eventually created the precondition for German unification—Mikhail Gorbachev's reforms in the Soviet Union and in particular his policy of *glasnost*. Proposals for greater openness were rejected by the GDR Politburo, which reacted by extending its censorship to embrace the Soviet press and literature. But this attempt at resistance was futile: it gave rise to a number of scandals which increased the pressure for change. Writers and intellectuals were keen to explore the possibilities of freer expression; they were particularly open to Gorbachev's argument that the stagnation into which the socialist countries had declined could be countered only by openness and unfettered discussion of the need for change. The Ninth Congress of the Writers' Association in 1983 was held under the motto of 'business as usual'. In a reference to the most recent wave of expulsions in 1979 Hermann Kant, the President of the Writers' Association from 1978 to 1989, stated that 'grass has since grown over many matters which upset us a lot at the time' (Zimmermann 1985:774), and the Congress remained uncontroversial compared to those of the 1970s. In contrast, the Tenth Congress in 1988 was a much more outspoken affair. Apart from Christoph Hein's widely reported attack on the censorship apparatus, the Congress featured a wide-ranging debate on another taboo issue, the physical environment. Jurij Koch, for example, spoke of his home in the Sorb area in the south-east: the area had the misfortune of being the GDR's only energy source, brown coal, with the result that villages and towns were destroyed by open-cast mining. For his part, Volker Braun argued for new attitudes in matters of ecological concern:

> But now we are aware of movement; things are starting to change, questions are beginning to be asked! The conflict of interests, the conflict of different value systems, in which the forest and the car, chemicals, and evening twilight are taking up battle positions. (*Schriftstellerverband* 1988:I.83)

Perhaps even more surprising than the discussion itself was the fact that it took place for the first time in the presence of West German journalists. Indeed the whole proceedings of the Congress were published uncensored, albeit after some delay, by Aufbau (*Schriftstellerverband* 1988). However, it is emblematic of the conflicting tendencies within the GDR leadership at the time that, in the same week as Honecker and other Politburo members attended and apparently supported this conference with its calls for more openness and concern for the environment, the *Stasi* raided the unofficial

Umweltbibliothek (ecological library) run by an East Berlin church con-
gregation; the *Stasi* planned to show that the library was antagonistic to the
state and close it down.

Another sign of increased openness in publishing was the introduction
by Aufbau of a new series, *Außer der Reihe* (Out of Line). As the name
indicates, this was dedicated to works which were outside the normal
range covered by the publishing house. The series was edited by Gerhard
Wolf, Christa Wolf's husband, who had done a great deal within the GDR
to promote young literary talent, particularly the young poets of the group
based on the Berlin district of Prenzlauer Berg. Younger experimental
poets and writers such as Bert Papenfuß-Gorek, Jan Faktor, Gabriele
Kachold, and Rainer Schedlinski, whose works had hitherto been published mainly in semi-official and unofficial magazines (and in West Germany) with only a limited circulation within the GDR, were made available
to a wider audience by their appearance in *Außer der Reihe*.

10.2 The contribution of GDR writers to the *Wende*

The small steps in the direction of liberalization which began in the mid-
1980s were overtaken by the events of 1989 which resulted in the unification with the FRG in October 1990. Many GDR writers played their own
parts in this process. Some of the younger writers and artists were instrumental in the formation of the protest groups such as New Forum and
Democracy Now. But the authors who were best known in the West did
not identify themselves closely with any of these groups, although they
supported many of their positions; in some cases at least they held on to a
belief in the capacity of reform of the GDR and its institutions for longer
than was justified by events.

The involvement of East German authors in political moves for reform
may be dated more or less arbitrarily to February 1989, when Christa Wolf
asked the PEN Centre of the GDR to express solidarity with Václav Havel
who had just been sentenced to nine months imprisonment in Czechoslovakia. On 1 March the PEN Centre called for Havel's immediate release, stating that controversial public discussion was necessary for peace,
literature, and socialism. By passing this resolution the PEN Centre placed
itself in opposition to the GDR authorities, who supported the repressive
stance of the Czech government. By September it was the liberal stance of
the Hungarian government which led Wolf, Helga Königsdorf, and five
other women authors (Daniela Dahn, Sigrid Damm, Helga Schütz, Gerti
Tetzner, and Rosemarie Zeplin) to express public opposition to official
GDR policy. The Hungarian borders were opened on 11 September and

within three days more than 15,000 East German citizens had left for the West. The seven authors put forward a resolution to a general meeting of the Berlin Writers' Association expressing concern at the mass exodus from the GDR and attacking official pronouncements that 'nothing in the GDR needed to be changed'. It identified the exodus as a sign of the basic problems which had built up at all levels of society and called for an open, democratic dialogue between the authorities and reformists to be initiated. The meeting accepted the resolution with a large majority. In so doing the Berlin Writers' Association was not forming public opinion but responding to a more widespread movement: New Forum, the first of the civil rights movements to organize openly, had published similar demands in its foundation manifesto just a few days before.

In early October, with the official celebrations for the fortieth anniversary of the foundation of the GDR and Gorbachev's visit to Berlin, the situation became even more acute. The violent treatment of demonstrators in Berlin and Leipzig provoked public responses from Wolf and Königsdorf among others (Wolf 1990a:77–100; Königsdorf 1990a:58–79). One example of Christa Wolf's involvement at this period is worth quoting at length as it is a particularly clear illustration of how critical authors in the GDR were perceived by ordinary East Germans and of how they perceived themselves. At the beginning of October Wolf gave a reading from her works to an audience of about 200 in a small town in Mecklenburg. The discussion that followed was not about literature but about the current political situation. One of the participants called on everyone present to speak out and express their own opinions freely, not to be intimidated and not to act against their consciences. A woman replied, 'We haven't learned how to do that,' and went on to describe how in her own experience she had been encouraged from childhood on to pay lip-service to political orthodoxy and keep any personal opinions to herself. Having a personal view, particularly a critical one, could only lead to difficulties; conforming ensured security and career progression. The subsequent discussion concentrated on how the structures of GDR society, and particularly the education system, had failed to promote critical awareness. In an article in *Wochenpost* on 21 October (1990a) Wolf described this discussion and reflected on the lessons to be drawn from it. The article provoked a huge response from readers, many of them teachers. While some accepted the validity of the criticisms, many even at this late date were vehement in their rejection of any suggestion that the schools had been dedicated to the production of passive, uncritical citizens. A selection from the over 300 letters received was published in book form in January 1990 as a contribution to further debate within the GDR (Gruner 1990).

This example (others could be quoted) shows the environment within which Wolf and other 'positively critical' authors operated. Communication with their readers functioned not simply through the private reception of literary works. Authors' readings (before large audiences, even in small towns) provided a focal point for those who identified with the authors' views to come together and discuss explicitly political matters in a way which was otherwise possible only under the aegis of the Church. The openness of the criticism in the *Wochenpost* article was a sign of the changing times. Readers were used to looking for, and finding, much more cryptic opposition expressed in essays and articles in *Wochenpost*, *Sonntag* and other publications that were regarded as relatively liberal.

It is difficult to refute the accusation that limited critical freedom of this kind served as a safety valve rather than to encourage people to take to the streets. In retrospect it is clear that the moral authority enjoyed by Christa Wolf, Stefan Heym, and others was limited to specific sections of the GDR population; in the rush of events in 1989 such authority had already lost much of its significance. But this was not evident at the time. The mass demonstration in the Alexanderplatz in Berlin on 4 November 1989 which had been organized by artists and writers and which called for a reformed socialist GDR marked a high point in the belief that literature had a role to play in defining the future of the GDR. This optimism is reflected in the speeches made by Heym, Wolf, and Christoph Hein (Schüddekopf 1990). Wolf focused on the slogans carried by demonstrators in Leipzig and elsewhere as examples of 'the people's literary ability'. Hein more realistically warned that slogans were not enough and that a great deal remained to be done. He referred to Erich Honecker as an old and lonely man who had also dreamed of setting up a better society. Although Hein's sympathetic reference seemed unwelcome and inappropriate at the time, the warning it contained has been given some justification by subsequent events; and the irony of his proposal to award the Stalinist title of 'hero city' to Leipzig was largely lost on contemporary commentators. Stefan Heym's much more rhetorical speech, calling for peaceful revolution, popular democracy, and a socialist GDR, most closely reflected the mood of the demonstration.

In the official television news programme *Aktuelle Kamera* of 8 November Christa Wolf appealed to those leaving the GDR to stay and 'help to shape a truly democratic society which also preserves the vision of a democratic socialism'. Speaking on behalf of representatives of the civil rights movements and fellow-authors including Heym, Hein, and Volker Braun, Wolf conceded that 'we are aware of the powerlessness of words when faced with mass movements, but we have no other means than our words'. The signatories to the appeal promised to fight for democratization, free elections, legal certainty, and freedom of movement. With the opening of the Berlin Wall the following day, this last aim was realized in a way which made the survival of a separate GDR much less likely.

Against the trend, Wolf, Heym, Königsdorf, and others continued to campaign for an independent socialist GDR. On 28 November Stefan Heym presented the petition *Für unser Land* (For our Country) at an international press conference in Berlin. The final wording of the petition had been drawn up by Christa Wolf. Heym described the petition as a response to Chancellor Kohl's 'attempts to take over' the GDR (Kohl's ten-point programme for developing relationships between the two countries was presented to the *Bundestag* on the same day). Apart from Wolf and Heym, the petition's initial signatories included Volker Braun (but not Christoph Hein) along with the filmmaker Konrad Weiss and other figures from political and intellectual life and the reform movements. The text called for the preservation of an independent GDR as a 'socialist alternative to the FRG' and claimed (unrealistically as hindsight demonstrates) that it was not too late for the protest movements to bring about a society in which 'peace and social justice, the freedom of the individual, freedom of travel for all and the conservation of the environment are ensured'; otherwise, 'as a result of strong economic pressures and unacceptable conditions which influential circles in the FRG attach to their help, a sell-out of our material and moral values will begin and sooner or later the German Democratic Republic will be taken over by the Federal Republic of Germany'. Popular support for this vision was dwindling in November 1989 and in March 1990 two elections revealed the extent of Heym's political influence: while Heym was elected Honorary President of the Writers' Association at an Extraordinary Congress, in the elections to the People's Chamber the citizens of the GDR chose Lothar de Maizière and his Conservative political grouping, the Alliance for Germany, which advocated unification as soon as possible.

10.3 After the *Wende*: the *Literaturstreit*

Since 1990 interest in GDR literature and GDR authors has proceeded in three main stages in the German media: first, the discussion of Christa Wolf's *Was bleibt*; second, the discovery that Sascha Anderson and Rainer Schedlinski had reported to the *Stasi*; and more recently, in 1993, the furore about Christa Wolf's and Heiner Müller's contacts with the *Stasi*. In general it can be said that questions of specific literary evaluation played only a very subordinate role in the *Was bleibt* discussion and featured hardly at all in the magazine articles and talk-show discussions that followed the *Stasi* revelations.

Christa Wolf's long short-story *Was bleibt* was originally written in 1979 but published only in 1990. It describes in the subjective style familiar from Wolf's other works a day in the life of an author and contains obvious autobiographical features. There are few events (a telephone call, a visit from a young woman who wants to write, a reading in the evening) but all the events of the day are pervaded by the awareness that the author is under the surveillance of the *Stasi*: three young men are (again) parked in a white Wartburg on the opposite side of the road and she must assume that all her contacts and correspondence are being recorded. This awareness, its effect on the author, and her analysis of her own weakness in reaction to it form the substance of the story.

The debate aroused by this work was marked by its volume, its intensity, and by the way in which the work itself was used by many primarily as a peg on which to hang an attack against Christa Wolf as well as against other GDR and even West German authors; the literary quality of the work was attacked, but almost as an afterthought. The debate became known as the *Literaturstreit* (the quarrel about literature) and was conducted largely in the literary pages of the (West) German press. Its prelude had been an article published in the *Frankfurter Allgemeine Zeitung* in 1987 (well before the demise of the GDR) by Marcel Reich-Ranicki, the elder statesman of West German literary critics (Anz 1991:35–40). Reich-Ranicki, well known for his outspoken views, attacked Christa Wolf on literary, political, and personal grounds: 'this author, whose artistic and intellectual ability is quite modest'. At the time such criticisms ran completely counter to the accepted West German view of Wolf's person and work. After the publication of *Was bleibt* Reich-Ranicki's position was taken up and further developed by the younger generation of literary editors of the main West German weeklies. The debate was initiated by an article by Frank Schirrmacher in the *Frankfurter Allgemeine Zeitung* of 2 June 1990 which recapitulated Wolf's biography, including her role as a GDR author and an acceptable voice of East Germany. The article accused Wolf of lack of courage on the grounds that she had not used her position to speak out against abuses in the GDR, an accusation at least related to the theme of *Was bleibt*; it went on, however, to draw parallels between the GDR and Nazi Germany and to criticize the role of intellectuals in supporting the East German state. In short, Wolf's slim volume was dismissed as the product of a bad conscience.

The response to this criticism was immediate. It included defences of Christa Wolf by Lew Kopelew, Günter Grass, Walter Jens, and others, but there were also further attacks. These attacks developed the themes of Schirrmacher's article: they criticized Wolf's works and her political involvement and in some cases questioned her personal integrity. They went on to equate the GDR with Nazi Germany as a totalitarian dictatorship and to condemn the whole concept of a political and social engagement in literature. Some commentators saw the attacks on Wolf as part of a concerted campaign to discredit her as the most respected representative of GDR literature. This stage of the literary debate is well documented in collections of articles (Anz 1991; Deiritz and Krauss 1991) .

Generally speaking, East German reactions were supportive of Christa Wolf or, at the very least, defensive. But some younger East German authors who had been part of the protest movement of the late 1980s and therefore counted themselves among the true opposition had long since rejected the type of involvement which Wolf and her generation saw as the function of literature. They aligned themselves with some aspects of the criticism of *Was bleibt* and accused Wolf of having herself reinforced typical GDR attitudes of reluctant but ultimately passive acceptance (Koziol and Schedlinski 1990).

Contributions to the debate on Christa Wolf and GDR literature were not restricted to the two Germanies. Foreign commentators tended to adopt less partisan positions. On the whole Austrian and Swiss commentators distanced themselves from the West German criticisms; some Austrian critics perceived them in terms of the cultural imperialism of a Greater Germany which could have repercussions for Austrian cultural life. In a gesture of official support by the French government Christa Wolf was made an 'officier des arts et des lettres' in September 1990, and the Socialist French Minister of Culture, Jack Lang, referred to the 'campaign' against *Was bleibt* as 'unjustified'; he described the book as a very beautiful work of memory, of pain, and of irony (Anz 1991:218, 227).

Literary reviews in Britain and the USA presented the German arguments surrounding *Was bleibt*. Summarizing the critical attacks on Wolf since the publication of *Was bleibt*, Peter Graves in the *Times Literary Supplement* of 24 August 1990 defended Wolf's integrity but criticized her political naivety and the timing of the publication, concluding that:

> Christa Wolf's earlier status as a moral authority is unlikely to recover from the damage, but in its place should come a clearer picture of this writer: a twentieth-century German romantic with a chronically bad conscience. (Graves 1990)

Graves qualified this apparently dismissive evaluation by adding: 'In time, that may come to be seen as a less reprehensible posture than it seems to some at present.' In the *New York Book Review* of 20 December 1990, Ian Buruma also discussed the background of the affair. He accused Wolf of political short-sightedness and of an unthinking rejection of Western values in favour of a romantic socialism, but he also opposed the calls of some West German critics for an absolute separation between literature and politics. British reactions were summarized for German readers by Ian Wallace who, while conceding that Wolf and others had been over-optimistic in their hopes for internal reform, argued against the view that they had prolonged the life of the state by remaining in the GDR after Biermann's expulsion (Wallace 1991).

In Germany the controversy over GDR authors and politically com-mitted literature smouldered on in the *Feuilletons* (literary review pages) and in literary journals until it was fanned back into life on the front pages by new revelations that the authors themselves had been involved in spying for the *Stasi*. The discovery that Sascha Anderson, one of the best-known literary figures of the younger generation, had been active as an informant for the Ministry for State Security marked the opening of this new stage of the argument. Now GDR authors could be accused not merely of having failed to protest openly enough against Communist repression; they could be shown to have actively collaborated with the repression apparatus.

10.4 The legacy of the *Stasi* files

After unification the German government set up an official body, the Gauck Office, specifically to administer access to the *Stasi* files. By law Germans have the right to examine material held on them by the former *Stasi*. However, the Gauck Office differentiates between so-called 'victim files', that is, material filed on someone who has been under surveillance, and the files on *Stasi* employees and informants themselves. The victims are not normally shown the latter files unless they can show a legal interest in their contents (Vinke 1993:295).

The Gauck Office opened the *Stasi* files to public scrutiny in January 1992. Allegations by Wolf Biermann and by Jürgen Fuchs in the *Spiegel* series *Landschaften der Lüge* (Landscapes of Mendacity) that Sascha An-derson had been a *Stasi* informant were immediately confirmed by evid-ence from the Gauck files (evidence was cited in the TV magazine programme *Kontraste* at the beginning of January and in articles by Ulrich Greiner and Iris Radisch in *Die Zeit* of 24 January 1992; the controversy has been documented by Peter Böthig and Klaus Michael (1993)).

Anderson's case is an excellent illustration of how and in what circum-stances *Stasi* surveillance worked. Until the mid-1980s Anderson had been the driving force behind the literary and artistic scene based on the Berlin district of Prenzlauer Berg. The Prenzlauer Berg group can scarcely be de-scribed as state poets. Anderson himself had excellent credentials as a dissident: he had spent some time in prison and had lived in the West since 1985.

The Prenzlauer Berg scene, as it was known, consisted of writers, poets and artists who for the most part were a generation younger than Christa Wolf: Wolf was born in 1929, Anderson in 1953. Having grown up within the GDR system they had little patience with its shortcomings and even less optimism that it could reform itself. They also conceived of their own role as writers and artists differently from their older counterparts and did not aim to achieve wide popularity through the existing publishing structures. In a radio interview before the move to German unification the critic and essayist Rainer Schedlinski, a prominent member of the group and editor of the most important of the unofficial literary magazines, *ariadnefabrik*, stated: 'I think it is more effective to communicate within a closed group that you know. I just get more out of that. These are people who listen' (Arnold 1991:12). It soon emerged that Schedlinski had also worked for the *Stasi*, who were well known as people who listened in another sense. The Prenzlauer Berg group was largely self-contained and inward-looking. Its publications, poems, and lyric prose (largely characterized by experimentation with encoded or defamiliarized language) were duplicated or printed in very small, often almost bibliophile editions and were intended for distribution only within the group and its fringes.

Although much of the work produced in Prenzlauer Berg can be seen both in form and in content as a provocation directed at the GDR and although the group was accorded recognition and publicity by critics and the media in West Germany, it would be a mistake to over-emphasize its importance within the wider spectrum of younger East German literature in the years before 1990. Other writers, both in Berlin and in other centres such as Leipzig and Dresden, had developed their own voices, partly in reaction to the stagnation that had characterized GDR literature since Wolf Biermann's expulsion in 1976. Prenzlauer Berg, however, was in the capital. It was a lively if sometimes rather self-regarding scene in which both literary and personal contacts flourished, relationships were formed and dissolved, and everything was constantly discussed and analysed by the participants. The literary production was an essential though not necessarily independent element of a whole way of life. It is scarcely surprising that the *Stasi* wanted to keep itself informed about these artists and intellectuals who had attracted attention in the West. What is more surprising is that the opening of the *Stasi* files showed that their informants had not been simply fringe figures trying to infiltrate the group but included Anderson and Schedlinski themselves.

The Prenzlauer Berg scene was a late GDR phenomenon. The availability of run-down housing for an alternative lifestyle, the possibility of finding non-demanding work (such as janitors or central heating stokers) or of living on the illegal income from publication in the West, the participants' awareness of themselves as dissident intellectuals and objects of *Stasi* interest, even the connivance of the authorities—all these factors combined to create a situation different from any Western literary *avant-garde*. It is not easy to disentangle the thread of *Stasi* involvement and to assess its importance in isolation from the various interactions within and outside the group. The articulate accusations, self-justifications, and counter-accusations of those involved do not make the judgement any easier. What does seem clear is that *Stasi* interest had always formed a part of the activities of the Prenzlauer Berg scene and that the writers involved were aware of this. In these circumstances the revelations that Anderson and Schedlinski had been informants for the *Stasi* were surprising rather than incredible. Schedlinski himself pointed out that the *Stasi* was the only authority in the GDR which was not obliged to represent the official view that things were as they should be. He claimed that the informants in the GDR were often people trying to achieve changes which could not be brought about through the normal channels (1992). An attempt to present the *Stasi* as pragmatic social reformers is clearly undialectic, but, if anything, the Prenzlauer Berg affair illustrates how complex the mutual involvement of literature and state surveillance could be. In that sense it has provided the material for one of the most thoughtful novels about the individual and the state in the aftermath of the GDR (Hilbig 1993a). After Anderson and Schedlinski the hunt was now on to discover the *Stasi* involvement of other GDR authors. Following the *Spiegel* comment that a re-evaluation of GDR literature was now required since previous analyses had failed to take the '*Stasi* context' into account (Peters 1992), journalists turned with renewed interest to the files of the Gauck Office.

The next major *Stasi* scandal broke a year later in early 1993. Dieter Schulze, a minor East Berlin poet whose works have remained largely unpublished, claimed that the Heiner who appeared as an informant in his own *Stasi* files was in fact the dramatist Heiner Müller. Apart from three filing cards naming an informant as Heiner and the coincidence of the name, Schulze could produce no convincing evidence for his claim but this was enough for *Spiegel TV* and *Die Zeit* to publish allegations about Müller's role. This was partly because no further evidence could be found and partly because Müller, while denying he had ever been a *Stasi* informant, made no apology for having spoken with *Stasi* officers on numerous occasions. He pointed out that this was part of his material as a writer and that he would have found it interesting to talk to Stalin and Hitler too, except that they were already dead. More cynically, he declared that he had no objection to drinking whisky with the *Stasi* as long as the bill could be charged to the 'firm' (Vinke 1993:178,186). In his press statement Müller allowed himself a further ironic commentary on the way the *Stasi* files were being handled: 'I begin to realize that the true secret function of the *Stasi* was to supply the successor state with material on potential enemies of the state' (Radisch 1993).

The main reason for the comparative loss of interest in Müller was that this affair was overtaken by the more sensational discovery of another major GDR author who had been a *Stasi* informant, Christa Wolf, once again. The *Spiegel* obtained a copy of files from the Gauck Office showing that Wolf had operated as an informant under the cover name of Margarete. Admittedly, the activity lay more than thirty years in the past and covered only a short period, between 1959 and 1962. The files show that the security officers dealing with Wolf had considered her to be honest and that she had been upset by the discussion of operative secrecy and by the requirement not to discuss her security contacts with third parties. The information supplied by Wolf was limited to her general assessment of the situation in the Writers' Association and did not include personal denunciations or betrayals of confidence of the kind contained in the allegations against Anderson. Wolf's files were far outweighed by the more recent forty-two volumes of *Stasi* documentation recording the surveillance of her and her husband, Gerhard Wolf, up to 1989 (the files and the subsequent media discussion have been well documented by Hermann Vinke (1993)).

The outcry in the popular media was exaggerated, as might be expected. In the serious press the reaction was more varied. Fritz J. Raddatz published an emotional denunciation of both Müller and Wolf in *Die Zeit* on 28 January 1993, while Frank Schirrmacher, who eighteen months before had been one of the initiators of the controversy over *Was bleibt*, wrote a very measured commentary for the *Frankfurter Allgemeine Zeitung* on the same day. Schirrmacher pointed out that much of the media response was based on very limited foundations, that writers like Müller and Wolf had been fêted in West Germany before 1989 despite the fact that they had never concealed their support for the GDR, and that the current outbreak of media shock and horror was simply diverting attention (and discussion) from what he considered to be the real issue, the relationship between politics and aesthetics.

However critical they were of the regime, authors who remained in East Germany until the end have been criticized for lending credibility to the GDR in one way or another. Volker Braun, who formerly stated that he would stay in the GDR unless he was faced with physical violence or the confiscation of manuscripts, has conceded that, if he had been aware of the full extent of censorship and of *Stasi* involvement in literature, he would have given up any hope of change and left: 'It is not possible to put up

234 JAMES MELLIS

consciously with an infamous situation where no struggle can be carried on because no opponent is visible, but instead everything is regulated by the All-Highest beneath the surface' (Quilitzsch and Kaufmann 1993). Ursula Heukenkamp describes the situation as follows:

> At present there is only one permissible distinction to be made among the writers coming from GDR literature: between those who stayed and those who left. Anyone who lived in the GDR was integrated into their appropriate area to some extent. The example of the autonomous groups shows particularly clearly how even they were formed by GDR conditions, so that actually there is no real evidence for autonomy. It was part of the existing structures that the requirement and compulsion to behave appropriately was placed much more directly and forcibly on the author than in other societies. (Deiritz and Krauss 1993:34)

During the *Stasi* debates the question of literature itself has been pushed into the background but has never been totally lost sight of. One of those who stayed, Günter de Bruyn, commented on the literary quality of GDR writers:

> The great advantage for GDR authors who stayed was that simply having the courage to say something truthful was rewarded. As if that in itself was an artistic achievement. It is only now after the end of censorship that it can become clear what was really good and of literary value. (Bruyn 1993)

10.5 The new market: prospects for east German writers

Enough time has elapsed since unification for it to be possible both to look back on the achievement of GDR literature and to consider what east German authors have produced since 1989 (Arnold 1991; Deiritz and Krauss 1993). The following section gives a brief survey of some of the more important works published since 1989 and mentions some of the younger authors who may be considered to be representative.

Speaking in March 1991 of her plans for the future, Christa Wolf said, 'At my age I do not know if I will manage, or if my generation can manage, anything other than to describe the collapse we have experienced and analyse the reasons for it' (Brandt 1991). Wolf's statement has proved to be accurate: the themes that she outlined have directly or indirectly provided the subject matter for most of the works published since by ex-GDR authors. Apart from the autobiographies (Hermann Kant, Stefan Heym,

Heiner Müller) and collections of essays and interviews (Heym, Christoph Hein, Helga Königsdorf, and Christa Wolf) which proliferated after the ending of censorship, the literary output on these themes has been considerable. So far Christoph Hein with his novel *Napoleonspiel* (Playing Napoleon, 1993) is the only major author to turn his sights elsewhere. In an interview at the height of the events of 1989 Hein had already made it clear that he did not intend to write immediately about the events he was living through, stating with some hyperbole that 'all this is certainly material for literature, but three generations after me' (Krebs 1989:180). Set in Germany his novel is the first person narrative of a murderer who kills not for passion or for gain but from boredom and as a gamble that he can commit murder and get away with it. The murder is presented as the ultimate extension of a series of business risks which present no further challenge. The central character, the lawyer Wörle, is bored, cynical, and no believer in utopias or in humanity; he regards risk-taking as the highest human activity and sees Napoleon as a suitably amoral role-model. Elsewhere Hein has pointed out what he sees as the danger of distortion in the literary treatment of the GDR after its disappearance: referring to a novel written before the *Wende*, he states:

> I am glad that I wrote *Der Tangospieler* (The Tango Player) before the collapse of the GDR; for one thing because it was possible to be precise then. When the dragon is dead there is an increasing tendency to inflate parts of it, for instance, in order to make one's own cowardices more understandable. (Hein 1993a)

The activities of the *Stasi* had featured in GDR literature before 1989, for instance in Hein's *Der Tangospieler* mentioned above, where the central character is pressurized to act as an informant. The theme of the *Stasi* and the writer as an informant lie also at the centre of Wolfgang Hilbig's novel *'Ich'* ('I', 1993a), but as the title suggests, this is not a book about the conflict between retrospective allocation of guilt and clear consciences. Hilbig, although born in 1941 and based in West Germany since 1985, may be considered as one of the younger generation of East German writers. He is one of the few true working-class authors to have been produced by the Workers' and Peasants' State, having worked as a semi-skilled labourer for over twenty years before his literary talents were promoted by Franz Fühmann. His narratives are characterized by a Kafkaesque combination of the surreal and the starkly realistic. The narrator of *'Ich'*, the writer M.W. alias Cambert, is commissioned by the security services to report on a Berlin colleague. On one level the novel presents a le Carré

world of duplicity where innocence is as impossible to define as truth; this
in turn serves as a metaphor of the quest for self, the 'I' of the title.

One of the most widely reviewed poems from East Germany has been
Volker Braun's *Das Eigentum* (Property), beginning *Da bin ich noch:
Mein Land geht in den Westen* (I am still here: my country's going West;
Braun 1992:84). The work has generally been interpreted as an example of
intellectual *hubris*, a complaint that the people had abandoned their poets.
Braun's play *Böhmen am Meer* (Bohemia by the Sea) was no more favourably received when it was premiered in Berlin early in 1992. The
play's subject is not the disappearance of the GDR as such but the wider
issue of the collapse of Communism and its consequences. It sees not 1989
but 1968 as the turning-point for the collapse, the year when Warsaw Pact
armies intervened to suppress the Prague Spring. Pavel, a Czech socialist
forced to emigrate with his wife Julia after 1968, now (in the 1990s) invites a Russian and an American to visit him, and their interactions re-
stage the historic development. The 1990s are not presented as the end of
history. The brave new world that is dawning faces ecological catastrophe
and a struggle between North and South. The 'victors of history' represented by the American, Bardolph, have still to reap the consequences of
the Vietnam War, the counterpart to the Russian invasion of Czechoslovakia. None of the characters has any real values left which can oppose
the tempest sweeping towards them.

As the GDR recedes further into the past other authors have begun the
attempt to re-examine it with the benefit of increased distance. Kerstin
Hensel (born 1961 in Karl-Marx-Stadt, now Chemnitz) was already beginning to make a name for herself in GDR times, for instance with her collection of short stories *Hallimasch* (1989). Her long short story *Im
Schlauch* (Treadmill, 1993) recreates an evocative picture of everyday
reality in the GDR. This is not the GDR of political fanaticism, *Stasi* terror
and resistance, conjured up by some *post hoc* commentators, nor the safe,
humane welfare state of GDR nostalgics. Hensel's GDR is grey, boring,
and ordered, threatening only in its oppressive mediocrity and narrow-
mindedness. It forms the background to the story of a dissatisfied and rebellious teenager, told with Hensel's characteristic blend of down-to-earth
realism, surrealism, and humour.

Like Hensel, Jurek Becker looks back at everyday life in the GDR not
uncritically but sovereignly and with humour. Becker has been based in
West Berlin since 1978 but his novel *Amanda herzlos* (Heartless Amanda,
1992) is set wholly in East Berlin over a period of several years up to
1988. It consists of first-person narratives by the three men involved seri-
ally with the eponymous Amanda: a well-integrated conformist and dogmatic Party member, a dissident author, and a West German journalist. To

a large extent the narrative is concerned to re-examine the day-to-day life in the later years of the GDR and the way in which the state was involved at all levels of public and private life.

In the last decade of the GDR the lyric poets and performance artists Hans-Eckardt Wenzel and Steffen Mensching built up a large and predominantly younger audience for their mixture of songs, poetry, and cabaret. Their satirical programme *Letztes aus der DaDaeR* (Latest from the DaDaeR) in autumn 1989 was revised performance by performance to keep up with the changes as they occurred. Wenzel and Mensching have remained very popular since unification: the irony, anger, and melancholy with which they described the stagnant society of the GDR have been transferred to their treatment of post-unification life in the new federal states. Their favoured targets now include the new bureacracy which has replaced the familiar socialist one (and which seems to many east Germans to be even more impenetrable), the experience of unemployment, homelessness and social cut-backs, the rise of neo-Nazi groups, and the stereotypes which east and west Germans have formed of each other. At the same time they ridicule any nostalgia for the old GDR.

While the output of East German authors since 1990 makes it clear that East German literature has not ended, it remains to be seen what the East German contribution to an all-German literature will look like. The big names of GDR literature such as Wolf, Müller, and Braun will make their characteristic contributions, as will writers like Becker, Hilbig, and Monika Maron, who are no less 'GDR authors' for having left before 1989. It also remains to be seen in what directions the authors of the younger generation, such as those from the Prenzlauer Berg group, will develop. Prediction is hazardous but a possible short-list of names to watch includes Brigitte Struzyk, Thomas Rosenlöcher, Jan Faktor, Durs Grünbein, and Stefan Döring, in addition to those already mentioned. These writers and others are well represented in the anthologies edited by Geist (1991), Döring and Steinert (1990), and Arnold and Wolf (1990).

There is another group of GDR writers who have not yet been discussed. These are the writers, many of them of the middle generation between Wolf and Anderson, who made their literary reputation in the GDR but did not achieve the high profile in the West of Wolf, Müller, Braun, Königsdorf, Hein, and Kant. Authors such as Fritz Rudolf Fries, Günter de Bruyn, and Karl Mickel did not fit into the categories of Party author or dissident which tended to inform Western interest in GDR literature. Equally, as writers with a long history of publication in the GDR, they cannot be regarded in the same way as the unknown writers of the younger East German generation. Their works stand on their own considerable merit, without having attracted any dissident bonus.

Clearly in one sense East German literature has ended. The structures peculiar to the GDR no longer exist. The Writers' Association of the GDR, wracked by dissension and self-criticism throughout the latter part of 1989 and 1990, ceased to exist in January 1991, not through any act of self-dissolution but because its funding was cut off with the end of the GDR as an independent state. Moreover the publishing landscape has been transformed. Some GDR publishers, including the main literary publishers Aufbau and Mitteldeutscher Verlag, have managed to privatize and survive. Other new publishing ventures have been set up in the east: the first of these, LinksDruck Verlag-GmbH, was established in Berlin in December 1989 and others, in particular smaller ventures, have followed. However, it is the large publishers based in western Germany who now dominate the book market.

It also has to be recognized that, just as the circumstances of production have changed radically for writers in the former GDR, so their readers have experienced equal or greater transformations. They face new problems and challenges in their everyday lives. Except for the unemployed the pace of life has increased enormously. In place of the limited range of information, entertainment, and cultural activity offered by the old system, east Germans are now able to choose from the overwhelming variety of leisure activities made available by the market: theatre, cinema, opera, new and previously unavailable literature of all kinds, attractively produced magazines and newspapers catering for every specialist interest, satellite television and video, and holiday travel to previously unimaginable destinations. Not surprisingly the breadth and depth of interest in literature which was partly the product of shared limitations within the GDR have receded, to be replaced by diversification and individualization. Hermann Kant, when he was the official representative of the Writers' Association, coined the description of the GDR as a 'country of readers' (*Leseland*). In 1990, shortly after the introduction of the West German mark and in consequence the West German book market, he gave the following forecast of the effect of unification on this readership:

> I think that [serious literature] has reduced chances, first because a need, or perhaps a supposed need, to catch up on what has been missed, will initially take over. Second, it hardly has any chance at the moment because people here are not at all inclined to read such books. People have other worries now. The traditional West German calculation now applies here too: if a book costs as much as a shirt, then you will probably buy yourself the shirt. So it has become a very uncertain occupation to write books that deserve the name. And where there is uncertainty, there are fewer people. That is, even if

you simply take the number of people involved in it, literature will no longer be as strongly represented as in other times. And that is without mentioning the so-called privileges, now gone, which provided an incentive to write books because writers believed that in this way they could obtain something they would never get otherwise. (Arndt 1991:872)

At this time bookshops across the GDR were pulping the bulk of their old stock in order to make room on their shelves for the newly-available range of west German publications, of which serious literature made up a relatively small proportion. Kant's comments on book sales, based as they are on the specifics of GDR book production and marketing, have been confirmed by subsequent developments. So far there seems to be little evidence to support his concern about an absolute drop in the number of authors, or at least of serious authors, although in 1991 Werner Liersch, in his capacity as editor of *neue deutsche literatur* (formerly the journal of the Writers' Association and currently the major forum for the discussion of contemporary east German literature), identified a 'considerable drop in the number of publications' by east German authors.

If east German writers, old and new, can no longer count on the loyalty or continued interest of their former readers, neither can they automatically assume that these losses will be balanced by the extension of their market to the old FRG. Books about the GDR and its literature have certainly sold well throughout Germany since 1990 but these have been discussions and documentations on GDR writers in the wake of the *Literaturstreit* and the *Stasi* allegations rather than original works of literature. Even the relative success of the publication of *Sei gegrüßt und lebe* (Regards and Keep Well), Christa Wolf's correspondence with Brigitte Reimann (1993) attests primarily to a biographic interest in the subject of the current *Stasi* scandal. Those 'critical authors' of the GDR whose works were widely read in the old FRG owed their popularity largely to the perception that they were criticizing East German society and drawing attention to the shortcomings there. This perceived position was agreeable to a wide compass of West German readers and reviewers across the whole political spectrum. The main exceptions to this generalization were Christa Wolf and Christoph Hein. Both could claim a readership in the FRG which was interested in their literary works *per se* and not primarily as a more or less coded commentary on life in the GDR. It remains to be seen to what extent Wolf can re-establish her reputation in Germany with future works. Significantly many of the criticisms that reviewers aimed at Hein's *Napoleonspiel* reflected their irritation that the novel was not what they had expected, a literary reckoning with the past. Instead Hein elected to deal with present realities and set the novel in the West.

The separate history and divergent experiences of German people in the new federal states ensure that, whatever view they have of the new Germany, they see it in a different perspective from that of their contemporaries in the old *Länder*. To the extent that literature draws on experience and engages at some point with social reality, these differences will find their reflection in German literature for some decades to come. In an interview in Jena in August 1993 Volker Braun spoke of the need for east Germans, once the first shock of unification had passed, to put forward their own views based on their unique history in its negative and positive aspects, rather than simply to take over the values and attitudes of the old FRG as if they were exemplary (Quilitzsch and Kaufmann 1993). Whether the specific features which characterized GDR literature will have any lasting effect within the new German literature is more problematic. As discussed above, many of these features arose directly or indirectly from the organization of GDR society and the role allotted to literature within that society and from the perception of GDR literature in the West. The disappearance of these institutions and the changed circumstances of reception fundamentally change the rules of the game for those authors of whatever grouping who never left the GDR. Even writers who went to the West before 1989 but whose works still dealt with the GDR in one way or another have been faced with an analogous task of adapting to the new circumstances.

The one characteristic of GDR literature which has not disappeared with the demise of 'real existing socialism' is its view of the function of literature. This view ranges from the loose notion of a socially involved and socially critical literature to the belief in the author as moral authority or delineator of a realizable utopia; it further encompasses the contrary reaction of a literature of subversion and provocation. Social involvement traditionally includes the attempt to reach a wider audience. This has not always meant renouncing formal experiment or conceptual difficulty, although neither were encouraged by official GDR cultural policy. The last major (West) German author to combine popular appeal, social involvement, and literary acclaim was Heinrich Böll. The combination came in for some fierce attacks during the 'literary debates' on Wolf, Müller, and other GDR authors in the West as well as in the East; these debates will no doubt be used as weapons in the arsenal of those literary critics and others who would prefer literature to limit itself to the specifically literary, however that may be defined. But whereas critics have frequently identified the political pressures under which authors operated in the GDR as inimical to literary quality, East German writers have seen free-market forces as equally threatening. In 1986, before he could have reasonably predicted that he would soon be exposed to the market, Christoph Hein had already analysed the contrast between producing literature under the bureaucratic censorship of the socialist countries and under free-market conditions. His conclusions did not favour the market. His comment that he was currently busy 'renovating his ivory tower' has to be read together with his 1986 argument that, in the context of a market-oriented culture, the ivory tower is 'an insolently *avant-garde* and revolutionary construction' (Hein 1992, 1986:189).

The ivory tower also featured in Fritz Rudolf Fries's critical comments about (west) German literature's failure to react in any way to major current events, specifically the Gulf War. Saying he is shocked by recent west German literature, he goes on:

> It has nothing to do with the ivory tower, or the constantly misunderstood concept of *l'art pour l'art* (which in nineteenth century France was directed against the levelling-down influence of the market). This is rather the prose of peaceful pink bunny-rabbits who have found their livelihood and their future within the enclosure allocated to them, secure in the consciousness that history, if it still exists at all, is sordid, and war, like the mass spectacle in the Gulf, is unworthy of literature. (Grambow 1991:882)

Jurek Becker also saw dangers ahead for German literature:

> A literature which reflects neither on its society's aspirations nor on the counter-model of that society, a literature which has no clearly defined social role and does not even know where to look for the centre of its society, a literature that knows no more about its readers than the trivia supplied by market research, is condemned to produce mass opportunism. (Becker 1990a:57)

Even the concrete poets of Prenzlauer Berg were aware of the challenge presented by the transition to the free market. In an interview in 1990 Rainer Schedlinski and Bert Papenfuß-Gorek felt that 'not much would change for them under the new conditions' (Gratz 1992:161). But Papenfuß went on to add the caveat: 'somehow we have to preserve this idea of subversiveness.' It is not clear that they have succeeded.

Further reading

The best and most up-to-date general treatment of the whole area of East German literature is the new (1994) edition of Emmerich's *Kleine Literaturgeschichte der DDR*. On the circumstances of literary production in the GDR before 1990, Lewis and Brumsack (1988) describe the general social background, Wallace (1984) deals particularly with literary aspects, and Jäger (1982) provides a well-illustrated survey of the interaction between politics and literature. Recent retrospects in English on East German literature include Reid (1990) on literature and *glasnost,* and the collection by Kane (1991), which emphasizes the literary importance of the East German contribution, while Goodbody and Tate (1992) re-examines GDR authors' relationship to political power. Volume 67 of the *Germanic Review* (1992) is a theme issue on 'the end of GDR literature' and contains relevant articles in German and English (especially Hörnigk 1992). Jurek Becker's remarks on the specifics of literature in East and West, made before (1990a) and during (1990b) the events which ended GDR literature's special position, have if anything become more relevant as our view of GDR literature has been rewritten. And Christa Wolf's recent articles and essays (1994) are a useful reminder that political responses to literature are not peculiar to the former GDR.

11
German Literature after Unification

JOCHEN ROHLFS

11.1 The *Literaturstreit*

While the previous chapter focused specifically on writers and artists of the former GDR, this chapter looks at the effects of unification from the wider perspective of German literature as a whole. The issues of the *Literaturstreit* are outlined against the background of the political debate which has been conducted in the new united Germany since 1990. There then follows a brief introduction to a selection of particularly significant texts published by major authors since unification.

Anyone who recalls the euphoria that greeted the fall of the Berlin Wall might be forgiven for assuming that German writers from East and West would have been the first to rejoice over the unification of their country. More than any other group they had been aware of their shared cultural inheritance as a unifying bond which existed even before 1871, when Germany began its troubled history as a nation. Such an assumption could not have been more wrong. The first shots in what has since been called the *Literaturstreit* (the quarrel about literature) were fired some months before 3 October 1990, the official date of German unification.

The outbreak of hostilities was occasioned by the publication in June 1990 of *Was bleibt* (What Remains, 1990b), a short narrative by one of the GDR's most acclaimed writers, Christa Wolf. What irritated predominantly West German critics and reviewers was the fact that Christa Wolf had published her outspoken critique of the GDR, written in 1979, in the relative safety of 1990. The story describes the alarming effects of *Stasi* observation on the mind of a narrator who was promptly identified with the person of the author. The ensuing debate became increasingly acrimonious. It engulfed a whole spectrum of German writers and critics from east and west and led to a concerted campaign, mounted by the literary critics of leading (west) German newspapers, for a 'new German literature'. They argued that the defeat of Germany in 1945 had marked the beginning of a new post-war literature in both Germanies, a literature which had now become redundant. The unification of 1990 should herald the beginning of a 'normalization' of literature.

Any such normalization, by which the reviewers and critics meant chiefly the ability of German authors to write works free from political and social pressures and expectations, seems some way off. The new Germany's ability to contain and integrate conflicting social and political views is still being tested and is likely to occupy the attention of German authors for some time. Much of the nationally and internationally acclaimed writing that was produced in both Germanies after 1945 drew its inspiration from the unique historical, political, and moral situation of Germany in the twentieth century. Even if we concede that with unification the post-war era has come to an end, another set of circumstances, less traumatic but no less momentous, has arisen which surely demands the attention not only of politicians, industrialists, and bankers but of writers as well.

The collapse of socialism in Eastern Europe in general and in East Germany in particular is commonly perceived as a victory for the West. Nowhere is this more the case than in the former West Germany which had been at the cutting edge of the East–West political divide throughout the post-war period and whose very existence had seemed threatened during the Cold War. Compared to, say, France and Britain this has made the former West Germany less ideologically forgiving, particularly where the GDR is concerned. Other Western European countries are less directly confronted with the aftermath of the demise of socialism in Eastern Europe and are inclined to let Poles, Slovaks, Czechs, and Russians settle their own differences in the hope that they will succeed in establishing democratic societies from within their own resources. Only with the emergence of enormous problems in the former USSR and the bloody break-up of Yugoslavia has the realization dawned that some kind of involvement, economic or even military, may be inevitable. At present, the former GDR alone benefits, and suffers, by virtue of unification, from the massive economic and political intervention of the West. That this situation creates a feeling of helplessness in east Germany, where yet again Germans are not in charge of their own future, need surprise no-one. The feeling is compounded by a certain triumphalism on the part of many (west) Germans who express their amazement (and sense of superiority) at the run-down state of the east's economy; they see nothing worth preserving and promptly proceed to demolish what cannot be modernized in order to impose upon the east their own hugely successful, profit-driven, model economy. At the same time the new Germany is beginning to realize that it may take decades rather than years for the east to catch up.

The *Literaturstreit* must be seen against this background. The continuing debate would not have arisen without the perception that one political and ideological system had defeated the other: the polemical nature of some reviews of *Was bleibt* betrays a desire to demolish the reputation of hitherto respected East German writers by alleging that they were as morally bankrupt as the foundations of their state.

The uncomfortable and repressive circumstances under which many writers in the GDR had worked are well documented. From the point of view of their relationship with the state one could crudely divide them into three groups: those like Hermann Kant who by and large supported the state, who proudly represented it abroad, and whose work often not only conformed to but also exemplified official cultural policy; those like Christa Wolf who stayed in the GDR but continued, within the confines of censorship, to voice their criticism of repressive reality, hoping in vain to be able to contribute to change from within; and finally, those who were allowed, or forced, to leave the GDR. These distinctions fall short of accounting for the full diversity. Of course there existed various degrees of conformism among the conformists: some denounced, others defended non-conformist authors. Many of those who stayed and voiced their criticism believed that only within the GDR could they work for a transition towards a truly democratic form of socialism. Some enjoyed the privileges of state support and recognition along with holiday homes and travel to the West; others were simply not prepared to pay the price of being uprooted from families and friends and deprived of the very core of their artistic concerns. The many who left for the West are perhaps the least homogeneous group. They range from writers like Wolf Biermann, expelled because of his commitment to a Communist ideal far removed from the repressive reality of GDR socialism, to poets whose aesthetic preoccupations were considered of no value to the state and whose work was rejected by the state publishing houses.

Before unification West German publishers had eagerly welcomed East German writers of all persuasions. Hermann Kant, Christa Wolf, and Wolf Biermann were all published in the West and their work received favourable attention, particularly if they contained any hint of criticism of the GDR. After unification those who had supported the GDR were cold-shouldered since they were deemed to have discredited themselves. Hermann Kant's admittedly vain and self-righteous autobiography *Abspann* (Unhitching, 1991) was not even considered a worthy document of the history of the GDR. Those who had left the GDR before unification, among them the novelist Erich Loest and the poet Sarah Kirsch, were exempt from criticism. Instead, it was those who had stayed in the GDR and had publicly opposed a rapid and wholesale takeover by the West, like

Christa Wolf and the dramatist Heiner Müller, who came under scrutiny. The controversy that began with *Was bleibt* turned into a full-scale attack on the literary establishment of the old GDR, regardless of how outspoken individual writers had been in their criticism of the state. Had not these *Staatsautoren* (literally: 'state authors'), as they were now labelled, accepted and enjoyed privileges normally afforded only to high-ranking party officials? Had they not become remote from the real concerns of the oppressed population? Christa Wolf's last-minute public plea to the citizens of the GDR (naive as it perhaps was) to stay and help build a socialist state worthy of the name (at a time when after forty years of empty promises those same citizens were voting with their feet) seemed only to confirm how remote this élite had become. And they berated their compatriots for heading for the bright lights of the capitalist consumer society! Had they really been unaware of how impoverished in every sense the lives of East Germans had become during forty years of socialist reality?

The tone of the debate has not been conciliatory though there have been moderate voices taking part in it. It was only a short step to accusations that the *Staatsautoren* had in fact been instrumental in retarding the revolution of 1989 and had prolonged the agony of a bankrupt state by trying to justify, in principle, its continued existence: naively, if misguidedly, or cynically, they had dangled the carrot of an impossible utopia before the people. In view of the loosening grip of censorship in the 1980s, was criticizing so little not synonymous with condoning so much? The provocative tenor of these allegations, triggered by *Was bleibt*, inevitably fuelled a wider debate, which was conducted in the *Feuilletons* (the review pages of German journals), and an unprecedented number of authors felt compelled to clarify their position. Among those from the West, Günter Grass defended Christa Wolf and others now labelled *Staatsautoren* against the 'hypocrisy of the West' as represented by critics who had showered praise and admiration on their works prior to unification. An active voice in German politics (and a member of the SPD until the end of 1992 when he resigned over the Party's consent to the tightening of the constitutionally guaranteed immigration policy), Grass had consistently warned against hasty reunification, declaring it to be little more than a takeover. He had courted unpopularity by reminding Germans, in the midst of all the reunification euphoria, of the real threat that a strong united Germany had been to the world in the past. The attacks on this 'German Cassandra' are symptomatic of the new assertiveness in the recently unified Germany where the terms 'nation' and 'patriotism' (frequently invoked by Chancellor Kohl) are no longer viewed with well-deserved suspicion. With the post-war period declared at an end, many Germans seem to share the view that introspection and retrospection are at best a hindrance in the new tasks facing their country. As once before, an 'economic miracle' is needed. In the recession of 1993 the prospects for an economic miracle which would rejuvenate and transform the dilapidated east seemed further away than ever, and appeals for solidarity fell by and large on deaf ears. Most west Germans have seen their living standards rise for decades and are unused to putting any kind of collective interest above individual aspirations.

At the same time 'normalization' is the catchword. That Germany, this 'economic giant' in the 'heart of Europe', should remain a 'political dwarf' is surely an anomaly. The present vigorous revision of Germany's identity and role in the world is indeed the key to an understanding of the *Literaturstreit*. As in the *Historikerstreit* ('historians' quarrel') of 1987, German intellectuals are crossing swords in a struggle for the territory of 'political correctness' (the *Historikerstreit* was sparked off by the conservative German historian Ernst Nolte arguing that the Third Reich and, in particular, the mass murder of Jews should be relativized against the background of Soviet atrocities). Despite pious routine affirmations of the 'powerlessness of writers and intellectuals', the dispute is essentially a struggle to determine the course of the new Germany by exploiting the power of the media. This time the left-wing liberals, once again branded 'the intellectuals' by none other than centre and right-wing intellectuals, are at a disadvantage. They have lost their common ground as the 'utopian' socialism of Wolf and the democratic socialism of Grass are discredited along with the socialism of the former GDR. Once again intellectuals of centre and right feel justified in fanning a simmering anti-intellectualism against their opponents on the left. They accuse their opponents in the west of unnecessarily prolonging the division of Germany by accepting it too readily as a consequence of Germany's historic guilt. Not content with the gift of reunification, they sound a note of triumphalism. Memories seem to be short: did not twenty years of Conservative government in the FRG (1949–69) help cement the division? Was it not the *Ostpolitik* of the Social Democrats that began the dialogue which paved the way to normalization? Not according to the new German revisionists who with hindsight condemn it as the politics of appeasement and some of whom condemn all left-wing liberals as having collaborated with an inhumane regime.

In the *Literaturstreit* even the dominant literary influence of *Gruppe 47* during the first twenty years of the FRG has come under review. This group was only a loose association, not some kind of literary mafia; but the most prominent members, such as Böll and Grass, are supposed to have transfixed all who followed them by occupying the high moral ground. It is now being argued that their belated literary opposition to National Socialism was, objectively speaking, of dubious merit: politically, such opposition provided the young West German republic with the redemption it sought in the eyes of the world by giving it a collective moral voice and identity; individuals were thereby absolved of the task of searching their conscience, which would have detracted from the task of rebuilding the devastated country. In other words what had hitherto been regarded as the non-conformist and uncomfortable post-war literature of the West had in reality served to legitimize the state.

Anyone familiar with the novels of Grass and Böll may find this re-evaluation perverse in three respects. First, these writers had clearly been too young to formulate their 'belated' opposition either from within National Socialism (even if that had been an option) or from exile. Second, their work consistently stressed individual over collective responsibility. Third, it was in fundamental conflict with the conservative restoration of the infant republic and opposed all efforts to consign the 'temporary aberration' of National Socialism to the dustbin of history.

What is entirely consistent with this fundamental revision is that the work of writers who opposed National Socialism from exile (that is, not 'belatedly') and who then settled in the GDR or expressed their sympathy for the young socialist GDR should also be downgraded. Heinrich Mann's politics have already been condemned as confused, Brecht's plays as infantile. The view that the writings of such authors are also somehow politically contaminated is gaining ground. Whatever one may think of their work, the timing of this downgrading is striking. It is to be hoped that it does not also herald an ideologically motivated re-appraisal of German national literature before 1945.

The other charge against the literature of post-war West Germany that has characterized the continuing *Literaturstreit* concerns allegedly misguided aesthetics. Rather than being guided by the aesthetics of pure literature, post-war writing was allegedly dominated by ethics. Precisely because it concerned itself with providing Germany with a conscience, it neglected (so the charge reads) the true purpose of literature, the pursuit and development of autonomous aesthetic qualities free from social, political, and moral obligations. Moreover, it was argued, this literature had been too dominant to allow the talented younger generation to develop independently, and had exercised a kind of tyranny of conscience over everything that had followed. Such a generalization conveniently ignores the contribution of writers outside *Gruppe 47* during the first decades after the war, and gives a quite false impression of a monolithic structure. In the two decades before reunification the literature of the FRG, far from being transfixed by the aesthetics of conscience, was characterized by diversity (without perhaps producing any towering giants of 'pure' artistry). This diversity was fed by the continuing exodus of East German writers. In the

GDR conditions were less favourable: a younger generation (increasingly unencumbered by moral pressure to identify with the official superiority of socialist ideology) created an alternative reservoir of individualism in the 1980s, but true diversity could not flourish even in this last phase as the pressures to conform had largely been internalized; several of the young alternative writers who formed the Prenzlauer Berg group have indeed since been implicated in dealings with the *Stasi*.

Early in 1993 German newspapers revealed that even two of the leading figures of GDR literature had not remained untarnished. The playwright Heiner Müller, now one of the directors of the famous Berliner Ensemble, had apparently over many years (and indeed until recently) taken part in conversations with the *Stasi*. His claim that rather than allowing himself to be used he had in fact been conducting his own investigation into the nature of power was greeted with scepticism and ridicule. Christa Wolf's recorded connections with the *Stasi* were brief and less substantial, lasting from 1959 until 1962. All this seemed to confirm that even respected GDR authors had been drawn into a web of deceit and collusion. The newspapers' response ranged from moral indignation to deep disappointment, not least at the refusal of both authors to clarify their involvement fully and publicly. It is worth noting that Christa Wolf did not help her cause by implying, during a television interview in California, that her situation was in some way comparable to that of writers forced into exile by the Nazis. Eventually the review editor of *Die Zeit*, Ulrich Greiner, who had been a prominent combatant in the *Literaturstreit*, wrote a resigned article calling for an end to the fruitless *Stasi*-debate, arguing that the basic positions had proved irreconcilable because of the absence of any common ground.

By 1993 the German literary debate seemed to have reached an impasse and the combatants were showing signs of fatigue. In the eyes of many, the reputation of several established authors has suffered irreparable damage, while literary critics and reviewers stand accused of having instigated a German Inquisition on a minor battleground in order to promote their own interests. The critics' demands and prescriptions for fundamental change are unlikely to be fulfilled in the near future: a new artistic direction seems more remote than ever as German writers from all quarters will want to deal with the attacks on their profession and on their individual morality and conscience. The time to write about trees seems some way off. The debate arose from political change and ideological turmoil and it looks as though its issues will occupy the literature of the new Germany for some time yet. It is conceivable that after a period of consolidation the much-evoked national 'normality' might set in and the pendulum swing back. But the central concerns of German literature, not just since 1945, are unlikely to be transformed overnight. Indeed, the tension between individual responsibility and collective identity, moral integrity and conscience may well acquire a renewed literary urgency, as a consequence both of unification and the vexed question of national identity in general, and also of a questioning of the future of literature in particular. In this respect the denigration of post-war literature and demands for radical aesthetic change could easily prove counter-productive.

11.2 Writers' responses to unification

Viewed from outside Germany, the literary opposition to repressive and immoral use of power has greatly enhanced the attraction of twentieth-century German literature. An early example of this opposition was Heinrich Mann's *Der Untertan* (Man of Straw, 1918). A satire on the Wilhelminian Empire, the novel had itself become a form of *Vergangenheitsbewältigung* (overcoming of the past) by the time it was fully published. Later examples were provided by the literature of (necessarily) belated opposition to National Socialism. If German literature has more than once in this century contributed to the rehabilitation of Germany through its vibrant reference to the shared experience of the nation, who would welcome its withdrawal from this main concern into a self-referential literary aestheticism?

Some German writers responded remarkably quickly and directly to the new situation. It is apparent that those from the east who, after all, have had to adapt to radically changed circumstances and expectations, have, with a few exceptions, been slower to respond than their western colleagues. What appears to be absent from the most recent writing is a sense either of triumph or of relief. Responses to the new situation have so far largely been predictable.

Stefan Heym's amusing and caustic stories from the immediate past in *Auf Sand gebaut* (Built on Sand, 1990) ridicule the absurdities of the old GDR almost affectionately, while warning of greater dangers to come. Unwilling to discard his deeply held convictions, Heym uses his stories to display his continued allegiance to socialism if not to a state whose moral bankruptcy belied its idealistic pretensions. Unfortunately the resulting stories, however cleverly handled, illustrate little more than a fully intact set of pre-unification clichés. In *Filz* (Felt, 1992) Heym expresses his thoughts on the new Germany in a way that is representative of the authors and intellectuals who were prepared to suffer the consequences of the GDR while remaining there. Both *Filz* and *Auf Sand gebaut* show an author painfully aware of the contradictions and shortcomings of the old GDR; it is an author who nonetheless remains true to his conviction that democratic socialism is possible. Unaffected by the widely diagnosed 'loss of utopia' (another catchphrase in the German debate) Heym concludes that to denounce this possibility would be tantamount to 'throwing away his entire life', a phrase he used in an interview with *Die Zeit* in 1991. This is precisely the attitude that his opponents in the German debate find unforgivable, not only in Heym himself but in all the intellectuals on both sides who cling to their dreams of a fairer and more caring society. There is a tendency to blame the dream for the reality that followed it and categorically to dismiss any chance of turning the original vision into a practicality. Not content with the triumphant victory of capitalism over socialism in Europe, the Right wants to root out any remaining 'utopian' aspirations. Such a reduced vision of humanity makes no allowance for the basic need of an ideal worth striving for. All too frequently this stance poisons the German debate and, by excluding a significant number of individuals who think differently, undermines any talk of solidarity.

An author from the west, Friedrich Christian Delius, 'records' the arrival in the Brandenburg village of Ribbeck of the first west German visitors as perceived by an ordinary farm labourer. *Die Birnen von Ribbeck* (Ribbeck's Pears, 1990) describes a classic clash of pre-unification values. On one hand there is the eternally dispossessed labourer with his awareness of the age-old predicament of his class. He reflects on the lives of his ancestors under the feudal conditions of the nineteenth century and traces the development forward to the wasteful centralized mismanagement of agriculture in the GDR. Despite this depressing perspective his defiant class-consciousness remains intact as he soberly observes the first signs of a takeover by the brash westerners. The central image, the pear tree reputedly planted by a former feudal Junker family, the Ribbecks, is both a literary allusion to a poem by Fontane and at the same time a symbol for the continuing falsification of history. This falsification stretches from the legendary benevolence of the feudal landlord in the poem to the sickening prospect of a heritage industry, managed by westerners and centred on the replanted pear tree. *Die Birnen von Ribbeck* is a cleverly constructed story full of ironies, but critics felt that it suffered from the same weaknesses as Heym's stories, chiefly an extensive use of stereotypes. The *Wessis* who arrive in their shiny new cars, eager to impose the crass values of their consumer society on the village, are a caricature of the spirit of the takeover. The shrewd old proletarian who observes the latest turn of the wheel of history, stoic in his acceptance of the role of eternal underdog, turns into a rather idealized figure who shares none of the real population's hopes and aspirations for a brighter future, however materialistic these may be. Clearly the scepticism of this short novel did not fit in with the euphoria of unification. The west German author was promptly criticized not only in the east for patronizing the reader and distorting the true mood in the former GDR, but also in the west for presenting the most recent events in the outmoded terms of class conflict, namely the continuing exploitation of the dispossessed.

Wolfgang Hilbig, born in Saxony in 1941, exemplifies many of the problems encountered by non-conformist authors in the GDR. While working as a labourer in various industries he attempted to gain recognition as an author of lyric poetry and prose fiction but met with indifference and rejection in the 1970s. His work did not conform to official cultural policy and he was forced to support himself as a manual worker while writing short pieces in his spare time and on nightshift. It is not surprising, therefore, that his writing is devoid of any notion of the political and social achievement of the GDR or of its perfectability. The rootlessness and alienation of the individual in a closed society, where any attempt to voice the widespread disillusionment and demoralization was stifled, is the bleak norm in Hilbig's work. As a result of his uncompromising stance Hilbig experienced *Stasi* supervision, interrogations, and arrest. The alienation and paranoia of these years are captured in the novel *Eine Übertragung* (A Translation, 1989) in which reality and nightmare merge. In 1985 Hilbig was forced to move to the FRG. *Alte Abdeckerei* (Old Knacker's Yard) was published in 1991. This short narrative is set in the author's native area south of Leipzig, an industrial wasteland notorious for the particularly ruthless devastation of the natural environment by outmoded industrial practices. But *Alte Abdeckerei* is not primarily an anti-*Aufbau* novel about the irresponsible exploitation and mismanagement of natural resources under the socialist regime, nor about the waste of human resources, however much it draws on the author's own experience of these processes. One hesitates even to call it a novel in the orthodox sense. The narrative draws the reader into the vile centre of one of the many taboos of that society. We follow the narrator on his compulsive walks through the repellent remnants of a countryside where a suffocating smell of decay and corruption lingers over slimy riverbanks, where deformed willows and grasses ooze with the vapours of substances carried in the greasy, foaming water. We sense the menace as we approach the source of this corruption and withdraw with the narrator as we come too close, weighed down by the oppressiveness of the leaden atmosphere, only to be drawn to it again. It is a nightmarish journey of discovery that leads the reader to the infernal source, the old slaughterhouse of the title, known to all in the region but mentioned by no-one: Germania II is a no-go area where a numbed underclass of untouchables, outcasts in their own depressed community, such as criminals, former SS officers, and dissidents, recognizable by their smell and demeanour, dispose of screaming lorryloads of diseased and deformed pigs and cattle, which all arrive after dark. *Alte Abdeckerei* is a relentless and powerful vision of putrefaction which transcends the actual setting from which it emerges. To reduce it to a mere critique of the GDR at its worst would not do justice to the narrative. But in the context of Hilbig's other works it is apparent that here we have a mode of writing which is more radical than anything the GDR could ever have tolerated and which, by implication, questions the very foundations of that state.

Hilbig is beginning to be recognized as perhaps the most powerful exponent of this kind of literature and as a most individual voice. Several of his most recent stories published in *Grünes grünes Grab* (Green Green Grave, 1993b) reflect his continued alienation in the new Germany. He places his narrators on shaky ground. The relative material security of the narrator of *Fester Grund* (Firm Ground) is undermined by his sense of not belonging in the smoothly functioning society of the West. Simple tasks like picking up a glass of beer become an impossibility, ordinary conversations seem menacing, as he feels that everyone around him is observing his transparent uneasiness with disapproval and disgust. The insecurity commonly experienced in the west by many former citizens of the GDR is heightened in this story until the 'weatherproof, fireproof, and bombproof model of a railway station' transforms itself in the narrator's mind into the sinking Titanic. Another story, *Die elfte These über Feuerbach* (The Eleventh Thesis on Feuerbach), describes a writer's return to Leipzig after the opening of the border. He has been invited to take part in a panel discussion on the topic of 'Utopia'. As the taxi takes him on an endless nightmarish journey through the desolate outskirts of Leipzig to his former home town in the industrial wasteland, he observes the effects of forty years of socialism on his homeland. The bitter conclusion is that the country was ravaged in pursuit of Marx's eleventh thesis on Feuerbach: 'The philosophers have only *interpreted* the world in various ways; the point, however, is to change it.' At the same time the first manifestations of change resulting from unification are hardly reassuring. The taxi driver's relentless, manic use of his brand new Mercedes on the still decrepit roads makes for an uneasy ride; the incongruous apparition of a brightly lit, state-of-the-art, green and yellow BP service station looms like a strange monument to a new cult along the dark, deserted country road. Is this the new utopia? As the taxi driver (in a shirt with the BP logo) enquires what his passenger is noting on his pad, the narrator is struck by the thought that, two years earlier, to be seen writing down his thoughts on the socialist utopia would have been foolhardy.

Hilbig's observation of concrete detail in these stories reveals a great deal about the problems facing a society in transition. Perhaps this is due to the absence of the ideological bias that has so far tended to prevail in writing dealing directly with the new Germany. It will be interesting to see how other east German writers, freed from the constraints of censorship more recently and under different circumstances, reflect the historic reality of the GDR in their works.

Two veterans of German literature, both at one time members of *Gruppe 47*, have published major novels since unification: Günter Grass, *Unkenrufe* (The Call of the Toad, 1992a) and Martin Walser, *Die Verteidigung der Kindheit* (The Defence of Childhood, 1991). Also published by both authors around the time of unification, two essay collections (consisting of newspaper articles and interviews) document their fundamental differences regarding Germany's future. *Über Deutschland reden* (Talk about Germany, 1989b) demonstrates how Walser arrived at the view that the division of Germany was a 'punitive measure' which had lasted long enough, that Germany had to determine its own future, and that any fears for this future as expressed in the continued evocations of Auschwitz were groundless. Grass's essays on Germany, *Gegen die verstreichende Zeit* (Against the Passing Time, 1991), include an interview in which he criticizes Walser's 'sentimental' view of the nation and his fluctuating political allegiances. Grass, for whom Auschwitz remains a valid warning of the effect of a strong, united Germany, has been a consistent opponent of unification. Considering the outspoken nature of both essayists, it may come as a surprise that references to Germany in their latest novels are veiled, rather than overt as in their previous works.

In *Die Verteidigung der Kindheit* Walser's protagonist Alfred Dorn is hardly politically motivated. Dorn is one in a long line of Walser's central characters who suffer from an inability to determine the course of their own lives and to find their identity. But it is significant that Dorn's psychological problems are at least aggravated by Germany's division. After his move from Dresden to West Berlin in the 1950s much of his time is spent arranging ever more difficult meetings with his mother. While centring on his pathological mother-worship the novel records the ups and downs in the relationship between the two German states over more than thirty years of Cold War. Walser locates Dresden as the root of Dorn's insecurity. Dorn's fear of loss dates back to his childhood experience of the devastation of the city in the air raids, and it is this fear that comes to determine his life, infringing on his studies and subsequent career. He devotes his time to the collection of childhood memories, an all-consuming obsession exacerbated by his mother's eventual death. The novel ends with his own bizarre death before the time of unification, but the density of references to the abnormality of the divided Germany suggests that both his trauma and his continuing search for identity are intimately linked with the division.

Walser let it be known that the figure of Dorn is based on documentary evidence of a real-life case made available to him.

In *Unkenrufe* Grass's narrator claims to have had the material for the narrative (diaries, letters, tapes) forced upon him by the protagonist Alexander Reschke, a former class-mate from pre-war Danzig. That this is no more than a formal device becomes apparent as the narrative unfolds with all the imaginative vigour characteristic of Grass's novels. It is set, as ever, against a detailed and concrete contemporary background: in this case the Danzig-Gdansk of 1989 where a German professor of art history, the widower Reschke, meets a Polish widow, Alexandra Piatkowska, who restores works of art. It is the love story of an elderly couple who channel their considerable vitality into establishing a 'German–Polish Cemetery Trust' which allows wealthy Germans who (like Grass) lost their homes in the East in 1945 to be buried in their native soil. Recent developments in Europe seem to make such a gesture of reconciliation possible, and any hesitation on the Polish side is quickly overcome by the lure of the German mark. The basic idea allows Grass, who for decades has promoted Polish-German reconciliation, to cast a satirical eye on the market forces which determine what is and what is not possible in the new Europe. While the events which led to German unification are registered in newspapers and on television screens, the fictional couple, having overcome old resentments on both sides but not new resentments amongst their grown-up children, lose control over the trust they founded because the trustees establish an agenda more in line with the economic spirit of the time. On this narrative level Grass expresses his worries about the expansionist drive of the powerful German economy. Rather than focusing (as he does in his essays) on the ill-prepared 'takeover' of the GDR by the capitalist West, he adopts the perspective of Germany's eastern neighbour, Poland, mindful of the painful history of German–Polish relations. While ostensibly criticizing his powers as a novelist, the more negative reviews of *Unkenrufe* in German newspapers duly voiced their irritation with the author's persistent scepticism. But by and large *Unkenrufe* was recognized as a major post-unification novel from the pen of Germany's most important contemporary novelist.

Rolf Hochhuth's play *Wessis in Weimar. Szenen aus einem besetzten Land* (West Germans in Weimar. Scenes from an Occupied Country) was a subject of controversy even before its première on 10 February 1993 in Berlin. The advance publication of the first scene featuring the murder of the first president of the Trust Agency, the organization created to sell off East Germany's state industries to private buyers, had provoked Chancellor Kohl into a public condemnation of play and playwright and caused uproar in the press. In a series of nine scenes Hochhuth's play presents a hastily united Germany in terms of takeover and occupation of the GDR by the West, and as torn by strife and civil war. According to the director Einar Schleef, Hochhuth decided to defuse the original (unpublished) version which could have been interpreted as a call for an uprising. Schleef claims to have based his production on the original rather than on the 'approved' version subsequently published by the author. Hochhuth in turn disowned the production.

Hans Magnus Enzensberger, poet, essayist, literary editor, and translator, who described his own intellectual migration from the radical left-wing opposition towards the FRG in the 1960s (Arnold 1992), reflects on the theme of migration and immigration in *Die Große Wanderung. Dreiunddreißig Markierungen* (The Great Migration. Thirty-three Markers, 1992). This collection of observations or 'markers' adds up to one of the more thoughtful contributions to the continuing political debate. The author's declared intention is to combat the blinkered views which have characterized the debate up to now. He looks at migration in a global and historical context before examining the factors underlying the present mass migrations. In particular he demonstrates the absurdity of territorial claims by 'native' populations who, not least in Germany, are themselves the product of migrations; in the process he explodes myths and catch-phrases such as 'the boat is full' and 'Germany is not a country for immigrants'. He looks also at the notion of an excessively high world population in the context of global demographic growth and notes that not so many years ago Germany and other European countries were more concerned about the decline of their populations. Observing that a policy of closed borders tends to be ineffective, he examines the vulgarization of the term asylum (as in shelters for alcoholics or for down-and-outs) and questions the appropriateness of a distinction between 'genuine' and 'economic' immigrants at a time when the political root causes for both categories are essentially identical. When on the basis of this analysis Enzensberger addresses the problems facing the new Germany, he does not offer any easy solutions. Having noted the universal nature of xenophobia he expresses his distaste for Germany's xenophobes and xenophiles alike. His reservations about an open-door policy at a time of rising structural unemployment are based on the conclusion that the system of welfare could not function under ever-increasing pressure and that a disintegration of the social consensus would be a serious threat to Germany's stability. A glance at the tribalism and armed conflict in multi-ethnic countries elsewhere appears to prove that the successful integration of various ethnic groups into a functioning multicultural society is the exception rather than the rule. Enzensberger states bluntly that it is usually a radical minority of those who consider themselves true natives who provoke conflict 'in defence of their territory', and then mentions neo-Nazis and skinheads for the first time. But he concedes that these groups are justified in their assumption that they have the backing of a considerable reservoir of other social categories. He concludes by stating his minimum requirements for an inhabitable civilized society, noting that these requirements have only rarely been fully met anywhere.

In a lengthy footnote, 'particulars of the manhunt', Enzensberger criticizes the German state's failure to enforce those basic requirements. He details the considerable repertoire of repression previously employed by the FRG in dealing with real or imagined threats to its existence and ironically asks why these well-tested powers have not been brought to bear on the neo-Nazis who are making the new Germany 'uninhabitable'. He suspects that the short-term political interests of the 'political class' may be responsible for that failure and warns that this is bound to lead to a 'culture of self-defence' which could ultimately threaten both the political class and even the state itself.

11.3 Conclusion

The xenophobic and neo-fascist tendencies that Enzensberger is concerned about are perhaps the strongest signs of how unstable and unpromising the situation in German society remains barely four years after unification. As the economic and social disparities between the old and the new federal states persist, many Germans from east and west continue to feel alienated from each other. The degree of alienation is echoed by the intransigence and lack of communication which has characterized the *Literaturstreit*. A strident tone is struck even in debates where the issues do not follow a neat east–west divide. An example is the heated controversy about Botho Strauss's provocative essay *Anschwellender Bocksgesang* (Rising Chant), in which he advocates a return to the unpolitical realm of pure art and aesthetics in order to save civilization (Strauss 1993). Symptomatic of the uncompromising climate is the latest sequel in the apparently never-ending series of revelations about the political entanglements of leading intellectuals. In the summer of 1994 it emerged from the publication of a secret file that Marcel Reich-Ranicki, the doyen of literary criticism in the FRG and one of the principal initiators of the campaign against Christa Wolf, was himself deeply involved in the activities of the Polish secret service during the 1950s. Not only have these revelations failed to moderate the tone of the contestants, Reich-Ranicki's evasiveness and lack of candour over the issue have served as powerful reminders of the uncompromisingly self-righteous and judgemental attitude that many western critics have adopted since unification towards writers of the former GDR.

In the current situation it is too early to speculate about the eventual out-come of the *Literaturstreit*. At the same time it must be hoped that the *Feuilletons* will eventually turn their attention away from this rather arid controversy and return to what they should be really about—literature. Texts discussed earlier, such as those by Hilbig, Walser, and Grass, are the genuine expressions of highly individual but also characteristically German experiences. Through the richness and complexity of their aesthetic form they, rather than heated literary debates, can help Germans to understand their differences and to bridge the current cultural divisions. Furthermore it is well to remember that Germany is reunited, not united for the first time, and initial signs suggest that the awareness of cultural continuity is still strong despite forty years of enforced separation. The literature produced since unification reflects the division between *Ossi* and *Wessi* and writers continue to be critical of existing conditions but there is no radical chal-lenge to the assumption of a shared national and cultural tradition.

Further reading

For overviews of the *Literaturstreit* see Deiritz and Kraus (1991), Anz (1991), Arnold (1992), and Brockmann (1994a); more specific aspects are covered in Brockmann (1994b), Gerber and Woods (1993), Lehnert (1991), Reed (1993), Vinke (1993), and Wolf (1994). For a general study of German literature since unification see Bullivant (1994). Interviews with authors can be found in Liersch (1991), Röscher (1992), and Wolf (1993b). For English translations of relevant texts by German authors see Wolf (1993a) and Grass (1990b, 1992b).

12
The German Theatre

MICHAEL PATTERSON

12.1 Introduction

This survey focuses on the upheavals in the theatre of the former GDR following unification. There have, of course, also been changes in west German theatre during this period. But apart from a freer cultural interchange with colleagues in the east, few of these changes can be traced to unification itself. They are rather a product of general European economic recession and the usual vagaries of theatrical taste. Since this volume sets out to explore the impact of unification on the new Germany, most of the following is devoted to an analysis of the emergent theatre scene of the new federal states.

12.2 The contribution of theatre to the revolution of 1989

The theatre in Germany has traditionally occupied a more central role in political life than is the case in most other countries, including Britain. What for the Anglo-Saxon is primarily a form of entertainment is for the German above all a source of cultural edification and a forum for political debate. In the eighteenth century German theatre provided a focus for national aspiration and for the establishment of the German language as something better than, in Frederick the Great's famous words, a way of talking to one's horse. Since then the German theatre has frequently expressed revolutionary dissent or been appropriated as a vehicle of propaganda, and it is no accident that the two most significant practitioners of political theatre of this century, Erwin Piscator and Bertolt Brecht, were German.

It is therefore unsurprising that theatre-workers contributed a disproportionate amount to the moves towards a united Germany in the late 1980s. This contribution culminated in the first officially sanctioned protest demonstration in East Berlin on 4 November 1989, which was organized by theatre-workers and which led within days to the breaching of the Wall.

The many complex factors leading to the downfall of the GDR are addressed in other chapters in this volume, but a few theatrical landmarks on the way to unification can be established. Here as elsewhere the influence of *perestroika* in the USSR was the initial impulse. In February 1986 Mikhail Gorbachev had insisted that a staging in Moscow of Mihail Shatrov's controversial piece *Diktatura sovesti* (The Dictatorship of Conscience) should go ahead despite concern from both the political and the theatrical establishment. Shatrov, who claimed that Russia had lived for fifty years in mental stagnation, was now able to present a provocative piece in which, for example, an Ernest Hemingway figure challenges a Communist apologist about acts of Stalinist terrorism in the Spanish Civil War (*Theater heute,* March 1988:30; the full German text of Shatrov's play is printed in this issue under the title *Diktatur des Gewissens*: 33–48). Such a controversial play was bound to generate colossal excitement in Moscow, where the public fought to obtain tickets. As in other areas the GDR approached *perestroika* more cautiously. Only after a decent interval of over a year and a half was Shatrov's play given its East German première in Leipzig in November 1987 under the direction of Karl Kayser, a trusted Communist and member of the Central Committee of the SED. Moreover the pretext for staging the play was the seventieth anniversary of the October Revolution. Despite these efforts to emasculate the piece, it touched a nerve in the East German public and raised questions that had for too long remained unasked.

In the same month as Shatrov's German première the dramatist Christoph Hein caused a stir at the influential Tenth Writers' Congress of the GDR by pleading for a relaxation of censorship. Hein's plea was to some extent answered by the East German Minister of Culture, Hans Joachim Hoffmann, in a long and frank interview for the West German magazine *Theater heute* in June 1988, an interview which was to earn him reproaches from his party bosses (*Theater 1988*:10–20). Hoffmann insisted that he had never banned a work for performance but that one might have to wait for the right moment for a production (Volker Braun's *Lenins Tod* (The Death of Lenin), for example, had to wait ten years for its East German première). In fact theatre-managements in the East were generally so cautious in their proposals that there was seldom any need for official censorship. Such caution proceeded not necessarily from fear but often from a genuine commitment to a Communist ideology which many intellectuals had no desire to undermine.

Inevitably though, there was a growing relaxation in deciding what was acceptable for performance and in who was allowed to work in the theatre. In June 1988 the director Adolf Dresen, who had ten years previously defected from the East, was permitted to return to stage *Eugene Onegin* at the Komische Oper in East Berlin. Rehearsals for Christoph Hein's play *Die Ritter der Tafelrunde* (The Knights of the Round Table) began in Dresden and the première was announced before official approval had been granted. Thinly disguised by its Arthurian cloak, this piece presented an image of an inflexible and bewildered Old Guard who had failed to find the Holy Grail and were now losing control of those over whom they exerted power. Towards the end of the play Arthur confronts his son Mordreth (*Theater heute*, July 1989:34–35):

ARTHUR	What about the Kingdom of Arthur, ordreth? Has it all been in vain?
MORDRETH	It is your kingdom, father. You and your knights made it. I don't want it.
ARTHUR	But we fought for it for your sake, my child.
MORDRETH	I don't want it. [...]
ARTHUR	We don't understand you. We don't understand what you want.
MORDRETH	I don't know myself. But all this here, I don't want it.
ARTHUR	It's not a bad table. I like sitting here. Do you really want to smash it?
MORDRETH	I'll put it in a museum.
ARTHUR	Yes, I thought you would. And how will that help you? Will it help to make anything clearer for you?
MORDRETH	It will make room. Room to breathe, father.
ARTHUR	I am afraid, Mordreth. You'll destroy so much.
MORDRETH	Yes, father.

[*Curtain*]

The audience had little difficulty in recognizing the relevance of Hein's drama to the contemporary situation in East Germany, where there was a clear opposition between a regime which, however well-intentioned, had signally failed to deliver the promised Grail of a prosperous democracy, and a disillusioned populace who knew only that they wanted something different from the *status quo*. Significantly, after its official première on 12 April 1989, only one more performance was given in that season and the reviews in the East German press were careful to present the play as a historical drama without drawing any parallels with the existing political situation.

Similarly, the dramatist Heiner Müller, who for years had suffered from official disapproval in East Germany and whose works were more often initially performed in the West, was now allowed to turn his critical eye on the GDR. His *Wolokolamsker Chaussee*, written as static dramatic monologues and duologues in five sections, was staged at the Deutsches Theater in Berlin in 1988 and subsequently in other regions of East Germany; significantly, the only production of all five sections together had taken place in France. Müller's piece pronounced judgement on the forty-year-long relationship between the Soviet Union and the GDR and was changed nightly in performance to correspond to events on the streets. Despite its forbidding undramatic structure it attracted colossal attention, especially amongst the young. As Frau Stingl of the Public Relations Department of the Leipzig Schauspielhaus recalls, when Müller's piece was being played there, the streets round the theatre would fill with bicycles (personal communication to the author, 18 May 1993).

Once again as it had so often done in its past, the theatre in East Germany was fulfilling the function of a political forum. Deprived of the opportunity for open debate within the traditional political structures and with the media firmly under the control of the government, progressive elements turned to the Church and to the theatre for the freedom and simply the physical space to discuss the future of their society. The actor Ulrich Mühe summed it up as follows:

> The theatre, at least in the ten years that I have been treading the boards, has been in the vanguard. It has drawn attention to what is wrong with our society and to what has been hushed up, although naturally only within permitted limits; there were plays that we were not allowed to stage. But a kind of unspoken understanding between public and performers developed over the years about the intentions of a production, including the classicial repertoire. The theatre isn't just a fellow-traveller. At the Deutsches Theater in 1988 [...] we already held meetings, passed resolutions and wrote letters, which were seldom if ever answered. A growing politicization took place within the ensemble, so that on 6 October 1989 we simply said: We'll open our doors to post-performance discussions which will not deal primarily with the production but consider the present political situation, something we shall announce to the public beforehand. (*Theater heute*, December 1989:6–7)

Mühe was one of the organizers of the colossal protest demonstration of 4 November, 'desperately rushing to kick in the door before it was opened,' as Heiner Müller cynically observed (*Theater heute*, December 1989:7). Mühe had caused a stir a few days previously by his public reading at the Deutsches Theater on 29 October of Walter Janka's book *Schwierigkeiten mit der Wahrheit* (Difficulties with the Truth) which was banned in East Germany. Janka had been one of the most prominent cultural leaders of the nascent GDR. Appointed to manage both the East German national film company DEFA and the Aufbau publishing house, he was condemned in 1956 for 'conspiring against the state', a typically Stalinist charge. Mühe's defiant and courageous act received a standing half-hour ovation and led to Janka's eventual rehabilitation on 24 November. Moreover it demonstrated how effective the theatre can be as a political instrument at the right moment. Although addressing only a tiny proportion of the public, Mühe cast yet another stone into the already troubled pond, creating a ripple that would join others to become a tidal wave.

While Berlin naturally became the focus for change and necessarily the site of the eventual breaching of the Wall, pressure for change was also considerable in the provinces, especially in Saxony. A major example of the involvement of theatre-workers was provided by the ensemble of the Schauspielhaus in Dresden. From 4 October 1989 the following demands were read out to the audience from the theatre stage every evening:

> We are stepping out of our roles. The situation in our country compels us to.
> A country that cannot hold on to its youth is endangering its own future.
> The leadership of a state that does not speak to its people is no longer credible.
> The leadership of a party that no longer questions whether its principles are still of use is condemned to go under.
> A people that have been denied a voice is beginning to become violent.
> Truth must out. We are committed to working in this country. We will not allow the country to be destroyed.
> We are using this platform to make the following demands:
> 1. We have a right to information
> 2. We have a right to dialogue
> 3. We have a right to independent thought and creativity
> 4. We have a right to pluralistic thinking
> 5. We have a right to contradict
> 6. We have a right to travel freely
> 7. We have a right to examine the leadership of the state
> 8. We have a right to think new thoughts
> 9. We have a right to get involved
> We are using this platform to declare our duty:

1. We have a duty to demand that lies and misrepresentation disappear from our media

2. We have a duty to insist on a dialogue between the people and the leadership of state and party

3. We have a duty to demand that both we and the state apparatus conduct this dialogue without violence

4. We have a duty to define the word socialism, so that it once again becomes an acceptable ideal for our people

5. We have a duty to demand of the leadership of the state and the party that they again win the trust of the populace. (*Theater 1990*:133)

With such idealism and with a continuing commitment to socialism, the progressive elements in the East German theatre intelligently, bravely, and conscientiously hoped they were at last going to give some substance to the word 'democratic' in the German Democratic Republic. That things turned out very differently was hardly their fault. As Heiner Müller ruefully observed in an interview with the New York magazine *Village Voice*, 'The Germans, they went from Hitler to Stalin to the Deutsche Mark' (*Theater 1990*:128).

12.3 The structure of theatre in the former GDR

Before the tidal wave of the *Wende* the GDR could boast one of the healthiest theatre structures in the world. With sixty-eight theatres (playing to some 200 different venues) the GDR had more subsidized theatres than any other nation relative to its size and population. In 1986 there were 28,190 performances of 1,813 different productions, generating 9,813 million theatre visits. Not only could the GDR congratulate itself on the sheer volume of its theatrical output, it also distinguished itself in other ways. The Berliner Ensemble, for all its tendency to fossilize Brecht's achievements in slavish copies of his *Modellbücher* (Production Models), was still one of the best theatre companies in Europe, and other stages, such as the Deutsches Theater Berlin and the Schauspielhaus Dresden, attracted international attention. The GDR had nurtured directing talents of the calibre of Manfred Wekwerth, Benno Besson, Ruth Berghaus, Peter Palitzsch, Wolfgang Engel, Alexander Lang, and Frank Castorf, even if some of these eventually felt the need to escape to the West to pursue their work more freely. There was a disproportionate number of gifted and experimental playwrights, including Peter Hacks, Volker Braun, Ulrich Plenzdorf, Heiner Müller, and Christoph Hein—even more if one adds those authors who left the GDR, like Hartmut Lange, Manfred Karge, and Thomas Brasch. The proportion of working-class theatre visitors was said to be higher than anywhere in Western Europe although it must be admitted that some of the tickets distributed through union organizations were not actually used. State encouragement of new writing for the theatre was also commendable: of 744 premières of both spoken and musical theatre in 1986, 182 (almost a quarter) were by GDR authors.

Despite this there was a concern that the East German theatre was stagnating. There was widespread suspicion of the vast bureaucratic structures of both the Ministry of Culture and the individual municipal theatres, sometimes scornfully referred to as 'culture-factories'. There was also a prevailing sense of artistic isolation from Western Europe. On a visit to Leipzig in 1975 the author was invited to address a meeting organized by the Union of Theatre-Workers. The talk was on contemporary British theatre. The hall in the depths of the Schauspielhaus was packed, every radiator and window-ledge filled to capacity with actors, technical personnel, Dramaturgs and others—not, the author is sure, because of the eloquence of the speaker, but simply because of a desperate thirst for knowledge of what was happening beyond the Wall. Today perhaps half a dozen people might turn up for such a talk.

There was also frustration about the enforced diet of classics and generally mediocre and unchallenging modern works. Despite the theatre's ability to relay coded messages, seen clearly in a production such as Hein's *Die Ritter der Tafelrunde*, the theatre seldom encouraged audiences to examine the society in which they lived. The author wrote the following about a visit to the Berliner Ensemble in 1986:

A Chilean guest-director staged an adventurous dramatization of Saint-Exupéry's *The Little Prince*, prefaced by a twenty-minute sequence set in East Berlin's main station, the Bahnhof Friedrichstrasse. This 'Prologue', suggesting the desert in which the Little Prince would find himself, consisted of a well-observed series of entrances and exits of several dozen typical figures of this urban milieu, all performed with considerable virtuosity by a handful of actors. It was clever and theatrical, but was studied with almost disturbing intensity by the audience present. When one of the cast was asked why the reaction to this bravura piece was so muted, he replied that one had to understand that this was the first time for years that Berliners had seen their own environment accurately represented on stage, and that this necessarily provided a shock. It is alarming to think that it was in Brecht's own theatre that it was such a rarity for 'the familiar to be seen as unfamiliar'. (Thomson 1994:275–76)

12.4 The theatre and unification: the immediate effects

When the Wall fell there were in the theatre, as in so many areas of life in the former East Germany, great hopes for renewal and for an unleashing of all the creative forces that had been suppressed by bureaucracy, censorship and plain gutlessness. Here, as with so many of the hopes for the new order, disillusionment rapidly followed.

The first major change, and the first major disappointment, was economic. The collapse of the East German state meant a reduction in the generous subsidies from which the theatres had lived (the state paid for about nine-tenths of every theatre ticket). Subsidies were to continue at a reduced rate, albeit still at a very generous level since the financial support to the west German theatre is about seven times the amount of funding for *all* the arts in the United States; but it was often unclear in the turmoil of the new situation who was to pay for what. Even the future of the Deutsches Theater in Berlin was in the balance for a while and it rapidly became clear that the theatres of the former GDR were no longer economically viable in their existing form. As in industry, overmanning was rife and the sixty-eight theatres which the state used to boast now seemed far too many for a population of sixteen million. Staff were made redundant and some theatres closed or were encouraged to merge.

More seriously perhaps, the economic changes in society as a whole had a more immediately damaging effect. While ticket prices increased sometimes as much as five-fold, salaries in the new federal states remained much lower than in the west. Furthermore the east German populace developed new ideas of how to use their disposable income. For years they had enjoyed low fixed rents, cheap food and transport, and often had to forego consumer goods and private motor-cars. It was a congenial part of the East German way of life that in the evenings the cafés, theatres, and opera-houses were usually packed to capacity, not least because there was little else on which to spend one's money.

After unification and the introduction of the West German mark in the east, those in the former GDR understandably began to compensate for years of seeming deprivation: money went towards consumer goods, cars and, now that the borders were open, foreign travel. If people wanted entertainment, then they now tended to seek it from television programmes that were at last worth watching without having to tune into Western stations, or in the sudden availability of videos, with the added excitement that pornography became freely accessible. In formerly bustling cities such as Magdeburg and Erfurt, hit by both unemployment and families' desire to save for what they regarded as a better life-style, public houses found themselves so empty that they opened only at weekends and were in the main dependent on the money of west German visitors and workers. Theatres similarly emptied. Even in large towns many were 'dark' for most of the week and, when they were open, were full only for major premières (average attendance at the Leipzig Schauspielhaus fell below 40% although it has now recovered to over 50%). Some years ago it was essential to queue for tickets at the Berliner Ensemble. On the author's last visit in 1992 the gallery and dress-circle were closed for that night's performance, an excellent staging of Kleist's seldom performed *Die Familie Schroffenstein* (The Schroffenstein Family), and even then the stalls were half-empty. Culture-factories were threatening to become morgues.

A further consequence of unification and the accompanying economic changes was the effect on the acting ensembles of east German theatres. Before the *Wende* East German actors enjoyed almost total job security. Except in cases of gross misconduct they could not be sacked; on joining a company they could, as Professor Guhr, Head of the Mendelssohn Academy for Music and Drama in Leipzig, wryly observed, 'already order their gravestones' (personal communication to the author, 23 May 1993). In an interview in June 1988 the Minister of Culture declared: 'while accepting the need for mobility, we want to hold on to the ensemble principle. We don't want to have any unemployed actors' (*Theater 1988*:12). This meant that there was great stability (some might say, stagnation) in the ensembles of the GDR and also that actors dared to be more outspoken since their jobs were not under threat. With the introduction of Western economics east German actors suddenly found themselves subject to the conditions prevailing in the FRG. These were much more favourable than in most other countries, but with a significant level of unemployment and with the prevailing operation of two-year contracts, actors were required to please the management if they hoped to be asked to stay on. Moreover salaries offered to east German actors were initially only a quarter to a third of those available in the west; this affected leading actors in particular, whose salaries in the GDR had not been very much higher than those of the junior members of the ensemble. Backed by excellent training and having no problems with the language, actors from the former GDR were now free to seek well-paid employment in western Germany or to work in the newly liberated television. There were gloomy predictions that east German theatres would lose all their best talents and have to survive on those who could not find employment elsewhere. Fortunately things have not turned out quite so badly. Some theatre-workers did indeed head west but many remained, whether because of domestic circumstances, continuing loyalty to the east, or because life in the new federal states is still much less stressful than in the west. Some went and came back and a few western actors transferred to the east. The situation is perhaps comparable to the attraction for British theatre-workers exercised by the Hollywood film-industry: the monetary rewards can be colossal but it has not meant that the British theatre has lost all its major talent to California.

Economic rationalization has also affected drama training in the east. Formerly, drama schools in the GDR offered a holistic approach combining both intellectual and practical approaches to the study of theatre, similar to the model provided by university drama departments in Britain. Now following the west German model, drama schools are perceived as conservatoires for professional training, while academics are to be transferred to the universities. It is another unfortunate development but is being gently countered, for example at the Mendelssohn Academy for Music and Drama in Leipzig which has introduced a course in practical dramaturgy.

Added to the upheaval created by the new economic circumstances, there was the perceived need to cleanse all former GDR institutions of members of the Communist establishment. In the theatre as elsewhere a vacuum was created in many leading positions. This was frequently filled by applicants from west Germany who were free of any possible collaboration with a discredited regime and who were familiar with the market principles which now governed the administration of theatres. Predictably this created resentment amongst those who had patiently suffered for years in the GDR, necessarily coming to some form of accommodation with the regime, and who now found themselves being treated as inferior to the new thrusting managers from the west. It was all part of the process described by the young actor/playwright Sewan Latchinian as *BRDigung der DDR* (BRD refers to the FRG, while *Beerdigung* in German means burial—hence the notion of being 'buried' by the FRG).

Perhaps the most insidious change affecting German theatre after the *Wende* was the sudden removal of the main target for protest. As indicated earlier East German theatre thrived in a society where it fulfilled the important function of being the only public forum for progressive political thought. When the battle was won the troops had no-one left at whom they could brandish their weapons and demoralization ensued—what Brecht called *die Mühen der Ebene* ('the tiresome journey across the plain'). As the Dresden director Wolfgang Engel said in 1990:

> The enemy has gone, and we must find a new one. I still think—that's the way I was brought up—that art must be subversive, and that we have to seek out the opposition. [...] Now we shall have to find out whether we are able to make theatre in a democracy. We have been conditioned to make theatre in a dictatorship. It's like a new birth now—I find it really exciting. Now I'll see what will happen, I'll see how I can carry on working. (*Theater 1990*:48)

Engel's positive response to the challenge posed by the changes in the east German theatre demonstrates that not everything is felt to be in decline.

The most obvious gain brought about by unification has been the aesthetic freedom accorded to the theatre. Formerly it was not only impossible to stage works that fundamentally challenged the Communist state (such as adaptations of George Orwell's *Animal Farm*, which has subsequently become popular) but also many standard works of Western theatre that reflected an absurdist or nihilistic world-view, notably the plays of Samuel Beckett. Sometimes it simply cost too much to stage standard works of the Western repertoire because the level of royalties, especially given the unfavourable exchange-rate, was prohibitive for smaller GDR theatres. This problem was removed with the currency union. Many theatre-workers in the east currently fear that there is a danger that the repertoire will now be determined by aesthetic considerations alone, and that any play that stimulates the director's imagination will be regarded as acceptable. For most of us in the west that is good enough. There is still a lingering hope in the east that each theatre production will remain immediately relevant to the day-to-day problems of society.

12.5 Post-unification: coming to terms with past and present

Predictably enough many plays have been written to examine the changes wrought in Germany in the last few years. Rudi Strahl, the most popular writer of comedies in the former GDR, spoke of 'the joy of being able to work at last without a censor sitting in his office or in the back of his head' (*Theater 1990*:143). Since unification many playwrights have begun a process of coming to terms with the past, in a manner reminiscent of the soul-searching that took place after the collapse of Hitler's Third Reich but with the added risk here that any rejection of former Communism may draw unwanted approval from right-wing elements. A case in point is a piece by the young writer Carl Ceiss, *An den XIII—Requiem fur einen Greis* (To the Thirteenth—Requiem for an Old Man), a monologue in which Erich Honecker lies on his sick-bed and tries to justify the way he ran the state.

Plays that set out specifically to analyse what is happening to Germany since unification are less frequent, although of course every new play with a contemporary German setting has to take into account recent changes in society. While there has been nothing in the theatre which has had the same resonance as the *Motzki* series on television, theatres in the west began to look with interest at the neighbour with whom they now had to share a bed. Within six weeks of the breaching of the Wall the Bavarian playwright Herbert Achternbusch had written an anarchic farce about the new Germany, *Auf verlorenem Posten* (Forlorn Hope), nominated by critics as the third best new play of the season. In Achternbusch's own production at the Munich Kammerspiele in April 1990 it began with a scene in which a Trabant chugs smoking onto the stage. Sixteen (sic) East Germans get out and begin to eat bananas (a symbol of the 'deprivation' endured by those in the East who were unable to buy tropical fruit). They throw their banana skins at a hitch-hiking East German actor who launches into a monologue which includes the statement: 'I am digesting myself in the hope that I shall digest the GDR in me ... If you have given up thinking you pay the price with thoughts' (*Theater 1990*:29).

In April 1991 a play by the young playwright Elfriede Müller, *Goldener Oktober* (Golden October), was premièred at the Landestheater Tübingen. The protagonist is a young woman from East Berlin in October 1990 who has given up her factory job to become a striptease-artiste, while an acquaintance, a young prostitute, solicits on the former 'death-strip', the no-man's land beside the Wall—Communist tyranny giving way to capitalist exploitation.

Probably the most significant play dealing with the contemporary German situation is Rolf Hochhuth's *Wessis in Weimar: Szenen aus einem besetzten Land* (West Germans in Weimar: Scenes from an Occupied Country), published in 1993. While only a mediocre playwright, Hochhuth has always possessed a considerable talent for spotting a controversial issue and recording it with documentary thoroughness. With a seductive measure of self-irony he makes one of his characters in *Wessis in Weimar* say: 'I could have written it much better myself, I just didn't have the idea' (Hochhuth 1993:178). His play *Der Stellvertreter* (The Representative, 1963), which accused Pope Pius XII of complicity in the persecution of the Jews, became one of the most notorious works of post-war German theatre. This was followed by *Soldaten* (Soldiers, 1967) whose theme was the alleged involvement of Churchill in the death of the Polish leader Sikorski. The piece once again stirred up considerable controversy and resulted in a lengthy libel trial.

In *Wessis in Weimar* Hochhuth, with his penchant for detail, examines different aspects of life in the new federal states since unification. Each scene addresses a different issue but the recurrent theme is that the West has betrayed the hopes of the East and is now concerned only to exploit this new market as best it can. Deliberately reminiscent of the structure of Brecht's *Furcht und Elend des Dritten Reiches* (Fear and Misery in the Third Reich), there is no continuous narrative or character development. Each scene forms part of a kaleidoscopic image of the 'new Germany'.

Written in his characteristic free verse, the play opens with a prologue in which the policies and attitude of the President of the Trust Agency, the organization empowered by the Unification Treaty to restructure and privatize East German concerns, are challenged by a lawyer who is a member of the SPD. Here we see the confrontation between socialism and capitalism that is to form the focus of the remaining scenes:

> PRESIDENT. In what sense am I 'robbing' a state, when I am
>   directing its economy on to a capitalist course
>   because socialism made it totally bankrupt?
> HILDEGARD. You're not robbing the state,
>   there isn't a state any more
>   and it didn't own anything that it hadn't stolen
>   from its own people first. You're robbing them,
>   the people. They're being robbed a second time:
>   forty years ago, at the end of the war
>   they were robbed by German Communists in the pay of Moscow
>   and now again by your Trust Agency ...
>   And without exception you carry out all your deals
>   as the last uncrowned absolutist monarch of Europe
>   without any accountability! (Hochhuth 1993:25)

At the end of this scene the President, an affable but determinedly capitalist figure, is, like the real-life President of the Trust Agency, assassinated by an unknown gunman.

Subsequent scenes show examples of the exploitation of the former GDR. The first, entitled Apple Trees (*Apfelbäume*), with obvious echoes of Chekhov's *The Cherry Orchard*, describes the clearing of a now unwanted apple orchard to make way for a golf course. Scene Two is set in Weimar in a hotel which is to be taken over by western entrepreneurs; it reveals the sham of Western multi-party 'democracy', as party allegiances are decided by the throw of dice. Scene Three, *Systemnah* (Collaborators), examines the unhappy situation of those in the east who reached an accommodation with the former regime and are now fired from their jobs, in contrast to the treatment of many former Nazis in the west who now enjoy comfortable retirement. Scene Four again portrays an assassination: it consists of a monologue by an official in Berlin who is killed by a letter-bomb. Scene Five is a pastiche of the popular nineteenth-century Viennese dramatist Nestroy in which former owners of property confiscated for the building of the Berlin Wall are refused compensation. A similar theme is explored in Scene Six, entitled Philemon and Baucis: an elderly peasant couple in Saxony are driven to suicide through unjust compensation for the loss of their farm and the threat of enforced rehousing. Scene Seven deals with the ironic situation in which the heads of the secret services of the former FRG and GDR both come from the small town in Swabia; in a further twist the West German spy-chief Klaus Kinkel (subsequently Federal Minister of Justice), demanded after unification that his eastern counterpart, Markus Wolf, be put on trial. The scene, played by an actor who was invited to perform in a television version of *Wessis in Weimar*, also addresses the question of censorship in the west. Pointing out that senior appointments in regional television are dependent on government approval, Hochhuth describes the censorship of the west as 'as bad as it was in the east, because it's subcutaneous' (Hochhuth 1993:183); it comes as no surprise that the actor is told that plans to screen *Wessis in Weimar* have been withdrawn. The next scene, *Abgewickelt* (Early Retirement), also refers to the sacred cow of Western 'free speech':

> the bosses find it chic to be criticized
> first because they are flattered
> if people think they're liberal;
> and secondly they know
> it doesn't matter a damn what is written or broadcast about them.
> (Hochhuth 1993:196)

The lines are spoken by a sympathetic radio reporter who interviews those who have been sacked (*abgewickelt*) from a light-bulb factory in central Berlin; the factory is threatened with closure because it occupies a prime site for property development. Here Hochhuth criticizes the capitalist practice of making every job dependent on immediate profit:

> If the inefficient GDR gave work and wages
> to six drivers,
> when the lucrative FRG makes five unemployed
> because it can make do with one, then the FRG is
> —in economic terms, four times
> more immoral than the decayed system,
> because it gives less work to four families,
> in order to be so efficient. (Hochhuth 1993:206)

In the final scene, entitled *Ossis: Diebe, Wessis: Hehler* (*Ossis:* Thieves, *Wessis:* Receivers of Stolen Goods), the attack on the treatment of east Germany develops an edge of aggression which verges on an incitement to violent resistance. The setting is a castle in Thuringia, formerly the property of an aristocratic family who discover that, although their inheritance has been seized in turn by the Nazis and the Communists, it will not be restored to them by the Bonn government, who use it instead to entertain foreign diplomats. Strengthened by an article in the Basic Law which guarantees the right to resist 'if other means are impossible', the ninety-year-old former owner and his granddaughter conspire to burn the castle down. As the building burns in a spectacular ending we learn that the security service has the names of all former members of the Communist Party in the area but not the telephone number of the local fire-brigade—a telling symbol of the new regime's inability to protect its people from the conflagration which may result from the indignities and exploitation the *Ossis* have suffered.

Just as playwrights like Hochhuth have explored the recent past, so have many directors used established texts to do the same. An example of this was the production of *The House of Bernarda Alba* by Federico Garcia Lorca, premièred at the Schauspielhaus Leipzig on 29 May 1993 and directed by Konstanze Lauterbach with Sybille Hahn in the title role. What was striking about Lauterbach's approach was the considerable freedom in the treatment of the text. This is of course nothing new for the German theatre where such experimentation in mainstream theatre is much more common than in Britain. It was not even new for East Germany where Ruth Berghaus and Frank Castorf have long been renowned for their iconoclastic approach to the classics. It is also undoubtedly true that in the melting-pot of ideas in the new unified Germany directors have more freedom than ever to challenge existing viewpoints. As the critic Christoph Funke observed in 1990: 'There is no certainty left, no truth is beyond question, every dream is at risk, even that of November 1989' (*Theater 1990*:131).

Of particular interest in Lauterbach's treatment was her use of Lorca's play as an opportunity to present an image of the GDR. Bernarda Alba attempts to protect her daughters by shutting them in their home and isolating them from the surrounding community, a discipline against which they eventually rebel with tragic consequences. Interestingly this production made little endeavour to explore the psychological depths of Lorca's theme of sexual repression; the actresses played in a strongly demonstrational style derived from Brechtian practice rather than with a Stanislavskian empathetic approach. Instead Lauterbach used the story as a political metaphor of the GDR's attempt to cut itself off from the West. Bernarda Alba was played by a smiling, chain-smoking, briefcase-carrying woman—more a benevolent Party functionary than a dominating tyrant. There is initial optimism about being shut away, and while imposing her strict rule of isolation, Alba liberally dispenses house-shoes, fur-coats, and honey to see her daughters through the hard years ahead. But her refusal to allow contact with the outside world is undermined by the rebelliousness of the sexier (= more subversive) daughters, and Alba's plan of protection and containment fails. The fact that the outcome (both in Lorca's original play and in this production) is not necessarily a happy one is a comment on the present situation in the former GDR to which many would subscribe.

In common with the whole of east Germany the mood in the theatre is one of disappointment, occasionally of despair, more often of quiet optimism. No-one longs for a return to the days of Stalinist rule. Even if some harbour secret yearnings, the most ardent Communist must acknowledge that, since unification, any return to a separate Communist state is impossible. In the theatre there is a general relief that the huge and unwieldy theatre structures have been dismantled and that the new, leaner institutions can be more flexible, adventurous, and analytical. It is a huge compliment to the seriousness and commitment of those making theatre in the east that they have so willingly abandoned the protected status of their profession and that the expected pain and sacrifice in terms of losing jobs and audience have not been as extreme as at first predicted.

Nevertheless theatre in the new federal states has to confront the rule of capitalism, expressed by the playwright and director Thomas Brasch in the simple phrase: 'Money now replaces ideology' (*Theater 1990*:130). The *Ossis* are now free to travel abroad, but foreign travel is not free; they are free to buy a good motor-car instead of having to wait years for a clattering Trabant, but Volkswagens and Renaults are not free. The newly-won freedom is a freedom for those with money, accompanied by the hope that, with the tough discipline of a market economy, eventually more and more will have enough money to become genuinely free. The rule of the Deutschmark in the theatre has made companies less wasteful but it has also introduced different pressures. A theatre is not a factory and cannot be evaluated in terms of output. But in the context of a European recession the theatre in east and west is called upon more and more to justify itself in economic terms. In Leipzig, for example, the venue for studio productions, Die Neue Szene, may, if the City Council has its way, be turned into a theatre permanently staging popular farces. In the summer of 1993 it was announced that the Director of the Schauspielhaus, Wolfgang Hauswald, would not have his contract renewed; the reasons were not fully explained but might have had something to do with his solid resistance to purely economic pressures. The whole staff of the Schauspielhaus were uncertain about their futures and struggled on bravely despite an inevitable atmosphere of demoralization.

Emerging from the feather-bed of the past, the theatre of the former GDR is standing in a cold wind which is at once invigorating and uncomfortable. Given the intelligence and commitment of those who work in the theatres of the new Germany it is virtually certain that after the understandable binge on foreign travel and consumer goods, eastern audiences will return to their theatres, perhaps in an endeavour to rediscover values more profound than a new dish-washer or a trip to Mallorca. In this way the *Ossis*, now treated as the poor relations of the west, may take a lead and guide the *Wessis* towards an understanding that some things, good theatre included, matter more than money.

Further reading

At the time of going to press no comprehensive survey of the effects of unification on German theatre has yet been published. The most immediate source of information is in the form of the excellent monthly theatre journal *Theater heute*, published by Friedrich Verlag, Velber bei Hannover. The East German equivalent, *Theater der Zeit*, published by Hensel in Berlin, is also useful but ceased publication between 1991 and 1993. Otherwise the following publications offer background reading to developments in German theatre since 1945: Daiber (1976), Innes (1979), Nössig (1976), Patterson (1976), Rischbieter (1967), Shaw (1963), *Theatre in the German Democratic Republic* (1965–).

13

German Film after the *Wende*

HELEN HUGHES and MARTIN BRADY

13.1 Introduction

The period encompassed by this chapter, November 1989 to 1993, was unique in the history of German cinema. The fall of the Wall, the opening up of the borders, monetary union, unification and its aftermath all provided ideal subject matter for documentary filmmaking in Germany, leading to an unprecedented flowering of the genre. The social and psychological impact of these events also left its mark, albeit less swiftly, on feature filmmaking. This chapter will focus on those films that responded to the process of unification and demonstrated an awareness in the historical significance of events as they unfolded.

Alongside unification three events of institutional significance for German filmmaking took place. These events were accompanied by a heated debate which reflected a good deal of anxiety about the future of German cinema. First, and most significantly, the DEFA film studios, the state-owned organization exclusively responsible for all film production in the GDR, was taken over by the Trust Agency and privatized in August 1992; majority-owned by a French company, the studios are now headed by the West German filmmaker Volker Schlöndorff. The story of the transformation of what was potentially one of the most lucrative assets of the GDR into the privatized concern of Babelsberg Studios GmbH was at the heart of a debate about not only the future of film in eastern Germany but also the industry as a whole.

Second, in 1992 the film subsidy law that provided financial support for filmmaking in Germany was extended to include the five new federal states and revised to allow for larger budgets. This was the culmination of an argument that had lasted throughout the 1980s in the FRG about the need for the German film industry to be more commercial and less concerned with film as a cultural product.

Third, at the GATT talks on international trade in Geneva in November 1993 forceful attempts were made to end or at least severely reduce the protection of European audio-visual industries through subsidy and quotas.

The talks almost foundered over this issue. In Europe—most vehemently in France but also in Germany—the dispute over film as a cultural medium was revived once again but the decision to exclude the audio-visual media from GATT confirmed that European subsidies would continue to protect national film industries.

The controversies surrounding these three events and their implications for the status of film culture in Germany have served to aggravate rather than resolve conflicts between those who wish to open the industry fully to market forces and those who are committed to the principle of state subsidy on the grounds that film art, like music, theatre, and opera, needs to be protected as part of the national heritage. This conflict forms part of a widespread sense of unease which has accompanied much of the so-called takeover of the GDR and which contrasted starkly with the joy and optimism felt by many over the end of the Cold War. The central issues focus on the film industry as a cultural institution and an entertainment industry and on the nature of German filmmaking as the expression of a national identity. These issues can be illustrated by two paradigmatic examples.

Die Mauerbrockenbande (The Wall Buster Gang) is a children's film with an East German director, Karl-Heinz Lotz, and a West German producer, Regina Ziegler. The actors are also from East and West. The film was planned and scripted before the *Wende* as an adventure story portraying the lives of children in the then divided Berlin. It was scheduled to be completed by late 1989 and shooting was already underway when the peaceful revolution began. The story was immediately rendered irrelevant. The script was hastily rewritten as events unfolded during filming so that it could incorporate the early stages of the unification process. It is a film which, as the American film magazine *Variety* put it, 'scores as the first genuine East/West German film' (Holloway 1990:4), although other films have also tried to lay claim to the title. The film never made it into the cinema (children's films rarely do) but was broadcast on German television in September 1990 just before unification. A small-scale production with a German director and cast, it catered unambiguously and exclusively for a German audience. Not so *In the Line of Fire*. A thriller released in Germany under the title *Die zweite Chance* (The Second Chance), this tells the story of an FBI bodyguard who witnessed and failed to prevent the assassination of President Kennedy in 1963. When contacted and mocked by a psychopathic killer determined to assassinate the current president, the ageing bodyguard is given a second chance to prove that he is capable of throwing himself before a bullet. The film was made in Hollywood by Wolfgang Petersen, the celebrated director of *Das Boot* (The Boat, 1980), Germany's most successful and prestigious recent film export. *In the Line of Fire* was released in November 1993 to coincide with the anniversary of

President Kennedy's assassination. It was the first Hollywood film directed by a German to have a budget of over a 100 million US dollars.

In the Line of Fire presents a chapter on German film with something of a problem. Despite the celebration of Petersen in the German press as a Hollywood success, it does not claim to be a German film. Yet the film's producer, Clint Eastwood, who was also its lead actor, hired Petersen in order to be able to exploit the perspective of a European director on an important event in American history. It is important to bear in mind that during this period, between the fall of the Wall and the third anniversary of German unification, the German film industry found itself increasingly threatened by competition from America and therefore ironically by Petersen himself. In 1992 US films accounted for 82·8% of the total turnover in Germany, rising to 86·27% between 26 November 1992 and 30 June 1993 (according to statistics published by the German film trade magazine *Filmecho/Filmwoche*).

A further dimension was added to this debate when a row blew up in 1992 over the film *Hitlerjunge Salomon* (Europa, Europa), pinpointing the issues confronting German film in the early 1990s. From the outset the film was attacked by none other than its script-writer Paul Hengge for glorifying the biography of a young Jew who had been forced to play the part of a keen Hitler youth in order to survive. Hengge attacked the film for exploiting the theme of National Socialism for popular entertainment. This criticism became more urgent when the film turned out to be extremely popular in the United States, achieving the kind of success that the German film industry had been striving for. The arguments came to a head when the film was not nominated by the German Committee for the Oscar as Best Foreign Film on the grounds that it was not German. The director, Agnieszka Holland, was Polish but the producer, Artur Brauner, was German; the finance came from both France and Germany and it is a German-language film.

When, therefore, is a film a German film? When it is funded in Germany? When it is made by a German director? What is the nationality of a co-production? Does the nationality of a film matter in a global industry? Could the German film industry on its own come up with an international blockbuster? Is it the role of government subsidy to finance the attempt to make a commercially successful film? In what circumstances does film, as a form of cultural expression, need a specific audience with a specific cultural heritage? These questions dogged German filmmaking in the early 1990s during a period when it was claimed, not least by Volker Schlöndorff in his attempt to promote the Babelsberg site as the new centre for European filmmaking, that German directors would be inspired, as they were during the golden age of Ufa in the 1920s and in the FRG during the

1970s and early 1980s, to produce films that would be of interest the world over.

This is not to say that no films of interest were produced in Germany at this time. Debates about the industry's institutional and financial problems should not obscure the fact that challenging and entertaining German films were made by resilient, often independent filmmakers in spite of the problems presented by subsidy law and the marketplace. It should also be remembered that for former DEFA filmmakers the marketplace was a new environment, often characterized as the exchange of one set of restrictions for another. The chapter will now focus on the films that were produced and the events on which they reflect.

13.2 Documentary films during the *Wende*

It comes as no surprise that the historically most significant films produced in Germany between 1989 and 1993 were documentaries. The forum for such films has remained the film festivals, above all in Berlin and Leipzig. At the end of 1989 films (some incomplete) which recorded the events of the previous October and November could already be seen at the Leipzig Documentary Film Week. In 1990 two documentary films recording the process of unification even achieved cinema release; in 1991 the number was fifteen and in 1992 twelve. Like the director of *Die Mauerbrocken-bande*, some filmmakers, including Thomas Schadt, whose *Magazine der Bilder* (Scrapbook of Images) documented impressions of life in the FRG and was planned before the *Wende*, found themselves in a position to record the historic events as they unfolded in late 1989. Helke Misselwitz's *Sperrmüll* (Rag and Bone), a film about an East Berlin punk rock band, was by chance also able to follow the events surrounding the fall of the Wall.

It must be remembered that documentary films of this period competed for their relevance with a powerful force in the form of live television. While filmmakers were the first to record events in Leipzig and elsewhere, television soon took over the function of informing the people about what was happening. Productions such as the opening film of the Leipzig Documentary Film Week, Andreas Voigt's *Leipzig im Herbst* (Leipzig in the Autumn), 'a rather cautious, intimate film of discussions about the explosive situation in Leipzig in October' (Roth 1990:4), were informative at the time they were released and have since become records of an important moment in history. Documentary filmmakers soon came to see their role as voicing an alternative view, taking more time to observe and show the effects of events on people and places outside the limelight. Thus they adopted a longer editing process to shape the material into a considered essay reflecting on what they had recorded. Johann Feindt and Helga Reidemeister's film *Im Glanze dieses Glückes* (In the Splendour of Happiness), for example, premièred at the Mannheim Film Week in 1990, is a collection of impressions of the GDR after the fall of the Wall. It uses techniques not employed by television. Against a background of black and white images of politicians making speeches, it shows scenes in colour from the everyday lives of GDR citizens. The camera waits for passers-by in the street to stop and talk, and a cross-section of people from all walks of life oblige, including a teacher, a school child, a *Stasi* psychologist, and a factory worker; there is no commentary.

Voigt's film *Letztes Jahr Titanic* (Last Year Titanic, 1990) picks up where *Leipzig im Herbst* leaves off, recording the period between December 1989 and December 1990, including the last months of the GDR. Again important as a historical document, it contains interviews from the *Wende* period and in 1992 received an Adolf-Grimme-Prize, the most important award in German television. Other films focus on the same period in various cities: Pavel Schnabel's *Brüder und Schwestern* (Brothers and Sisters, 1991) documents everyday life in Weimar between 1988 and 1991; Ulrike Ottinger's *Countdown* (1990) takes a long slow look (189 minutes) at Berlin during the ten days leading up to currency union on 1 July 1990; it provides no commentary and allows the events time to speak for themselves. In *Countdown* the camera remains at a distance from its subjects: only twice in over three hours does it come within earshot of people talking about the economic change that is about to take place. A comparison with Ottinger's documentary *Taiga* (1992), an eight-hour film about the nomads of Mongolia, indicates that such reticence represents an attempt to use time and distance to respect the authenticity of what is portrayed. Moving out of the city, Manfred Wilhelm's *Rostige Bilder* (Rusting Images, 1992) focuses on the industrial landscape of the former GDR, following an artist as he takes photographs and transforms them into super-realist paintings. In all these films there is the strong sense that the camera is not only recording and informing but also creating a memory of landscapes and cityscapes which are about to undergo, or are already undergoing, a process of rapid change.

One of the most striking documentary films about unification, both as a film and as a thought-provoking essay on the emotional and historical significance of the fall of a unique monument, is Jürgen Böttcher's *Die Mauer* (The Wall, 1990). The film was produced by the DEFA Studio for Documentary Films which in 1990 was operating under the Trust Agency; its future was uncertain, no suitable buyer having come forward. Disarmingly simple in concept, *Die Mauer* dares to focus on the centre of attention during the *Wende*: it can be seen as a last attempt to capture the significance of the Berlin Wall on film before it finally disappeared. One difficulty which the film overcomes is what has been described as the Wall's lack of dramatic potential (Hickethier 1991:6); it records people from all over the world looking at, touching, walking through, and hacking away at the Wall. Fragments of concrete are turned into commercial stock and whole panels taken away to be stored like sculptures or gravestones in bizarre museum-like yards. The film registers the sense of relief inherent in this process of transformation and of familiarization. It also becomes a comment on how a symbol of world separation has metamorphosed into a target for collectors of objects, memories, experiences, and images of history.

At the centre of *Die Mauer* are two sequences which confront the Wall's status as a fetish object. One sequence records a CNN news team making a programme about the Wall to be broadcast throughout the world. The same script is read over and over again in an attempt to get it right for sound and image. In the same portentous tone that eventually begins to sound comic the reporter repeatedly asks where the road is leading now that the Brandenburg Gate is open. The second sequence consists of scenes from the history of the Wall and the Brandenburg Gate projected onto the remains of the Wall itself. These images, compiled from archive footage, become unclear on the uneven surface, appearing and dissolving like ghosts. The virtue of these two sequences is that the historical images of the Wall paradoxically become less portentous. It becomes possible to sense emotionally that the Wall's history is already over. The images of the Wall being dismantled towards the end of the film become a narrative beyond the pain of its history. As the slow, ineffectual attempts by individual bounty-hunters to hack away at the concrete are replaced by the efficient forces of huge machinery, the sense of acceleration does not yet feel out of control; rather there is a sense of exhilaration.

13.3 Documentary films: looking back

After unification it was a natural step for documentary filmmakers to explore and attempt to exorcise the past. Although a sense of loss is perceptible in many of the films, none goes so far as to mourn the demise of the GDR. Two films did, however, portray attractive pockets of artistic life, the loss of which is a genuine source of regret: Petra Tschörtner's DEFA film *Berlin—Prenzlauer Berg—Begegnungen zwischen dem 1 Mai und dem 1 Juli 1990* (Berlin—Prenzlauer Berg—Encounters between 1 May and 1 July 1990) about the life led by artists living in Prenzlauer

Berg, and Wolfgang Pfeiffer's *Der letzte Applaus* (The Final Curtain Call, 1991), which records the last show put on by the GDR state circus. Both films are part of a complex emotional balancing act brought about by the knowledge that the fragile and creative life-styles portrayed were in different ways dependent on a sterile regime that brought suffering to many.

The more common approach to the work of memory has been to investigate the crimes against humanity committed by the SED and its agents, particularly the *Stasi*. Such films have taken up the theme of *Vergangenheitsbewältigung*, or coming to terms with the past, applying it not to the Nazi period but to the legacy of the Communist years. Ralf Marschallek's *Streng vertraulich oder Die innere Verfassung* (Strictly Confidential or The State Within), Andreas Fischer and Fayd Jungnickel's *Lindenhotel* (The Hotel Linden), and Heinz Brinkmann and Jochen Wisotzki's *Komm in den Garten* (Come into the Garden), all sought to expose and analyse the mechanisms of suppression and punishment of dissenters in the GDR. Sibylle Schönemann's *Verriegelte Zeit* (Locked Up Time, 1990) was significant because of the way in which the filmmaker personalized the process of investigating and identified those responsible for the mistreatment of individual citizens. In the film Schönemann researches her own history. A filmmaker in Potsdam, she was arrested with her husband in 1984 and sentenced to fourteen months in prison for applying to go abroad. When the FRG bought her freedom she found herself exiled in the West. *Verriegelte Zeit* records her return to the former East Germany in 1990 to interview those responsible for her sentencing and imprisonment. As she interviews the prison guards, the lawyers, the witnesses who gave evidence against her, the DEFA *Generaldirektor* who handed in a negative report about her, a *Stasi* officer who provided information, and others, her individual sense of outrage becomes less important than the nature of the psychological and administrative mechanisms that were responsible for her persecution. The interviews focus on the question of moral and personal guilt versus duty to the state; parallels are also drawn between the situation after the Second World War and unification. None of the interviewees acknowledges a sense of guilt or makes apologies: it is clear that they all understand their actions as acceptable in the terms of the time at which they were carried out.

The brutal reality of state oppression in the GDR is also confronted in the documentary by Joachim Tschirner, Lew Hohmann, and Klaus Salge, *Ein schmales Stück Deutschland* (A Small Piece of Germany). This film focuses on the individual tragedies of those who were shot crossing the border from East to West. For all its use of manipulative techniques to dramatize the tragedy of the deaths, the film was a timely reminder of the true horror of the border. It was shown towards the end of 1991 when the first waves of unemployment and fears of economic insecurity had brought about a cooling in relations between the old and new federal states.

A second wave of documentary films shown in 1992 took advantage of the new opportunities to explore the now historical GDR in more depth. For some time the West German filmmaker Helke Sander had been researching her film about the mass rape of German women by Russian soldiers after the Second World War. *BeFreier und Befreite: Krieg— Vergewaltigungen—Kinder* (Liberators Take Liberties: War, Rape, and Children) was able to make use of records released in East Berlin which provided further material on a hitherto suppressed chapter in the city's history. In *J. K. Erfahrungen im Umgang mit dem eigenen Ich* (J. K. Encounters with the Self) Fosco and Donatello Dubini experiment with cinematic form in an attempt to create a portrait of an eighty-eight-year-old GDR academic, Jürgen Kuczynski, that reflected the contradictions in his life: a scientist who worked for the Party, Kuczynski was also a dissident who argued the case for Communism. In *Der schwarze Kasten* (The Black Box) Johann Feindt and Tamara Trampe explore and investigate the mechanisms of state control in an extended interview with a former *Stasi* officer, Jochen Girke, whose job it was to educate agents in developing methods for gaining the trust of citizens willing to inform on their friends and relatives. There are uncomfortable similarities between the intrusive methods the film uses to investigate and portray the personality of the *Stasi* officer Girke (who volunteered himself as a subject) and Girke's own manipulation of psychological techniques to control the informers and their victims.

13.4 Documentary films on Germany after unification

Two films shown in late 1992 focus specifically on unification: they are Thomas Heise's *STAU—Jetzt geht's los* (JAMMED—Let's Get Moving) and Helga Reidemeister's *Rodina heißt Heimat* (Rodina Means Homeland). A third film, *Grenzland—eine Reise* (Borderlands) by Andreas Voigt, eventually found its way into the cinema in 1993. All three deal with economic and social problems experienced in the wake of the collapse of Communism. *Rodina heißt Heimat*, shot between February and August 1991, depicts a Soviet military unit as it leaves its base in the GDR. *Grenzland—eine Reise*, based on a journey along the Oder–Neisse frontier between Germany and Poland, provoked criticism in some quarters for portraying the Poles as a nation of gentle philosophers and the Germans as 'evil profiteers whose narrow horizons render them unable to think beyond the question of ownership' (Rother 1992). The film's fascinating mix of interviews, ranging from an unemployed engineer describing the types of sausage for sale in his new business to a fanatical youth expressing the racist views of the extreme right-wing, presents a sad, thought-provoking, and visually arresting portrait of a neglected region that highlights the relationship between the emotionally charged subject of national borders and the practical need to do business and to live.

Heise's controversial *STAU—Jetzt geht's los* (premièred in Duisburg in 1992 and awarded a German Documentary Film Prize) homes in on one of the themes addressed in *Grenzland—eine Reise*, the rise of the New Right. The film was to have its Berlin première at Bertolt Brecht's famous theatre, the Berliner Ensemble, but before it could be screened, fliers proclaiming 'no right to free speech, no right to organize, no freedom for fascists to produce propaganda' demanded a boycott of the film and the decision was made not to show it. The dramatist Heiner Müller, one of the theatre's directors, justified the decision by arguing that the theme of fascism could not be given objective treatment in the prevailing climate (*Tagesspiegel*, 6 December 1992). The film is a portrait of five right-wing youths in Halle-Neustadt. It shows them with their parents and friends in surroundings of unemployment and drabness as ideological victims of unseen manipulators, unable to articulate their beliefs convincingly. The film strains to provide an objective viewpoint: rather than asking questions Heise waits for the youths to talk and edits together sequences of embarrassed and embarrassing grinning silences with short bursts of articulated unhappiness, all tempered with a rosy belief in the heroic achievements of National Socialism. The film was refused an FBW predicate (a quality rating designed to promote films of artistic merit) in 1993 on the grounds that it was 'a document portraying no more than the inability of both the subjects and the filmmakers to articulate themselves'. In defence of the film it was pointed out that the method of observing the youths was more revealing than any artificial discussion or attempt to convert the youths to a better cause. A similarly virulent debate has since accompanied another film about right-wing extremism, Winfried Bonengel's *Beruf Neonazi* (Occupation Neo-Nazi, 1993). The decisions not to predicate films such as *STAU—Jetzt geht's los* and *Grenzland—eine Reise* have led to accusations of bias (*epd Film* August 1993:47) and to the suggestion that the jury both fails to recognize the worth of the filmmakers of the new federal states and is exercising a form of censorship on films that tackle sensitive issues.

Whilst these films have taken documentary filmmaking towards a controversial future, the release of two unusual films has signalled the end of an era. *Kinder, Kader, Kommandeure* (Children, Cadres, Commanders,

1991), a tragi-comic film compiled by Wolfgang Kissel and promptly released on video, consists of clips from propaganda and educational films made during the forty years of GDR history. It moves from the energy and optimism of the late 1940s and 1950s, through state rituals startlingly reminiscent of National Socialist rallies, and ends with the celebrations of the fortieth anniversary of the GDR in 1989. The second film, *Drehbuch, die Zeiten* (Film Script, In Days Gone By, 1961–93) by Winfried Junge, is a documentary about the making of Junge's own film *Lebensläufe* (Biographies). Begun in 1961, *Lebensläufe* follows the fortunes of a class of schoolchildren from the East German village of Golzow for three decades. This film and *Drehbuch, die Zeiten* have become unique documents of the history of the GDR and of the DEFA documentary film.

13.5 Feature films: unification and the new hope for filmmaking

Initially unification appeared to offer the German feature film much needed topical subject matter. If anything characterized the West German cinema of the 1970s it was the response to domestic politics; this was also true at least in principle for the officially preferred *Gegenwartsfilm* in the East, which aimed to depict contemporary society and issues. The hope was widely expressed both at home and abroad that the events following the fall of the Wall would provide the impetus to stimulate a revival in the making of feature films; in the words of the film historian Lotte Eisner: 'German artists need a certain creative desperation, a certain feverish exaltation in order to be truly creative' (Fischer and Hembus 1980:145). A body of feature films has indeed appeared that addresses directly or indirectly the subject of unification. Taken together, however, they add up to a curious mix of quirky light entertainment and political timidity.

Very few feature films are unequivocally positive about unification; those that are tend to be allegorical. Percy Adlon's *Salmonberries*, for example, an English-language film released in 1991, addresses the division and unification of Germany obliquely through the story of a relationship between two women living in Alaska. The older woman, Roswitha, is an East German whose husband was shot in 1969 as they attempted to flee together across the border to the West. Ten years later she is earning a living as a librarian in a tiny Eskimo village, unable to rid herself of her traumatic memories which she bottles up together with the fruits of summer in beautifully glowing jars. The younger woman, Kotzebue, played by the country and western singer k.d. lang, is a lesbian in search of her true national and sexual identity. Believing she may have been left stranded in the snow by Russian parents, she turns to the librarian for help in tracing her ancestry, only to discover that she is an Eskimo. The film is a remarkable if quirky conglomeration of romantic landscape imagery, gender issues, the search for identity, friendship, love, and forgiveness, with a potted history of Germany thrown in for good measure. At the heart of the film are two strikingly simple images of unification: a spring thaw, and a tentative love affair between two very different women.

Rudolf Thome's *Liebe auf den ersten Blick* (Love at First Sight, 1991) is a love story that explores the relationship between two people as an expression of hope for the union of the two countries. A futurologist, a single mother from West Berlin, meets an archaeologist, a single father from East Berlin, in a children's playground. She immediately falls in love with him and invites him and his two children to her home for tea. By the end they have become one big family of five and plan to have a child together. The film was celebrated by the critics as a significant achievement, its chief virtue lying in its portrayal of likeable characters from both East and West. Thome does not indulge in the facile images that were soon to become the well-worn clichés of unification, except perhaps in the overly schematic parallel between the couple's first love-making and the union of the two states.

These two films are exceptional in their optimistic treatment of unification. The fact that *Apfelbäume* (Apple Trees, 1991) by the West German director Helma Sanders-Brahms is structured around striking documentary footage of rows and rows of East German apple trees being ripped out of the ground indicates a more critical response to some of the consequences of unification. The story moves from the idealism that accompanied the planting of the trees in East Germany in the 1950s (an apple tree for each and every GDR citizen) to betrayal and sterility, reconciliation, and the planting of a new tree after the borders have come down. Paradoxically the film appears to be more a criticism of the cold and calculating West than an attempt to come to terms with GDR history. As in many other films the one-dimensional representation of the evils of Western capitalism tends to project an image of life in the former GDR that is uncomfortably similar to the clichés of community life propagated by the GDR government itself. The distortion is compounded by the implication that life in the East was more natural, less polluted and altogether more healthy than in the West. In addition the portrayal of GDR citizens as simple, almost mindless provincials caused considerable offence in the east.

13.6 Reunification comedies

> The present German-German situation gives little cause for laughter: yet reunification is providing the setting [...] for numerous, diverse comedies. (Schäfer and Schobert 1993:49)

Perhaps it was the fear of an overly didactic, moralizing tone that led so many directors to resort, often rather desperately, to humour when confronting the disappointments of post-unification Germany. An early example, Jörg Foth's *Letztes aus der DaDaeR* (Lastest from the DaDaeR), was one of the last films to be produced by DEFA. While Foth's film brings together a group of cabaret artists to sing and dance the GDR to its end, one of the first West German comic treatments of the subject, Christoph Schlingensief's *Das deutsche Kettensägenmassaker—Die erste Stunde der Wiedervereinigung* (The German Chainsaw Massacre—The First Hour of Reunification, 1990) adopts an altogether more macabre approach. In this trash horror movie the new Germany becomes an underworld in which a manic West German family, equipped with axes and chainsaws, hunts down East Germans just over the border and turns them into sausages. West Germans are capitalist cannibals devouring the East whilst the East Germans are optimistic but helpless victims unable to defend themselves in an evil world of unfettered commerce. The scenario is frequently recycled, albeit less extremely, in various guises in the new genre of the *Wiedervereinigungskomödie* (reunification comedy).

One of the most successful reunification comedies was Vadim Glowna's *Der Brocken* (Rising to the Bait, 1991), which tells the story of an elderly East German woman living on the north coast of Germany. When the borders come down she finds herself visited by a constant stream of West Germans interested in purchasing her house, which is beautifully situated with views across the countryside and the sea. The plot involves complications about the ownership of the house, a *Stasi* agent who is redeemed by helping out the old lady with a little secret police magic, and a new business venture in which the locals pull themselves up by their bootstraps and grow natural and healthy produce for the new unified German market. With more than a touch of irony the film consciously reduces the severe problems facing the new federal states to a set of wacky east–west clichés, topped with a mysterious ending in which the old woman's house appears to have developed strategic military significance.

The American film *Trabbi goes to Hollywood*, starring the popular German actor Thomas Gottschalk, was one of three Trab(b)i films to appear in 1990; the others were Peter Timm's *Go, Trabi, Go* and *Der Superstau* (Super Jam) by Manfred Stelzer, both German productions. In

Trabbi goes to Hollywood a GDR inventor takes his precious car to Hollywood where it is stolen. In searching for it he manages to procure himself sixteen million dollars and a beautiful wife. The East German is portrayed throughout as a lucky, lovable, naive country bumpkin, a characterization extreme enough to include the detail that his Trabi is fuelled by beetroot juice. Timm's film on the other hand is an altogether more German affair as the travel-hungry East Germans set off for Italy in their Trabi, armed with a well-thumbed copy of Goethe's *Italienische Reise* (Italian Journey). The East Germans, a teacher and his family from Bitterfeld, plan to follow in Goethe's footsteps through Regensburg, Munich, and on to Rome during the summer of 1990. When the *Ossis* come back from Italy to be confronted with the task of operating in a capitalist world, the film again suggests that the morally superior GDR citizens do not possess the financial acumen of their Western brothers and sisters. A very popular film, it was nominated for a *Bundesfilmpreis* (National German Film Prize). In 1992 it spawned a less successful sequel, *Das war der Wilde Osten* (That Was the Wild East) also known as *Go, Trabi, Go II*, directed by Wolfgang Büld and Reinhard Kloos.

In 1993 feature films about post-unification Germany continued to resort to humour to reflect on the more sober political situation. Philip Gröning's *Die Terroristen* (The Terrorists) is sometimes categorized as a comedy, although Chancellor Helmut Kohl, who spoke out against the film, appeared along with most of the critics to have missed the joke. It deals with a 'fourth generation' of terrorists, inauthenticity, and senseless violence, and portrays the fall of the Wall as a media event rather than a historical occasion. Three twenty-year-olds plan to assassinate a fat statesman but fail, killing the wrong person. They clean up and go their separate ways as if nothing special has happened. Although the trio appear to be nostalgic for a time when radical action is relevant, their behaviour is unmotivated. It is this that distinguishes them from, for example, the West German terrorist groups active in the 1970s. They play computer games obsessively and their preparations for robbery and assassination take place against an incessant background of collaged sound from political advertising, pop music, and the fireworks of unification. Above all the film provoked moral outrage for the way in which it seemed to pour scorn on the unification celebrations.

13.7 Looking to the east

Two films in particular have offered a more promising vision of the future, Detlev Buck's popular *Wir können auch anders ...* (We Can Change ...,

1992) and *Gorilla Bathes at Noon* (1993) by the Yugoslav Dušan Makavejev. Both films look towards the east and introduce a new character, the Red Army deserter. *Wir können auch anders ...* is a 'German western, a road-movie' in which two men, both illiterate, go into business together. They travel not towards the west but to the east to claim property as an inheritance and they pick up a Red Army deserter on the way. Arriving at their destination they find the property is a country cottage, run down, and in need of repair. The film argues for a different way of living altogether, for a rejection of metropolitan life in favour of the flat landscapes of the east.

A Red Army deserter is also the hero of *Gorilla Bathes at Noon*, which attempts to find a balance between regret at the demise of socialism and the sense of a new future with all its potential for self-expression. When a Russian soldier leaves hospital to find his battalion has gone (he is not really a deserter at all; the Red Army has abandoned him) he decides not to leave Berlin but to remain in the city that has become his home. Whilst the soldier affirms his affection for the city by staying, his life-style (sleeping on roofs and in cellars, moving among different nationalities, finding food from the zoo, and looking after a baby) becomes an anarchic exploration of a cosmopolitan and confused city. On his odyssey he is forced to confront new perils thrown up by the free market and by increasing nationalism. The film is quietly humorous, gaining a warmth generally lacking in the German *Wiedervereinigungskomödie* through its unsentimental treatment of the sense of loss experienced by a Russian soldier who once loved Lenin. During production Makaveyev managed to film the removal of the famous Lenin monument from Berlin Friedrichshain to the depot in Köpenick where it was stored along with other GDR monuments. In the film the Russian soldier sits on top of the statue, attempts to clean off the yellow paint that has been thrown at it, and lovingly escorts it to its final resting place. A surreal moment of release comes when, in a dream sequence, he talks with Lenin and manages to extract the bullet from his hero's brain. Although reminiscent of Schlingensief's *Kettensägen-massaker* in its goriness, the scene manages to paint an image of reconciliation with the past which has eluded so many recent German films.

13.8 New German Cinema

Perhaps one of the most remarkable (some might say disappointing) features of post-unification film has been the lack of incisive debate and engaged, topical filmmaking from those directors who were once internationally renowned for their radical contributions to German cultural and political life. These directors had been in the vanguard of the New German Cinema during its heyday from 1969 to 1982. For many of them, notably Jean-Marie Straub and Danièle Huillet, Volker Schlöndorff, Alexander Kluge, Wim Wenders, Werner Herzog, and Herbert Achternbusch, unification appears to have passed by almost unnoticed and without altering thematically or aesthetically the course that their work had followed during the 1980s. Kluge, for example, was not tempted out of what he claims to be temporary retirement from cinema to produce either an essay film or a collaborative venture to mark the historic changes. This is despite the fact that *Deutschland im Herbst* (Germany in Autumn), the title of the film made collectively in 1977 by nine German filmmakers, would once again have been an appropriate title. Hans Jürgen Syberberg's stage production *Ein Traum, was sonst?* (A Dream, What Else? 1991) was planned with a cinema adaptation in mind; the result could turn out to be one of the most striking and visionary films about unification. The work is a recitation by Edith Clever of texts by Euripides, Kleist, and Goethe; the narrative framework is based on events from 1945 to 1989 and uses as source material Marion Dönhoff's autobiography *Namen, die keiner mehr nennt* (Dönhoff 1964). The stage production, premièred at the Hebbel-Theater in Berlin, was enthusiastically received at the Edinburgh Festival in 1992.

Regardless of the critical acclaim their films have received (which in the case of Straub/Huillet and Achternbusch has been considerable), the directors of the New German Cinema have, to put it generously, consolidated their positions. In *Paul Cézanne im Gespräch mit Joachim Gasquet* (Paul Cézanne in Conversation with Joachim Gasquet, 1990) and *Antigone* (1991) Straub and Huillet continued their dialogue with Friedrich Hölderlin which began with *Der Tod des Empedokles* (The Death of Empedocles, 1986). *Paul Cézanne* is a sixty-five-minute documentary about an artist whom Straub and Huillet see as a seminal influence on their own work. It is a complex and stimulating essay drawing connections between what Straub has termed Hölderlin's 'Communist utopia', the paintings and writings of Cézanne, Flaubert's *Madame Bovary* (including Jean Renoir's film of the novel), and Straub/Huillet's own *Tod des Empedokles*. Beautifully shot by the veteran French cameraman Henri Alekan, this film is in many ways a stock-taking of Straub/Huillet's Brechtian style of filmmaking. The same can be said of their Sophocles adaptation, *Antigone*, which ends with an overt and topical reference to the Gulf War. Literary adaptation, an important genre for the New German Cinema, has retained a significant presence in post-unification filmmaking, thanks not only to Straub/Huillet but also to Werner Schroeter (in his 1990 adaptation of Ingeborg Bachmann's novel *Malina*), Volker Schlöndorff (*Homo Faber*, Voyager, 1990, based on the novel by Max Frisch), and Hans W. Geissendörfer (*Justiz*, Justice, 1993, based on Dürrenmatt's novel).

Auteurist filmmaking, the German variant of which is known as the *Autorenfilm*, has been kept alive (if not always kicking) by directors of this generation, though with varying degrees of critical acclaim. Wenders' maximalist road movie *Bis ans Ende der Welt* (Until the End of the World, 1990/91), starring Jeanne Moreau and Max von Sydow, was praised more for its soundtrack than its narrative coherence; his sequel to *Der Himmel über Berlin* (Wings of Desire, 1987), *In weiter Ferne, so nah!* (Faraway, So Close! 1992), scripted by the relatively unknown Berlin writer Ulrich Zieger and featuring amongst others Lou Reed and Mikhail Gorbachev, was received with considerable disdain in Germany and abroad. Nevertheless this film does attempt to confront the climate of post-unification Berlin, albeit from a fallen angel's view. Werner Herzog retreated to Patagonia for his most recent allegory of man's triumph over adversity, the mountain-climbing saga *Schrei aus Stein* (Scream of Stone, 1991), based on an idea by the mountaineer Reinhold Messner. Messner subsequently distanced himself from the film's unsuccessful marriage of commercial production values with Herzog's idiosyncratic romanticism. More notable has been Herzog's return to form with documentary films on Bokassa and the war in Kuwait (*Lessons in Darkness*, 1992).

Achternbusch, the Bavarian filmmaker likewise renowned for his exotic locations, deserted Germany in favour of Mongolia in *Niemandsland* (No-Man's-Land, 1991) only to resurface personally in the silent film *I Know the Way to the Hofbrauhaus* as Hick, his American Buddhist alter-ego. One of the most original, visionary, and anarchic filmmakers of his generation, Achternbusch has continued to produce films at the consistent rate of over one a year (twenty-four in all by 1993), earning great critical success. His most recent films, including *Ich bin da, ich bin da* (I'm Here, I'm Here, 1992), a maverick contribution to the Columbus anniversary celebrations, and *Ab nach Tibet* (Off to Tibet, 1993), have been shot on a shoe-string budget.

Like Achternbusch, Rosa von Praunheim has continued to cater to a small but loyal niche audience (in this case the gay community), although his recent films have been successful beyond the parameters of sexual orientation. The 1990 AIDS Trilogy, *Positiv* (Positive), *Schweigen = Tod* (Silence = Death) and *Feuer unterm Arsch* (Fire under Your Arse), demonstrated von Praunheim's remarkable talents as a documentary filmmaker. The docu-fiction drama *Ich bin meine eigene Frau* (I Am My Own Woman, 1992), based on the extraordinary life of Charlotte von

Mahlsdorf, a transvestite who was born Lothar Berfelde in 1928 and experienced persecution as a homosexual in the Third Reich and subsequently in the GDR, is a unique, part-tragic, part-comic, and ultimately uplifting history of gay subculture in Berlin. A film also about unification, this biography of a survivor is one of von Praunheim's most engaging works, ending worryingly with renewed attacks on Charlotte and the Berlin gay community, this time by neo-Nazis.

Although experimental film extends beyond the scope of this chapter, mention should also be made, in the context of New German Cinema filmmakers, of a significant experimental contribution to the theme of unification. *Candida* by Dore O. (a leading figure in the first generation of German experimental filmmakers of the mid-1960s) is an extraordinary and vibrant celebration of female dynamism and of the breaking down of physical, metaphorical, and linguistic barriers. A kaleidoscope of classic structural filmmaking techniques, Dore O.'s encyclopaedic odyssey follows a tight travel narrative based on Frans Masareel's 1920 series of woodcuts, *Die Idee* (The Idea). *En route* Candida visits the Ruhr, Hamburg, Berlin (where she encounters the *Mauerspechte*, the Wallpeckers), Vienna, New York, Paris, and Bahia, unifying them all in a musical, dynamic rhythm of ecstatic forward motion. *Candida* is undoubtedly one of the most exhilarating products of post-unification optimism.

13.9 The second *Stunde Null*?

Since 1989 a new wave of films either set in the Third Reich or dealing with its aftermath has appeared. Some of these have been box office successes. Examples are Hans W. Geissendörfer's *Gudrun* (1991), a story about children under National Socialism, and Helmut Dietl's *Schtonk!* (1992), a comedy on the Hitler Diaries fiasco. Other films in this category deal more seriously with issues relevant to Germany after unification. The issue of *Vergangenheitsbewältigung* in the former GDR, together with the suggestion that November 1989 was a second *Stunde Null* (zero hour), have made National Socialism and its aftermath a source of material for historical analyses in post-unification Germany. The trend was heralded just before the *Wende* by a film which was enthusiastically received by critics at home and abroad, Michael Verhoeven's *Das schreckliche Mädchen* (The Nasty Girl, 1989). This addressed the question of individual guilt in a fresh and engaging manner and Verhoeven injected topicality and relevance into the theme by basing the film on the true story of Anja Rosmus's single-handed and highly controversial battle with the legacy of

Nazism in her conservative home town of Passau. Furthermore it is one of the first films to depict, in the form of the neo-Nazi thugs who repeatedly attack the protagonist, the all-too real resurgence of fascism amongst young people.

During the 1960s protracted debates took place concerning Germany's so-called 'inability to mourn'. The phrase was derived from the title of a book by Margarete and Alexander Mitscherlich who argued that the German people had suppressed their mourning for the loss of the National Socialist dream and had been unable to face up to the reality of the crimes committed in the name of that dream (Mitscherlich 1967). It is therefore both telling and appropriate that one of the feature films to draw implicit historical and psychological parallels between 1945 and 1989 should be directed by a member of the same family, Thomas Mitscherlich. The subject of *Die Denunziantin* (Just a Matter of Duty, 1992) is Helene Schwärzel, the informer whose naive sense of duty led to the execution of the civilian head of the 20 July conspiracy against Hitler, Dr Carl Goerdeler. After the war Schwärzel became the first person to be tried before a German court for a crime against humanity. The significance of this film lies in the way in which it implicitly links an exploration of the motivation and consequences of denunciation during the Third Reich to the current debate about *Stasi* informers and the legacy of the GDR.

The parallels between 1945 and 1989, in particular the implication from the new wave of right-wing extremism that historical lessons have not been learnt, have led some directors to express their desperation and frustration in a kind of frenzied hysteria. According to the film critic Helmut Schödel this hysteria is paradigmatically articulated in the work of one of the most controversial young directors, Christoph Schlingensief (whose film *Kettensägenmassaker* is discussed above). For some Schlingensief is the Fassbinder of the 1990s. Schödel points out that his celebrated comedy *Terror 2000—Deutschland außer Kontrolle* (Terror 2000—Germany out of Control, 1992) has echoes of Fassbinder's futuristic terrorist film *Die dritte Generation* (The Third Generation, 1979). At the same time it is unmistakably a product of post-unification disillusionment: 'Fassbinder reacted to Germany by making melodramas. That period is now over; Schlingensief has good reason to be hysterical' (Schödel 1992:59). Schödel convincingly captures the essence of Schlingensief's work: it is old-fashioned and regressive as well as disturbingly topical. The furore surrounding Schlingensief's 1993 multimedia adaptation for the Berlin stage of the life of Michael Kühnen, the neo-Nazi leader who died of AIDS, suggests that he has indeed struck a raw nerve. The same may be true for Jörg Buttgereit, the controversial director of the *Nekromantik* films

(1987, 1991) which use horror, splatter, and gore to represent necrophiliac eroticism as a metaphor for absolute self-fulfilment.

13.10 The diversity of cinema in the 1990s

Despite the danger of over-simplification it could be said that Schlingensief's *Terror 2000* and Katja von Garnier's unexpected box office hit *Abgeschminkt* (Making Up, 1992), a light-hearted, romantic debut comedy, mark out the stylistic parameters of German feature filmmaking in the 1990s. On the one hand there is an obsessive and violent vision of an apocalyptic future in a neo-fascist society and on the other a rare example of a German film that is entertaining without leaving an aftertaste of heavy pessimism. Von Garnier's success can be measured by the fact that she received an offer from Hollywood to document the making of Petersen's *In the Line of Fire*.

Besides *Abgeschminkt* other films by young directors have succeeded in breathing new life into tried and trusted themes or genres. Examples include: Sönke Wortmann's *Kleine Haie* (Little Sharks, 1992), a parochial comedy about young acting hopefuls; Joseph Vilsmaier's Second World War drama *Stalingrad* (1992); Peter Sehr's prize-winning *Kaspar Hauser—Verbrechen am Seelenleben eines Menschen* (Kaspar Hauser—Crimes against the Soul of a Human-Being, 1993), a reworking of the *enfant sauvage* theme; Wolfgang Becker's *Kinderspiele* (Child's Play, 1991), a drama of conflicting generations set in the 1950s; and Marcel Gisler's *Die blaue Stunde* (The Blue Hour, 1991), a sensitive and arresting portrait of a young Berlin call-boy who enters into a relationship with his female neighbour. These films are distinctly heterogeneous in style and content, as are those by women directors who came to prominence in the 1980s, including Dorris Dörrie's *Happy Birthday, Türke* (Happy Birthday, Turk, 1991), Monika Treut's *My Father is Coming* (1991), and Cynthia Beatt's *The Party—Nature Morte* (1991). Even so they demonstrate continuity with pre-unification cinema and use diverse strategies to reach both niche home markets and audiences abroad.

13.11 The preservation of film history

Towards the end of 1993 an important centre for German filmmakers and audiences, the Frankfurt *kommunales Kino*, was threatened with closure. A repertory cinema funded by the community to show non-mainstream films and films of historic interest, the *kommunales Kino* was founded in 1971 as the first of its kind in Germany and acquired immense symbolic importance as an institution supporting a community-based cinema culture. Several other cities in Germany subsequently founded their own *kommunale Kinos*. In Lübeck, Kiel, Cologne, and Frankfurt, the need to cut local government spending in the wake of the unexpectedly high cost of unification and the worsening recession led to proposals to discontinue financial support for these centres.

The threat to the existence of the Frankfurt *kommunales Kino* provoked a storm of protest of a kind not experienced in the film world in Germany since the late 1970s. The administration's suggested solution, to turn the cinema into a video library, added insult to injury. This was surely a far cry from the optimistic prognoses of people like the film-historian and producer Rolf Giesen who in 1990 had spoken of a bright future for German cinema as 'part of a giant media network stretching from Tokyo to New York' (Becker 1990:6). Angry letters and expressions of support flooded in from critics, producers, and filmmakers from the whole spectrum of the German film industry. Typical of the tone of these protests was the letter sent by Edgar Reitz, who could speak out with the added authority of a string of successful television collaborations to his name (including *Die zweite Heimat* (The Second Heimat: A New Generation) which was shown on German and British television in 1993). For Reitz, cinema is the medium of the future, an expression of community, identity, and humanity:

> As international statistics are already showing, cinema will experience an impressive renaissance in the second century of its history. The reason for this is that people are once again looking for a sense of community and are trying to escape the isolation of city life which is imposed upon them by television and video. Discussions with others, the exchange of thoughts and feelings, and the experience of relaxed togetherness—these are at the heart of cinema culture, this is what makes the art of film immortal. (Reitz 1993)

In an even more pugnacious letter Danièle Huillet launched a spirited defence of cinema. Likening the proposed act of cultural vandalism to the environmental devastation brought about by uncontrolled economic growth, she offered an apocalyptic vision of a Europe without culture. Her letter is an eloquent and much-needed celebration of the value of a medium whose history Germany has in the past decisively influenced and enriched:

> Is the art form of the twentieth century to disappear, to be forgotten in Goethe's city, just at the moment when it is about to reach its

hundredth year? (For without a cinema, without a place to show films, without a public, without technology the art form cannot exist.) Is the space to be cleared for the business of mass communication? What kind of Europe do they have in mind? A desert for robots? As with our air and with our water, there will be no going back; we will not be able to put things right again: what is dead is dead. (Huillet 1993)

After much debate it was decided not to close the Frankfurt *kommunales Kino*.

Further reading

The state of German film today is a frequent discussion topic in the German national newspapers; it appears occasionally in international film magazines such as *Sight and Sound* and *Screen International*. The main German film magazine is the monthly *epd Film*. A good publication that has hit hard times since unification is *Film und Fernsehen*, originally a GDR film magazine. Other important publications include the biannual *Frauen und Film* and the weekly trade journal *Filmecho/Filmwoche*.

There is a plethora of books on the New German Cinema in the FRG during the 1960s, 1970s, and early 1980s. Elsaesser (1989) and Sandford (1980) are standard textbooks. Fischetti (1992) contains interviews with eight women directors active in filmmaking in the FRG from the late 1970s into the 1990s. There are fewer books on film in the GDR and this is likely to be one of the major areas of publication in the next few years. Blunk and Jungnickel (1990), begun before the *Wende*, gives an insight into the organization of filmmaking in DEFA. Jacobsen and others (1993) contains essays on all periods of German filmmaking; there are also extensive bibliographies and a chronology highlighting the important events in the history of German cinema. For a history of Ufa see Kreimeier (1992). Pflaum and Prinzler (1992), also published in English translation under the title *Cinema in the Federal Republic of Germany* (1993), is one of the most useful publications after unification. The new and expanded edition is the first to provide information on both east and west German filmmakers. The book covers all aspects of film in Germany, including funding, prizes and awards, training facilities, and numerous bio-filmographies. It also lists major journals and books.

14

The German Language
From Revolt to Division

DEREK LEWIS

14.1 Introduction

> Every revolutionary movement also liberates language. What up to
> now was so difficult to articulate suddenly comes freely from our
> lips [...]. (James and Stone 1992:127–29)

These words—part of an address by the East German author Christa Wolf
to a mass demonstration in Berlin on 4 November 1989—capture the joy
of linguistic liberation which accompanied the political changes of the
Wende. Dismissing the language of the SED and of the state-controlled
media as the straitjackets of the old regime, Wolf saw the new eloquence
as actively contributing to the process of political reform. She noted that
ordinary citizens were beginning to express their opinions freely and were
reading newspapers that contained genuine information instead of government propaganda; for the first time in the GDR's history, dialogue,
spontaneous expression, and the flow of information were assisting in the
development of a popular revolutionary consciousness. Another speaker at
the Berlin rally, the author Stefan Heym, declared that the East Germans
had 'overcome their speechlessness and learned to walk erect' (James and
Stone 1992:125).

These observations indicate how the 1989 revolution was not just a political event but also a 'revolt of language'—according to Peter von Polenz
(1993) the term *Sprachrevolte* was first used at this time by the GDR linguist Reinhard Hopfer. This chapter will investigate the nature of this revolt, tracing it from its origins before the *Wende* to its climax in late 1989.
One striking aspect of the fall of the Berlin Wall is revealed in the televised
reactions of ordinary citizens to the event. While Westerners responded
confidently to interviewers, the East Germans were markedly reticent: for
them the events were beyond words (typical utterances included:
Wahnsinn, unbeschreiblich, das muß man gesehen haben). This
'speechless' phase demonstrates how the impact of the *Wende* was differ-

ent for East and West Germans. It also raises the issue of how a people held within the strict parameters of SED polit-speak would react to the articulate Western society to which they were suddenly exposed. After unification, language usage in Germany reflects the uncertainties of the transition process and the problems of achieving a sense of genuine unity. Finally, the chapter discusses how east Germans are adapting linguistically to the post-unification period and what, if anything, they will retain of their pre-*Wende* linguistic heritage in the longer term. The material for this chapter is derived mainly from surveys and observations made by German linguists since 1989. Given the volume of German material presented, translations are provided only exceptionally.

14.2 The origins of Marxist-Leninist rhetoric

To understand the interplay between the *Wende* and the German language it is helpful to review the origins of the public rhetoric of the Communist regime in East Germany. The language of the SED was rooted in the political theory of Marxism-Leninism. Marxism-Leninism was a compulsory subject in GDR schools, and extensive knowledge of its principles was a prerequisite for Party membership and professional advancement. The term Marxism-Leninism originated in the late 1920s, when it referred as much to the institutions of state Communism in the Soviet Union as to the ideology which underpinned them (Kernig 1973:78); at any rate it is clear that Communist political theory was early on closely identified with the bureaucracy of the Party machine. Marxism-Leninism claimed to be dogmatic, universalist, and scientific. It was dogmatic in that it asserted a set of fixed and immutable axioms which explained social and political processes. It was universalist inasmuch as it claimed to provide the basis for explaining all natural and human phenomena; it also went a stage further by combining this explanatory world-view with prescriptions for political and personal behaviour. But it was the pretension to scientific method and the emphasis on the role of social class which was at the centre of Marxism-Leninism's view of itself as superior to all other philosophies. Under the leadership of Walter Ulbricht (1949–71), the SED saw itself as a 'scientific party' uniquely able to analyse political processes and to provide utopian solutions.

The second source of SED-rhetoric was the language of the Communist Party as used during the 1920s in the Soviet Union and Germany. Features of this language betrayed the mentality of an embattled proletarian party. They included a tone of belligerent stridency, a fondness for working-class expressions, deviations from standard forms, and the use of military and religious vocabulary (Oschlies 1989a). The twin traditions of bureau-cratism and militant activism produced a curious mixture of stereotype and aggressiveness in the political language of the GDR.

From the 1960s onwards the official linguistic and philosophical author-ity on Marxism-Leninism in the GDR was Georg Klaus, co-author of the *Wörterbuch der Philosophie*, a compendium of officially approved polit-ical terms and definitions. First published in 1964, the work appeared in fourteen editions and became the standard reference authority on every censor's desk. As a result of the Soviet tradition and Klaus's linguistic po-licing, public language in the GDR degenerated into preformed stereo-types. This trend was exacerbated by geriatric and unimaginative SED leaders whose level of formal education was low. East Germany never produced an inspired rhetorician, and linguistic elegance was disparaged as a relic of the bourgeoisie (Bergmann 1992).

14.3 The SED's reaction to the reform movement

The political stagnation of the SED and its inability to appraise the need for reform emerged linguistically in two ways. First, at a time when the SED needed open dialogue and a frank exchange of information with its own members (not to mention with the people as a whole), communication within the Party became increasingly formal and standardized (Fix 1992). Decades of control from the political centre had established an inhibiting model of communication which meant that reports of discontent in the country were progressively censored the further they were passed up the hierarchy. Second, the state-controlled media continued to churn out in-appropriate propaganda in response to the mounting protests of 1989. They either reiterated hackneyed formulae about the *gute Entwicklung des Sozialismus* and *Einheit von Kontinuität und Erneuerung* or they reverted to the shrill rhetoric of the Cold War; such rhetoric was strongly reminis-cent of the language of National Socialism:

Frontberichterstattung
stabsmäßig vorbereitete Heim-ins-Reich-Psychose
illegale Nacht- und Nebel-Aktion
berufsmäßige Dreckschleuder
geistige Fossile von Gestern
wüste Schlammschlacht der Kalten-Kriegs-Hysterie
antikommunistischer Taumel

In their collective myopia and constrained by their narrow ideological horizons, the SED-leadership failed to realize that both strategies belonged to a thoroughly discredited past.

Erich Honecker's personal response to the crisis of 1989 was typically unsophisticated. Ever fond of the homely cliché, he uttered trite observations about the irreversible 'wheel of history', or the 'march of socialism' which neither 'ox nor ass' could hold up (*den Sozialismus in seinem Lauf hält weder Ochs noch Esel auf, Neues Deuschland* 15 August 1989:1). Alternatively he would resort to abuse: for example, he derided *glasnost* as 'the whining of a demented petit-bourgeoisie' (*das Gequake wildgewordener Spießer*). Honecker's successor Egon Krenz made a similar error when in his inaugural speeches he revealed himself to be 'a prisoner of that language which for most people had nothing more to say' (Eppler 1993:76).

The leaders of the SED thus countered demands for reform with a fundamentally anachronistic language that betrayed their hostility to change. In the eyes of the people Marxist-Leninist rhetoric was irretrievably compromised as an instrument of oppression; it was a further manifestation of political stagnation and official indifference. Stefan Heym forcefully confirmed this view when he spoke of liberation from 'the years of torpor and staleness, of phrasemongering and bureaucratic arbitrariness, of official blindness and deafness' (James and Stone 1992:125). Just when they most needed it the SED's leaders showed that they lacked the intellectual capacity for renewal. Recalling how the Politburo responded to the unrest from September 1989 onwards, Günter Schabowski stresses its 'speechlessness' and its inability to progress beyond 'standard phraseology' (Schabowski 1990). Old habits died hard: after unification an observer at the trial of the former East German Defence Minister Heinz Kessler saw him as 'a man who clung to the language of real existing socialism' (*Süddeutsche Zeitung* 8 December 1992:2).

14.4 Language as the barometer of the revolution

Language played a special role in the process of emancipation in all the Soviet satellite countries (Oschlies 1990a). This role took the form of manifestos (although these were less prominent in East Germany), popular slogans (*Wir sind das Volk!*) that ignited and spread the enthusiasm for change, and, above all, non-violent dialogue with the authorities (*Keine Gewalt!*). Oschlies distinguishes four phases of language change during the *Wende*. The first is the collective awakening to new insights and truths (*das Aha-Erlebnis*). The prevailing metaphors of this period included the throwing opening of windows, the tearing down of walls, and the collapse of the fortress of Communism. During the second phase political concepts and terms which had been ignored or used only in propagandistic senses were brought to life and openly discussed (*Gulag, Totalitarismus, Mafia, Pluralismus, Marktwirtschaft*). The third phase saw the discarding of the ideological linguistic ballast of the old society (*sozial, sozialistisch, Überzeugungsarbeit, Errungenschaften*). Street and place names were also discarded, as were forms of address in socialist organizations (such as *Jugendfreund*, widely used in the youth movement). Left-wing reformers in the GDR made valiant but futile efforts to revitalize the concept of socialism by assigning fresh attributes to it, such as 'modern', 'humanistic', or 'genuinely democratic', which suggested a positive alternative to bureaucratic socialism. But attempts to restrict the revolution to a version of reformed socialism, a *Wende des Sozialismus*, deeply underestimated the legacy of popular disillusionment with the 'real existing socialism' that the state had propagated since the 1970s. The final phase of the language revolution was, according to Oschlies, a 'linguistic disarmament', that is, the abandonment of the military metaphors (*Kampf, Front, Stab, Feind, liquidieren*) and the superlative style favoured by the SED (*immer mehr, immer vollständiger, noch nicht konsequent genug, noch besser machen*).

In addition to these changes, former euphemisms were discarded and negative ideas that had been hitherto suppressed were allowed to surface. Thus *Mauer* was now used for *befestigte Staatsgrenze*, *Mangel* for *Mißwirtschaft*, and *Engpässe* and *Ladenhüter* replaced *Überplanbestände*. Stigmatized groups were rehabilitated, so that *Randalierer, Provokateure, Rädelsführer* became *Demonstranten*, while *Konterrevolutionäre, antisozialistische Elemente* or *Verräter* were now referred to as *Oppositionelle*. At the same time new objects of hostility emerged, especially the relics of the old regime (*Stalinismus, Betonköpfe, Wendehals*). There was a marked increase in Western linguistic imports, notably the jargon of West German political ideology (*Pluralismus, Meinungsvielfalt, artikulieren, Offenlegung, Koalition, mündiger Bürger, Konsens*). The gentler and more conciliatory language of the Churches also made its presence felt as East Germans were encouraged to 'bring in' (*einbringen*) their experiences to enrich the new society.

While SED-jargon was swiftly abandoned, public speakers in the GDR occasionally committed indiscretions by reactivating politically sensitive language. An example is *zuführen*, the euphemism for arrest and detention widely employed by the *Stasi* but unwisely used in September 1990 by an official referring to the arrest of football fans in Leipzig. Ulla Fix (1992) gives an interesting example of how pre-*Wende* habits of public communication lived on. She describes how a government minister remarked on the difficulties of continuing to provide school meals and nursery care in the former GDR; despite official denials, the public instantly took this to mean that the facilities would be withdrawn. This incident illustrates how East Germans had gleaned information by reading between the lines of official statements and recognizing implicit threats. Even after unification some easterners felt compelled to deliver politically 'correct' language. Thus a group of parents, drawing up proposals for changes to their school, altered the sentence *Wir wollen unsere Kinder zu fröhlichen Menschen erziehen* to *Unser Ziel ist die Erziehung unserer Kinder zu lebensfrohen Menschen*. The revisions correspond closely in syntax and lexis to the approved 'official' style of the old GDR.

14.5 'The street is the tribunal of the people' (slogan)

Slogans at mass demonstrations played a prominent role in what has been described as the 'search for a new rhetoric' (Volmert 1992). The early slogans show a variety of emotions and attitudes, including anxiety, insecurity, and naivety:

> *Gorbi, hilf uns!*
> *Reformer an die Macht!*
> *Wir sind keine Rowdys!*
> *Reisefreiheit statt Massenflucht*
> *'Neues Forum' zulassen!*
> *Demokratie—jetzt oder nie!*

A more confident note emerges with the inclusion of homely, everyday expressions:

> *Trittbrettfahrer zurücktreten!*
> *Gehen ist Silber, Bleiben ist Gold*

Occasionally the tone is vulgar:

> *Sozialismus, so ein Dreck, alle Roten müssen weg!*
> *Wir lassen uns nicht mehr verarschen!*

Some slogans highlighted specific injustices:

> *Keine Priviligien für uns Berliner!*

Pässe für alle–Laufpaß für die SED!

Political leaders were suddenly addressed directly and informally. This was a reaction to the titlemania of the GDR leadership, who cultivated remoteness from the people:

Erich, laß die Faxen sein, laß die Perestroika rein!
Egon Krenz, wir sind nicht deine Fans!
Helmut und Hans, macht uns Deutschland ganz!
Grüß Dich, Helmut, nimm's nicht schwer, wenn wir bleiben DDR

The wit, rhyme, and word-play in many slogans draws on a long tradition of political humour in Communist countries:

Sägt die Bonzen ab, schützt die Bäume!
Kein Artenschutz für Wendehälse!
Rücktritt ist Fortschritt
SED—das tut weh.
BeKRENZTt—wie lange?
Macht die Volkskammer zum Krenz-Kontrollpunkt
Krenz(en)lose Demokratie
eGOn
Mehr Ökonomie statt EGONomie!
Gegen KOHLonie DDR
Wir lassen uns weder beKRENZen noch verKOHLen
Laßt euch nicht BRDigen!

Some slogans relied on ambiguity for their effect:

Wider Vereinigung!
Reiht euch ein in die Einheizbewegung!
Herr Kohl, Sie wollen nur unser Bestes, aber Sie bekommen es nicht!

Numerous slogans parody the old socialist rhetoric, as used by its leaders and theoreticians. Traditional Marxist war-cries and statements by SED-leaders are satirized mercilessly. There is no mistaking the bitterness of the attacks on the broken promises of socialism:

Stalin entsorgen
Egon, wir haben einen Plan
Eure Politik war und ist zum Davonlaufen.
Proletarier aller Länder, verzeiht mir (Karl Murx)

Priviligierte aller Länder, beseitigt euch
Mafiosi aller Länder, vereinigt euch
Es lebe die Oktoberrevolution 1989!
Ein Gespenst geht um in Europa

One slogan, *Tapetenwechsel*, specifically recalled an interview with Polit-buro member Kurt Hager: referring to *perestroika* in the Soviet Union, he asserted that no-one would replace the wallpaper in his own flat merely because his neighbour had done so (*Neues Deutschland* 10 April 1987). Another slogan mocked Erich Mielke's fatuous statement, *Ich liebe doch alle*, which he addressed to the People's Chamber on 13 November 1989.

A small number of slogans provided a commentary on important themes and issues. These slogans evolved over time and reflected changing attitudes. Popular reactions to the *Stasi*, for instance, ranged from demands for its disbandment to calls for retribution:

Stasi raus!
Rechtssicherheit spart Staatssicherheit
Stasi in die Volkswirtschaft!
Stasi in die Produktion!
Stasigelder in die Wälder!

The *Volk* slogan originated in Leipzig, when demonstrators exhorted the security forces not to use violence against their own people. Reaching its climax in the demand for unification, it ended up as an expression of regret over a lost identity:

Wir sind das Volk
Wir sind auch das Volk PDS
Wir sind ein Volk
Wir sind vielleicht ein Volk
Wir sind ein blödes Volk
Wir waren ein Volk

The slogan finally became an expression, not of unity but of division when western Germans, weary of the financial burdens of unification, cynically observed: *wir auch!*

The slogans formed an important part of the spontaneous development of a collective identity and of open forms of public discourse during the early days of the *Wende*. East Germans rejected the past and anticipated their future, not so much by direct political action as by openly ridiculing the old rhetoric and experimenting with a new one. Slogans were repeated, quoted, and adapted from one user to another, a process to which Christa Wolf contributed in her address on 4 November 1989.

The demonstrations of 1989 represented the final verdict by the people on their masters and contrasted starkly with the ritualized parades of the old GDR, in which the people filed dutifully past their political leaders. During the demonstrations the roles were reversed, a situation which Bertolt Brecht prefigured in a poem written after the Workers' Uprising of 1953 in which he ironically suggested that the SED should dissolve the East German people and elect a new one that is worthy of the Party. Fittingly, Brecht's suggestion was recalled in a slogan of 1989: *Ein Vorschlag für den 1. Mai: Die Führung zieht am Volk vorbei* ('A suggestion for the 1 May: the leadership will parade past the people').

The slogans not only expressed solidarity, they also acted as a means of consolidating and spreading the revolution (Hopfer 1992). Slogans belonged to a broader 'repertoire of discourse' that embraced various channels of communication. These included pamphlets, discussions, hecklings, tape recordings, television and radio interviews, as well as graffiti and car stickers; non-linguistic forms of expression were silent marches, torch-lit processions, and candles to remember the many political prisoners of the regime (Polenz 1993).

14.6 The origins of the new rhetoric

Despite the dominance of official polit-speak in the GDR, other varieties of language existed and may well have contributed to the linguistic renaissance of the *Wende*, including the slogans noted above.

According to Fraas and Steyer (1992) communication in the GDR operated on at least three levels. The first was the official, jargon-dominated level of public discourse which predominated in schools, mass organizations, and the media. The second was the quasi-public discourse used by opposition groups and Church circles and found in the arts and literature; it was also employed informally within the SED. The third was the private discourse of family and close friends (idioms from Western television entered at this level). During the 1980s the second type of discourse was tolerated by the authorities although it contained implicit criticisms of SED jargon. It appeared in cabarets, songs, satirical journals, literature, and in some cultural programmes on television and radio. Its principal weapons were jokes and satire, usually directed at officialdom and life under Communism. Example expressions include: *Tal der Ahnungslosen* (valley of the innocents) for the area around Dresden unable to receive western television transmissions; *die Firma Horch, Guck und Greif* (the firm

Eavesdrop, Spy and Snatch) for the secret police; *Camping Afghanistan* for the Soviet Army; and *Bückware* (literally: 'bend-down goods') for consumer goods in short supply (so-called because they were kept 'under the counter' for special customers; Polenz 1993).

Certain groups in the GDR consciously employed language to assert their identity and to set themselves apart from authority. The group jargon of East German soldiers, for instance, may have originated during the Second World War as a reaction by the troops against the propaganda of National Socialism; after 1945 the jargon entered the language of the working class (Bobach 1993). More influential than the language of barrack-room or prison was that of young people. Until the 1970s the language of teenagers was officially derided because of its openness to Western popular music and consumerism. But with the publication of Ulrich Plenzdorf's novel *Die neuen Leiden des jungen W.* (The New Sufferings of Young W.) in 1973, youth jargon attracted academic attention. A small lexicon of terms used by young people appeared (Heinemann 1989); teaching materials for foreigners also included elements of youth language, although the tendency of such language to satirize the establishment was not stressed. Examples of youth jargon include *Wessi* (for West German), *Kosakendollar* (GDR money), *Bunte* (West German marks) and *dumm wie ein Konsumbrot* (literally: 'as daft as a loaf of bread from the state-owned food store')(Oschlies 1989a, 1989b).

Finally, it is worth briefly noting the status of dialects in the GDR. During the 1950s and 1960s dialects were regarded with some suspicion by the SED. This was due in part to sensitivity to political criticism of the then East German leader, Walter Ulbricht, who spoke with a marked Saxon accent (Oschlies 1989a). Under Honecker dialects were encouraged, partly to counter the sense of alienation which the regions had long felt towards the Berlin government as a result of economic neglect and industrial pollution. But although dialect was employed in official circles, its use could still imply an element of opposition towards the authorities in the capital. While no-one would argue that dialects cause revolutions, it was no accident that in 1989 peaceful dialogue with demonstrators started, not in Berlin, but in the regions, where the regime's authority had also started to collapse.

14.7 From the *Wende* to unification

By December 1989 the period in which spontaneous street slogans functioned as vehicles of popular expression was coming to an end. Thereafter East Germans were preoccupied with how to achieve unification and integration with the West. Enthusiastic to assimilate West German models, East Germans imported whole areas of vocabulary from the political, social, and economic life of the FRG. These imports included terms for general concepts (*Rechtsstaat, Marktwirtschaft*) and specific institutions (*Datenschutz, Arbeitsamt*), and they encompassed the positive concerns of Western society (*Umweltverträglichkeit*) as well as its negative aspects (*Armutsgrenze, Talsohle*). Observers noted how the style of West German political argumentation entered public debate, with its repertoire of devices for highlighting issues and for persuading and affirming (*auf den Weg bringen, es ist angesagt, Eckpunkt, letztendlich, schlußendlich, einerseits—andererseits*)(Polenz 1993).

14.8 Increasing divisions

After 1990 the euphoria produced by unification gave way to disillusionment and scepticism: while eastern Germans were disappointed about economic and social conditions, westerners questioned the financial burdens of unification. In line with the changing mood, the vocabulary of the post-unification period as used in newspapers and the media reflected the failure to achieve a genuine sense of national unity.

A common post-unification image was that of tiredness, the hangover after the party (*einheitsmüde, einheitsernüchtert, Vereinigungskater, Katerstimmung*). In particular the imagery of the Cold War enjoyed a revival. References to *them* and *us*, *over here* and *over there* (*wir–ihr, bei uns, bei euch, drüben*) persisted. Old metaphors of division were resurrected and modified to express a new alienation. The symbol of the Wall, and its counterpart, the trench, reappeared:

> *die innere Mauer*
> *die unsichtbare Mauer*
> *die Mauer in den Köpfen*
> *tiefe Gräben*
> *der Graben zwischen Ost und West*

Now the east-west barrier was variously described as invisible, emotional, mental, inner, social, or even (from the perspective of the poorer east) golden. Related images involved cutting, fracturing, and splitting (*Gegensatz, Kluft, Knatsch, Schere, Spaltung, Riß, auseinandergeraten, auseinanderklaffen, auseinanderdriften*). Bridges (*Brücken*) were needed to span obstacles that had grown more subtle and complex.

Formerly positive images were turned into their opposites. The 'European house', a popular metaphor at the end of the Cold War, conveyed the idea of solidity, harmony, and communality. But the house became a rickety structure, threatened by the strains of unification and the collapse of the economies of former Eastern Europe. Alternatively, it was fortified into a barricade, an island redoubt against the eastern poor:

> *das wacklige Haus Europa*
> *das verriegelte Haus Europa*
> *Festung Europa*
> *Handelsfestung*
> *Wohlstandsinsel*
> *Wohlstandsfestung Europa*

Houses, of course, have ghosts. This time, it was the ghost of nationalism and racism which replaced the spectre of Communism originally evoked by Karl Marx (*Ein Gespenst geht um in Europa*). Architectural imagery also served to highlight the bunker mentality which West Europeans were developing to preserve their own culture and living standards.

Geographically speaking, the 'blossoming landscapes' (*blühende Landschaften*) of the east anticipated by Chancellor Kohl were replaced by depressed valleys, de-industrialized wastelands, and economic deserts (*ökonomishes Jammertal, Wüste, Dürregebiet, Industriebrache*). Images of organic failure included devastation, deforestation (*Kahlschlag*), and medical illness (*nicht überlebensfähig, Infarkt*). A variation on the wilderness theme was the (western) view of the eastern federal states as *der wilde Osten* ('the wild east'). This ambiguous image not only pinpointed the economic depression and increased criminality in the east, it also evoked images of a land of opportunity for swashbuckling entrepreneurs. The slogan *Go East, Go West* denoted the two-way traffic of pioneers heading from west to east and of east Germans commuting to work in the west.

As fears about financial transfers to east Germany focused the national debate on the material costs of unification, a process originally fired by an optimistic vision of a new Germany turned into political haggles over subsidies. The new federal states were increasingly seen in negative terms. The run-down, materially deprived east was cynically portrayed as a high-earning, parasitic burden. These views emerged in labels like *Hochlohnland DDR, Kostenstelle DDR*, even *Ostbauch*. The motif of the burden (*Lasten*), whether financial, economic, ecological, political or mental, recurred frequently. The *Treuhandanstalt*, the Trust Agency responsible for regenerating or closing down eastern concerns, provided linguistically fertile ground for satire which played on the literal senses of this archaic sounding term (*treu* = loyal, *Hand* = hand). To easterners, the hand appeared as grasping, clutching, choking, and with crooked fingers (*im Würgegriff der Treuhand, die krummen Finger der Treuhand*); since it had perverted the notion of loyalty and trust (*Untreuhand, Veruntreuungshand*), it should be allowed to wither and die (*die Treuhand verdorren lassen*).

Early in 1990 the spontaneous street slogans of the early *Wende* were replaced by the propaganda of campaigning political parties. The established parties of the FRG set the tone at this point. The Conservative 'Alliance for Germany' was particularly assiduous in presenting its Western credentials. The CDU election newspaper, published in Bonn, printed in West Berlin, and distributed free of charge in the GDR, contained photographs of Chancellor Kohl and not a single picture of an East German candidate. Western preoccupations dominated the language of the campaign and reflected 'the collective anxieties of the [West] Germans' (Hermanns 1992). The following slogan of the CDU, for instance, was designed to appeal to general feelings of nationhood, unity, and working for a future:

Ja zu Deutschland
Ja zur Zukunft
Gemeinsam schaffen wir's

And the following slogan could have appeared at any time in the FRG from the 1950s onwards:

CDU
Freiheit
Wohlstand
Sicherheit

Freiheit (freedom) was a leitmotif of anti-Communist rhetoric from the Cold War; during the *Wende* in East Germany it implied that not to vote CDU would allow a return to GDR-type socialism. *Wohlstand* (prosperity) referred to the FRG's economic post-war success. *Sicherheit* (security) had associations with the NATO military umbrella. Such images indicate how Western fears and interests were simply transplanted eastwards.

After unification the language of a new governmental and economic bureaucracy proliferated. New euphemisms appeared in order to disguise unpleasant realities. East Germans could be forgiven a degree of cynicism on learning that they were to be 'let go' (*freisgesetzt* or *freigestellt*) instead of being made redundant (the idiom is a loan translation from English). Widely perceived as a euphemism for shutdown and mass dismissals was the term *Abwicklung*. *Abwicklung* in the Treaty of Unification denoted the transfer of mainly cultural, scientific, and medical institutions of the former GDR to the new Germany, but it could also imply their closure. Hitherto *Abwicklung* had been used as a technical term for a specific legal process, the liquidation or reorganization of a company. In east Germany it rapidly developed negative connotations, in particular the high-handed dismantling of eastern institutions by Germans from the west. The term also extended its reference: not only were cultural institutions objects of *Abwicklung*, it was applied to everything from agriculture to the army, and even to human beings (*Politiker abwickeln, unsere abgewickelten Menschen, abgewickelter Soziologieprofessor*). For east Germans *Abwicklung* was synonymous with the annihilation of everything associated with the old GDR. The leader of the SPD in the east, Wolfgang Thierse, spoke of how their entire history was being wound up (*Abwicklung unserer Geschichte*) or, more accurately, confiscated (he uses the words *Überwältigung* and *In-Besitznahme*)(Preußen 1993).

Abwicklung spawned numerous compounds, such as *Abwicklungsstelle, Abwicklungsbeauftragte, Abwicklungsbeschluß* and *Abwicklungssyndrom*, including the ironic nomen agentis *Abwickler*. It was also the title of a department of the Trust Agency. By August 1991 the term was felt to be such a political liability that a public competition was held to find a positive alternative. The result was *Rekonstruktion*. Unfortunately this word had different meanings in east and west Germany. For westerners it meant destroying and replacing old buildings. In the east it implied renovation or restoration. Neither sense captured the role of the Agency, and the change of name could not alter the economic realities.

14.9 Linguistic uncertainties and problems of identity

The upheaval of the *Wende* produced uncertainties about the meanings of certain words and ignited debates about the most appropriate language to use. The term *Bürgerbewegung* (citizens' movement), for instance, fluctuated in its designation. The founders of the group Democracy Now introduced it in September 1989 to denote popular participation in the revolution. Later *Bürgerbewegung* referred in turn to the following: the name of a particular group; the entire protest movement; those organizations which participated in the Round Table; any organization that saw itself as an alternative to a recognized political party (Wielgohs 1993). The term always excluded the SED and the Block Parties, but it was less clear what oppositional groups it encompassed and whether it included individual protesters who, while not members of an organization, were acting in concert.

While the meaning of *Bürgerbewegung* reflected the imprecisions of a rapidly changing situation, the word *Wiedervereinigug* (reunification) awakened spectres from the German past. For some, reunification implied a restoration of the 1937 boundaries of the Third Reich, which included parts of present-day Poland and Russia. Willy Brandt criticized its use and from mid-1990 it was displaced by the more neutral terms *Vereinigung, Einigung* (unification) and *Beitritt* (accession). For a while a variety of expressions were used (*Neuvereinigung, Herstellung der Einheit Deutschlands, Überwindung der Teilung, Zusammenwachsen*)(Polenz 1993).

Reservations about the one-sided nature of the unification process appeared in images of being sold out, swallowed up, or steam-rollered (*vereinnahmen, einverleiben, überrollen, plattgewalzt, Planierraupe*). Parallels were drawn with the Nazis' seizure of power (*Machtergreifung*) in 1933 and the annexation of Austria in 1938 (*Anschluß*). Unification was depicted as a colonial takeover, with west Germans as the colonizers and easterners as a subjugated people under at best a benevolent protectorate. West German civil servants seconded to the east received additional salary, sarcastically called *Buschgeld* (officially: *Solidaritätsabgabe*). Memories of the Second World War resurfaced in the (eastern) view of the west Germans as occupiers (*Besatzungsmacht*). Even the notion of social class re-appeared, with east Germans as the underclass in a new dual class structure (*Zweiklassensystem*).

As the GDR progressively lost its political identity between 1989 and 1990, the country itself was referred to it in a variety of ways. *Die neue DDR* or even *künftige DDR* (counterpart: *die alte DDR* for the pre-*Wende* period) indicated optimism about the prospect of a reformed but separate GDR. When this prospect faded, the designation *Noch-DDR* predominated. The prefix *noch* was readily transferred to institutions and individuals, as in *Noch-DDR-Bürger, Noch-NVA, Noch-Justiz-Organe der DDR, Noch-Innenminister, Noch-Außenminister,* and even *Noch-Werktätiger der DDR* (= someone about to lose their job). Adjectives of transition and extinction conveyed the terminal condition of the state (*vergehende DDR, dahinsterbende DDR, verblichene DDR*). At the same time constructions with *Staat* and *Republik*, which suggested stable and legitimate political structures, were less frequently applied to East Germany even before it formally ceased to exist.

After unification *Ex-DDR* was most often used to denote the former GDR, with *frühere DDR* and *ehemalige DDR* as close contenders. The desire to avoid reference to the defunct GDR and to highlight its new status within the FRG produced *die (fünf) neuen Bundesländer* ('the five (new) federal states'), abbreviated by officials to *FNL* and caricatured as *FOB* (*Faß ohne Boden*). The old GDR was most commonly referred to as a geographical, not a political entity (thus: *Gebiet, Land/Länder, Neuländer, Territorium*). Overcoming its associations with the Hitler period, the attribute 'east' proved popular, as in *östliche/ostdeutsche Bundesländer, Ostländer, Ostdeutschland,* and *Ostrepublik.* The official expression for the accession of East Germany was *Beitritt* (as in *Beitrittsgebiet, Beitrittsländer,* even *Beitrittsdeutsche* and *Beigetretene*), but the term seldom appeared in the media, and the Unification Treaty mostly refers to the former GDR as a geographical entity, that is, as a 'territory' or an 'area'. Three years after unification it was felt that the eastern *Länder* were no longer 'new': 'young' is now the preferred term (*die jungen Bundesländer*).

During the period of political transition the problem arose as to what to call the former FRG. The official, little-used title was *Bundesrepublik Deutschland*. Most popular even before the *Wende* were compounds with *Bund-* (*Bundesrepublik, Bundesgebiet*). After 1989 forms with *West-* (*der Westen Deutschlands, westdeutsche Republik*) became common (Glück 1991). The abbreviation *BRD* appeared only rarely, reflecting a long-standing official disapproval within the FRG of an acronym which allegedly undersold the notion of 'Germany' and which was perceived as resembling too much the title *DDR* (Berchin 1979). Although there were never as many designations for the western part of Germany as for the east (*Ex-BRD*, for instance, was not used; Fleischer 1992:23), the status of the FRG had clearly changed. The change was expressed in various attributes (*Alt-Länder, bisherige BRD, früheres Bundesgebiet*). After unification the title *Bundesrepublik Deutschland* was felt to be too closely identified with the old FRG to be appropriate to the new Germany. Preferred terms were based on *Deutschland*, either as part of a compound (*Gesamtdeutschland*) or with an adjective emphasising the new status (*neues, größeres, (wieder)vereinigtes, ganzes Deutschland*). *Deutschland* without attributes has since achieved widespread currency.

Nationhood did not bring a sense of national communality to Germans. East Germans had long referred to West Germans colloquially as *Bundis* or *Wessis*, while *Ossi* was not unknown in the West (the terms originated in the youth culture of Berlin). When every German became a citizen of the new FRG, *Bundi* became redundant (the coinages *DIN-Deutschi, Neubundi* and *Gesamti* led a mercifully brief existence), but *Ossi* and *Wessi* came to be widely employed in written and spoken German (*Ossa* appeared in a cartoon as a humorous gesture to feminism; *Süddeutsche*

Zeitung 22–23 August 1992). According to a survey by the Allensbach Institute in March 1991, neither term was considered flattering by either east or west Germans. The suffix *-i* is generally reserved for pet names and nicknames, and although such forms are seldom malicious, *Ossi* was often used with explicit contempt to imply an inhabitant of a remote third-world country: *armer Ossi, doofer Ossi, Jammer-Ossi, der Ossi–diese Lachnummer, Ossis raus, Ossiland, Ossinesien*. *Wessi*, on the other hand, conveyed self-important arrogance and condescension: *Angeber-Wessi, Wessi-Arroganz, Besserwessi, Wessibesserwisserei*. Should the *Wessi* look kindly on his eastern colleague, the *Wessi-Helfer*, he could earn the title *Wossi*, which at least implied a degree of integration into eastern society.

14.10 The future: new terms from the *Wende*

At this stage it is appropriate to ask what new concepts and words coined during the *Wende* are likely to remain in the German language.

An obvious candidate is *Wende*, which means a turning-point or change of direction. *Wende* had been used before 1989 to denote a political sea-change: thus Helmut Kohl's election in 1982 was seen as a 'Conservative *Wende*' (Derbyshire 1991:73). The term has now become a synonym for the fall of the GDR. But its adoption did not go unquestioned. Believing that *Wende* failed to capture the dynamic nature of the changes, Christa Wolf had suggested 'revolutionary renewal' (*revolutionäre Erneuerung*) as an alternative. Stefan Heym spoke of the 'peaceful revolution' (*friedliche Revolution*). Other terms included *Umbruch*, with its emphasis on social upheaval, and *Aufbruch*, which implied a journey towards a new future. The attraction of *Wende* was that it conveyed the peaceful nature of the changes. It also lacked political bombast, and East Germans had had enough of that.

A vogue word, *Wende* appeared in numerous variations after 1990. Notably *Wendehals* (literally: wryneck) denoted opportunist turncoats from the old system, such as Egon Krenz, who sought to maintain their position in the new order (also: *wendehälsig, Wendehälsigkeit*). *Wende* and its derivations (including the verb *sich wenden*) appeared as a general attribute for anything linked to the events of 1989–90 (*Wendekirche, Wendesieger, Wendewunder, Wendewut*). It was coupled with attributes of time (*nachwendlich, Nachwendezeit, Nach-Wende-CDU, Vor-Wende*) and was even applied to countries other than Germany (*die Schweiz braucht eine Wende*).

An institution closely associated with the *Wende* is the Round Table (*Runder Tisch*; see Chapter 3, Section 3.3.2). Although the original Round

Table was disbanded after March 1990, the term was soon applied to any kind of forum for minority groups or for the disadvantaged, such as Jews, asylum-seekers, women, and children (*Jüdischer Runder Tisch, Runder Tisch für Asylbewerber, Runder Tisch der Frauen Dresdens, Runder Tisch für Kinder, Runder Tisch von unten*). Like the citizens' committees (*Bürgerkomitees*), such bodies illustrated a widespread desire to find new methods of dialogue between the state and society at a time of profound change.

Of all the slogans of the early *Wende*, the one which has remained most clearly in the German consciousness is *Wir sind das Volk!*. In 1991 the slogan was taken up in protests against the Gulf War, in South Tyrol, and by ethnic Germans in Russia seeking an independent Republic of the Volga. It also appeared in western Germany in wage disputes and in the campaign to retain Bonn as the capital (*Wir sind das Volk—bald auch in Bonn*). The ingenious slogan, *Wi(e)der Gewalt!*, first seen in Leipzig during the early *Wende*, was later used by protesters condemning racial violence.

In the longer term it is, however, unlikely that the language revolt of the *Wende* will contribute more than a handful of period-bound curiosities. Examples include *Übersiedler* (an immigrant from East Germany), *aufrechter Gang* (the 'upright walk' of a people that has regained its self-respect), *Mauerspecht* (a 'wallpecker' who chipped away at the Berlin Wall) and *Blockflöten* (a pun on the primary sense of 'wind recorder' and the GDR Block Parties who played to the SED's tune). The list is short, but the distinctive popular base for the democratic movement of the *Wende* was rapidly usurped by the powerful political and cultural forces emanating from West Germany. German observers saw the very transience of the language revolt as a symptom of the crisis of identity for east Germans. Pressure to conform to Western linguistic models reflected the one-sided nature of the political takeover (see Polenz 1993:17). In this context it is worth noting that only a handful of East Germanisms had succeeded in entering Western usage before the *Wende*. Examples include *Größenordnung* (for *Menge*), *Exponat, Überzeugungsarbeit, Kulturerbe, Autorenkollektiv, Elternbeirat, Hochschulgruppe, Postzusteller, Straßenbenutzungsgebühr, wertgemindert* and compounds with *Spitzen-*. None of these forms is now felt to be specifically East German.

14.11 German in east and west: a continuing division?

Given the problems which have accompanied the integration of the eastern states into the new Germany, it is useful to consider to what extent the varieties of German in the old FRG and GDR were separate linguistic entities and, if so, whether they will continue to remain different.

Soon after the division of Germany in 1949 German linguists ardently debated the differences between the languages of the two states. Ignoring regional usage, they focused on language in political and formal contexts. During the 1950s and 1960s most Western observers equated East German with the politicized language of the Communist Party, dubbing it 'SED language' or 'Soviet German'. The stance was consciously hostile to the GDR and assumed that the language in the East was being undermined by an alien political system. Although the Germanist Hugo Moser warned against using linguistic analysis for political polemic, he noted that East German was developing distinctive features: as some words fell into disuse others emerged as neologisms and existing meanings were altered. But while he acknowledged that these changes were the products of a different social system and a deliberate policy of ideological control, Moser rejected the notion that East German was becoming a separate language: a shared orthography, morphology, syntax, and phonemic system preserved its essential unity. West Germans were not alone in linking observations about language with political propaganda: East German commentators were also guilty of this, especially after the erection of the Berlin Wall. But despite their own anti-FRG stance, East Germans saw the social changes occurring in the GDR as contributing to a common linguistic heritage, not destroying it. Even when emphasizing the GDR's separate identity, its leaders acknowledged the unity of the language. Erich Honecker declared that the 'communality of language' (*Gemeinsamkeiten in der Sprache*) did not alter the fact that the social structures of the two Germanies were incompatible (*Neues Deutschland* 29 May 1973 and 15 October 1982).

The West German linguist Walther Dieckmann was among the first to query the assumptions underpinning earlier comparisons of East and West German (Dieckmann 1967). Rejecting political motivation as a basis for linguistic investigation, he argued in favour of an objective critique of lexical innovation in the GDR. He pointed out that the GDR had not invented the core vocabulary of Marxism, which had in fact existed in German since the nineteenth century. Dieckmann also questioned the assumption that West German was the norm and that East German had deviated most from a notional pre-war standard language (in word-lists and dictionaries it was always the Eastern, not the Western forms that were marked as deviant). West Germans further overlooked the fact that they were more open to adopting foreign loans, coining neologisms, and employing new varieties of style than the more conservative Easterners (although the East Germans enthusiastically adopted many Anglo-American loans; Oschlies 1989b). While Dieckmann demonstrated the need for a more objective methodology, the lack of proper data and a comparative base for the two language communities posed considerable problems. Contrasting individual word entries in East and West German versions of the Duden, for instance, could never indicate differences in actual usage.

By the late 1970s academic interest in the topic had declined in the FRG. The field was left to a small group of scholars, notably Manfred Hellmann, who applied computerized techniques to compare significant amounts of language data. At the time of unification Hellmann estimated the total number of GDR-specific words in German at over 2,000, mainly in the areas of political and social organization (Hellmann 1990). These terms were either neologisms or forms whose meanings differed from Western usage. Other studies (for example by Frein-Plischke 1987) confirmed that the main variations occurred in particular registers (public and official language) and subject domains (especially politics). Thus the political terms *Fraktion, Initiative, Parlament, Partei* existed in both Germanies but were functionally distinct, since the entities they denoted behaved in very different ways.

Most pre-*Wende* studies relied on published texts and lexika to gain an insight into GDR language. But with the opening up of the country, researchers have been able to do field work, including interviewing east Germans to establish how they used language in communicative situations. An example of such work is provided by Manfred Hellmann, who took 'looking for a flat' as a basis for comparing actual usage (Hellmann 1991). Interviews with twenty GDR citizens indicated that home-hunters had to master very different vocabularies. There were significant differences in the types of flats, their availability, quality and facilities, and, of course, in the systems which people had to navigate in order to acquire a home. While it was normal for East Germans to file a formal application (*Antrag stellen*), often more than once, to obtain any type of accommodation, West Germans would do this only when applying for a council flat (*Sozialwohnung*). Age, number of children, qualifications, membership of the Communist Party, job, and past history all influenced the outcome of the application. Since viewing and comparing homes or negotiating with a landlord did not arise in the GDR, such vocabulary was inappropriate there. East Germans were versed in categories such as *Neubauwohnung, Altbauwohnung, Reko-Wohnung, Neu-Altbauwohnung*, and *Ausbauwohnung*. Where these terms existed in the West, they denoted different things. Thus, while an *Altbauwohnung* to an Easterner meant a dilapidated pre-war hovel where nothing worked, it could suggest to a West German a fashionable, carefully renovated period apartment. Terms such as *Kontingente* (quotas of flats reserved for members of organizations) or *nicht-*

erfaßte Zimmer (flats for which keys were not available) were unknown in the FRG.

Other studies have confirmed the link between language and economic circumstances. Thus while the West German would ask about the price of an article in a shop, the East German tended to enquire whether it was in stock. Having decided to buy something, the Westerner would say 'Can I please have ...' (*Geben Sie mir ...*); the East German, especially if the item was in short supply, would probably ask 'How much can I have?' (*Wieviel geben Sie davon ab?*)(Leciejewski 1991).

The language of advertising also revealed cultural differences between East and West. Promotional advertising in the GDR was by Western standards unsophisticated. The difference was shown in the East German preference for the term *Reklame* as opposed to the West German *Werbung* (whose associations with the business world emerge in the compounds *Werbeagentur, Werbefachmann, Werbekampange*). A comparison by Ekkehard Schmider (1990) of 200 pre-unification advertising slogans from East and West Germany reveals interesting differences in preferences for key terms. In the West the predominating concepts were taste, enjoyment, life, fun, beauty, and health. Those for the GDR stressed reliability (for the home market) and quality, performance, tradition, and innovation (for export goods). Typically, a limited number of key terms were used more frequently, and also interchangeably, for different products. Such terms became devalued, for they could not identify specific qualities with individual products. Adjectives and prepositional constructions occurred twice as often as in the West, reinforcing the monotony of tone (for example: *Leuchten aus Zeulenrode, Citrusfrüchte aus Kuba, Ein Program für vorteilhaften Handel*). Schmider concludes that advertising in the GDR did not produce a full-scale culture of language but displayed similar artificiality and restrictions to the rhetoric of the SED.

It is clear from the above evidence that differences between East and West German were not restricted to names of objects or institutions: they also involved styles of communication, inter-personal negotiation, and even promotional advertising. But although such differences resulted from divergent social and economic systems, it must be recognized that they occur in principle in language communities throughout the world. By themselves they are not enough to support the notion of two distinct 'German' language varieties to the extent that British and American English have diverged over a much longer period. The German language continued to be the 'unifying band' across the political division (Oschlies 1989a).

14.12 Conclusion

Contemporary observers of the *Wende* who stressed the unity of the German language were in tune with the optimism of the time (Drosdowski 1991; Oschlies 1989b, 1990b). They felt that most differences between East and West German would not outlive the political context in which they had been created. Of course, some differences would continue as regionalisms in the new federal states, marking their users as easterners. Examples of regionalisms include: *Broiler* (for West German *Huhn*), *Plaste* (West: *Plastik*), *Zielstellung* (West: *Zielsetzung*), *Havarie* (a Russian word denoting a minor technical hitch), *Territorium* (West: *Gebiet/Gegend* or *Stadtteil*), *Getränkestützpunkt* (West: *Getränkemarkt* or *Getränkeservice*), *Anlieferungszone* (West: *Ladezone*), *einfrosten* (West: *tieffrieren*), and *Grobmüll* (West: *Sperrmüll*). To this category belong a number of verb constructions: *auf etwas orientieren* (where West Germans would use *über*), *einschätzen, daß* (West: *schätzen, daß*), and *informieren* (in the sense of announce or *bekanntgeben*). Some regional forms would become archaic and disappear (*Datsche, Brigade*).

In a survey of East German newspapers and radio broadcasts between March and June 1990, Manfred Hellmann (1990) registered many eastern forms that were still in active use. These included names of institutions, economic terms, and job titles, whose chances of survival were already slim in view of impending unification. Hellmann envisaged better prospects for everyday words that could be used in a variety of contexts. Alongside some already mentioned (*Datsche, Territorium*), these included *Organ* (for an official body or authority), *Objekt* (any kind of building, but especially a shop or restaurant), *Kader* (trained specialists, not necessarily with political functions), *Perspektive* (in the sense of chances or prospects), *Selbstlauf* (an unwanted development), *Feierabendheim* (West: *Altenheim*), *andenken* (to plan or consider) and *gesellschaftlich* (in the Western sense of non-private or public). As part of a reassertion of identity after 1990—the 'We are still here' movement (*'Es gibt uns noch' Bewegung*)— some east German producers resurrected the pre-unification brand names for their goods; examples include the soft drinks *Club-Cola* and *Spreequelle*.

Many commentators suspected that such linguistic differences would mirror a continuing east–west split. It was even suggested that east Germans might carry on using words such as *Brigade* or *Kollektiv* as gestures of defiance (Roche 1991). They might also assert their group identity by code-switching to exclude west Germans. Such predictions of linguistic alienation between east and west Germans may be exaggerated but they confirm the metaphor of the mental wall discussed earlier. If east Germans

revert to pre-*Wende* language in defiance, then the SED's linguistic indoc-
trination will prove to have been more successful than originally thought.
After all, most spheres of activity were politicized in the GDR and the effect on everyday communication was always difficult to gauge. Although
some east Germans explicitly denied such influence (Schlosser 1991:7–
17), the reaction to it was very real. Non-political words, for instance,
were avoided in private situations because official overuse had devalued
them. Examples include *freiwillig, herzlich, freundlich* and *Freundschaft*
('socialist friendship' was widely propagated in the mass organizations;
Frein-Plischke 1991).

Many business terms from the West had negative associations in the
former GDR, where socialism had allegedly overcome the evils of ex-
ploitative capitalism. In the following examples the 'positive' socialist alternative is given in brackets: *Profit (Gewinn), Konkurrenz (Wettbewerb),
Manager (Leiter), Teamwork (Arbeitsgemeinschaft), Geschäftsführung
(Betriebsleitung)*. With the introduction of a free market economy the
Western terms have been rehabilitated. But the economic ruin which
overtook the new federal states after 1990 has prompted some easterners
to see the vocabulary of socialism as more appropriate to their personal
experiences of the 'wolf's law of capitalism' *(Wolfsgesetz des Kapitalis-
mus)*(Good 1993:256–58).

However, east Germans are unlikely to revert in significant measure to
the language of the SED, if only because the system of linguistic control
and censorship that sustained its use no longer exists. The lingering associations of such language have even prevented some groups from participating in the democratic renewal. Young people are refusing to join a
political party because *Partei* is still equated with the SED's slogan 'The
party is always right' *(die Partei hat immer recht)*. Similar inhibitions are
hindering efforts to revitalize the trade unions and to establish a context in
which the language of socialist activism (which predates the GDR) can
again be used freely. Many terms that originated in the pre-GDR tradition
of social democracy are discredited because they were monopolized by the
SED (examples: *Solidarität, Funktionär, Aufklärung, Bewußtsein, Einheit,
Massenorganisation, soziale Sicherheit*; Good 1993:256). On the other
hand, words that can be detached from political usage, such as *herzlich*
and *freundlich*, will doubtless soon lose their negative associations.

Whatever the long-term consequences of political unification for the
German language, east Germans have had to cast off much of their former
linguistic identity. The lexicographer Marianne Schröder (1992) provides
an interesting example of this. After the *Wende* she was given the task of
revising a dictionary produced originally for GDR students but now intended for the post-unification market. In line with job titles and names for

GDR institutions which disappeared with unification, educational terms such as *EOS* (*Erweiterte Oberschule*), *Horterzieherin*, and *Pionierhelfer* had become obsolete and were removed from the dictionary. *Firma* and *Unternehmen*, on the other hand, were added as titles of market-orientated economic institutions. Sometimes a basic concept was retained but its semantic components were altered or redefined. Thus East German *Muttersprachenunterricht* became *Deutschunterricht*, while *Literaturunterricht* became *Literaturkunde*. Adjectives describing personal characteristics of school pupils, previously restricted to academic excellence and personal enthusiasm, now included more realistic attributes: *schwatzhaft*, *lernbehindert*, *konzentrationsschwach*, *lese- und rechtschreibschwach*, *verhaltensgestört*. Most changes of all were required in the fields of commerce and banking, work, the social system, and education. Vocabulary associated with family and religion was least affected. A small number of archaisms from the pre-GDR period, such as *Hauptschüler* and *Gymnasium*, were restored. Overall the study shows that large areas of GDR vocabulary became redundant overnight as western usage displaced eastern terms in most areas of public, commercial, and social life.

While processes of lexical change can be found in any language, they normally occur gradually over a period of time. But for east Germans the changes have been abrupt and are continuing on a massive scale. All the signs are that the process is one-way and that a more dominant, high prestige culture is engulfing a smaller and less confident one. While the fundamental unity of the language is not in question, it is almost inevitable that west German usage will become the standard and that eastern forms will be relegated to the status of regionalisms.

Further reading

For analyses of how comparisons of East and West German reflected the political climate before the *Wende* see Frein-Plischke (1991) and Domaschnew (1991). Oschlies (1989a, 1989b) and Schlosser (1990) review usage in the GDR before 1989; Fleischer (1987) provides an East German perspective on this topic. For an overview of linguistic developments during the *Wende* see Polenz (1993); Hellmann (1990) gives a snapshot of East German forms observed in the media during 1990. Much of the material presented in this chapter is documented in the journal *Der Sprachdienst*, published by the *Gesellschaft für deutsche Sprache* in Wiesbaden (see contributions by M. Kinne, G. Müller, and E. Eppler). The GfdS also publishes the periodical *Muttersprache*, a useful source of articles on the German language.

Chronology of Events
January 1989 – December 1994

1989

15 January: East Germans demonstrate in Leipzig for free speech, a free press, and the right to associate. Eighty are arrested.

6 February: Twenty-year-old Chris Gueffroy is killed by East German border guards as he attempts to flee to West Berlin.

7 May: Local elections are held in the GDR. Opposition groups contest the official figures of a 98·5% victory for the SED and its puppet parties. On the 7 June in Berlin 120 are arrested for trying to register evidence of electoral fraud.

8 August: The FRG closes its Permanent Representation in East Berlin where 130 East Germans attempting to leave the GDR have sought refuge.

13 August: Crowded with 180 East Germans wanting to escape to the West, the FRG's embassy in Budapest is temporarily closed. On 24 August 108 are allowed to leave for the West.

2 September: Over 3,500 East Germans wait in Hungary to emigrate to the West.

10–11 September: Hungary opens its borders to the West. By the end of the month over 25,000 East Germans have fled via Hungary to the FRG.

11 September: Eleven are imprisoned and 104 fined after demonstrating in Leipzig.

12 September: The opposition group Democracy Now is founded in the GDR.

19 September: The opposition group New Forum seeks official recognition but is condemned as 'hostile to the state'.

30 September: 5,500 East German citizens in Prague and 800 in Moscow are given permission to go to the West.

2 October: 20,000 demonstrate in Leipzig for reforms.

4–5 October: The GDR provides special trains to transport East Germans from Prague and Warsaw to the West.

5 October: Security forces violently break up mass demonstrations in Magdeburg and Dresden.

6–7 October: At official celebrations marking the fortieth anniversary of the GDR, the Soviet leader Mikhail Gorbachev urges the SED to adopt reform.

9 October: 70,000 demonstrate in Leipzig; this time the authorities do not intervene.

10 October: 500 detained demonstrators are released.

18 October: Erich Honecker resigns as head of the SED and is replaced by Egon Krenz.

23 October: Demonstrations for free elections take place throughout the GDR.

3–4 November: The GDR allows East Germans in Czechoslovakia to go to West Germany; 40,000 have left by 9 November.

4 November: One million East Germans demonstrate in East Berlin, the largest gathering in GDR history.

6 November: Several hundred thousand East Germans demonstrate in Leipzig for freedom to travel and free elections.

7 November: The GDR government resigns.

8 November: Egon Krenz becomes leader of a reconstituted Politburo. New Forum is legalized.

9 November: The Berlin Wall is opened.

10 November: The SED announces a programme to provide free and secret elections.

13 November: The reform Communist Hans Modrow is elected Prime Minister.

18 November: 50,000 attend the first officially approved rally of New Forum in Leipzig.

27 November: Demonstrators in Leipzig demand reunification.

28 November: Chancellor Helmut Kohl announces a ten-point plan for reunification.

1 December: The People's Chamber strikes the SED's claim to political leadership from the Constitution.

3 December: The Politburo and Central Committee of the SED resign. The Party expels Erich Honecker.

7 December: The Round Table meets in East Berlin. It decides to draw up a new Constitution, sets a date for national elections (6 May 1990), and demands the disbanding of the *Stasi.*

8 December: The SED elects Georg Gysi as leader; a week later it re-names itself SED-PDS (PDS = Party of Democratic Socialism); the SED in the title is dropped on 4 February

1990.

19–20 December: Kohl and Modrow agree to start negotiations on an inter-German partnership.

31 December: 343,854 East Germans emigrate to the FRG in 1989 (40,000 in 1988).

1990

15 January: Crowds storm the headquarters of the *Stasi* in East Berlin.

21 January: The SED-PDS expels Egon Krenz.

29 January: To restore confidence in the GDR's interim government the Round Table advances national elections to 18 March. A warrant is issued for the arrest of Erich Honecker.

30 January: Gorbachev announces that he has no objections to German reunification.

31 January: 58,043 East Germans emigrate to the FRG in January.

1 February: Modrow announces his plan for reunification. On 3 February Kohl announces economic aid for the GDR.

4 February: The FDP is founded in the GDR.

5 February: The Conservative Alliance for Germany is formed.

7 February: The opposition groups New Forum, Initiative for Peace and Human Rights, and Democracy Now combine to form Alliance 90.

12 February: Liberal Parties in the GDR form the Alliance of Free Democrats.

13 February: Modrow and Kohl set up a commission to prepare to merge the economies of the GDR and FRG.

21 February: The People's Chamber formally commits itself to unification.

18 March: The first free national

elections to the People's Chamber see a landslide victory for the Conservative Alliance.

12 April: Lothar de Mazière (GDR-CDU) becomes leader of a coalition government of the GDR's major parties. The government's main objective is rapid reunification.

24 April: 1 July 1990 is set as the date for economic, monetary, and social union.

28 April: An extraordinary summit of the EC approves German unification.

5 May: Foreign ministers of the FRG and the GDR (the two) and the USA, USSR, UK, France (the four) begin the Two+Four Talks in Bonn.

16 May: The German Unity Fund is established to support the GDR. The Fund is to provide 115 billion DM for the period 1990–94.

1 July: The West German Mark is introduced in the GDR.

6 July: Negotiations begin in East Berlin on the Treaty of Unification.

14–16 July: Gorbachev agrees to a united Germany's membership of NATO.

22 July: The People's Chamber passes a law creating federal states (*Länder*) after the West German model. *Land* elections are set for 14 October 1990.

11 August: The East and West German Liberal Parties (FDP) merge.

23 August: The People's Chamber agrees to accede to the FRG according to Article 23 of the Basic Law, which it will adopt from 3 October 1990.

31 August: The FRG and GDR sign the Treaty of Unification. The Treaty is ratified by the People's Chamber on 20 September and by the West German Parliament a day later.

12 September: The Two+Four Treaty is signed in Moscow. It restores to the united Germany full sovereignty over its internal and external affairs, ending all post-war allied rights in Germany.

20 September: 20% of the East German workforce are on short time.

27 September: The East and West German SPD parties merge.

1 October: The East and West German CDU parties merge.

3 October: Germany is united.

14 November: The first all-German draft budget is presented to the *Bundestag*. It envisages transfers of 35,000 million DM to the eastern *Länder*.

2 December: The national election to the enlarged *Bundestag* (644 seats) results in victory for the CDU-FDP coalition.

1991

2 January: East German students protest at the closure of university departments and institutes.

17 January: Chancellor Kohl is re-elected Chancellor of an CDU-FDP coalition. The main issue for the government is how to finance unification.

24 January: Postal workers in the east strike for three days, protesting at increased living costs.

29 January: The trial of the former GDR trade union leader and Politburo member Harry Tisch opens in Berlin. The first East German leader to face trial, Tisch is accused of breach of trust and misappropriation of funds. Sentenced on 9 June to eighteen months imprisonment, he is released after one year.

12 February: The government admits it has underestimated the problems of unification and announces the Upswing East programme. Some 24,000 billion DM will be injected into the eastern economy over two years. By the end of February unemployment in the east is 8·9% (7% in the west).

12 March: The government proposes tax increases to finance unification.

19 March: The cabinet drops plans for an amnesty for former *Stasi* agents.

25 March: Over 60,000 protest in Leipzig over unemployment and economic decline. There are calls for the resignation of Chancellor Kohl.

1 April: Terrorists murder Detlev Rohwedder, head of the Trust Agency. The Agency faces increasing protests against the closure of east German concerns.

7 April: In Erfurt, where he was fêted in February 1990, Chancellor Kohl is jeered and pelted with eggs.

9 April: The government announces tax concessions for civil servants moving to the east; pensions in the east will rise to half of western levels.

14 May: Wolfgang Berghofer, former Mayor of Dresden, is charged with electoral fraud in the May 1989 elections in the GDR. On 7 February 1992 he receives a one-year prison sentence.

19–21 May: Visiting the USA, Chancellor Kohl comes under pressure to increase Germany's military involvement outside the NATO area.

20 May: The former East German leaders Willi Stoph (Chairman of the Council of Ministers), Heinz Keßler (Defence Minister), Fritz Streletz (Deputy Defence Minister), and Hans Albrecht (regional SED party leader) are charged with incitement to manslaughter over the shoot-to-kill policy at the East–West border. Two days later Erich Mielke, former head of the *Stasi*, is charged with incitement to murder.

28–31 May: The SPD approves German military participation in UN peace-keeping missions.

31 May: Neo-Nazi leader Rainer Sonntag is shot dead in Dresden, now a centre of extreme right-wing activity. 2,000 neo-Nazis hold rallies in Dresden on 15 and 22 June; these are accompanied by anti-Semitic acts and attacks on foreigners.

20 June: The *Bundestag* votes to move the seat of government to Berlin.

10 July: The cabinet approves a draft budget for 1992 to increase spending by 3% and raise subsidies to eastern Germany while cutting those for the west. Unemployment in the east is 9·5%, with almost two million on short time and production down by two-thirds since early 1990. Over 20,000 are emigrating westwards every month.

9 September: Following allegations that he spied for the *Stasi*, Lothar de Mazière resigns from all offices. The CDU's popularity in the east plummets.

24 September: Markus Wolf, the East German spymaster, is arrested and later charged with with treason, espionage, and corruption. His trial begins on 4 May. On 6 December he is sentenced to six years imprisonment. The sentence is overturned on 23 May 1995.

29 September: In elections in Bremen the neo-Nazi DVU, campaigning against foreigners and asylum-seekers, gains seats. Violent attacks on foreigners in Saxony and west Germany reach a peak. The government seeks to limit the influx of asylum-seekers but cannot get all-party support to change Article 16 of the Basic Law, which guarantees an unrestricted right of asylum.

14 November: The *Bundestag* passes legislation regulating public access to the *Stasi* archives.

1992

20 January: Former GDR border guards Ingo Heinrich and Andreas Kühnpast are found guilty of the manslaughter of Chris Gueffroy.

13 February: The state of Brandenburg sets up a commission of enquiry to examine links between its Minister President, Manfred Stolpe, and the *Stasi.*

12 March: The *Bundestag* sets up a commission to investigate the history and consequences of the SED-dictatorship.

5 April: The right-wing Republicans and DVU win seats in *Land* elections in Baden-Württemberg and Schleswig-Holstein.

27 April: Public sector unions in west Germany strike for a 9·5% pay increase. The strike spreads to engineering workers and ends on 7 May when unions accept a 5·4% pay rise. Similar agreements follow in other industries.

24 May: The Republicans win 8·3% of votes in the Berlin communal elections.

3 June: Eastern CDU members of the *Bundestag* form a parliamentary group to represent the interests of eastern Germany.

26 June: The *Bundestag* agrees a uniform abortion law for east and west Germany. CDU MPs bring an injunction before the Federal Constitutional Court to halt its im-plementation.

1 July: A draft budget for 1993 provides for increased transfers to the east.

12 July: A number of east German politicians and intellectuals, led by Gregor Gysi (PDS) and Wolfgang Diestel (CDU), call for the founding of Committees for Justice (*Bürgerrechtskomitees*). Their aim is to combat social and economic injustices in the east that have resulted from unification.

29 July: Erich Honecker is brought back from Moscow to face charges of manslaughter and misappropriation of state funds.

22 August: Neo-Nazis begin a five-day attack on a reception centre for asylum-seekers in Rostock. Bystanders sympathize with the attackers and local authorities are criticized for inaction. Demonstrations against racist violence are held in Rostock and other cities. Right-wing attacks continue in east and west Germany.

8 September: Chancellor Kohl announces that annual transfers of 150,000 million DM to east Germany are needed for the foreseeable future; tax increases are unavoidable. Kohl appeals for a Solidarity Pact between political parties, employers, and trade unions to find ways of financing unification.

12 November: The trial begins of former GDR leaders Erich Honecker, Heinz Keßler, Fritz Streletz, and Hans Albrecht. Willi Stoph and Erich Mielke are too ill to stand trial.

16–17 November: At a special congress the SPD agrees to amendments to Article 16 of the Basic Law which will restrict the numbers of asylum-seekers.

22 November: A Turkish woman and two girls die in an arson attack in Mölln, near Hamburg. Seventeen have died in 1,760 racist attacks so far in 1992.

27 November: The government bans the neo-Nazi Nationalist Front.

2 December: The *Bundestag* ratifies the Maastricht Treaty on European Union. Full ratification is delayed until 12 October 1993 when the Federal Constitutional Court rules that the Treaty does not violate national sovereignty. The Treaty comes into force on 1 November 1993.

31 December: Unemployment for 1992 in west Germany is 6·6% (2,030,000); in east Germany it stands at 13·5% (1,100,000). The number of asylum-seekers totals 438,000 (256,112 in 1991).

1993

12 January: The charges against Erich Honecker are dropped. He leaves for Chile where he dies on 29 May 1994.

13 January: The Federal Government agrees on amendments to the Basic Law which allow German troops to join international peace-keeping operations outside the NATO area.

19 January: The government unveils its Solidarity Pact and plans tax increases. The SPD rejects the Pact for its cuts in social welfare.

30 January: Lothar Bisky replaces Gregor Gysi as president of the PDS.

7 March: In communal elections in Hesse the Republicans gain 8·3% of the vote (9·5% in Frankfurt). Support for the SPD and CDU falls.

13 March: The government, the opposition, and the *Länder* agree on

the Solidarity Pact. This includes a 7·5% surcharge on income tax from 1 January 1995, with no cuts in welfare benefits. Transfers to the east for 1995 are set at 110,000 million DM.

20 April: Hans Modrow, former SED chairman in Dresden, is placed on trial for rigging the May 1989 local elections in the GDR. He is found guilty on 27 May and cautioned.

3 May: Metal workers in the east strike for wage parity with the west by 1994. The strike ends after three weeks when employers agree to raise wages to western levels by 1996.

16 May: Twenty-two German troops arrive in Somalia as part of a UN peace-keeping force. This is the first time that armed Federal German soldiers have participated in operations outside the NATO area.

25 May: *Bundestag* MP Rudolf Krause defects from the CDU to the Republicans, who thus gain their first seat in the national Parliament.

26 May: The *Bundestag* approves restrictions to the right of asylum, which come into force on 1 July.

28 May: The Federal Constitutional Court rules against the uniform abortion law. Counselling should encourage the mother to continue the pregnancy, with no right to state funds for abortion.

29 May: Five Turkish women and girls die in an arson attack in Solingen.

16 June: Chancellor Kohl announces measures to control right-wing extremists and reform nationality laws. Attacks on foreigners continue. Neo-Nazi groups are banned in Baden-Württemberg and Bavaria.

25 June: The SPD elects Rudolf Scharping as Party Chairman.

11 August: The government proposes large cuts in welfare spending from 1994.

16 September: Former GDR leaders Heinz Keßler, Fritz Streletz, and Hans Albrecht are sentenced to up to seven years imprisonment for the shoot-to-kill policy at the border with the FRG.

19 September: In communal elections in Hamburg neo-Nazi parties increase their share of the vote at the expense of the main parties.

26 October: Stasi chief Erich Mielke is sentenced to six-years imprisonment for the murder of two policemen in 1931.

5 December: The CDU loses heavily to left-wing parties in communal elections in Brandenburg. 22% vote for the PDS, indicating easterners' disillusionment with unification.

8 December: Two neo-Nazis receive maximum sentences for the murder of three Turks in Mölln a year earlier.

1994

11 January: Figures confirm that the west German economy suffered its worst decline in 1993 since the Second World War. The economy in the east shows signs of recovery after the post-unification collapse.

4 March: Engineering workers in Lower Saxony vote to strike in protest at a zero pay offer and cuts in holiday pay.

21 March: In communal elections in Schleswig-Holstein the Green Party wins seats at the expense of the SPD.

4 April: Thousands of Germans take part in Easter marches deploring racism and anti-Semitism.

15 May: Controversy grows over official inaction after sixty neo-Nazis violently attack foreigners in Magdeburg on Ascension Day.

23 May: Roman Herzog, Bavarian right-winger and President of the Federal Constitutional Court, is elected German President to succeed Richard von Weizsäcker. His election is seen as boosting support for Chancellor Kohl.

12 June: The CDU gains a clear victory over the SPD in the European Elections.

25 June: CDU and SPD gain almost equal numbers of seats in *Land* elections in Saxony-Anhalt. On 15 July the SPD and Alliance 90/Greens form a minority 'red-green' administration which the CDU attacks as dependent on PDS support.

11 July: On an official visit to Germany US President Bill Clinton acknowledges Germany as America's leading ally in Europe.

12 July: The Federal Constitutional Court rules that, subject to parliamentary approval, German troops may be used outside the NATO area.

17 August: Since the introduction of the new asylum law in July 1993, the number of asylum-seekers admitted into Germany has fallen from 50,000 a month to under 10,000; numbers of illegal immigrants fall by 50%.

21 August: The crime rate falls for the first time in five years. This is attributed to a drop in crimes committed by foreigners.

31 August: The PDS surrenders its claim to the assets of the former SED, estimated at 2 billion DM.

1 September: The last Russian troops leave Germany.

12 September: In *Land* elections the SPD and CDU gain overall majorities in Brandenburg and Saxony.

The FDP and Alliance 90/Greens fail to clear the 5% hurdle.

15 September: Chancellor Kohl announces that the Trust Agency is making 500 million DM available in 1994 for privatized concerns in the east; he declares that unemployment has passed its peak.

23 September: Bundestag and *Bundesrat* agree a comprehensive reform of the Basic Law, committing the state to environmental protection, rights for the disabled, and greater equality for women; in return for their approval the *Länder* gain more powers.

24 September: In state elections in Bavaria the CSU is returned to continue its 3-year rule; the FDP and Republicans fail to clear the 5% hurdle.

5 October: Unemployment in September falls to under 3·5 million. It stands at 7·9% in the west and 13·8% in the east.

11 October: IG-Metall demands wage increases of up to 6%, rejecting attempts by employers to defer implementation of the agreed 35-hour week.

16 October: In national elections the government coalition (CDU/CSU and a much weakened FDP) is returned with a reduced majority of ten seats over the SPD and Alliance 90/Greens. The PDS wins 30 of the 672 seats.

16 November: Chancellor Kohl forms a CDU-FDP cabinet pledged to reform taxation and reduce government spending.

17 November: The Council of Economic Experts predicts slow economic growth for 1995 (2·5% in the west, 9% in the east) and stresses the need to reduce state spending and unemployment.

25 November: Despite opposition from the *Bundesrat* the German government is ready to deport thousands of asylum-seekers, mainly to Turkey and former Yugoslavia.

31 December: The Trust Agency is wound up and its functions transferred to other government agencies. From January 1995 Germany begins a two-year term on the United Nations Security Council, where it hopes to gain permanent representation.

Glossary of Terms and Abbreviations

The following glossary covers most of the institutional terms and abbreviations used in this book. Terms not covered here are explained in the chapters in which they occur.

Abitur: German school-leaving certificate qualifying for university entrance

Administrative Council (*Verwaltungsrat*): body responsible for the daily management of a regional broadcasting service in the FRG

ADN (*Allgemeine Deutsche Nachrichtenagentur*): the official news agency of the former GDR

Alliance 90 (*Bündnis 90*): alliance of civil rights organizations formed to contest the GDR national elections of 18 March 1990

Alliance for Germany (*Allianz für Deutschland*): alliance of Conservative parties in the GDR national elections of 18 March 1990

Alliance of Free Democrats (*Bund Freier Demokraten*): alliance of Liberal parties in the GDR national elections of 18 March 1990

Allianz für Deutschland: →Alliance for Germany

ARD (*Arbeitsgemeinschaft der öffentlich-rechtlichen Rundfunkanstalten Deutschlands*): main national television network of the FRG

Assembly of Constituent States (*Bundesrat*): assembly of the sixteen →federal states of the FRG

Aufbau: literally 'construction', a term widely used after 1952 in the GDR to refer to the establishment of a socialist society after the war

Aufschwung Ost: → Upswing East

Basic Law (*Grundgesetz*): the constitutional framework for the FRG; adopted in 1949, the Basic Law was amended in 1990 to include the territory of the former GDR

Betriebsrat: →Works Council

Betriebsverfassungsgesetz: →Works Constitution Act

Bezirk: an administrative region in the former GDR

Broadcasting Council (*Rundfunkrat*): body responsible for the running of a regional broadcasting authority in the FRG

Bund: →Federal Parliament

Bund Freier Demokraten: →Alliance of Free Democrats

Bundesbank: →Federal German Bank

Bundesrat: →Assembly of Constituent States

Bundesregierung: →Federal Government

Bundesrepublik Deutschland: →Federal Republic of Germany

Bundestag: →Federal Parliament

Bundesverfassungsgericht: →Federal Constitutional Court

Bundeswehr: Federal German Army

Bündnis 90: →Alliance 90

cadre (*Kader*): a group of politically reliable and highly trained personnel who were also members of the →SED; senior party officials were usually recruited from cadres

CDU/CSU (*Christlich Demokratische Union/Christlich Soziale Union*): Christian Democratic Union/Christian Social Union, an alliance of the two main Conservative parties in the FRG; the CSU campaigns exclusively in Bavaria

CDU: →CDU/CSU

Central Committee (*Zentralkomitee*): the main administrative organ of the SED in the GDR

Co-determination (*Mitbestimmung*): a system of worker participation in management in the FRG

COMECON: Council for Mutual Economic Assistance, an economic alliance of satellite states of the USSR, set up initially to counter →Marshall Aid

Concerted Action (*Konzertierte Aktion*): series of annual meetings initiated in 1967 to prepare guidelines for economic policy in the FRG

Council of Economic Experts (*Sachverständigenrat*): panel of experts set up in 1963 to advise the FRG government on economic policy

Council of Ministers (*Ministerrat*): cabinet of government ministers in the GDR

Council of State (*Staatsrat*): organ set up by the →SED in 1960 to increase its control of the GDR government

CSU: →CDU/CSU

DBD (*Demokratische Bauernpartei Deutschlands*): Democratic Landworkers' Party of Germany, founded in 1948 to organize agricultural workers in the GDR

DEFA (*Deutsche Film AG*): film studios founded in 1946 in the Soviet zone; from 1952 DEFA was the centre of film production in the GDR

Democracy Now (*Demokratie Jetzt*): opposition group founded in the GDR in September 1989

Democratic Awakening (*Demokratischer Aufbruch*): opposition group founded in the GDR in October 1989

Demokratie Jetzt: →Democracy Now

Demokratischer Aufbruch:→Democratic Awakening

Deutsche Demokratische Republik: →German Democratic Republic

DFD (*Demokratischer Frauenbund Deutschlands*): Democratic Women's Federation of Germany, a mass organization for women in the GDR

DVU (*Deutsche Volksunion*): German People's Union, an extreme right-wing party in the FRG

East Germany: →GDR

east(ern) Germany: the five new →federal states, comprising the territory of the former GDR

EC: →European Economic Community

EEC: →European Economic Community

EMS: →European Monetary System

EMU: →European Monetary Union

EOS (*Erweiterte Oberschule*): →Extended Upper School

EU: →European Union

European Community: →European Economic Community

European Economic Community (EEC): an economic association of Western European states established by the Treaty of Rome in 1957; the deepening of links led to the formation of the European Community (EC) in 1967 and to the →European Union (EU) in 1993

European Monetary System (EMS): a system established in 1979 to link and stabilize European currencies

European Monetary Union (EMU): a common European currency, a key objective of the →European Union

European Union (EU): union of the twelve member states of the →European Community established in 1993 by the Treaty of Maastricht; the EU's objectives include monetary union and a common security and foreign policy; the EU comprised fifteen members on 1 January 1995

Extended Upper School (EOS): sixth-form school in the former GDR

FDGB (*Freie Deutsche Gewerkschaftsbund*): Free German Trade Union Federation, the officially approved trade union organization of the GDR

FDJ (*Freie Deutsche Jugend*): Free German Youth, the national youth movement of the GDR

FDP (*Freie Demokratische Partei Deutschlands*): Free Democratic Party of Germany, orientated towards the middle classes and small business interests in the FRG

Federal Constitutional Court (*Bundesverfassungsgericht*): the supreme court of the FRG, established in 1951 to enforce and interpret the Basic Law

Federal German Bank: FRG Central Bank responsible for regulating the national money supply and largely independent of government and Parliament

Federal Government (*Bundesregierung*): national government of the FRG

Federal Parliament (*Bundestag*): national assembly of the FRG

Federal Republic of Germany (FRG): the FRG was formed in 1949 from the post-war Western occupation zone, incorporated into the →European Economic Community in 1957, and merged with the former →German Democratic Republic in 1990

Federal state (*Land*; plural: *Länder*): one of the sixteen regions comprising the FRG; the relationship between the states and the →Federal Parliament is laid down in the →Basic Law

Federation of Culture of the GDR (*Kulturbund der DDR*): umbrella organization for cultural and artistic activities in the GDR

Federation of Metal and Electrical Industry Employers' Associations (*Gesamtmetall*): association of employers in the engineering and electrical industries of the FRG

Fonds 'Deutsche Einheit': →German Unity Fund

Framework Law for Higher Education (*Hochschulrahmengesetz*): law regulating higher education in the FRG from 1976

FRG: →Federal Republic of Germany

GATT: →General Agreement on Tariffs and Trade

Gauck Office: body set up after unification to regulate access to the *Stasi*-files and headed by Joachim Gauck, co-founder of →New Forum

GDR: →German Democratic Republic

General Agreement on Tariffs and Trade (GATT): international treaty in operation since 1948 for the promotion of global trade and economic development; a new GATT agreement involving 117 nations was concluded in December 1993

German Democratic Republic (GDR): the GDR was formed in 1949 from the post-war Soviet occupation zone and governed by the →SED until merged with the →Federal Republic of Germany in 1990

German Unity Fund (*Fonds 'Deutsche Einheit'*): fund established by the →Treaty of Unification to meet the costs of merging the FRG and the GDR

Gesamtmetall: →Federation of Metal and Electrical Industry Employers' Associations

Grundgesetz: →Basic Law

Gruppe 47: group of poets and authors who met in western Germany in 1947 to re-establish German creative writing after the Second World War

Historikerstreit: 'historians' quarrel', a controversy generated by the conservative German historians Ernst Nolte and Andreas Hillgruber who claimed in 1986–87 that the genocide committed by the Nazis was inspired by Soviet atrocities and therefore not uniquely evil

HO (*Handelsorganisation*): state-owned food distribution organization in the GDR

Hochschulrahmengesetz: →Framework Law for Higher Education

IG-Metall: →Metal Workers' Trade Union

IM (*informeller Mitarbeiter*): literally 'informal collaborator', a term for citizens who were engaged by the *Stasi* to spy on their friends, colleagues, and relatives

Initiative for Peace and Human Rights (*Initiative Frieden und Menschenrechte*): founded in 1985, the oldest independent opposition group in the GDR

Initiative Frieden und Menschenrechte:→Initiative for Peace and Human Rights

Kader: →cadre

KB: Federation of Culture of the GDR

KMK (*Kultusministerkonferenz*): →Standing Conference of State Ministers of Education

Konzertierte Aktion: →Concerted Action

Kulturbund der DDR: →Federation of Culture of the GDR

Kultusministerkonferenz: →Standing Conference of State Ministers of Education

Land (plural: *Länder*): →federal state

Landesmedienanstalt: →State Media Authority

LDPD (*Liberal-Demokratische Partei Deutschlands*): Liberal-Democratic Party of Germany, formed in 1945 to appeal to middle class elements in the GDR

Literaturstreit: 'literary quarrel', an often acrimonious debate among writers and critics about the degree to which GDR authors had supported the Communist state

Maastricht, Treaty of: →European Union

Marshall Aid: programme initiated by the USA in 1947 to provide post-war economic aid for Western European

Mediation Committee (*Vermittlungsausschuß*): committee comprising members of the *Bundestag* and *Bundesrat* which agrees on legislation that will be mutually acceptable to both chambers

Metal Workers' Trade Union (*IG-Metall*): engineering workers' union in the FRG

Ministerrat: →Council of Ministers

Mitbestimmung: →co-determination

Nationalist Front: neo-Nazi organization founded in the FRG in 1985; after unification the Front set up groups in the east; banned in 1992, it demanded the repatriation of all foreigners, denied the genocide of Jews during the Third Reich, and advocated street violence

Nationalistische Front: →Nationalist Front

NATO: →North Atlantic Treaty Organization

NDPD (*National-Demokratische Partei Deutschlands*): National-Democratic Party of Germany, established in 1948 to appeal to right-wing elements in the former GDR

Neues Forum: →New Forum

Neues Ökonomisches System: →New Economic System

New Economic System (*Neues Ökonomisches System*): programme of economic reforms introduced in the GDR in 1963

New Forum: opposition group formed in the GDR on 9 September 1989

North Atlantic Treaty Organization (NATO): alliance of North American and West European states formed in 1949 to defend Europe against Soviet aggression; NATO had sixteen members in 1982

OPEC: →Organization of Petroleum Exporting Countries

Organization of Petroleum Exporting Countries (OPEC): association of leading oil-producing countries established in 1960 to co-ordinate trade and policies

Ossi: disparaging term for eastern Germans

Parlamentarischer Rat: →Parliamentary Council

Parliamentary Council (*Parlamentarischer Rat*): elected body established in 1948 in the West German occupation zone to draw up the →Basic Law

PDS (*Partei des Demokratischen Sozialismus*): Party of Democratic Socialism, the successor party to the →SED

PEN (Poets, Playwrights, Essayists, Editors, Novelists): international writers' organization founded in 1921, widely known for its commitment to human rights and for assisting persecuted artists

People's Chamber (*Volkskammer*): national Parliament of the GDR

PH (*Pädagogische Hochschule*): Pedagogical University or teacher training college in the FRG

Politburo (*Politbüro*): supreme policy-making organ of the →SED

Politbüro: →Politburo

Polytechnic Upper School (POS): standard school for secondary education in the GDR

POS (*Polytechnische Oberschule*): →Polytechnic Upper School

real existierender Sozialismus: →real existing socialism

real existing socialism (*real existierender Sozialismus*): term used in GDR ideology from the mid-1970s to emphasize the achievements of socialism

Republicans, the (*die Republikaner*): extreme right-wing party in the FRG which performed well in regional elections between 1986 and 1994

Republikaner, die:→Republicans, the

Rundfunkrat: →Broadcasting Council

Sachverständigenrat: →Panel of Economic Experts

Schriftstellerverband der DDR: →Writers' Association of the GDR

SDS (*Sozialistischer Deutscher Studentenbund*): Federation of Socialist German Students, a left-wing opposition group active in the FRG during the 1960s

SED (*Sozialistische Einheitspartei Deutschlands*): Socialist Unity Party of Germany, the ruling Communist Party in the GDR from 1946 to 1989

Social market economy: an economic model which aims to achieve a balance between free market forces and state intervention; it was adopted as the basis for post-war economic reconstruction in the FRG

Solidarity Pact: agreement concluded in March 1993 between business associations, trade unions, political leaders, and the →federal states in order to help finance unification

Solidarpakt: →Solidarity Pact

SPD (*Sozialdemokratische Partei Deutschlands*): Social Democratic Party of Germany, the leading moderate left-wing party of the FRG

Staatsrat: →Council of State

Standing Conference of State Ministers of Education (KMK): committee of regional ministers responsible for co-ordinating education policy in the federal states

Stasi: short for *Staatssicherheitsamt* (Office of State Security), the secret police of the GDR

State Media Authority (*Landesmedienanstalt*): body responsible for overseeing the operation of broadcasting services in a →federal state

tariff system (*Tarifsystem*): binding agreements drawn up between employers and trade unions in the FRG

Tarifsystem: →tariff system

Trabant: popularly known as a 'Trab(b)i', a cheap, noisy and notoriously inefficient car produced in the GDR

Treaty of Unification: treaty between the FRG and the GDR embodying the terms of unification; its main provision was that the GDR would accede to the FRG and adopt its →Basic Law

Treuhand Anstalt: →Trust Agency

Trust Agency (*Treuhand Anstalt*): organization set up by the →Treaty of Unification to privatize state-owned concerns in the former GDR; the Agency was dissolved in December 1994

Ufa (*Universum-Film AG*): founded in 1917, the largest film-producing company in Germany during the Weimar period

UFV (*Unabhängiger Frauenverein*): Independent Women's Association, founded in the former GDR in 1989

UN: →United Nations

United Nations: international organization set up in 1945 to promote peace, security and co-operation throughout the world

Upswing East (*Aufschwung Ost*): two-year programme of economic aid for the new →federal states announced in February 1991

USSR: Union of Soviet Socialist Republics

Volkskammer: →People's Chamber

VPDE (*Verkehrsprojekte 'Deutsche Einheit'*): Transport Projects for German Unity, a programme to develop east–west German infrastructure after unification

Warsaw Pact: Soviet-led military alliance of Communist states established in 1995 in response to the founding of →NATO

Wende: 'turning-point', a term for the revolutionary period in the GDR between the summer of 1989, when opposition mounted against the →SED, and unification in October 1990

Wessi: disparaging term for western Germans

West Germany: →Federal Republic of Germany

west(ern) Germany: the eleven →federal states that comprised the original →Federal Republic of Germany between 1949 and 1990

Works Constitution Act (*Betriebsverfassungsgesetz*): law regulating →co-determination in the FRG

Works Council (*Betriebsrat*): body elected by employees and entitled to consultative rights in companies as laid down in the →Works Constitution Act of the FRG

Writers' Association of the GDR (*Schriftstellerverband der DDR*): state-approved organization for writers in the GDR

ZDF (*Zweites Deutsches Fernsehen*): the second national television channel in the FRG

Zentralkomitee→Central Committee

Bibliography

Abbey, W. (1993) *Two into One: Germany 1989–1992: A Bibliography of the 'Wende'*, London: University of London, Institute of Germanic Studies.

Abelshauser, W. (1983) *Wirtschaftsgeschichte der Bundesrepublik 1945—1980*, Frankfurt (Main): Suhrkamp

Abromeit, H. (1992) *Der verkappte Einheitsstaat*, Opladen: Leske und Budrich

Allen, C.S. (1989) 'Corporatism and Regional Economic Policies in the Federal Republic of Germany: the "Meso" Politics of Industrial Adjustment', *Publius. The Journal of Federalism*, Vol. 19 : 147–64

Anderson, C. (ed.) (1993) *The Domestic Politics of German Unification*, London: Lynne Rienner Publications

Anthony-Woods, P. (1992) 'Nihilist Cinema—Part Two: Buttgereit, Der Todesking', in Dwyer: 52–70

Anweiler, O. (1990) 'Die Wende in der Bildungspolitik der DDR', *Bildung und Erziehung*, 1 March 1990: 97–107

Anz, T. (ed.) (1991) '*Es geht nicht um Christa Wolf': Der Literaturstreit im vereinten Deutschland*, Munich: edition spangenberg

Arbeitsgruppe Bildung und Erziehung (December 1989), Dresden

ARD Jahrbuch, Hamburg: Hans-Bredow-Institut (appears annually)

Arndt, A. (1991) 'Gespräch mit Hermann Kant', *Sinn und Form*, Vol. 43: 853–78

Arnold, H.L. (ed.) (1991) *Literatur in der DDR. Rückblicke*, Munich: Text+Kritik (Special Issue)

Arnold, H.L. (ed.) (1992) *Vom gegenwärtigen Zustand der deutschen Literatur*, Munich: Text+Kritik 113

Arnold, H.L. and Wolf, G. (eds) (1990) *Die andere Sprache: neue DDR-Literatur der 80er Jahre*, Munich: Text+Kritik (Special Issue)

Arntz, J. (1993) 'Als der Kämmerer das Loch entdeckte', *Die Zeit*, No. 40, 1 October 1993: 22

Asmus, R. (1993) 'The Future of German Strategic Thinking', in Geipel:137–82

Baerns, B. (1990) *Journalismus und Medien in der DDR: Ansätze, Perspektiven, Probleme und Konsequenzen des Wandels*, Bonn: Jakob-Kaiser-Stiftung

Bahro, R. (1977) *Die Alternative. Zur Kritik des real existierenden Sozialismus*, Cologne: Europäische Verlagsanstalt

Baier, L. (1993) 'Selbstverstümmelnde Literatenschmäh: Über den neuen deutschen Intellektuellenhaß', *Freitag*, No. 5, 29 January 1993: 9–10

Baumbach, J. (1992) *Einige Thesen zum Transformationsprozeß für die Entwicklung des ostdeutschen Bildungswesens*, Berlin: WFO

Becker, J. (1990a) *Warnung vor dem Schriftsteller. Drei Vorlesungen in*

Frankfurt, Frankfurt (Main): Suhrkamp

Becker, J. (1990b) 'Die Wiedervereinigung der deutschen Literatur', *German Quarterly*, Vol. 63: 359–66

Becker, J. (1992) *Amanda herzlos*, Frankfurt (Main): Suhrkamp

Becker, W. (1990) 'Des Kaisers neue Kleider', *Film und Fernsehen*, May 1990: 2–6

Benz, W. (ed.) (1983) *Die Bundesrepublik Deutschland*, Vol. 2, Frankfurt (Main): Fischer Taschenbuch

Berchin, H. (1979) *Deutschland—ein Name im Wandel*, Munich/Vienna: Olzog Verlag

Berghahn, S. (1992) 'Frauenrechte im Einigungsprozeß', in Faber and Meyer: 78–79

Berghahn, V.R. and Karsten, D. (1987) *Industrial Relations in West Germany*, Oxford/New York, Hamburg: Berg

Bergmann, C. (1992) 'Parteisprache und Parteidenken. Zum Sprachgebrauch des ZK der SED', in Lerchner: 101–42

Berufsbildende Schulen in Berlin (1992) Berlin: Senatswerwaltung für Schule, Berufsbildung und Sport

Bischof, R. (1993) *Senioren 2000, Forum Deutsche Einheit: Aktuelle Kurzinformationen*, Nos 1–2, Bonn: Friedrich Ebert Stiftung

Blacksell, M. (1981) *Post-War Europe—A Political Geography*, 2nd edition, London: Hutchinson

Blacksell, M. (1982) 'Reunification and the Political Geography of the Federal Republic of Germany', *Geography*, Vol. 67: 310–19

Blacksell, M. (1994) 'State and Nation: Germany since Unification', *Europa*, Vol. 1, No. 1: 11–22

Blacksell, M. (1995) 'Reunification, Property Rights and Legal Services: Law without Lawyers in Germany's New *Bundesländer*', *European Urban and Regional Studies*, Vol. 2, No. 1: 71–77

Blacksell, M. and Brown, M. (1983) 'Ten Years of *Ostpolitik*', *Geography*, Vol. 68: 260–2

Blacksell, M. and Williams, A.M. (1994) *The European Challenge. Geography and Development in the European Community*, Oxford: OUP

Blumenthal, V. von, Brämer, R. and others (1981) *Grundfragen der Vergleichenden Erziehungswissenschaft*, Munich: Verlag Minerva

Blumenwitz, D. (1992) 'Zur strafrechtlichen Verfolgung Erich Honeckers', *Deutschland Archiv*, Vol. 25, No. 6: 567–79

Blunk, H. and Jungnickel, D. (eds) (1990) *Filmland DDR: Ein Reader zur Geschichte, Funktion und Wirkung der DEFA*, Cologne: Verlag Wissenschaft und Politik

Bobach, R. (1993) 'Mentale Konversion? Kulturelle Aspekte der deutschen Vereinigung', *Deutschland Archiv*, Vol. 26, No. 1: 7–20

Böthig, P. and Michael, K. (1993) *MachtSpiele: Literatur und Staatssicherheit im Fokus Prenzlauer Berg*, Leipzig: Reclam

Brämer, R. (1981) 'Bildungssystem und Sozialstruktur', in Blumenthal and others: 87

Brandt, L. (1991) 'Zeitschleifen', *Freitag*, No. 13, 22 March 1991: 21

Braun, V. (1979) *Training des aufrechten Gangs*, Halle: Mitteldeutscher Verlag

Braun, V. (1990) 'Das Eigentum', *Neues Deutschland*, 4 August 1990: 8; *Die Zeit*, No. 33, 10 September 1990: 36; in Braun 1992: 84

Braun, V. (1992) *Die Zickzackbrükke*, Halle: Mitteldeutscher Verlag

Brockmann, S. (1994a) 'German

Literary Debates after the Collapse', *German Life and Letters*, Vol. 47, No. 2: 201–10

Brockmann, S. (1994b) 'Preservation and Change in Christa Wolf's *Was bleibt*', *German Quarterly*, Vol. 67, No. 1: 73–85

Bruyn, G. de (1991) *Jubelschreie, Trauergesänge: deutsche Befindlichkeiten*, Frankfurt (Main): Fischer

Bruyn, G. de (1993) 'Nachträglich noch so ein Krieg', *Wochenpost*, 8 July 1993: 22

Bryson, P.J. (1992) 'The Economics of German Unification: A Review of the Literature', *Journal of Comparative Economics*, Vol. 16:118–49

Bullivant, K. (1994) *The Future of German Literature*, Oxford: Berg

Bulmer, S. (1989a) 'Territorial Government', in Smith, Paterson, and Merkl: 40–59

Bulmer, S. (ed.) (1989b) *The Changing Agenda of West German Public Policy*, Aldershot: Association for the Study of German Politics

Bulmer, S. (1989c) 'Unity, Diversity and Stability: the "Efficient Secrets" behind West German Public Policy', in Bulmer 1989b: 13–39

Bulmer, S. and Paterson, W. (1987) *The Federal Republic of Germany and the European Community*, London: Allen and Unwin

Bulmer, S. and Paterson, W. (1989) 'West Germany's Role in Europe: Man-Mountain or Semi-Gulliver?', *Journal of Common Market Studies*, Vol. 28, No. 2: 95–117

Bundeszentrale für politische Bildung (1990) *Verträge zur deutschen Einheit*, Bonn

Burkhardt, A. and Fritzsche, K.P. (eds) (1992) *Sprache im Umbruch*, Berlin/New York: de Gruyter

Bürklin, W. and Roth, D. (eds) (1994) *Das Superwahljahr*, Cologne: Bundverlag

Busch, F.W. (ed.) (1993) *Wege entstehen beim Gehen—Erziehungswissenschaft in Dresden*, Dresden: Technische Universität Dresden

Christ, P. and Neubauer, R. (1991) *Kolonie im eigenen Land. Die Treuhand, Bonn und die Wirtschaftskatastrophe der fünf neuen Länder*, Berlin: Rowohlt

Conradt, D. (1993) 'Putting Germany Back Together Again: the Great Social Experiment of Unification', in Geipel: 3–18

Cornelsen, D. (1989) 'Die Volkswirtschaft der DDR', in Weidenfeld and Zimmermann: 258–75

Corrin, C. (ed.) (1992) *Superwoman and the Double Burden*, London: Scarlet Press

Crouch, C. (1993) *Industrial Relations and European State Traditions*, Oxford: Clarendon

Dähnhardt, W. (1992) 'Mein Traum—ein Monopol', *Der Spiegel*, Vol. 46, No. 21,18 May 1992:76–83

Daiber, H. (1976) *Deutsches Theater seit 1945: Bundesrepublik Deutschland, Deutsche Demokratische Republik, Österreich, Schweiz*, Stuttgart: Reclam

Dalton, R. (ed.) (1993) *The New Germany Votes*, Oxford: Berg

Darnton, R. (1991) *Berlin-Journal 1989–1990*, New York: W.W. Norton

Deiritz, K. and Kraus, H. (eds) (1991) *Der deutsch-deutsche Literaturstreit: oder 'Freunde, es spricht sich schlecht mit gebundener Zunge'*, Hamburg: Luchterhand

Deiritz, K. and Kraus, H. (eds) (1993) *Verrat an der Kunst?*, Berlin: Aufbau

Delius, F.C. (1991) *Die Birnen von*

Ribbeck, Hamburg: Rowohlt

Demokratischer Neubeginn in der DDR (1990) Bonn: Gesamtdeutsches Institut

Dennis, M. (1993) 'The Vanishing Opposition; the Decline of the East German Citizen Movements', in Padgett: 193–224

'Der Deutsche Frühling im November', *Berliner Illustrierte Zeitung*, 19 November 1989

Derbyshire, I. (1991) *Politics in Germany*, Edinburgh: Chambers

'Deutschstunde', *Berliner Illustrierte Zeitung*, 26 November 1989

Die Fachschulbildung in der DDR (1980) Leipzig: Autorenkollektiv des Instituts für Fachschulwesen der DDR

Dieckmann, W. (1967) 'Kritische Bemerkungen zum sprachlichen Ost-West Problem', *Zeitschrift der deutschen Sprache*, Vol. 23, No. 3: 136–65

Döbert, H. (1993) 'Neuaufbau zwischen Kopie, Eigenständigkeit und Barrieren', *Deutsche Lehrerzeitung*, No. 10: 1

Dokumentation der Schulgesetze der Länder (1992) Bonn: Sekretariat der Ständigen Konferenz der Kultusminister

Dölling, I. and others (1992) *Unsere Haut. Tagebücher von Frauen aus dem Herbst 1990*, Berlin: Dietz

Domaschnew, A.I. (1991) 'Ade, DDR-Deutsch!', *Muttersprache*, Vol. 101, No. 1: 1–12

Dönhoff, M.G. (1964) *Namen, die keiner mehr nennt*, Munich: dtv

Doormann, L. (1990) 'Die neue Frauenbewegung: Zur Entwicklung seit 1968', in Herve: 255–89

Döring, C. and Steinert, H. (eds) (1990) *Schöne Aussichten. Neue Prosa aus der DDR*, Frankfurt (Main): Suhrkamp

Drawert, K. (1993) 'Der Text und die Freiheit des Textes', *Freitag*, No. 5, 18 June 1993: 12

Drosdowski, G. (1991) 'Deutsch—Sprache in einem geteilten Land', in Stölzel: 21–35

Drummond, S. (1993) 'Germany: Moving Towards a New Ostpolitik?', *World Today*, Vol 49: 132–35

Dwyer, S. (1992) *Rapid Eye 2*, London: Annihilation Press

Ebert, A. and others (1989, 1990) *Räumt die Steine hinweg. Geistliche Reden im politischen Aufbruch*, Munich: Claudius

Einhorn, B. (1992) 'The German Democratic Republic. Emancipated Women or Hardworking Mothers?', in Corrin: 125–54

Einhorn, B. (1993) *Cinderella Goes to Market, Citizenship, Gender and Women's Movements in East Central Europe*, London: Verso

Elsaesser, T. (1989) *New German Cinema. A History*, Houndmills and London: Macmillan/British Film Institute

Emmerich, W. (1994) *Kleine Literaturgeschichte der DDR*, Darmstadt: Luchterhand

Enzensberger, H.M. (1992) *Die große Wanderung. Dreiunddreißig Markierungen*, Frankfurt (Main): Suhrkamp

Eppler, E. (1989) 'Ist die DDR noch zu retten?', *Die Zeit*, No. 48, 24 November 1989: 10

Eppler, E. (1993) 'Tod der Sprache—Ende der Politik', *Der Sprachdienst*, Vol. 37, Nos 3–4: 76

Erbrecht, R. and Klein, J. (1990) *'Thesen zur Weiterentwicklung der polytechnischen Bildung', Schule in der Diskussion*, Berlin: Volk und Wissen Verlag

Ermischer, I. and Preusche, E. (September 1992) *Betriebsräte zwischen Mitbestimmung und Abwicklung—'Komanagement'*, Chemnitz Institut für Wirtschafts- und Sozialforschung

Ernst, T. (1992) *Privatkommerzieller Rundfunk in Deutschland*, Bonn: Bundeszentrale für politische Bildung

Exler, U. (1992) 'Financing German Federalism: Problems of Financial Equalization in the Unification Process', *German Politics*, Vol. 1, No. 3: 22–37

Faber, C. and Meyer, T. (eds) (1992) *Unterm neuen Kleid der Freiheit— das Korsett der Einheit*, Berlin: Sigma

Falkner, T. (1990) 'Die letzten Tage der SED', *Deutschland Archiv*, Vol. 23, No. 11: 1750–62

Falter, J.W. (1994) *Wer wählt rechts*, Munich: Beck

Faludi, S. (1992) *Backlash*, London: Vintage

Ferner, A. and Hyman, R. (1992) *Industrial Relations in the New Europe*, Oxford: Blackwell

Fichter, M. (1993) 'A House Divided: German Unification and Organized Labour', *German Politics*, Vol. 2, No. 1: 21–39

Filmstatistisches Taschenbuch, published annually by the *Spitzenorganisation der Filmwirtschaft*

Fink, H.-J. (1990) 'Die SPD in der DDR', *Deutschland Archiv*, Vol. 23, No. 2: 180–85.

Fischer, E. (1956) 'The Passing of *Mitteleuropa*', in Moodie and East: 60–79

Fischer, R. and Hembus, J. (1980) *Der Neue Deutsche Film 1960– 1980*, Munich: Goldmann

Fischetti, R. (1992) *Das Neue Kino:*

Acht Porträts von deutschen Regisseurinnen, Frankfurt (Main): tende

Fix, U. (1992) 'Rituelle Kommunikation im öffentlichen Sprachgebrauch der DDR und ihre Begleitumstände', in Lerchner: 3–99

Fleischer, W. (ed.) (1987) *Wortschatz der deutschen Sprache in der DDR*, Leipzig: Bibliographisches Institut

Fleischer, W. (1992) 'DDR-typische Benennungen und ihre Perspektive', in Welke: 15–34

Flockton, C. (1993) 'The Federal German Economy in the Early 1990s', *German Politics*, Vol. 2, No. 2: 311–27

Floren, F.J. (1991) *Wirtschaftspolitik im vereinten Deutschland*, Paderborn: Schöningh

Fraas, C. and Steyer, K. (1992) 'Sprache der Wende—Wende der Sprache?', *Deutsche Sprache*, Vol. 20: 172–84

Freese, G. (1993) 'Poker um Medien', *Die Zeit*, 21 May 1993: 20

Frein-Plischke, M.-L. (1987) *Wortschatz Bundesrepublik–DDR*, Düsseldorf: Schwan

Frein-Plischke, M.-L. (1991) 'Erziehung in der DDR zwischen öffentlichem Anspruch und Familie', in Schlosser: 131–35

Frevert, U. (1990) *Women in German History*, London: Berg

Freyermuth, G.S. (1993) *Der Übernehmer: Volker Schlöndorff in Babelsberg*, Berlin: Links Verlag

Fricke, K.W. (1991) *MfS intern*, Cologne: Verlag Wissenschaft und Politik

Friedheim, D.V. (1993) 'Regime Collapse in the Peaceful East German Revolution', *German Politics*, Vol. 2, No. 1: 97–112

Fründt, B. (1993) 'Babelsberg Studios', *Kino*, January 1993: 10–11

Fulbrook, M. (1991) '"Wir sind ein

Volk?" Reflections on German Unification', *Parliamentary Affairs*, Vol. 44, No. 3: 389–404

Fulbrook, M. (1992) *The Two Germanies 1945–1990*, London: Macmillan

Funk, N. and Mueller, M. (eds) (1993) *Gender Politics and Post-Communism*, London: Routledge

Futasz, M. (1990) 'Darf ich Einheitsschule sagen?', *Deutsche Lehrerzeitung*, No. 3: 12

Gabriel, O.W. (1993) 'Institutionenvertrauen im vereinigten Deutschland', *Aus Politik und Zeitgeschichte*, B 43/93, 22 October 1993: 3–12

Gaus, G. (1983) *Wo Deutschland liegt*, Hamburg: Hoffmann und Campe

Geipel, G. (1993) *Germany in a New Era*, Indianapolis: Hudson Institute

Geist, P. (ed.) (1991) *Ein Molotow-Cocktail auf fremder Bettkante: Lyrik der siebziger/achtziger Jahre von Dichtern aus der DDR*, Leipzig: Reclam

Geißler, R. (1991) 'Soziale Ungleichheit zwischen Frauen und Männern im geteilten und im vereinten Deutschland', *Aus Politik und Zeitgeschichte*, No. 29 (March): 39–45

Gemeinschaftsarbeit der APW (1983) *Das Bildungswesen der DDR*, Berlin: Volk und Wissen Verlag

General-Anzeiger: Bonner Stadtanzeiger Vol. 103, No. 31482, 7–8 August 1993: 1

Gensicke, T. (1992) 'Mentalitätswandel und Revolution', *Deutschland Archiv*, Vol. 25, No.12: 1266–83

Gerber, M. and Woods, R. (eds) (1993) *The End of the GDR and the Problems of Integration*, Lanham, New York: University Press of America

Geyer, T. (1991) 'Le Dr Thomas Geyer décrit les effets de l'ouverture des frontières à l'Est', *le film français*, 15 February 1991: 26

Gibowski, W. (1993a) *Zur politischen Stimmung in Deutschland. Januar 1993*, Bonn: Presse- und Informationsamt der Bundesregierung

Gibowski, W. (1993b) *Zur politischen Stimmung in Deutschland. Juni/Juli 1993*, Bonn: Presse- und Informationsamt der Bundesregierung

Gill, D. and Schröter, U. (1993) *Das Ministerium für Staatssicherheit*, Hamburg: Rowohlt

Glaeßner, G.-J. (1992) *The Unification Process in Germany*, London: Pinter

Glastetter, W., Högemann, G., and Marquardt R. (1991) *Die wirtschaftliche Entwicklung in der Bundesrepublik Deutschland 1950–1989*, Frankfurt (Main): Campus

Gluchowski, P. and Mnich, P. (1993) 'Alter, Generationen und Parteipräferenzen', *Aus Politik und Zeitgeschichte*, B 43/93, 22 October 1993: 13–23

Glück, H. (1991) 'Kleines Glossar zum Thema Deutschland', *Der Sprachdienst*, Vol. 35, No. 1: 6–11

Goldberger, B. (1993) 'Why Europe Should Not Fear the Germans', *German Politics*, Vol. 2. No. 2:288–310

Golombek, D. and Ratzke, D. (eds) (1990) *Dagewesen und aufgeschrieben. Reportagen über eine deutsche Revolution*, Frankfurt (Main): IMK

Good, C. (1993) 'Über die "Kultur des Mißverständnisses" im vereinten Deutschland', *Muttersprache*, Vol. 103, No. 3: 249–59

Goodbody, A. and Tate, D. (1992) *Geist und Macht: Writers and the*

State in the GDR, Amsterdam: Rodopi

Grambow, J. (1991) 'Gespräch mit Fritz Rudolf Fries', *Sinn und Form*, Vol. 43: 880–91

Grass, G. (1990a) *Deutscher Lastenaugleich. Wider das dumpfe Einheitsgebot. Reden und Gespräche*, Frankfurt (Main): Luchterhand

Grass, G. (1990b) *Two States—One Nation. The Case against German Unification*, London: Secker & Warburg

Grass, G. (1991) *Gegen die verstreichende Zeit: Reden, Aufsätze und Gespräche 1989–1991*, Hamburg, Zurich: Luchterhand

Grass, G. (1992a) *Unkenrufe*, Göttingen: Steidl

Grass, G. (1992b) *The Call of the Toad*, London: Secker & Warburg

Gratz, M. (1992) 'Was sollte sich daran ändern?', *neue deutsche literatur*, Vol. 40, No. 472: 159–163

Graves. P. 'Not Above Reproach', *Times Literary Supplement*, 24 August 1990: 890

Greiner, U. (1993) 'Plädoyer für Schluß der Stasi-Debatte', *Die Zeit*, 5 February 1993: 60

Gruner, P. (ed.) (1990) *Angepaßt oder mündig? Briefe an Christa Wolf im Herbst 1989*, Berlin: Volk und Wissen

Haase, H.E. (1990) *Das Wirtschaftssystem der DDR*, Berlin: Berlin Verlag

Hage, J. (1990) 'Schule im Umbruch', *Die Deutsche Schule*, No. 5: 20–21

Hahn, H. (1993) 'Ossis, Wessis and Germans: an Inner-German Perception of National Characteristics', *Journal of Area Studies*, No. 2: 114–27

Hampele, A. (1993) 'The Independent Women's Association', in Funk and Mueller: 180–93

Hancock, M.D. and Welsh, H. (eds) (1994) *German Unification*, Boulder, San Fancisco, Oxford: Westview Press

Hanesch, W. and others (1994) *Armut in Deutschland*, Hamburg: Rowohlt

Hannover, I. (1990) 'Von Ost nach West. Und umgekehrt', in Golombek and Ratzke: 63–72

Harmon, M.D. and Heisenberg, D. (1993) 'Explaining the European Currency Crisis of September 1992', *German Politics and Society*, No. 29: 19–51

Harris, C.D. (1991) 'Unification of Germany in 1990', *Geographical Review*, Vol. 81: 170–82

Haug, F. (1986) 'The Women's Movement in Germany', *New Left Review*, Vol. 155; also in Haug (1992): 185–217

Haug, F. (1992) *Beyond Female Masochism*, London: Verso

Hauptmann, H. (1989) 'Anzeige mit Komplimenten. Landolf Scherzers Visite beim Ersten', *neue deutsche literatur*, Vol. 37, No. 434: 27–32

Häußermann, H. and Heseler, H. (1993) 'Massenentlassungen, Mobilität und Arbeitsmarktpolitik: Das Beispiel zweier Ostdeutscher Großbetriebe', *Aus Politik und Zeitgeschichte*, B 35/93, 27 August 1993: 16–30

Heigemann, S. (1988) *Kabel und Satellitenfernsehen*, Bonn: Bundeszentrale für politische Bildung

Hein, C. (1986) 'Maelzel's Chess Player Goes to Hollywood: Das Verschwinden des künstlerischen Produzenten im Zeitalter der technischen Reproduzierbarkeit', in Hein (1987): 165–94

Hein, C. (1987) *Öffentlich arbeiten*,

Berlin: Aufbau

Hein, C. (1989) *Der Tangospieler*, Berlin: Aufbau

Hein, C. (1992) 'Es gibt sie längst, die neue Mauer', *Die Zeit*, 7 February 1992: 21

Hein, C. (1993a) 'Der Waschzwang ist da, also muß gewaschen werden: Gespräch mit Christoph Hein über Christa Wolf und die Wirkung von Stasiakten', *Freitag*, No. 3, 29 January 1993: 3

Hein, C. (1993b) *Das Napoleonspiel*, Berlin: Aufbau

Heinemann M. (1989) *Kleines Wörterbuch der Jugendsprache*, Leipzig: Bibliographisches Institut

Hellmann, M.W. (1990) 'DDR-Sprachgebrauch nach der Wende—eine erste Bestandsaufnahme', *Muttersprache*, Vol. 100, Nos 2–3: 266–86

Hellmann, M.W. (1991) '"Ich suche eine Wohnung"', in Schlosser:19–32

Helwig, G. (1987) *Frau und Familie in der Bundesrepublik Deutschland—DDR*, Cologne: Verlag Wissenschaft und Politik

Hensel, K. (1993) *Im Schlauch*, Frankfurt (Main): Suhrkamp

Hermann, R. (1987) 'Reise der zwiespältigen Gefühle', *Süddeutsche Zeitung*, Vol. 43, No. 200, 2 September 1987: 3; also in Golombek and Ratzke: 15–22

Hermanns, F. (1992) 'Ein Wort im Wandel: Deutsch—was ist das?', in Burkhardt and Fritzsche: 253–65

Herve, F. (1990) (ed.) *Geschichte der deutschen Frauenbewegung*, Cologne: PapyRossa Verlag

Heuven, M.H.A. van (1993) 'Testing the New Germany: the Case of Yugoslavia', *German Politics and Society*, No. 29: 52–63

Heym, S. (1990) *Auf Sand gebaut*,

Munich: Bertelsmann

Heym, S. (1992) *Filz*: Munich: Bertelsmann

Hickel, R. (1993) 'Transforming the East German Economy', *Debatte*, Vol. 1, No. 1: 65–84

Hickel, R. and Priewe, J. (1994) *Nach dem Fehlstart*, Frankfurt (Main): Fischer

Hickethier, K. (1991) 'Neue deutsche Filme auf der Berlinale', *epd Film*, May 1991: 5–7

Hilbig, W. (1989) *Eine Übertragung*, Frankfurt (Main): Fischer

Hilbig, W. (1991) *Alte Abdeckerei*, Frankfurt (Main): Fischer

Hilbig, W. (1993a) *'Ich'*, Frankfurt (Main): Suhrkamp

Hilbig, W. (1993b) *Grünes grünes Grab*, Frankfurt (Main): Fischer

Hilmer, R. and Müller-Hilmer, R. (1992) 'Es wächst zusammen', *Die Zeit*, No. 40. 1 October 1993: 17–21

Hochhuth, R. (1993) *Wessis in Weimar. Szenen aus einem besetzten Land*, Berlin: Volk und Welt

Hodge, C.C. (1992) 'The Federal Republic and the Future of Europe: a Reassessment', *German Politics*, Vol. 1, No. 2: 223–38

Hoffmann, A. (1990) *Die Entschulung der Schule*, Berlin: Volk und Wissen Verlag

Hoffmann, L. (1993) *Warten auf den Aufschwung*, Regensburg: tv Transfer

Hofmann, G. and Perger, W. (1994) 'Ohnmächtige Riesen. Die strategische Basis der Volksparteien im Superwahljahr 1994', in Bürklin and Roth: 293–307

Holldack, E. (1992) *Veränderung der Schulsysteme und Bildungsweggestaltung in Ostberlin und dem Land Brandenburg*, Berlin: WFO

Holloway, R. (1990) '"Wall Buster Gang" Tagged First True East-West film', *Hollywood Reporter*, 14 August 1990: 1–4

Holzweißig, G. (1989) *Massenmedien in der DDR*, Berlin: Verlag Gebr. Holzapfel

Holzweißig, G. (1991) *DDR-Presse unter Parteikontrolle*, Bonn: Gesamtdeutsches Institut

Hopfer, R. (1992) 'Christa Wolfs Streit mit dem "großen Bruder"', in Burkhardt and Fritzsche: 111–33

Hörner, W. (1991) 'Auf dem Weg zur Bildungseinheit—Die Umgestaltung des Bildungswesens in der DDR', *Jahresbericht der Arbeitsstelle für vergleichende Bildungsforschung*, Bochum Ruhr-Universität: 1–20

Hörnigk, F. (1992) 'Die Literatur bleibt zuständig: Ein Versuch über das Verhältnis von Literatur, Utopie und Politik in der DDR—am Ende der DDR', *Germanic Review*, Vol. 67, No. 3: 99–105

Hoyningen-Heune, G. and Meier-Krenz, U. (1988) 'Flexibilisierung des Arbeitsrechts', *Zeitschrift für Arbeitsrecht*, Vol. 19, No. 3: 293–318

Hrbek, R. (ed.) (1993) *Der Vertrag von Maastricht in wissenschaftlicher Kontroverse*, Baden-Baden: Nomos

Huelshoff, M., Markovits, A., and Reich S. (eds) (1993) *From Bundesrepublik to Deutschland. German Politics after Unification*, Ann Arbor: University of Michigan Press

Huillet, D. (1993) Unpublished Letter to the Mayor, Frankfurt (Main), dated 27 October 1993

Huinink, J. and Mayer, K.U. (1993) 'Lebensläufe im Wandel der DDR-Gesellschaft', in Joas and Kohli: 151–71

Humphreys, P. (1994) *Media and Media Policy in Germany*, Oxford & Providence: Berg

Informationen Extra (1991) No. 7, a European Community Publication

Innes, C. (1979) *Modern German Drama: a Study in Form*, Cambridge: Cambridge University Press

Jacobi, O. and others (1992) 'Germany: Co-determining the Future', in Ferner and Hyman: 218–69

Jacobsen, W., Kaes, A. and Prinzler H.H. (eds) (1993) *Geschichte des deutschen Films*, Stuttgart: J.B. Metzler

Jäger, M. (1982) *Kultur und Politik in der DDR: Ein historischer Abriß*, Cologne: Verlag Wissenschaft und Politik

James, H. and Stone, M. (eds) (1992) *When the Wall Came Down. Reactions to German Unification*, London: Routledge

Jeffery, C. (1992) 'Electoral Volatility in United Germany', in Osmond: 115–32

Jeffery, C. (1993) 'Plus ça change ... The Non-Reform of the German Federal System after Unification', University of Leicester Discussion Papers in Federal Studies, No. FS 93/2

Jeffery, C. and Savigear, P. (eds) (1991) *German Federalism Today*, Leicester and London: Leicester University Press

Joas, H. and Kohli, M. (eds) (1993) *Der Zusammenbruch der DDR*, Frankfurt (Main): Suhrkamp

Jones, A. (1994) *The New Germany. A Human Geography*, Chichester: Wiley

Jones, P.N. and Wild, T. (1994) 'Opening the Frontier: Recent Spatial Impacts in the Former Inner German Border Zone', *Regional Studies*, Vol. 28: 259–73

Joppke, C. (1993) 'Why Leipzig? "Exit" and "Voice" in the East

German Revolution', *German Politics*, Vol. 2, No. 3: 393–414

Jungnickel, D. (1990) 'Produktionsbedingungen bei der Herstellung von Kinospielfilmen und Fernsehfilmen', in Blunk and Jungnickel: 47–59

Kahlau, C. (ed.) (1990) *Aufbruch! Frauenbewegung in der DDR*, Munich: Frauenoffensive

Kaiser, C.-C. (1989) 'Die Ruhe täuscht', *Die Zeit*, No. 43, 20 October 1989: 5

Kaiser, K. (1990/1) 'Germany's Unification', *Foreign Affairs*: 179–205

Kamp, K.-H. (1993) 'The German *Bundeswehr* in Out-of-Area Operations: to Engage or Not to Engage?', *World Today*, Vol. 49: 165–68

Kane, M. (ed.) (1991) *Socialism and the Literary Imagination: Essays on East German Writers*, New York: Berg

Kant, H. (1991) *Abspann*, Berlin: Aufbau

Kaplan, G. (1992) *Contemporary Western Feminism*, London: University College London Press/Allen & Unwin

Kernig, C.D. (1973) *Marxismus im Systemvergleich*, Frankfurt: Herder & Herder

King, R. (1994) 'Migration and the Single Market for Labour', in Blacksell and Williams: 218–41

Kirchner, E. (1994) 'The Impact of German Unification on the New European Security Order', in Miall, H. (ed.) (1994) *Shaping the New Europe*, London: Pinter/Royal Institute of International Affairs

Klatt, H. (1992) 'German Unification and the Federal System', *German Politics*, Vol. 1, No. 3: 1–21

Kleinfeld, G. (1993) 'The Integration

of a Unified Germany: Update and Outlook', in Geipel: 49–60

Klemm, K., Böttcher, W., and Weegen, M. (1992) *Bildungsplanung in den neuen Bundesländern*, Munich: Juventa

Klump, R. (1985) *Wirtschaftsgeschichte der Bundesrepublik*, Bamberg: Franz Steiner

Koch, K. (ed.) (1989) *West Germany Today*, London: Routledge

Kohl, H. (1991) *Our Future in Europe*, Edinburgh and London: Europa Institute/Konrad Adenauer Stiftung

Kohl, H. (1993) 'European Union—a Challenge of Our Times', *German Comments*, No. 32: 4–10

Köhler, K. (1989) 'Wenn Mal um Mal die Stasi stürmt', *Die Zeit*, No. 42, 13 October 1989: 2

Kolinsky, E. (1992) 'Women in the New Germany: The East-West Divide', in Smith, Paterson, Merkl, and Padgett: 264–80

Kolinsky, E. (1993) *Women in Contemporary Germany*, Oxford: Berg

Königsdorf, H. (1990a) *1989 oder ein Moment Schönheit*, Berlin: Aufbau

Königsdorf, H. (1990b) *Adieu DDR. Protokolle eines Abschieds*, Hamburg: Rowohlt

Korka, J. (1990) 'Nur keinen neuen Sonderweg', *Die Zeit*, No. 43, 21 October 1990: 11

Koziol, A. and Schedlinski, R. (eds) (1990), *Abriß der Ariadnefabrik*, Berlin: Galrev

Kramer, W. (1989) 'Deutschland hüben, Deutschland drüben', *Frankfurter Allgemeine Zeitung*, No. 92, 20 April 1989, *Reiseblatt*: 3; also in Golombek and Ratzke: 23–36

Krebs, D. (1989) 'Interview mit Christoph Hein', *neue deutsche literatur*, Vol. 38, No. 3: 177–80

Kreimeier, K. (1992) *Die Ufa Story*, Munich and Vienna: Carl Hanser

Krenz, E. (1990) *Wenn Mauern fallen*, Vienna: Paul Neff

Krockow, C. von (1993) *Die Deutschen vor ihrer Zukunft*, Berlin: Rowohlt

Kühl, J. (1993) 'Arbeitslosigkeit in der vereinigten Bundesrepublik Deutschland', *Aus Politik und Zeitgeschichte*, B 35/93, 27 August 1993: 3–15

Kurbjuweit, D. (1993) 'Wir waren das Volk', *Die Zeit*, No. 46, 12 November 1993: 17–19

Land Brandenburg: Ministerium für Bildung, Jugend und Sport (1993) *Nach der 10. Klasse*

Land, R. (1990) *Zur Erneuerung des Sozialismus in der DDR*, Berlin: Volk und Wissen Verlag

Laux, S. (1993) 'Das Maastricht-Urteil des Bundesverfassungsgerichts', *Europaarchiv*, Vol. 48: D459–77

Leciejewski, K. (1991) 'Ökonomische Grundbedingungen in der DDR', in Schlosser: 55–63

Lehnert, H. (1991) 'Fiktionalität und autobiographische Motive. Zu Christa Wolfs Erzählung *Was bleibt*', *Weimarer Beiträge*, Vol. 37, No. 3: 423–44

Leicht, R. (1989) 'Was hält uns eigentlich noch hier?', *Die Zeit*, No. 46, 10 November 1989: 3

Leidecker, G. and others (1991) *Ich weiß nicht, ob ich froh sein soll. Kinder erleben die Wende*, Stuttgart: Metzler

Leonardy, U. (1992) 'Federation and *Länder* in German Foreign Relations', *German Politics*, Vol. 1, No. 3: 119–35

Leptin, G. (1991) 'Systemvergleich: Wirtschaftssystem', in Weidenfeld and Korte: 653–59

Lerchner, G. (ed.) (1992) *Sprachgebrauch im Wandel*, Frankfurt (Main): Leipziger Arbeiten zur Sprach- und Kommunikationsgeschichte, Vol. 1

Leusmann, C. and Klausnitzer, P. (1993) 'Zum Zusammenwachsen der alten und neuen Länder im Schulbereich', *Pädagogik und Schulalltag*, February 1993: 133–42

Lewis, D. and Brumsack, S. (1988) *The GDR: A Background to East German Studies*, Blairgowrie: Lochee

Liegle, L. (1988) 'Erziehung zur Anpassung?', in Meyer and Schröder: 80–95

Liersch, W. (1991) 'Brief an Dr. Josef Neubauer', *neue deutsche literatur*, Vol. 39, No. 9: 167

Link, J. (1993) 'La Réunification allemande comme événement symbolique', *Actes de la Recherche en Sciences Sociales*, Vol. 98: 59–61

Lohneis, H.-W. (1992) 'Appendix: the Legal Context of Unification', in Smith, Paterson, Merkl, and Padgett: 349–58

Mackinder, H.J. (1904) 'The Geographical Pivot of History', *Geographical Journal*, Vol. 23: 421–37

Malarski, R. (1993a) *Jugend und Gewalt: Jugend ohne Wertvorstellungen*, *Forum Deutsche Einheit: Aktuelle Kurzinformationen*, Nos 3/4, Bonn: Friedrich Ebert Stiftung

Malarski, R. (1993b) *Aus Politik und Zeitgeschichte*, B 46–47/93, 12 November 1993

Markovits, A. and Reich, S. (1993) 'Should Europe Fear the Germans?', in Huelshoff, Markovits, and Reich: 271–90

Maron, M. (1993) *Nach Maßgabe meiner Begreifungskraft: Artikel und Essays*, Frankfurt (Main): Fischer

McElvoy, A. (1992) *The Saddled Cow*, London: Faber and Faber

McLaughlin, C. (1993) 'Cold Light of Free-Market Dawn', *Scotsman*, 26 October 1993: 10

Media Perspektiven, Frankfurt: Arbeitsgemeinschaft der ARD-Werbegesellschaften

Menge, M. (1989a) 'Daß ich das noch erleben durfte', *Die Zeit*, No. 46, 10 November 1989: 2; and in Golombek and Raztke: 111–18

Menge, M. (1989b) 'Pläne schmieden für die neue Zeit', *Die Zeit*, No. 48, 24 November 1989: 4

Merian, S. (1980) *Der Tod des Märchenprinzen*, Hamburg: Buntbuch Verlag

Merkel, A. (1991) 'Chancengleichheit in den neunziger Jahren: Frauenpolitik im vereinten Europa', *Informationen Extra*: 1–2

Meyer G. and Schröder J. (eds) (1988) *DDR Heute*, Verlag Narr: Tübingen

Meyn, H. (1992) *Massenmedien in der Bundesrepublik Deutschland*, Berlin: Colloquium Verlag

Mitscherlich, A. and M. (1967, 1991) *Die Unfähigkeit zu trauern: Grundlagen kollektiven Verhaltens*, Munich: Piper

Mitscherlich, M. and Burmeister, B. (1991) *Wir haben ein Berührungstabu*, Hamburg: Klein

Modrow, H. (1993) 'The Dream of Unity Crashes', *Morning Star*, 9 October 1993: 5

Momper, W. (1991) *Grenzfall*, Munich: Bertelsmann

Moodie, A. and East, W.G. (1956) *The Changing World*, London: Harrap

Moore, O. 'Owning Up to the Past', *Screen International*, 10 December

1993: 9

Mudry, A. (ed.) (1991) *Gute Nacht, du Schöne. Autorinnen blicken zurück*, Frankfurt (Main): Luchterhand

Müller, B. and others (1990) 'Weg vom alten Stiefel der Einheitsschule', *Deutsche Lehrerzeitung*, No. 32: 1

Murphy, A.B. (1991) 'The Emerging Europe of the 1990s', *Geographical Review*, Vol. 81, No. 1: 1–17

Naftzinger, J.E. (1994) *Policy Making in the German Democratic Republic: The Response to West German Transborder Television Broadcasting*, Ph.D. dissertation, University of Maryland

Nave-Herz R. (1989) *Die Geschichte der Frauenbewegung in Deutschland*, Bonn: Bundeszentrale für Politische Bildung

Neather, E.J. (1993) 'The Abitur Examination', *Language Learning Journal*, No. 7 (March): 19–21

Neuner, G. (1989a) 'Mehr Individualität, mehr Leistung', *National-Zeitung*, 29 November 1989: 3

Neuner, G. (1989b) *Allgemeinbildung: Konzept—Inhalt—Prozeß*, Berlin: Volk und Wissen Verlag

Nickel, H.M. (1990) 'Frauen in der DDR', *Aus Politik und Zeitgeschichte*, No. 13 (April), Bonn: 39–45

Noelle-Neumann, E., Schulz W., and Wilke, J. (eds) (1989) *Fischer Lexikon Publizistik Massenkommunikation*, Frankfurt (Main): Fischer

Noelle-Smith, G. and Wollen, T. (1991) *After the Wall*, London: British Film Institute

Nössig, M. (ed.) (1976) *Das Schauspieltheater der DDR und das Erbe (1970–1974): Positionen, Debatten, Kritiken*, Berlin: Akademie-Verlag

Oschlies, W. (1989a) 'Sprache der Deutschen: Reißt, hält oder festigt sich das "einigende Band"?' in *Die DDR im vierzigsten Jahr*, Edition *Deutschland Archiv*, Cologne: 106–17

Oschlies, W. (1989b) *Würgende und wirkende Wörter. Deutschsprechen in der DDR*, Berlin: Verlag Gebr. Holzapfel

Oschlies, W. (1990a) *'Wir sind das Volk'*, Cologne and Vienna: Böhlau Verlag

Oschlies, W. (1990b) *'Vierzig zu Null im Klassenkampf?'*, Deustchland-Report 9, Melle: Konrad-Adenauer Stiftung

Osmond, J. (ed.) (1992) *German Reunification. A Reference Guide and Commentary*, Harlow: Longman

Padgett, S. (1989) 'The Party System', in Smith, Paterson, and Merkl: 122–47

Padgett, S. (1992) 'The New German Economy', in Smith, Paterson, Merkl, and Padgett: 187–207

Padgett, S. (ed.) (1993a) *Parties and Party Systems in the New Germany*, Aldershot: Association for the Study of German Politics

Padgett, S. (1993b) 'Introduction: Party Democracy in the New Germany', in Padgett 1993a: 1–21

Paetz, A. and Pilarczyk, U. (1990) *Schulen, die anders waren*, Berlin: Volk und Wissen Verlag

Paterson, T. (1993a) '300 Towns That Just Can't Find a Mayor', *The European*, No. 182, 5–11 November 1993: 1

Paterson, T. (1993b) 'A Landscape that Refuses to Blossom', in *The European*, No. 184, 26 November–2 December 1993: 10

Paterson, T. (1993c) 'Political Vacuum Alarms a 40-Year-Old Democracy', *The European*, No. 174, 2–5 September 1993: 8

Paterson, W.E. (1993) 'Muß Europa Angst vor Deutschland haben?', in Hrbek: 9–18

Patterson, M. (1976) *German Theatre Today: Post-war Theatre in West and East Germany, Austria and Switzerland*, London: Pitman

Peters, P. (1992) 'Der Satellit—ein inoffizieller Mitarbeiter?', *neue deutsche literatur*, Vol. 40, No. 2: 163–69

Pflaum, H.G., and Prinzler, H.H. (1979, 1992) *Film in der Bundesrepublik Deutschland*, Munich and Vienna: Carl Hanser

Piazolo, M. (1992) 'Ungeklärte Eigentumsfragen als Hauptinvestitionshindernis in den neuen Bundesländern', *Deutschland Archiv*, Vol. 25, No. 5: 481–84

Picht, G. (1964) *Die Deutsche Bildungskatastrophe*, Freiburg: Walter

Pilz, F. (1974) *Das System der Sozialen Marktwirtschaft*, Munich: Reinhardt

Polenz, P. von (1993) 'Die Sprachrevolte in der DDR im Hersbt 1989', manuscript from the *Institut für Deutsche Sprache*, Mannheim

Pollack, D. (1993) 'Zum Stand der DDR-Forschung', *Politische Vierteljahresschrift*, Vol. 34, No. 1: 119–39

Popplewell, R. (1992) 'The Stasi and the East German Revolution', *Contemporary European History*, Vol. 1, No. 1: 37–63

Porter, V. and Hasselbach, S. (1991) *Pluralism, Politics and the Marketplace. The Regulation of German Broadcasting*, London: Routledge

Portune, G. (1992) 'Was wird aus der Schule?', Paper given to the Thomas-Morus-Akademie, Bensberg

Preußen, H.-P. (1993) 'Abwicklung',

Deutschland Archiv, Vol. 26, No. 1: 91–93

Priewe, J. and Hickel, R. (1991) *Der Preis der Einheit*, Frankfurt (Main): Fischer

Prützel-Thomas, M. (1993) 'The Abortion Issue and the Federal Constitutional Court', *German Politics*, Vol. 2, No. 3: 467–84

Quilitzsch, F. and Kaufmann, U. (1993) 'Sich ernst nehmen—Volker Braun: Gedanken zur Zeit', *Thüringische Landeszeitung*, Wochenendbeilage, 14 August 1993: 1

Radisch, I. (1993) 'Krieg der Köpfe. Heiner Müller und die Stasi', *Die Zeit*, 22 January 1993: 47

Reed, T.J. (1993) 'Disconnection in the 1990 *Literaturstreit*: "keine akademische Frage"?', in Skrine and others: 211–18

Reich, J. (1991) *Rückkehr nach Europa*, Munich: Hanser

Reich, J. (1992) *Abschied von den Lebenslügen: Die Intelligenz und die Macht*, Berlin: Rowohlt

Reid, J.H. (1990) *Writing without Taboos: the New East German Literature*, New York: Berg

Reif, K. (1993) 'Ein Ende des "permissive consensus"', in Hrbek: 23–38

Reiher, D. (1990) 'Für die Demokratisierung der Schule', in Hoffmann: 21–31

Reimann, B. and Wolf, C. (1993) *Sei gegrüßt und lebe*, Berlin: Aufbau

Reinschke, K.J. (1991) 'Alltag in der DDR', *Informationen zur politischen Bildung. Geschichte der DDR*, No. 231: 48–51

Reitz, E. (1993) Unpublished Letter to the Mayor, Frankfurt (Main), 27 October 1993

Richter, P. (1993) *Kurzer Prozeß*,

Berlin: Elefanten Press

Rischbieter, H. (ed.) (1967) *German Theatre Today*, Velber: Friedrich Verlag

Roberts, G.K. (1991) '"Emigrants in their Own Country": German Reunification and its Political Consequences', *Parliamentary Affairs*, Vol. 44: 373–88

Robinsohn, S.B. and Kuhlmann, J.C. (1967) 'Two Decades of Non-Reform in German Education', *Comparative Education Review*, Vol. 11, No. 3: 311–30

Roche, R. (1991) 'Nach Tische liest man's anders', *Muttersprache*, Vol. 101, No. 4: 297–307

Rolff, H.-G. and others (1992) *Jahrbuch der Schulentwicklung*, Vol. 7, Munich: Juventa

Rolff, H.-G. and others (1994) *Jahrbuch der Schulentwicklung*, Vol. 8, Munich: Juventa

Röper, H. (1993) 'Formationen deutscher Medienmultis 1992', *Media Perspektiven*, No. 2: 56–74

Röscher, A. 'Aufhören, auf leere Hoffnung zu setzen. Gespräch mit Günter Grass, *neue deutsche literatur*, Vol. 40, No. 9: 7–28

Rösner, E. (1989) *Abschied von der Hauptschule*, Frankfurt (Main): Fischer

Rost, P. and Wessel A. (1992) 'Schulwahl—Ein neues Problem für Schüler und Eltern in Ostberlin', *Die Deutsche Schule*, March 1992: 272–81

Roth, W. (1990) 'Programmänderung Leipzig 1989', *epd Film*, January 1990: 3–5

Rother, H.J. (1992) *Neue Zeit*, 30 October 1992

Rust, V. (1992) 'Bedingungen für einen radikalen Wechsel', *Deutsche Lehrerzeitung*, No. 10: 3

Rutz, W. (1991) 'Die Wiedererrichtung der östlichen Bundesländer', *Raumforschung und Raumordnung*, Vol. 9, No. 15: 279–86

Sächsisches Staatsministerium für Kultus (1992) *Die Sächsische Mittelschule*, Dresden

Sandford, J. (1976) *The Mass Media of the German-Speaking Countries*, London: Oswald Wolff

Sandford, J. (1980) *The New German Cinema*, London: Eyre Methuen

Sandford, J. (1985) '"Wollt ihr das totale Fernsehen?": The New Media Debate in West Germany', *Journal of Area Studies*, No. 12: 24–30

Sandford, J. (1988) 'What Are the Media For? Philosophies of the Media in the Federal Republic and the GDR', *Contemporary German Studies*, No. 5: 5–24

Sandford, J. (ed.) (1990) *Günter Wallraff: Der Aufmacher*, Manchester: Manchester University Press

Sandford, J. (1992) '"Wer zu spät kommt ...": *Neues Deutschland* and the *"Wende"*', *German Life and Letters*, Vol. 45, 3 July: 268–78

Sandford, J. (1993) 'The Transformation of the Media in East Germany since the *Wende*', *Journal of Area Studies*, No. 2: 25–36

Saunderson, A. (1993) 'Caution Greets German Recovery', *The European*, No. 188, 17–23 December 1993: 15–16

Schabowski, G. (1991) *Das Politbüro*, Hamburg: Rowohlt

Schäfer, H. and Schobert W. (eds) (1993) *Fischer Film Almanach 1993*, Frankfurt (Main): Fischer

Schayan, J. (1993) 'Dresden', *Deutschland*, No. 2, 11 December 1993: 21–26

Schedlinski, R. (1992) 'Die Unzuständigkeit der Macht', *neue deutsche literatur*, Vol. 40, No. 6: 75–105

Schenk, H. (1990) *Die feministische Herausforderung: 150 Jahre Frauenbewegung in Deutschland*, Munich: Beck

Scherzer, L. (1988) *Der Erste. Eine Reportage aus der DDR*, Rudolstadt: Greifenverlag

Schlosser, H.D. (1990) *Die deutsche Sprache in der DDR zwischen Stalinismus und Demokratie*, Cologne: Verlag Wissenschaft und Politik

Schlosser, H.D. (1991) *Kommunikationsbedingungen und Alltagssprache in der ehemaligen DDR*, Hamburg: Helmut Biske Verlag

Schmider, E. (1990) *Werbedeutsch in Ost und West*, Berlin: Berlin Verlag

Schmidt, H. (1993a) *Handeln für Deutschland*, Berlin: Rowohlt

Schmidt, H. (1993b) 'Hände weg von der Steuerschraube', *Die Zeit*, No. 10, 5 March 1993: 1

Schmidt, M. (1992) 'Political Consequences of German Unification', *West European Politics*, Vol. 15: 1–15

Schmitt-Beck, R. and Dietz, R.G. (1993) 'Satellitendirektempfang in vier Ländern Westeuropas', *Media Perspektiven*, No. 8: 366–73

Schneider, B. (1992) 'Die ostdeutsche Tagespresse—eine traurige Bilanz', *Media Perspektiven*, No. 7: 428–41

Schneider, P. (1990) 'Die Kühlschranktheorie und andere Vermutungen', *Extreme Mittellage*, Hamburg: Rowohlt

Schödel, H. (1992) 'Götter der Pest', *Die Zeit*, 19 October 1992: 59

Schriftstellerverband der DDR (1988) *X. Schriftstellerkongreß der DDR*, Berlin: Aufbau

Schröder, M. (1992) 'Lexikographische Nach-Wende. Ein Über-arbeitungsbericht', in Lerchner: 263–96

Schüddekopf, C. (ed.) (1990) *'Wir sind das Volk!': Flugschriften, Aufrufe und Texte einer deutschen Revolution*, Hamburg: Rowohlt

Schulenberg, W. (1993) 'Employers Scorn Antiquated Pay System', *The European*, No. 24, 30 December 1993: 18

Schuster, R. (ed.) (1978) *Deutsche Verfassungen*, Munich: Goldmann

Schütze, Y. (1992) 'Vereinbarkeit von Familie und Beruf', in *Familien im wiedervereinigten Deutschland*, edited by B. Jans and A. Sering, Bonn

Schwartau, C. and Vortmann, H. (1989) 'Die materiellen Lebensbe-dingungen in der DDR', in Weiden-feld and Zimmermann: 292–307

Schwarz, G. and Zenner, C. (eds) (1990) *Wir wollen mehr als 'ein Vaterland'*, Hamburg: Rowohlt

Schwarzer, A. (1975) *Der 'kleine Unterschied' und seine großen Folgen*, Frankfurt (Main): Fischer

Schwitzer, K.-P. (1993) 'Alte Men-schen in den neuen Bundesländern: Das andere deutsche Alter', *Aus Po-litik und Zeitgeschichte*, B 44/93, 29.10.1993: 39–47

Shaw, L.R. (ed.) (1963) *The German Theater Today*, Austin: Texas University Press

Siedler, W.J. (1989) 'Berlin ist tot, es lebe Berlin!', *Die Zeit*, No. 48, 24 November 1989: 52

Sinnhuber, K. (1954) 'Central Europe—Mitteleuropa—Europe centrale: An Analysis of a Geo-graphical Term', *Transactions, In-stitute of British Geographers*, Vol. 20: 15–39

Skrine, R., Wallbank-Turner, R.E., and West J. (eds) *Connections:*

Essays in Honour of Eda Sagarra on the Occasion of her 60th Birthday, Stuttgart: Akademischer Verlag

Smith, F.M. (1992) 'Changing Sig-nificance of Space. Politics, Popula-tion and German Reunification', Applied Population Research Unit, University of Glasgow, Discussion Paper 92/4

Smith, G. (1992) 'The Nature of the Unified State', in Smith, Paterson, Merkl, and Padgett: 37–51

Smith, G., Paterson, W., and Merkl, P. (eds) (1989) *Developments in West German Politics*, Basingstoke and London: Macmillan

Smith, G., Paterson, W., Merkl, P., and Padgett, S. (eds) (1992) *Devel-opments in German Politics*, Lon-don: Macmillan

Smyser, W.R. (1992) *The Economy of United Germany*, London: Hurst & Company

Søe, C. (1993) 'Unity and Victory for the German Liberals: Little Party, What Now?', in Dalton: 99–134

Spence, D. (1991) *Enlargement with-out Accesssion: the EC's Response to German Unification*, London: Royal Institute of International Affairs

Stamm, K.-D. (1991) 'Das Ham-burger Abkommen', *Pädagogik und Schulalltag*, No. 2: 188–91

Staupe, J. (1991) *Schulrecht von A-Z*, Munich: dtv

Stefan, V. (1975) *Häutungen*, Mun-ich: Verlag Frauenoffensive

Steinmayr, J. (1989) 'Die Tage, die Deutschland erschüttern', *Die Zeit*, No. 41, 6 October 1989: 3

Stölzel, G. (ed.) (1991) 'Die deutsche Frage. Sprachwissenschaftliche Skizzen', *Sprache und Literatur in Wissenschaft und Unterricht*, Vol. 22, No. 67

Stolper, G. (1967) *The German Economy*, London: Weidenfeld and Nicolson

Strauss, B. (1993) 'Anschwellender Bocksgesang', *Der Spiegel*, Vol. 47, No. 6, 8 February 1993: 202–7

Streeck, W. (1984) *Industrial Relations in West Germany*, London: Heinemann

Streul, I.C. (1991a) 'Rundfunk und Fernsehen in den neuen Bundesländern—eine Zwischenbilanz', *Deutschland Archiv*, Vol. 24, No. 1:7–10

Streul, I.C. (1991b) 'Zum Stand der Neuordnung des Rundfunkwesens in den neuen Bundesländern', *Deutschland Archiv*, Vol. 24, No. 10: 1073–83

Sturm, R. (1992a) 'The Changing Territorial Balance', in Smith, Paterson, Merkl, and Padgett: 119–36

Sturm, R. (1992b) 'Government at the Centre', in Smith, Paterson, Merkl, and Padgett: 103–18

Sturm, R. and Jeffery, C. (1992) 'German Unity, European Integration and the Future of the Federal System: Revival or Permanent Loss of Substance?', *German Politics*, Vol. 1, No. 3: 164–76

Süßmuth, R. and Schubert, H. (1990) *Gehen die Frauen in die Knie?*, Zurich: Pendo

Syberberg, H.J. (1990) *Vom Unglück und Glück der Kunst in Deutschland nach dem letzten Kriege*, Munich: Matthes & Seitz

Taylor, P.J. (1993a) 'Geopolitical World Orders', in Taylor 1993b, Chapter 1: 31–61

Taylor, P.J. (ed.) (1993b) *Political Geography of the Twentieth Century. A Global Analysis*, London: Belhaven

Templin, W. (1990) 'Die DDR Opposition am runden Tisch', *Die*

Neue Gesellschaft. Frankfurter Hefte, No. 1: 77–80

Theater heute, Zurich: Orell Füssli & Friedrich Verlag

Theatre in the German Democratic Republic (1965–), Berlin: Zentrum des Internationalen Theaterinstituts

Thies, J. (1994) 'Germany: an Era Draws to a Close', *The World Today*, Vol. 50: 222–23

Thoma H. (1992) 'Wir sind die Säbelabteilung', *Der Spiegel*, Vol. 48, No. 41, 5 October 1992: 59–73

Thomaneck, J.K.A. (1984) 'Anna Seghers', in Wallace: 67–82

Thomson, P. (ed.) (1994) *The Cambridge Guide to Brecht*, Cambridge: Cambridge University Press

Verfürth, H. 'Spurensuche nach Glasnost', in Golombek and Ratzke: 37–42

Verträge zur deutschen Einheit (1990), Bonn: Bundeszentrale für politische Bildung

Vinke, H. (ed.) (1993) *Akteneinsicht Christa Wolf*, Hamburg: Luchterhand

Voigt, J. (1990) 'Irgendwie Niemandsland', *epd Film*, March 1990: 14–15

Volmert, J. (1992) 'Auf der Suche nach einer neuen Rhetorik', in Burkhardt and Fritzsche: 59–110

Wallace, I. (1991) 'Deutscher Literaturstreit aus britischer Sicht', *neue deutsche literatur*, Vol. 39, No. 3: 150–55

Wallace, I. (ed.) (1984) *The Writer and Society in the GDR*, Dundee: The Hutton Press

Wallraff, G. (1977) *Der Aufmacher: Der Mann, der bei Bild Hans Esser war*, Cologne: Kiepenhauer & Witsch

Walser, M. (1989a) 'Kurz in Dresden', *Die Zeit*, No. 42, 20 October 1989: 67–68

Walser, M. (1989b) *Über Deutschland reden*, Frankfurt (Main): Suhrkamp

Wander, M. (1989) *Guten Morgen, du Schöne*, Darmstadt: Luchterhand

Wanklyn, H. (1941) *The Eastern Marchlands of Europe*, London: G. Phillips and Son

Watts, R. (1991) 'West German Federalism: Comparative Perspectives', in Jeffery and Savigear: 23–39

Weber, H. (1991) *DDR. Grundriß der Geschichte 1945–1990*, Hannover: Fackelträger Verlag

Weck, R. de (1989) 'Im besten Sinne deutsch', *Die Zeit*, No. 48, 24 November 1989: 3

Weidenfeld, W. and Korte, K.-R. (eds) (1991) *Handwörterbuch zur deutschen Einheit*, Bonn: Bundeszentrale für politische Bildung

Weidenfeld, W. and Zimmermann, H. (eds) (1989) *Deutschland Handbuch*, Bonn: Bundeszentrale für politische Bildung

Weiler, H. (ed.) (1991) *Wirtschafts-Partner Ostdeutschland*, Bonn: Economica

Weishaupt, H. and Zedler, P. (1994) 'Aspekte der aktuellen Schulentwicklung in den neuen Ländern', in Rolff (1994)

Welke, K. (ed.) (1992) 'Die deutsche Sprache nach der Wende', Hildesheim (=*Germanistische Linguistik* 110–11)

Wielgohs, J. (1993) 'Auflösung und Transformation der ostdeutschen Bürgerbewegung', *Deutschland Archiv*, Vol. 26, No. 4: 426–34

Wiggershaus, R. (1979) *Geschichte der Frauen und der Frauenbewegung in der Bundesrepublik Deutschland und in der Deutschen Demokratischen Republik nach 1945*, Wuppertal: Hammer

Wild, T. and Jones, P.N. (1993) 'From Peripherality to New Centrality? Transformation of Germany's "Zonenrandgebiet"', *Geography*, Vol. 78, No. 3: 281–94

Wild, T. and Jones, P.N. (1994) 'Spatial Impacts of German Unification', *The Geographical Journal*, Vol. 160, No. 1: 1–15

Williams, A. (1976) *Broadcasting and Democracy in West Germany*, Bradford: Bradford University Press

Winkler, G. (ed.) *Frauenreport '90*, Berlin: Die Wirtschaft

Winters, P.J. (1990a) 'Zum ersten Mal frei', *Deutschland Archiv*, Vol. 23, No. 4: 497–501

Winters, P.J. (1990b) 'Deutschland nach der Wahl', *Deutschland Archiv*, Vol. 23, No. 12: 1817–19

Wirth, G. (1990) 'Pädagogische Institution, Erlebnis der Jugend und Elternrecht', in Hoffman: 72–92

Wistrich, E. (1994) *The United States of Europe*, London: Routledge

Wolf, C. (1983) *Kassandra. Vier Vorlesungen. Eine Erzählung*, Berlin: Aufbau

Wolf, C. (1990a) *Reden im Herbst*, Berlin: Aufbau

Wolf, C. (1990b) *Was bleibt*, Berlin: Aufbau

Wolf, C. (1993a) *What Remains*, London: Virago

Wolf, C. (1993b) 'Auf mir bestehen—Christa Wolf im Gespräch mit Günter Gaus', *neue deutsche literatur*, Vol. 41, No. 5: 20–40

Wolf, C. (1994) *Auf dem Weg nach Tabou, Texte 1990–1994*, Cologne: Kiepenhauer & Witsch

Wolf, M. (1991) *In eigenem Auftrag: Bekenntnisse und Einsichten*, Munich: Schneekluth

Zank, W. (1993) 'Noch ein Mezzogiorno', *Die Zeit*, No. 46, 12 November 1993: 31

Zimmer, J. (1993) 'Satellitenfernsehen in Deutschland', *Media Perspektiven*, No. 8: 358–65

Zimmermann, H. (1989) 'Deutschland 1989', in Weidenfeld and Zimmermann: 699–718

Zimmermann, H. (ed.) (1985) *DDR-Handbuch*, Cologne: Verlag Wissenschaft und Politik

Index